Khilafat in History
and
Indian Politics

Khilafat in History
and
Indian Politics

Zaheer Ali

AAKAR

KHILAFAT IN HISTORY AND INDIAN POLITICS
Zaheer Ali

First Published 2017

ISBN 978-93-5002-493-5

Published by
AAKAR BOOKS
28 E Pocket IV, Mayur Vihar Phase I, Delhi 110 091
Phone : 011 2279 5505 Telefax : 011 2279 5641
aakarbooks@gmail.com; www.aakarbooks.com

Laser Typeset at
Arpit Printographers, Delhi 110 032

Printed at
Mudrak, 30 A, Patparganj, Delhi 110 091

For
Fatma R. Zakaria

Contents

Preface

I

The term Khilafat has unfortunately acquired a sinister and fear-provoking connotation in the contemporary world thanks to the incessant terrorist activities of the Islamic State (IS) whose chief Abu Bakr al-Baghdadi claims to be the modern-day Khalifa and intends to establish the Khilafat of yore throughout the world. His devotees, followers, admirers, sympathisers some ideological adherents, with or without his sanction, have unleashed a series of terrorist attacks against the Muslims who beg to differ with Baghdadi's brand of Islam, against Shias and non-Muslims all across the world. When I started writing these lines sitting in a friend's house in Orlando, a couple of weeks ago, a few miles away, a 29-year-old American born young man of Afghan origin, Omar Mateen, pledging allegiance to the IS gunned down 49 innocent people at Pulse, a gay nightclub. Later it was reported that the terrorist who was also killed by the police in the exchange of fire, was not directly associated with the IS but was only inspired by the ideology of hate that Baghdadi preaches. It was not the first terrorist assault on unconnected, innocent non-Muslims by a self-appointed *mujahid* (holy warrior) of the IS and regrettably it was not the last one. In a month's time when I reached Chicago, quite a few heinous crimes were committed across Europe by the purported agents of the IS. The most reprehensible was the attack on a church in the Normandy town of Saint-Etienne-du-Rouvray in northern France, where the demons of hate who masquerade as "the Mujahideen of Islam" had slit the throat of an elderly priest in his mid-eighties.

Most Muslim apologists usually argue that organisations such as al-Qaeda and IS have nothing to do with Khilafat or even Islam; they are misinterpreting the tenets of Islam and in the process maligning the 'religion of peace'. Though the argument is true to a large extent, they say almost nothing about the rampant human rights violations in the Muslim-dominated societies and also do nothing about making Islam compatible with a liberal-democratic state. Moreover, the exaggerated enthusiasm with which the Muslim apologists remember the institution of Khilafat, in particular the reign of the four rightly guided companions of the Prophet Muhammad, as an ideal form of governance is problematic as their mindset seems to be trapped by a state-model that was suitable to the limited needs and demands of a pre-modern tribal society.

Islam does not distinguish between the religious and political realms. Consequently, any system of governance based on Islamic teachings is bound to be a theocracy. An all-inclusive democratic state guaranteeing equal socio-political and economic rights to all is foreign to a theocracy based on any religion. Khilafat is a theocratic order of governance though its characteristics keep changing from time to time and place to place. The brief historical survey of the Caliphate that this book puts out covering an extended period of about a millennium and a half present shifting hues of a system of governance that is by all accounts ingrained in Islam. In its infancy, the reign of the *'Rightly Guided Caliphs'*, Caliphate for the first time provided a well-ordered, transparent and responsible governance to the Arab peninsula. Nonetheless, bragging about its democratic foundation as quite a few Muslim *ulama* do is an exercise in futility. The issue gets discussed here in the relevant chapter.

The end of the reign of the first four Caliphs also put an end even to the 'democratic' pretention that prevailed till then. The Umayyads not only converted the Caliphate into a hereditary monarchy but also put into practice racism in contravention of Islamic teachings. The Muslim conquests outside the peninsula brought in a huge population of non-Arab people within the world of Islam. Most of these people embraced Islam but failed to acquire identical rights and privileges that the Arabs enjoyed during the Umayyad period. The non-Arab people (Persians, Egyptians, Armenians, Berbers and others) who embraced Islam came to be known as *Mawali*, the plural for *Mawla*, a term usually applied to a non-Arab Muslim. It must be noted that a *Mawla* was not a non-Muslim for whom the customary term was *Zimmi*. Nonetheless, there was not much difference between the socio-political standing between a *Mawla* and a *Zimmi* except that the latter was to pay an additional poll-tax (*Jiziya*) and was mostly exempted from military service. The *Mawalis* constituted the majority outside the peninsula, they were better educated, belonged to much superior cultural backgrounds, had acquired mastery over Arabic and yet were contemptuously discriminated against by the Umayyad Caliphs particularly in the economic sphere. Concisely, the Umayyad Caliphate was in essence a reign of Arab imperialism.

With the establishment of the Abbasid Caliphate the situation changed for the better and at its peak it was regarded as one of the most advanced empires the world had ever seen. The conditions also improved for the *Mawalis* in the middle of the Abbasid Caliphate but they could not achieve complete equality for as per the *ulama* only an Arab, preferably a descendant of the Quraish tribe, could become the Caliph. It must, however, be acknowledged that during the Abbasid period not only *Mawalis* but Jews, Christians and Zoroastrians were appointed to high positions and in turn they contributed significantly to the grandeur of the Caliphate. With the establishment of the Ottoman Caliphate in the fourteenth century, the Arab power declined and the focal point of political power of the Muslims was shifted to the Turks who ruled over a huge empire spread over the swathes of land of three continents till the beginning of the twentieth century.

British victory in the First World War heralded the disintegration of the Ottoman Caliphate and passing of most of the Muslim-dominated regions under the control of European imperial powers that were predominantly Christians. It was also the period when Arabs, living under the yoke of Ottoman imperialism for centuries, had discovered nationalism. The Arab population of the Middle East, in particular, of the Arab peninsula, therefore had not only welcomed the end of the Ottoman rule but had actively cooperated with the Allied Powers during the course of the war. In contrast, the Indian Muslims were appallingly unaware of the international political scenario. Many of them interpreted the downfall of the Ottomans as a conspiracy of the

British to denigrate Islam. Accordingly, the Indian Muslim political elite, Bombay businessmen and privileged Muslim class of North India launched a movement, which soon got the support of the Muslim masses, for the restoration of the Ottoman Caliphate. It was a strange movement in the sense that but for the Indian Muslims no Muslim population of other nationalities including the Turks were eager for the continuation of the institution of Khilafat. Nonetheless, because of its religious tenor and emotional pull, the Khilafat movement was the first mass movement of the Muslims of undivided India. Gandhi's patronage turned it into a national movement and augured for the first time an era of Hindu-Muslim unity. Even so, the unity of the two major religious communities did not last long and with the fizzling out of the Khilafat movement, the Hindu-Muslim camaraderie also petered out. The Khilafat movement failed to achieve its professed objectives but it proved a point that had the Hindu and Muslim leaders shown some more sagacity and thorough political wisdom by shunning their egoistic streak, a united Hindu-Muslim front against the British was possible. Had this happened, the partition of the country could have been avoided.

The Central Khilafat Committee in Mumbai survived despite the dissolution of the Khilafat movement. A chapter here deals with the activities of the CKC in the post-movement time. In the changed circumstances the CKC, especially under the guidance of the late Dr. Rafiq Zakaria, transformed itself into an educational institution in conjunction with espousing the ideal of Hindu-Muslim unity. The present management has plans to establish a research centre at the institution devoted exclusively to the study of Hindu-Muslim relations, which will certainly help reinforce the foundations of secularism in India.

II

It is needed to explain the spellings of Arabic, Persian and Turkish names and terms that appear frequently in the book owing to its theme. Phonetically speaking, certain alphabets of Arabic such as ا (alif) and ع (ain) and at times ه (haa), ت (ta) and ط (taa), ث (tha), س (siin) and ص (saad), ح (haa) and ه (haa), ح (khaa) and ق (qaaf) and ذ (dhaal), ز (zaay), ز (daad) and ظ (zaa) do not have separate and distinct sounds so far as most South Asian speakers are concerned. For instance a speaker of Hindustani/

Urdu/Hindi does not pronounce ا (alif) and ع (ain) or ذ (dhaal), ز (zaay), ض (daad) and ظ (zaa) distinctly. These Arabic letters have their use and significance in Urdu as most proper names of persons and a considerable percentage of vocabulary of the language have been borrowed from Arabic and Persian and while writing such names and words the usage of these letters make sense. Nonetheless, except for those who recite the Quran frequently (*huffaz* and *qaarian*) these Arabic letters are not pronounced the way Arabs do. What is more, all Arab people do not follow a solitary phonetic system. The Arabic pronunciation of the Egyptians (supposed to be the standard one because of the endorsement of Jamia Azhar) and the people of Saudi Arabia differ markedly. Some English writers usually use diacritics with Arabic and Persian names and words in an attempt to put across the exact sound. It hardly helps and in most cases makes the typing and composing cumbersome. I, therefore, have avoided doing it. I have followed the Hindustani/Urdu phonetic system and spelled the Arabic, Persian and Turkish names and words the way most speakers of the Indian subcontinent pronounce them. Therefore, instead of *Khalifah* I have spelled it as Khalifa and in place of *hadith* (traditions and sayings of the Prophet), I prefer to spell it as *hadis* for most people in India, Pakistan and Bangladesh can hardly distinguish between the sound of its ending letter ث. They pronounce it the way they do س and ص.

The standard spelling of the name of the Prophet of Islam is Muhammad. It is usually spelled this way universally even if it is used as part of someone else's name. I have retained this. Still, some persons bearing it as part of their names themselves spell it differently. For instance, one of the key figures of the Khilafat Movement would spell his name as Mohamed Ali. Obviously I have to respect his right to spell his name the way he liked. I cannot spell it otherwise. Thus, wherever I refer to the younger of the Ali brothers I have spelled it as Mohamed Ali. The same applies to citations. I have refrained from changing the spellings of the names and places that appear in the citations that I have made use of.

III

I am indebted to scores of people who have helped me in different capacities. It is not feasible here to thank everyone of them individually. Nonetheless, I must acknowledge the selfless support of a few of them. This study was assigned to me as a research project by Ms. Fatma R. Zakaria, the Chairperson of the Central Khilafat Committee, Mumbai, and I sincerely thank her for choosing me to carry out the project. As a token of my gratitude, I dedicate the book to her. Similarly, I wish to thank Sarfaraz Arzoo, the Vice-President of the CKC who made my access easy to the documents and official records* of the Khilafat Committee. My much cherished friend S.M. Khan (Zia) merits my genuine gratitude for helping me obtain and accomplish the study within the stipulated time. During my research tour of the USA, a few young people helped me in myriad ways to make my stay at different places comfortable. I, in particular, express my thanks to Nizam Khan (Taher) and Qamar Khan (Ather) both from Orlando, Gurpreet Singh of Atlanta, Shandon Lee who is a student in San Francisco and my younger sister Fahim Magrabi (Shameem) who lives in Chicago.

I thank Dr. A.G. Khan, Director of Dr. Rafiq Zakaria Centre for Higher Learning and Research, Aurangabad, who has been steady in extending the necessary collaboration during the course of the research. Among friends, I express my gratitude to Afaq Khan, Surendra Jondhale, Munawwar Ali, Sibtain Naqvi, Flory D'souza, Mohammed Fayyaz, Gautam Gawali and Ramesh Kambale for their encouragement. My wife Madhuri and son Zeeshan merit special thanks for backing me up all through the stint of the study. Similarly, my brothers, Syed Hamid Ali (Saleem) and Dr. Syed Khalid Ali (Khusrau), ought to be thanked for a host of reasons that helped me complete this project. Lastly, Shariq Khan, Registrar of the Khilafat College of Education, Mumbai deserves my appreciation for his consistent cooperation.

Zaheer Ali
Chicago

* According to a recent newspaper report (*Mumbai Mirror*, August 20, 2016) that four registers belonging to the halcyon days of the Khilafat Movement were found. "The registers", Sarfaraz Arzoo, the Vice-Chairman of the CKC informed, "were kept in a rarely accessed area of the house. We stumbled upon them while looking for some documents that we have to submit to the BMC for lease extension." However, the contents of these registers do not add to or contradict the account of the Khilafat Movement presented in this book.

1

Theoretical Framework

Allah has promised, to those among you who believe and work righteous deeds, that He will, of a surety, grant them in the land, inheritance (of power), as He granted it to those before them; that He will establish in authority their religion—the one which He has chosen for them; and that He will change (their state), after the fear in which they (lived), to one of security and peace. 'They will worship Me (alone) and not associate aught with Me.' If any do reject Faith after this, they are rebellious and wicked.

—The Holy Quran, 24: 55

Prophethood shall remain among you as long as Allah shall will. He will bring about its end and follow it with Khilafat on the precepts of prophethood for as long as He shall will and then bring about its end. A tyrannical monarchy will then follow and will remain as long as Allah shall will and then come to an end. There will follow thereafter monarchial despotism to last as long as Allah shall will and come to an end upon His decree. There will then emerge Khilafat on precept of Prophethood.

—The Holy Prophet

I

Islam, is a faith that aims at spreading its message all across the world. All devout Muslims seriously believe that all men and women throughout the world would ultimately embrace Islam. Nevertheless, there is not a solitary discourse of Islam. There are schisms mostly on account of feuds that had their roots in political polarisation in early Islam. Who should have succeeded the Prophet as the Khalifa was the first issue that divided the nascent *ummat*. It is necessary to understand the exact meaning of the word *Khalifa* (Caliph) in the light of the Quran and the traditions. First of all, there is a need to make clear that Islam has not created an institution similar to that of a Pope. Though among a few Shia sects some degree of divinity is associated with the Imam, the overwhelming Muslims across the world do not correlate divinity with anyone except the Prophet of Islam. Westerners, therefore, wrongly believe that the Khilafat is an institution similar to that of Papal authority. The Khalifa is not endowed with any spiritual quality. As leader of the Muslims, he is also called the Imam and in that capacity he has the right to lead the prayers, in particular, the noon prayer on Fridays and prayers on special occasions such as *Eid-ul-Fitr* (the popular festival celebrated on the first of the Hijri month of Shawwal after the conclusion of the month of Ramzan during which the Muslims observe fasts) and *Eid-ul-Adha* (Festival of the Sacrifice, celebrated on the 10th day of the Islamic month Zul-hijah). Leading the Muslim congregation at the time of prayer does not give the Imam any position of privilege, nor does it require any special qualifications. An ordinary Muslim can also lead the congregation at the time of prayer.

It was Abu Bakr who suggested, after the death of the Prophet in 632, to designate the leader of the Muslim community as Khalifah Rasul Allah (successor of the Apostle of God) There is, however, no evidence that the Prophet himself recommended Khakifa as the title of the leader of the Muslims after his death. The word connoting the successor of the Prophet or leader of the Muslims, does not appear in the Quran as well. Wherever the term Khalifah or its plural form Khulafa appeared in the Quran it conveys the meaning of successor/successors in general terms. It does not specifically refer to a political head of the Muslim community who would assume responsibility to guide the adherents of Islam in secular and religious matters. For instance, the term Khalifa and its variants appear in the sense of successors in general terms in the following verses:

> Allah has promised, to those among you who believe and work righteous deeds, that He will, of a surety, grant them in the land, inheritance [of power], as He granted it to those before them; that He

> will establish in authority their religion—the one which He has chosen for them; and that He will change [their state], after the fear in which they [lived], to one of security and peace: 'They will worship Me [alone] and not associate aught with Me. 'If any do reject Faith after this, they are rebellious and wicked'.[1]

The variant of the term used in this verse is *istakhlaf,* which is translated as *inheritance [of power],* in the above rendition. It is obvious, therefore, the term is used here not to connote a specific ruler of the believers but as a common parlance. In another verse the plural form of the term *Khalaif* appears, which is translated as *agents, inheritors of the earth*. The verse is as follows:

> It is He Who hath made you [His] agents, inheritors of the earth: He hath raised you in ranks, some above others: that He may try you in the gifts He hath given you: for thy Lord is quick in punishment: yet He is indeed Oft-forgiving, Most Merciful.[2]

There are two more verses wherein another plural form of the term Khulafa gets expressed and at both places the term has been translated as *inheritors* without any particularity.

"Do ye wonder that there hath come to you a message from your Lord through a man of your own people, to warn you? Call in remembrance that He made you inheritors after the people of Noah, and gave you a stature tall among the nations. Call in remembrance the benefits [ye have received] from Allah: that so ye may prosper."[3], and

"And remember how He made you inheritors after the 'Ad people and gave you habitations in the land: ye build for yourselves palaces and castles in [open] plains, and carve out homes in the mountains; so bring to remembrance the benefits [ye have received] from Allah, and refrain from evil and mischief on the earth."[4]

Nevertheless, there are two verses wherein the term refers to two specific individuals, viz. Adam and Daud (David). The first verse pertains to the intention of Allah to create Adam and He conveys the plan to the angels:

> Behold, thy Lord said to the angels: "I will create a vicegerent on earth." They said: "Wilt Thou place therein one who will make mischief therein and shed blood? Whilst we do celebrate Thy praises and glorify Thy holy [name]?" He said: "I know what ye know not."[5]

The verse in which David figures goes like this:

> O David! We did indeed make thee a vicegerent on earth: so judge thou between men in truth [and justice]: Nor follow thou the lusts [of thy heart], for they will mislead thee from the Path of Allah: for those who wander astray from the Path of Allah, is a Penalty Grievous, for that they forget the Day of Account.[6]

These two verses are very significant from the point of view of theoretical framework of Khilafat. It is obvious that in the two verses mentioned above the meaning of the term Khalifa is more than a mere successor, agent or inheritor. There are commentators who maintain that in the verse figuring Adam the term Khalifa does not mean more than a successor because Allah intended to appoint Adam the successor of angels who resided on earth before the creation of man. The other commentators, however, argue that the usage of the term Khalifa in the two verses is very significant because Adam and David were assigned extremely crucial functions of the highest order by the Almighty to carry out on earth. In view of this, the term Khalifa in these two verses goes beyond its literal meaning of successor. Here it is used to mean a vice-regent or a deputy of Allah on earth. In that capacity both Adam and David guided men to be on the right path and follow the commands of Allah.

The two verses mentioned above along with a few *ahadis* serve as the foundation for Islamic scholars to develop theoretical discourse of Khilafat though we cannot completely rule out the impact of the later praxis on the theory. It is clear from the *ahadis* that the primary qualification for a Caliph is that he must be a member of the Quraish tribe. In support of this view the following hadis is often cited:

The Prophet (peace be upon him) said: "The leaders are from Quraysh. The righteous among them are the leaders of the righteous, and the wicked among them are the leaders of the wicked."[7]

Though this qualification is obviously at variance with the purported egalitarian brotherhood of the Muslims and it also negates the major thrust of the sermon the Prophet delivered at the conclusion of his last Hajj eliminating all kinds of racial, ethnic, class and tribal differences, it has been strictly abided throughout the Umayyad and Abbasid Caliphate and also by the Shia Khilafat of the Fatmis of Egypt. Nevertheless, there is no absolute unanimity among the scholars that the Khalifah *must always* be from the tribe of the Quraish. Though the majority view favours the literal interpretation of the hadis under consideration, it is reported that Qazi al-Iyad has asserted: "Being from the tribe of Quraysh is regarded by all scholars as a condition for being the supreme political leader. They have considered it a point of consensus (*'ijmâ'*). No disagreement about this has been related to us from any of the Pious Predecessors, nor from any of those who came after them the prominent scholars of the provinces."[8] It must be pointed out that within the group of scholars which insists that the Khalifa must be from the tribe of the Quraish, there is divergence whether the office is open to all the members of the tribe or only to particular clans such as Banu Abd al-Muttalib or Banu Umayyah. The Shias insist that the Khalifah or Imam, the title they usually prefer, must be a member of the former clan while most Sunnis go along with the membership of the Quraish tribe but do not usually hold that to which clan he should belong.

The group of scholars that seems to differ with the opinion that a Khalifa must always be from the tribe of the Quraish argues that the real significance of the *hadis* in question is that the member of the Quraish tribe may be given preference if he happens to be among the group of equally suitable candidates for the post of the Khalifah. The *hadis* does not insist that a member of the Quraish must be appointed as the leader of the believers even if he is not fit for the job. Ibn al-Uthaymin commenting on the *hadis* under discussion writes: "The Prophet (peace be upon him) meant this only for a case where there is a choice between candidates. When we want to choose a supreme leader for the Muslims, we should choose someone from Quraysh. Yet, who from Quraysh should be chosen? He should be someone who adheres to the faith. It is not just a mere question of ancestry, of being able to trace your lineage back to Quraysh as a tribe or even to the Prophet (peace be upon him). There is no special distinction in this without true piety. If an iniquitous man from Quraysh comes forward and says he is entitled to the office, we would not appoint him. We would say to him that the primary consideration of a leader is that he must be just."[9] Though this seems to be a reasonable explanation of the *hadis*, the fact remains that its core is at variance with the principle of universal, egalitarian brotherhood of Islam. To this quite a few scholars respond that the *hadis* should be read contextually when Islam was confined to the Arab peninsula where only the Quraish tribe had all the necessary socio-political clout. Later, when Islam spread far beyond the Arab lands and particularly after the establishment of the Ottoman Caliphate, many scholars seem to have come around to the view that the supreme political leader of the Muslims need not be from the tribe of the Quraish.

There are other *ahadis* that help understand the attributes of the Caliphate that can be truly called a genuine Islamic rule observing and implementing the true message of the Quran and *ahadis* in letter and spirit which later came to be known as *Khilafat-e-Rashidun* (Rightly Guided Caliphate) and its perverted form that is Caliphate only in name but having all the trappings of an absolute, hereditary monarchy. This point gets conveyed in a famous *hadis*:

> Prophethood shall remain among you as long as God wills. Then Khilafat on the pattern of prophethood will commence and remain as long as He wills. A corrupt monarchy shall then follow and it shall remain as long as God wills. There shall then be a tyrannical despotism which shall remain as long as God wills. Then once again Khilafat will emerge on the precept of prophethood.[10]

Sunnis, therefore, believe that true to the prophecy of the Prophet the first four Caliphs were the Rightly Guided and thereafter a perverted rule began when the rulers were outwardly Muslims but they completely went astray from the path shown to them by the Prophet of Islam. A point worth noting is that the Muslim population of a perverted and fraudulent absolute monarch is not exactly expected to rebel against or make attempts to dislodge the corrupt ruler from his position. A *hadis* in this regard suggests that the Muslim subjects will not be held responsible for silently suffering the transgressions of a dishonest ruler. The *hadis* is as under:

> Rulers after me will come who do not follow my guidance and my tradition (*sunnah*). Some of their men will have the hearts of devils in

> a human body. You should listen and obey them even if the ruler strikes your back and takes your wealth, even still listen and obey.[11]

Based on these fundamental sources of the Quran and *ahadis*, the Muslim scholars developed the theoretical framework of the Khilafat that included the qualifications, appointment and legitimacy as its most pronounced constituents. The verses that pertain to Khilafat in the Quran do not help us get an inkling about procedure of its establishment, the powers of the Caliph or its tenure. In the first verse of the Quran cited above (24:55), the Almighty informs us that the Khilafat has been presented to the believers for their collective devoutness. It is argued by quite a few scholars that this particular feature should serve as the foundation of an Islamic rule implying that the collective piety of the Muslims is the primary constraint of an Islamic polity. Though, most scholars concur that the principle of election must be followed in choosing a Khalifa, the praxis shows that this principle was almost not adhered to even during the period of *Rightly Guided* Caliphs. An Islamic state cannot assert to be sovereign because according to Islamic precepts, it is Allah who enjoys sovereignty over the entire universe. Since Islam also does not classify the believers in terms of ethnicity and nationality, the Caliphate too is supposed to be discounting the ethnic and national considerations. The legitimacy of a Khilafat depends on the righteous and pious behaviour of the Caliph who is expected to guide the lives of the Muslims in the light of the Quran and *ahadis*.

II

In spite of the tall claims of the Muslim brotherhood and the unity of the Muslim *ummat* across the world usually propagated by the pan-Islamists, the reality is that there is not one single discourse of Islam. It is divided into more than seventy sects. According to a tradition (*hadis*), the Prophet himself had predicted Islam splitting into seventy-three sects. The *hadis* is: "Wahb ibn Baqiyyah told us from Khaalid from Muhammad bin 'Amr from Abu Salamah from Abu Hurayrah who said: the Messenger of Allaah (peace and blessings of Allaah be upon him) said: 'The Jews were divided into seventy-one or seventy-two sects, and the Christians were divided into seventy-one or seventy-two sects, and my Ummah will be divided into seventy-three sects'."[12] Discounting the inexactness of the number of Christian (as per an estimate the number of Christian denominations vary between 2,000 and 4,0000) and Judaic (it is claimed that there are not more than 20 sects of Judaism), the Muslim scholars maintain that there are in fact 73 sects in Islam. Interestingly, the sects that sprouted in the Indian subcontinent, viz. the Ahmadiya, Deobandi and Barelvi are not counted among the proper sects of Islam. Though the core beliefs are common among all the adherents of Islam irrespective of sectarian differences, there are certain issues on which there is no consensus among all the Muslims. This must be underscored that all the contentious issues that divide Islam into various sects made their appearance after the death of the Prophet. At least three major areas of disputation can be identified. They are: i) the controversy over the appointment of the first Caliph; ii) different sets of traditions (*ahadis*) and iii) different schools of *shariat* (Islamic law). These are all post-Prophet developments. The emergence of the Islamic sects was, therefore, the logical culmination of the differences that cropped up when the Prophet of Islam was gone.

It is appropriate to make a mention of an incident that, if scrutinised without prejudice, corroborates the Shia position in respect of Khilafat. After completing *Hajjat-ul-Wida* (the last pilgrimage to Mecca), the Prophet along with his seventy thousand companions—another source reports that there were 1,20,000 companions—[13] stopped at a place known as Ghadir Khumm, which is a short distance from the city of Juhfah in present-day Saudi Arabia. It appears that the primary reason that made the Prophet halt and deliver the subsequent sermon was the revelation of the following verse.

"O Apostle! Proclaim the (Message) which hath been sent to thee from thy Lord. If thou didst not, thou wouldst not have fulfilled His Mission. And Allah will defend thee from men (who mean mischief). For Allah guideth not those who reject Faith."[14] This verse read along with the sermon of the Prophet helps us understand the urgency which caused the Prophet to let his companion know about the precious gifts he was bequeathing to the *ummat*. There are detailed versions of the sermon that the Prophet delivered at Ghadir Khumm on that day (18th of Zil-Hijjah, 10 AH/March 10,

632 AD)[15] but in order to underscore the point under discussion a brief version of it may suffice. The prophet addressing a huge gathering of the companions had said:

> O people, Allah is my Lord and I am the lord of the believers. I am worthier of believers than themselves. Of whomsoever I had been Master (Mawla), Ali here is to be his Master. O Allah, be a supporter of whoever supports him (Ali) and an enemy of whoever opposes him and divert the Truth to Ali... I will ask you about the two weighty things that I have left for you when you come to me to see how you dealt with them. The greater weighty thing is Allah's book—the Holy Qur'an. One end is in Allah's hand and the other is in your hands. Keep it and you will not deviate. That other weighty thing is my family (Ahl al-Bayt) and my descendants. The Most Kind the Omniscient had told me that both of them, would not separate until they come to my Pond.[16]

There are more than a hundred versions of the sermon in both Sunni and Shia accounts. Sunni accounts do not deny the Prophet's declaration of Ali to be Mawla of the *ummat* after his death. Nevertheless, they argue that the Prophet was instructing the audiences to show respect to Ali. Shibli Nomani, a famous biographer of the second Caliph Umar writes in his book *Al-Farooq* that "the Prophet was just praising Ali."[17]

Now, it seems a bizarre logic that the Prophet would command more than one lakh of his companions to applaud his son-in-law! We must not lose sight of the Quranic verse that got revealed a short while before the sermon of the Prophet and that exhorted him to convey *"the (Message) which hath been sent to thee from thy Lord"* to his companions. In that sermon the Prophet inter alia announced the two *'weighty'* gifts that he was leaving behind. One was of course the Quran and the other was the nomination of Ali as *mawla* of the *ummat* after his demise. Sunnis point out that the word *mawla* has many meanings such as friend, guide, supporter, master, successor, etc. If we keep in mind the context, the Prophet had declared his inevitable death so it was natural on his part to name his successor. After making the heartrending announcement it was unlikely that he would eulogise his son-in-law. Though according to the experts there are about 27 connotations of the term *mawla* but by any stretch of the imagination it cannot be used to admire someone. The only meaning that comes to mind considering the circumstance is the *successor*. What is significant is that almost all the Sufi orders cite this sermon to bring into focus the *spiritual authority* of Ali, conveyed to the audiences by the Prophet himself. In view of this, one is justified to construe that the Prophet had hinted that after his death the successor / Khalifa / imam should have temporal as well as *spiritual authority*. The Shias, therefore, contend that in view of the Prophet's intention only Ali should have been nominated as the first Caliph and one has to be in accord with their position after a dispassionate reading of the Ghadir Khumm episode. The Ghadir Khumm incident has the foremost effect on the Shia concept of Khilafat.

It is, therefore, obvious that the principal reason for the schism in Islam into Sunnis and Shias was political. The party (literal meaning of the word Shia is party) that insisted on complying with the will of the Prophet that he had expressed in his last sermon at Ghadir Khumm came to be referred by the latter term while those who preferred to ignore the wish of the Prophet on account of a flawed interpretation were designated by the former. The most significant point in the Shia doctrine of Khilafat (the Shias prefer to use the term Imamat) is that it is not a temporal office that can be left for the common people to decide its fate. The office is divine in nature and for that reason the Imamat constitutes one of the core beliefs of Islam. Like a Prophet, an Imam is also nominated by Allah and the Quranic verse (5:70) revealed just prior to the Ghadir Khumm sermon had exhorted the Prophet (*Proclaim the (Message) which hath been sent to thee from thy Lord*) to let the *ummat* know about his successor. An imam, like a prophet, is after all a human being and therefore, mortal. When the time of the demise of an imam draws near, he nominates his *wasi* or successor. The Ghadir Khumm *khutba* (sermon) was the occasion when the Prophet had disclosed that after his death the Prophethood would end permanently, however, the *ummat* would have an imam and the first one would be Ali. It was unfortunate that the companions of the Prophet paid no heed to the divine will and chose others as the Caliphs. Despite the will of the Prophet expressed on the cue of the Quranic verse, Ali was deprived of his rightful position, and therefore, the Shias assert that the first three Caliphs were usurpers.

The Shias also assert that the right of imamat belongs only to Ali and his scions through his wife Fatima, the daughter of the Prophet. Thus, after Ali, Hasan, his elder son, was the second imam followed by his brother Husain as the third one. Thereafter, all the imams who followed traced their descent from Husain. The Shias assign superhuman attributes to the imam such as he is infallible (*Masoom*) who can never commit a sin. Moreover, an imam cannot go astray and carry out something wrong. All his words and deeds are perfect and moral and, therefore, he is not accountable for his words or actions before the people.

With the exclusion of Sunnis and the Khawarij, most of the other Islamic sects can be technically classified as Shia. Nevertheless, they differ from each other on various counts like the method of choosing a Caliph, the legitimacy of the first three Caliphs, the discontinuity of imamat, etc. The most moderate of the Shia sects is that of the Zaidis who concur with the Sunnis that the institution of Khilafat is elective. Nonetheless, they assert that the descendants of Ali have always been better suited for the position. If a scion of the Ali family does not stake his claim for the post of Khalifa, then the *ummat* is justified to elect any other man as the Caliph. On account of this the Zaidis do not consider the first three Caliphs as illegitimate rulers of the Muslims. Zaidis maintain that if the necessity arises, there can be two imams. For instance, if the territory of the Caliphate is too large or if one land mass of the territory is separated by a sea or ocean from the other part of the territory then the people can appoint two imams reigning over two parts.

The first civil war in the world of Islam was also fought on the issue of Khilafat. After the assassination of the third Caliph, Usman, the controversy arose on his successor. Though Ali was chosen as the Caliph, Muawiya, the governor of Syria and cousin of the departed Caliph along with a few more anti-Ali groups refused allegiance on the alleged reason that prior to the formal nomination of the fourth Caliph, the killers of Usman should be brought to justice. It was, obviously a ploy to oppose Ali's Caliphate, which led to the first violent confrontation between two groups of Muslims in less than quarter of a century after the death of the Prophet. The first civil war, known as the Battle of Siffin was fought between the forces of the Caliph Ali and the supporters of Muawiya in 657.[18] The army of the Caliph Ali had been towering above the rebellious forces right from the beginning of the battle. When Muawiya was on the verge of defeat, he asked his men to hoist the copies of the Quran on their spears, a sure sign of the ceasing of fighting. Then he suggested that the dispute should be resolved by means of arbitration in the light of Quranic guidance. At this point of time a section of Ali's army opposed arbitration as a means of resolving the issue of the Caliphate for, in its opinion, Allah alone could decide the issue. Ali conceded to Muawiya's suggestion for arbitration primarily because he wanted to put an end to the killings of the Muslims by Muslims.

Nevertheless, those who were part of Ali's armed forces and intensely objected to arbitration on the ground that the fate of an armed conflict should be decided on the battlefield as it was Allah who would determine the victor and the loser. On this issue they deserted Ali's army and for that reason came to be known as the Khawarij (literally 'those who seceded or went out').[19] The group later adopted an extremist position on quite a few theological issues and in the process got a separate identity of a sect popularly referred to as the Khawarij though the members of the sect call themselves Ash-Shurât (literally 'buyers') "those who have traded the mortal life (al-Dunya) for the other life (with God)".[20] It is one of the most extremist sects of Islam who differ with both Shias and Sunnis on many religious positions including that of Khilafat. It was a Kharji, Abdur Rahman bin Muljam, who ultimately assassinated Ali in 661.

Unlike the position of most of the Sunnis, the Khawarij argue that it is not necessary that a Caliph must necessarily be a descendant of the Quraish. At the same time they also oppose the Shia viewpoint that the descendants of Ali through his first wife Fatima, the daughter of the Prophet, are alone qualified to be the Caliph/imam. The Khawarij maintain that any devout and honest Muslim can be elected a Caliph. They insist that a Caliph must be elected not by a handful elites based in Dar-ul-Khilafa (capital) but the free vote of all Muslims. Refuting Shia's contention that a Khalif is infallible and, therefore, not accountable to the people, the Khawarij contend that a Caliph being a human being is likely to commit mistakes or even sins. If he does so then, in their opinion, he must be deposed or even killed. They also have a different view about the first four Khulfa-e-Rashidun (The Rightly Guided Caliphs) from the Sunnis and the Shias. The Khawarij acknowledge the Caliphate of Abu Bakr and Umar as just but insist that Usman did deviate from the path of justice and truth in the later part of his reign. On Ali the Khawarij argue that he began as a 'Rightly Guided Caliph' but committed a sin by agreeing to arbitration in the course of the Battle of Siffin. Therefore, they justify Ali's assassination by one of the members of their sect.[21]

III

The first proper attempt to theorise the institution of the Caliphate was made in the eleventh century by an Islamic jurist, Abul Hasan Ali bin Muhammad Mawardi, who had also written a classic treatise explaining the Shafai School of Sunni jurisprudence. Besides being a profound jurist, Mawardi also excelled in diplomatic assignments and oratory. It was Abbasi Khalifa, al-Qadir who first appointed Mawardi as one of the Qazis in the Caliphate. Mawardi ultimately occupied the position of the Chief Qazi in Baghdad. Additionally he also served as the chief negotiator from the side of the Caliphate conducting the diplomatic parleys with Iranian Buwaihids and later with the Seljuqs. By the eleventh century the power and grandeur of the Caliphate had almost gone astray and the Iranian Buwahids had become the de facto rulers. Thereafter, the Seljuqi dynasty overwhelmed the authority of the Abbasi Caliphate without completely decimating it. The province of Egypt by this time had seceded from the Abbasi rule and a parallel Fatimid Caliphate had emerged there. This impelled the Abbasi Caliph to ask Mawardi to write an Islamic political treatise explaining the essence of the legitimate Caliphate and dispel the Fatimid Caliphate of Egypt. In this manner, the most celebrated work of Mawardi, *Al-Ahkam as-Sultaniyyah* (The Laws of Islamic Governance), got published, which was the first systematic study of Islamic political theory.

The Laws of Islamic Governance (also translated as *Ordinances of Government*) provides an exhaustive description of the powers and functions of the Caliph. The book was ironically published at a time when the Abbasid Caliphate had become subservient to the Buwahid rulers. A scholar-translator of the work, Wafaa H. Wahaba, sums it up in these words. "For al-Mawardi the Caliphate symbolized an entire politico-religious system that regulates the lives of men in a Muslim community to the smallest detail. Hence the emphasis in [The Ordinances] placed on the qualifications, power and duties pertinent to [a given office of government]... This approach to the matter would explain the working arrangement finally reached by the Buyids and the Abbasid Caliphs, later followed also by the more efficient Seljuqs, whereby the military held actual power while recognizing the Caliph as the supreme head of government and receiving from him, in turn, recognition of their mundane authority."[22]

Mawarid enunciates a juristic theory of the Caliphate relying heavily on the Shariat canons to substantiate his arguments. He contends that the institution is an elective institution in the sense that either a Caliph is chosen by a larger congregation of the believers or by an exclusive group of prominent and influential members of the community nominated by the outgoing Caliph. Adopting such an approach for the appointment of the highest leader of the Islamic state, Mawarid has very tactfully legitimised the principle of heredity that has happened to be the norm of the appointment of the Caliphs since the Umayyad period. The elective principle is insisted upon to dispel the position of the Shias who swear by the code of divine nomination. It is also not clear who the electorates are. Are the believers living in the *Dar-ul-Khilafah* (capital of the Caliphate) alone qualified to be the voters or do all the believers living across the Caliphate also have the right to vote? Mawarid seems to favour that the residents of the capital should only have the suffrage because there should not be an interruption in the continuity of authority in the event of the death or removal of the previous Caliph. His second line of reasoning is too bizarre for he says that people possessing necessary qualifications to be the electorates—piety, uprightness, wisdom, etc.—as a rule reside in *Dar-ul-Khilafa*.

Mawarid also maintains a diplomatic silence on the issue of election or nomination of a profligate, incompetent or an outright imbecile person as the Caliph. This was obviously in view of the exigencies of his assignment and the circumstances in which he had to function. At that time the Buwahids controlled real power and they would often nominate a thoroughly incompetent person from the Abbasi lineage who would comply to their dictates. Mawarid also asserts that there must only be one Caliph lording over the entire Muslim world and firmly rules out the existence of two or more Caliphs. Some schools of Islamic thought like the Asharis are of the view that depending on the size of the Caliphate the number of Caliphs could be determined. If the territorial size of the Caliphate is vast and some parts of it are also separated by a sea or ocean then more than one Caliph may be appointed. Mawarid's insistence on a single Caliph was to delegitimize the Fatimids of Egypt and the Umayyads of Spain.

In the twenty chapters, Mawarid meticulously discusses the powers, functions and responsibilities of the Caliph. The methodology that he has employed to write this tome is, except the first chapter, empirical. It is only in the first chapter that he briefly discusses the theory of the Caliphate; the rest of the book is an exercise in legitimizing the governance of the Abbasi Caliphs. By way of theory of the Islamic state, Mawarid does not add anything new which can be considered his original contribution. His primary sources in developing a theory of an Islamic polity are obviously the Quran, Sunnah and the Shariat. He could not even firmly establish the linkages between Islam and democracy while critiquing the appointment of the Caliph. In doing so he would have to counteract the principle of heredity and nomination that got set in not only since the time of Muawiya but even earlier. It must also be acknowledged that for someone who is assigned the job of expounding a political theory of an Islamic polity in the light of the received wisdom, it is not possible to add anything new. Mawarid's significance lies in the fact that his was the first attempt which can be rightfully identified as the theoretical discourse of the Islamic state in the light of the Sunni Shariat. It is also reported that he contributed the "doctrine of necessity"[23] to political literature which implies a highly centralised governance wherein absolute powers must be vested in the Caliph.

The empirical methodology that is employed in discussing the administrative aspects of the Caliphate including the powers and functions of the Caliph, Mawarid relies heavily on the praxis of the Abbasi Caliphate justifying its legitimacy and disapproving other administrative models, in particular the governance of the Fatimid Caliphate. In enlisting the administrative functions of the Caliph he emphasises issues such as appointment of governors of various provinces, administrative officers responsible to various departments, judges and military commanders. Mawarid advocates that marking out the powers, functions and responsibilities of all the officials is also the job of the Caliph. Moreover, he stresses that a Caliph is duty bound to punish the apostates, rebellious sections of the people and organised criminals. It is the Caliph who is the final authority in dividing the spoils of war, demarcating boundaries between countries, repossession of lands, fixing the rate of taxation, alms and tithes. It is the function of the Caliph to stipulate punishments for crimes like rape, fornication, adultery, theft and consumption of intoxicating drinks. A close analysis of the vast powers that Mawarid vests in the post of the Caliph may reveal that he has created a head of the state in whom are vested all the legislative, executive and judicial powers. The officials he appoints are only there to carry out his commands. In such a dispensation the question of sovereignty turns out to be bewildering. In the strict Islamic sense the supreme power is that of the Almighty and the political chief executive of an Islamic state (Caliph/Imam or Emir-ul-Mominin) has to conduct the affairs of such a state in accordance with the stipulations laid down in the Quran and the Sunnah. In Mawarid's treatise, nevertheless, the Caliph enjoys absolute powers and the history of the Khilafat is testimony to the fact that, more often than not, the religious obligations went out of the window. In fact the title of the very first chapter which is about the selection of the Caliph is 'Appointment of the Sovereign.' Here Mawarid uses the term 'sovereign' as it is used in the mainstream political literature. At other places, however, the sovereignty of the Almighty has also been avowed.

In the contemporary world, Mawarid's works are usually revisited in many Muslim-dominated nations and in some of them he is put on a high pedestal as a great political thinker. Objectively speaking such a claim is far from the truth. Mawarid has almost nothing to contribute by way of original political theory. Such an exercise is not feasible for someone who is expected to expound conceptual postulations within the bounds of an inflexible framework of religious beliefs. Had he done that he would have been prosecuted for innovation or even blasphemy. Secondly, *Al-Ahkam as-Sultaniyyah* was written on the orders of the Abbasid Caliph. Mawarid was therefore, carrying out an assignment with a specific brief. Considering these facts, Mawarid's work could not have been any different than what he had written. He was essentially a jurist; not a political philosopher. The significance of *Al-Ahkam* lies not in its originality or profundity but, as has been already commented upon, in its chronological precedence among a few treatises that belong to the category of Islamic polity.

IV

Abu Hamid Muhammad Ghazali (1058-1111) was born in Tus, a famous city of Iran, where he was trained in Islamic studies. At that time the power of the Caliph had become ceremonial and the Seljuq sultans, who were by origin Turkish and therefore Sunnis were the de facto rulers of the so-called Abbasi Caliphate. The Grand Vizier Nizam-ul-Mulk was also from the city of Tus and on his recommendation the Seljuq Sultan Malik Shah appointed Ghazali a tutor at Madarsa-e-Nizamiya, in Baghdad. He was too serious a scholar to remain as a teacher for long at any educational institution. He was extremely well read and his areas of studies, in addition to the standard disciplines of Islamic learning, theology, exegeses of the Quran, Ahadis, Shariat, etc. included Greek philosophy and natural sciences.[24]

He was inclined towards rationalism and logic. The books he wrote during his stay at Baghdad included *Al-Iqtisad fi-l-itiqad* (Moderation in Belief) and *Fayasl al-tafriqa bayn al-Islam wa-l-zandaqa* (The Criterion of Distinction Between Islam and Clandestine Unbelief), which along with another book, *Nasihat al-Muluk* (Counsel for the Kings) that he wrote later constitute the sources of his political ideology. Ghazali believed that so far as the Islamic theory of knowledge was concerned, politics was not a self-regulating science but an integral part of the science of religion. Gradually, nevertheless, he became sceptical about the absolute dominance of reason and rationality over knowledge. This made him restless and in that state of mind, four years after teaching at Madarsa-e-Nizamiya, he resigned from his teaching job in 1095. Thereafter, for about a decade, he got involved in mysticism and for some time actually led the life of a Sufi.[25]

During Ghazali's absence from Baghdad, the political situation turned quite capricious that further weakened the position of the Caliph. To begin with, some disgruntled elements made an attempt to depose the Seljuq Sultan; then the crusaders had posed a real threat to the Muslim world as by this time they had occupied Syria and the Ismailis, in particular, the assassins of Hasan bin Sabah, had created mayhem all across the Caliphate. For Ghazali, however, this sabbatical proved extremely productive as he could complete his monumental work, *Ihya Ulum ad-Din* (Revival of Religious Sciences), because of which he is revered in the world of Islam and widely referred to as *Hujjat al-Islam* (Proof of Islam).[26]

It is unavoidable to keep the socio-political conditions of the Abbasid Caliphate in the times of Ghazali for critiquing his concept of the Khilafat. In this sense, he too like Mawarid a century earlier, responding to the prevalent political scenario while contemplating the notion of the Caliphate. Both were expected by the reigning political masters to deride the Fatimid Caliphate of Egypt. The major difference, however, was that Mawarid wrote his treatise on the command of the Abbasi Caliph who, at that time, was merely a titular head and the real power was in the hands of the Shia dynasty of the Buwahids while Ghazali expounded his political theory when the Caliph was still a ceremonial head but the real wielders of power were the Sunni Sultans of the Seljuqi dynasty. It was this state of political affairs that induced Ghazali to present a diarchal theory of the Caliphate wherein the de facto political authority is controlled by the Sultan who looks after the temporal affairs of the Islamic state while the de jure power is that of the Caliph who is vested with religio-spiritual powers.

It is needless to add that Ghazali's theory of the Caliphate was based neither on the Quranic injunctions nor on the *ahadis* that deal with the issue of Khilafat. It was his own innovation that he had developed to provide legitimacy to the real centre of political power that had been a different one than the Caliph for long. It seems that

Ghazali's ultimate aim was to secure the power of the Islamic state and in order to accomplish it he could only think of a strong central authority. With this intention he vested the de facto power in an absolute monarch, the Sultan. One can also discern the bearings of the non-Islamic, in particular that of pre-Islamic Iranian traditions, on the political ideology of Ghazali. A major example of intermingling non-Islamic elements in the theory of the Khilafat can easily be identified in the Zoroastrian guideline, "religion and empire are brothers". Thus, he combines religious stipulations with that of political power in his theory of the Caliphate and interestingly, he himself claims that his theory of the Caliphate is an exercise to seek the unity of the Islamic world.

Like most Muslim scholars, Ghazali too maintains that the Caliphate is a divine state, which cannot be governed by the laws made on the basis of reason and rationality but is regulated by the divine law, which is Shariat. In this manner he puts the Caliphate outside the purview of the secular discipline of Political Science. At any rate, his opinion about the discipline of politics is that it is not an independent area of knowledge but a part of the science of religion. The end of the state, in the political thought of Ghazali, is also very different from that of the one usually found in the mainstream political literature. By endowing a transcendental dimension to Aristotle's observation, ('polis continues to exist for the welfare of the people'), Ghazali has transformed the discipline of politics into theology because he contends 'politics continues in existence for people's welfare in this world and the bliss in the hereafter'.

Having conferred divinity to the study of politics, Ghazali makes an attempt to separate powers of the state into two distinct categories. While, day-to-day political affairs, appointments of viziers and of high officials including military commanders, administrative matters, finance, commerce, control of crimes and punishments, international relations, war and peace are vested in the temporal segment of the Muslim state headed by the Sultan, the religious and spiritual functions are to be taken care of by the Caliph who, according to Ghazali, is the *Zill-e-Ilahi* (Shadow of Allah) on earth. He expects the Caliph to lead a life of piety and be judicious while adjudicating feuds of religious nature because he is supposed to be the 'fountain of justice'. He also has a word of advice for the Caliph that he should be well-versed in Shariat and for that purpose he must constantly be in consultation with the ulama and fuqha (jurists). Another innovation of Ghazali is that he calls a Caliph Khalifa Allah (representative of Allah). This title was not even used by the rightly guided Caliphs who preferred to call themselves only as the 'representative of the Prophet Muhammad'.

Ghazali enlists obligations that a Caliph is duty bound to discharge to justify his position as the religious head of an Islamic state. Though in Ghazali's theory Khalifa is a mere figurehead, he must be competent enough to conduct jihad even if indirectly whenever the inevitability arises. A Caliph should also be well-versed in theological matters and for that reason should always be seeking counsel from the ulama. A life of simplicity and piety is prescribed for the Caliph because in Ghazali's theory he is expected to guide the people on how to lead a life in accordance with the Quranic commands and the traditions of the Prophet. Such a leader is obviously required to set a precedent himself in piety and devoutness. A Caliph must also be capable enough to administer justice in the light of the Shariat. It means a Caliph must also have a thorough knowledge of the Islamic law, which he can gain by consulting the leading *fuqha* of his times. A Caliph must always move in the company of scholars and men of letters who may lend a hand to him in carrying out his assigned functions. A Caliph is expected to monitor the functioning of the officials who work under him such as judges (*qazis*) and the rectors of the *madaaris* (seminaries). A Caliph should never seek pride in his position because being a devout man he must always be humble and acquiescent in this transient world.

A close critique of Ghazali's political views brings to light a startling fact that he anticipated the future of the Muslim state under the domination of an absolute monarchy. The position of a Caliph, for him, was that of an appendage as a religious attribute of the Islamic state. It is the Sultan who wields the real power in the state envisaged by Ghazali. It is the Sultan who is actually empowered to maintain the unity and integrity of the state. He recognises the significance of the ulama and fuqha who render an Islamic aura to the state and can also serve as a connecting channel between the

Sultan and the Caliph. He believes that in order to fortify a Muslim state the people should unreservedly submit to the authority of the Sultan who looks after the secular functions of a Muslim state. Ghazali demands absolute obedience to the dictates of the Sultan even if he acts in contravention of the Shariat or degenerates into an unjust ruler. Like Thomas Hobbes, he denies the right of the people to depose an unjust head of the state. He equates political dissent with *fitna* (civil war) that is bound to weaken the Muslim state. The internal disturbances can only be suppressed by an absolute monarch and, therefore, the Sultan should have a free hand in managing the affairs of the state as per his will. Ghazali's theory of Khilafat is not only a departure from the principles laid down for such a political entity in the Quran and *ahadis* but it is also different from the model set forth by the rightly guided Caliphs. His idea of the Caliphate defies the praxis of the institution of the Caliphate that existed during the Umavi and the initial phase of the Abbasi regimes. It is true that what Ghazali had envisaged in the eleventh century ultimately turned out to be true for the Islamic world.

A mention must also be made of the views of Abu Zaid Abdur Rahman Ibn Khaldun (1332-1406) on Khilafat. As a matter of fact, he has not written exclusively on the issue but while replicating the Aristotelian plan with reference to the kinds of state, Khilafat is mentioned as one of the kinds. Ibn Khaldun contends that there are four kinds of state. The first one in his classification is the Khilafat, which he defines as the ideal Islamic state because it is divine having the sanction of the Prophet Muhammad and perfectly governed by the *Khulfa-e-Rashidun*. This state was governed according to the divine law of the Shariat, so long as the four rightly guided Caliphs were in power. Ibn Khaldun asserts that the office of the Caliph was elective but corroborates that the Caliph must be a Quraish. During the reign of the first four Caliphs the Caliphate not only took care of the people in this world but also prepared them for their salvation in the hereafter. The deterioration set in when the elective principle was replaced by the heredity and family affiliations that created the second type of state, the Mulk under Shariat. Ibn Khaldun, however, maintains that this kind of state was the second best because, though the elective principle was abandoned, the Shariat continued to be the law of the state and for that reason it was still an Islamic state. The third type, according to Ibn Khaldun is called Mulk under the Siyasat-e-Aqliya. At this stage there seems to be a complete severance of Islamic laws from political processes. The head of the state would not bother about either the elective principle or the Shariat. The absolute monarchy based on the principle of heredity came into existence wherein the monarch was the law-maker, implementer of the laws and also the final adjudicative authority. He had complete control over the administration and armed forces. He would lead a life of luxury and grandeur and to maintain such a lifestyle huge sums of public money would be spent. In a way religion was almost banished from the affairs of state. Ibn Khaldun, therefore, says that the third type of state cannot be called an Islamic but a Muslim-dominated state. Ibn Khaldun does not explain the fourth kind of state which he names Siyasat-e-Madaniya, a hypothetical model that never existed anywhere.

It is obvious that conceptually Ibn Khaldun does not add anything new to the theoretical framework that was created by his predecessors. His classification of the state, a device that he had borrowed from Aristotle suffers from the similar glitch that existed in the Aristotelian model. There can never be types of state but the governing system may be classified in different categories.

2

The Rightly Guided Caliphs

Yet the abstinence and humility of Umar were not inferior to the virtues of Abu Bakr: his food consisted of barley bread or dates; his drink was water; he preached in a gown that was torn or tattered in twelve places; and a Persian satrap, who paid his homage as to the conqueror, found him asleep among the beggars on the steps of the mosque of Muslims.

– Edward Gibbon

The birth, the alliance, the character of Ali, which exalted him above the rest of his countrymen, might justify his claim to the vacant throne of Arabia. The son of Abu Talib was, in his own right, the chief of the family of Hashem, and the hereditary prince or guardian of the city and temple of Mecca. The light of prophecy was extinct; but the husband of Fatima might expect the inheritance and blessings of her father; the Arabs had sometimes been patient of a female reign; and the two grandsons of the Prophet had often been fondled in his lap, and shown in his pulpit, as the hope of his age, and the Chiefs of the Youth of Paradise.

– Edward Gibbon

I

The anglicised version Caliph of the Arabic word *Khalifa* means 'representative' or 'successor'. The word is used in the Quran in the context of Adam who had to act as the representative (*Khalifa*) of Allah on earth. In Islamic history the word acquired the connotation of 'the head of the Muslim *ummah*' possessing mostly temporal powers. The death of Prophet Muhammad in 632 necessitated the appointment of a leader to administer the affairs of the nascent *ummah* and also promote the interest of the Islamic community. Since most people believe that the Prophet had not named a successor[1], Abu Bakr, a close friend and the father-in-law of the Prophet was nominated as *Khalifat ur Rasul Allah* (the political successor to the Messenger of God). Caliph (*Khalifa*) is thus the shortened version of *Khalifat ur Rasul Allah.* Though there are alternative titles for the leader of the Muslim community such as *Emir ul Muminin* (Commander of the Muslim community), *Imam ul Ummah* and *Imam ul Muminin*, Caliph has been more popular and remained in use for long.

The Sunnis believe that the first four Caliphs—Abu Bakr-as-Siddiq, Umar ibn al-Khattab, Usman ibn Affan and Ali ibn Abi Talib—were the 'Rightly Guided Caliphs' (*Khulfa ur Rashidun*) because they were not only the close companions of the Prophet Muhammad but had also suffered, strived and fought along with the Messenger of God to establish the sovereignty of Allah in the Arab peninsula and beyond. The Shias, however, do not recognise the Caliphate of the first three successors to the Prophet; they assert that only the reign of Ali and the short regime of Ali's eldest son, Hasan were the genuine periods of the Caliphate.

There was no standard method of selecting a leader among the Arabs. Historians, nevertheless, identify two practices that were traditionally followed by the Arabs to choose a chieftain. One, the prominent men of a tribe would gather after the death of their leader and would nominate from amongst them the most capable man as leader. There was no specific procedure for the constitution of this consultative forum (*shura*).[2] Two, the hereditary principle was also in existence according to which the eldest male member of the deceased leader's family would be automatically accepted as the new ruler. The Sunnis cite the former and the Shias the latter as the legitimate method for selecting a Caliph. The Sunnis argue that the method by which Abu Bakr was elected as the political successor to the Prophet was in conformity with the principle of democracy. Also it helped in choosing the most competent and skilful member of the community to lead the *ummah*. Shia argument is based on the primacy of the lineage; they further point out that the Prophet, on quite a few occasions, had hinted that Ali, his cousin and son-in-law, would be his political heir. In view of such indications, the

Shias maintain, the question of application of the democratic principle does not arise. This controversy was so intense that it caused the first major divide among the Muslims. In this sense the primary cause for the emergence of Sunni and Shia sects was essentially political.

Nevertheless, choosing a political heir was not the only difficulty that the budding Muslim community had to confront after the death of Prophet Muhammad. The size and nature of the powers of the successor, the Caliph, was also a complex one. Muhammad was the Prophet of Allah as well as the leader of the *ummah*. Therefore, he rightfully enjoyed the spiritual as well as temporal powers. However, his successors were not the messengers of God and for that reason could not enjoy the spiritual powers. Nonetheless, they were expected to conduct the affairs of the *ummah* in the light of Quranic endorsements. The vexed issue was whether to accept the authority of a Caliph in the religious domain or to restrict his powers only to the worldly sphere. So far as the powers of the first four Caliphs are concerned the Sunnis believe that they combined both religious and temporal because they were the *rightly guided* as companions of the Prophet and strictly adhered to the teachings of the Quran and *ahadis* (traditions of the Prophet) in all matters. Thereafter, the gradual codification of Islamic law (Shariat) and with that the emergence of the experts in Islamic faith and law, the ulama, corroded the powers of the Caliph considerably. The ulama, i.e. Islamic jurists, lawyers, judges, scholars et al. insisted that they alone would determine what was religiously just and the Caliph would have to act upon their advice. In modern parlance it was a tussle between the judiciary (ulama) and the executive (Caliph) that ended ultimately in the triumph of the former.

The Shia doctrine of the Caliphate is different; they stress that the spiritual as well as temporal leadership, as per the wish of the Prophet himself, passed on to Ali and thereafter to Ali's descendants by Fatima, the daughter of the Prophet. Thus, Ali was the first legitimate Caliph and after him Hasan, who reigned for a very short period was the last Caliph of the *Ahl-e-Bait* (House of the Prophet). At this point it is pertinent to clarify the distinction Shias make between Caliphate and imamate. Caliphate signifies the political leadership to be conducted without disregarding any injunction of the Quran while imamate is purely spiritual. Ali and Hasan, therefore, were both Caliphs as well as imams for they provided political and spiritual leadership to the Muslims. In 661, when Muawiya got hold of the right of leadership from Hasan, the concept of Caliphate in actuality came to an end. Although Muawiya and the successive rulers of the House of Ommeyyad did use the title of the Caliph they were in fact absolute monarchs. Similarly, the Abbasids, the Fatimids, the Ommeyyades of Cordova and the Ottoman Turks, all styled themselves as Caliphs which they were not in the pure Islamic sense.

Since the time Hasan relinquished the Caliphate no member from the House of Muhammad could acquire political leadership of the Muslims. Nevertheless, the spiritual leadership, the imamate "descended in succession to his (Ali's) and Fatima's posterity in 'the direct male line' until it came to Imam Hasan al-Askari, eleventh in descent from Ali, who died in 874 A.C. or 260 of the Hegira in the reign of Abbasid Caliph Mu'tamid."[3] Hasan al-Askari was in fact deported from Madina to Sammarra and imprisoned there by the Abbasid ruler Mutawakkil. His five-year-old son Muhammad al-Mahdi, the twelfth imam, also vanished mysteriously. With his disappearance the imamate came to an end. The Shias believe that though the twelfth imam is not physically present, he bestows spiritual guidance to the true believers and they call him the *Muntazar* (the Expected) imam who will appear at the appropriate time to cleanse the world from evil and tyranny. For this reason the major Shia sect is known as *Isna-e-Asharia*, as they are the followers of the twelve imams of the House of Muhammad.

Notwithstanding Shia's repudiation of the reigns of the first three Caliphs, the fact remains that an overwhelming majority of the Muslims of the world who profess to be Sunnis hold all the four *Rightly Guided Caliphs* in high esteem and regard their period of supremacy as the finest in the history of Islam. For most of the Sunnis it is almost a part of their faith to look forward to the setting up of the kind of rule that existed at the time of the *Khulfa ur Rashidun*. A devout Sunni is expected to strive, wherever possible, for the reconstruction of the socio-political structure after the model that had been built up by the first four Caliphs. It is, therefore, relevant to have a cursory look at the life and reign of each one of the rightly guided Caliphs.

II

In the *jahilya* (prior to the rise of Islam), the tribe of Qureish was the most powerful in the Arab peninsula which increasingly got divided into two factions: Banu Hashim and Banu Umayyah. Most of the historians including Ibn Khaldun concur that in matters of worldly affairs such as commerce, social dealings and political power, Banu Umayyah surpassed Banu Hashim. The birth of the Prophet Muhammad, however, granted enviable spiritual pride and sacred honour to Banu Hashim. During the lifetime of the Prophet the traditional jealousy and resentment between the two factions of the *ummah* remained dormant. Nevertheless, the death of the Prophet caused the old rivalry to raise its ugly head. Since the Prophet, according to Sunnis, had not named any successor, the issue of his political heir turned into a major controversy that finally caused the great divide among Muslims.

During his brief illness, however, the Prophet had ordained Abu Bakr to lead the congregational prayers. This, according to the Sunni School, was enough indication for selecting the political representative of the Prophet. The original name of Abu Bakr (literally the 'owner of camels') was Abdul Kaaba ibn Usman abu Quhafa. He came to be popularly known as Abu Bakr when he started raising camels, which was his main business. Later his real name was changed by the Prophet from Abdul Kaaba to Abdullah. His title, al-Siddiq (testifier of the truth), too was conferred on him by the Prophet. He was born in Mecca in c. 573 to Usman Abu Quhafa and Salma Umm-ul-Khair. Most accounts inform us that he was exceptionally handsome and because of his good looks he was nicknamed Atiq which means a handsome gentleman.[4].His family was quite affluent and as was the practice among the well-heeled Meccans to let their children grow among the nomads of the desert, the Bedouins, so that they could become tough and strong, Abu Bakr too spent his childhood playing among the children of the Bedouins.

Abu Bakr was about three years younger than the Prophet and they first became friends when ten-year-old Abu Bakr accompanied his father in a merchants' caravan to Syria; Muhammad too was in the caravan. His class affiliation helped him seek education and develop a taste for poetry. Traditions point out that he would attend the poetic conventions that were a part of the annual fair at Ukaz.[5] At the age of 18, he joined the family business of trading in cloth and started travelling to distant places with the caravans. In those days these travels were in reality a source of gaining experience and knowledge and thus Abu Bakr, besides becoming a rich businessman also became a mature and well-informed member of Meccan society. Consequently, he was appointed as an honorary judge to decide blood-money in cases of murder. After his marriage to Khadija bint Khuwailid, Muhammad shifted to her house that was in the same locality as that of Abu Bakr. Thus, their acquaintance that was first initiated in their boyhood in a caravan developed into a close friendship during their adulthood.

Abu Bakr got to know about Muhammad's Apostleship of Allah when he returned from Yeman where he had gone on a business trip. He met the Prophet and immediately submitted to the sovereignty of Allah. He was the third male who embraced Islam on the call of Muhammad and "in his sincere, earnest and unvarying attachment to Mohammed he might almost be compared with Ali."[6] The Prophet would often speak about Abu Bakr's conversion to Islam thus: "To whomsoever I invited to embrace Islam he either took some time to think over it or showed some reluctance except Abu Bakr bin Quhafa who neither took time to think over it nor hesitated in accepting the call."[7] On becoming a Muslim he completely devoted himself to the cause of Islam and till his death remained steadfast in his mission. One of his wives, Qutaylah bint Abdul Uzza refused to embrace Islam and, therefore, he divorced her. His other wife, Umme Ruman, however, willingly joined the fold of Islam. All his children with the exception of Abdur Rahman too got converted to Islam. Abu Bakr got separated from his son Abdur Rahman.

Abu Bakr earnestly got engaged in inviting people to embrace the monotheistic faith of the Prophet and many of his friends and acquaintances responded positively to his call. The prominent persons who got converted to Islam on the invitation of Abu Bakr were, Usman bin Affan, Zubair bin Awwam, Abdur Rahman bin

Awf, Saad bin Abi Waqqas, Talhah bin Ubaidullah, Abu Ubaidah ibn Jarrah, Abudullah bin Asad, Khalid ibn Said and Abu Hudaifah ibn Mughairah.[8] Slavery was an accepted institution those days not only in Arabia but in most parts of the world. Though Islam did not specifically abolish the evil institution, it strongly recommended a just and humane treatment of slaves. Abu Bakr, in fact, allocated a huge fund for the cause of Islam out of which he would purchase the slaves who embraced Islam and then release them from bondage. The most prominent slave who was thus released by Abu Bakr was Bilal ibn Ribah. Abu Bakr would mostly purchase and release women and old slaves to free them from brutal suffering. Sunni ulama maintain that the following verses of the Quran are about the compassionate acts of Abu Bakr:

> As for him who giveth and is dutiful (towards Allah) and believeth in goodness; Surely we will ease his way unto the state of ease."[9] Also, "Who giveth his wealth that he may grow (in goodness), and none hath with him any favour for reward, except as seeking (to fulfil) the purpose of his Lord Most High. He will be content.[10]

Though Abu Bakr was a rich man, he had to face similar persecution at the hands of the Qureish as other Muslims did. On one occasion he was beaten so mercilessly that he fell down unconscious. Reacting to such brutality of the Qureish, Abu Bakr's mother embraced Islam at this point of time. In 617, when the Qureish ostracised almost the entire clan of Banu Hashim forcing them to seek refuge in a gorge some distance away from Mecca, Abu Bakr had to migrate first to Yemen and then to Abyssinia (the present Ethiopia) where a delegation of Muslims had migrated earlier. By 622, the Muslims, on the invitation of the Ansars, started migrating to Medina in batches. When the Prophet settled on migrating himself he let Abu Bakr know that "Allah has given permission to me to emigrate." When Abu Bakr anxiously inquired if he could accompany him, the Prophet replied, "Yes, you too will emigrate with me."[11]

The significance of Abu Bakr in the history of Islam is also evident from the fact that the Prophet chose him as his companion on the hazardous journey to Medina that proved momentous for the progress of Islam. Prior to the actual day of emigration, Abu Bakr had made meticulous arrangements so that the Qureish should not pursue them. He had hired the services of Abdullah bin Arqat, a polytheist, as a guide. Then on the appointed day the Prophet went to the house of Abu Bakr and both of them used the back window of the house to embark on the journey. They did not take the way to Medina but moved in the opposite direction and, as planned, took refuge in a cave in mount Saur, located in the south of Mecca. Abu Bakr had instructed his son Abdullah to keep him informed about the plans of the Qureish. Thus, Abdullah would inform the Prophet and his father about the affairs of Mecca daily. Every evening Asma, the daughter of Abu Bakr, would arrive at the mouth of the cave with food. Abu Bakr's released slave, Aemir bin Fahira would also bring the flock of goats to the entry of the cave to supply milk to the Prophet and Abu Bakr. The Qureish announced the reward of one hundred camels to anyone who would help bring back the fugitives to Mecca.[12] According to an account a search-party had come to the mouth of the cave but could not see them. A verse of the Quran speaks about it:

> If ye help him not, still Allah helped him when those who disbelieve drove him forth, the second of two; when they two were in the cave, when he said unto his comrade: Grieve not. Lo! Allah is with us. Then Allah caused His peace of reassurance to descend upon him and supported him with hosts ye cannot see, and made the word of those who disbelieved the nethermost, while Allah's word it was that became the uppermost. Allah is Mighty, Wise.[13]

The Prophet and Abu Bakr stayed in the cave for three days and when they felt it was safe to proceed further they undertook the journey to Medina. The first person who noticed them on the outskirts of Medina was a Jew. It was a Monday and the date as per CE was September 20, 622. Ahead of entering the city they stayed for three days in Quba, a suburb of Medina.[14] In Medina too Abu Bakr got engaged in cloth trading and quickly achieved success in the business. His daughter, Aisha who was engaged to the Prophet about a year earlier was handed over to her husband in a simple wedding ceremony at the beginning of 623. His friendship with the Prophet was further strengthened when Aisha, his daughter became the wife of the Messenger of God.

Thereafter, in various battles that were fought in the life span of the Prophet, Abu Bakr had always been present along with the

Messenger of God. Nevertheless, there are different versions in Sunni and Shia accounts about Abu Bakr's military achievements. Obviously the Shia chroniclers tend to compare the military accomplishments of Ali with those of Abu Bakr and find the latter wanting in this respect. It is a fact but comparing the two regarding their fighting prowess is an exercise in futility. Abu Bakr was a businessman, not a warrior. Prior to the Battle of Badr, perhaps he had not seen any military action. He was also much senior to Ali when the series of battles of Islam commenced. Yet, he took part in almost all the battles on the command of the Prophet.

In the Battle of Badr he was not an actual combatant but was assigned the job of guarding the tent of the Prophet. In the Battle of Uhud that was fought a year later in 625, Abu Bakr's son Abdur Rahman[15] who was still an idol worshipper was in the army of the Qureish, and as per the accounts, he dared his father for a one-on-one combat. Abu Bakr stepped forward to accept the challenge but was held back by the Prophet. The Battle of Uhud was a disaster for the Muslims and in the second phase of it many Muslim soldiers had escaped from the battlefield. In the Sunni accounts, however, Abu Bakr was one of the few who remained steadfast guarding the Prophet who was severely injured. A few months later, Abu Bakr took part in the operation against the Jewish tribe of Abu Nadir. Subsequently he was in action in the Battle of the Trench and the Battle of Banu Qurayza, both fought in the year 627. The following year he joined the drive against the Jews of Khaybar and at one point he was handed over the command of the Muslim forces that attacked the Jewish citadel of Qamos. In 629, he was also the joint commander with Umar of the reinforcement army that went to Zaat-ul-Sallasal to assist Amr ibn Aas. An important event took place in the life of Abu Bakr just before the conquest of Mecca that his father got converted to Islam. Abu Bakr took part in the Battle of Hunain as well as in the Siege of Taif. He accompanied the Prophet in the campaign of Tabuk that was incidentally the last military conquest of the Messenger of Allah.

Muhammad became unwell on return from the farewell Hajj. The Sunni accounts reveal that the Prophet despite being ill went to the mosque, sat on the pulpit and spoke in front of the people who were present, "No doubt, I am indebted to Abu Bakr more than to anybody else regarding both his companionship and his wealth. And if I had to take a Khalil from my followers, I would certainly have taken Abu Bakr, but the fraternity of Islam is sufficient. Let no door of the mosque remain open, except the door of Abu Bakr."[16] On hearing the news of the demise of the Prophet Abu Bakr first went from his house to the mosque of the Prophet and then entered the quarters of Aisha. As per the popular accounts, he went straight to the dead body of the Prophet, kissed him on the forehead and cried profusely. At the time Umar was in a state of disbelief and was giving expression to his state of mind in front of the people who had gathered in Masjid-e-Nabawi: "By Allah, he is not dead but has gone to his Lord as Musa ibn Imran went and remained hidden from his people for forty days. Musa returned after it was said that he had died. By Allah, the Messenger of Allah will come back and he will cut off the hands and legs of those who claim his death."[17]

Abu Bakr returned to the mosque and tried to soothe down Umar who could not be easily pacified. Then Abu Bakr addressed the congregation arguing that those who worshipped Muhammad, then Muhammad was dead for them. However, for those who worshipped Allah, then Allah was alive and eternal. In support of his reasoning he cited the following verse of the Quran:

> Muhammad is but a messenger, messengers (the like of whom) have passed away with him. Will it be that, when he dieth or is slain, ye will turn back on your heels? He who turneth back doth no hurt to Allah, and Allah will reward the thankful.[18]

The soothing words of Abu Bakr, in particular, the appropriate verse of the Quran helped Umar recover his poise and finally he realised that the Prophet was indeed no more. The death of the Prophet led to a power struggle among the Muslims who at the time constituted three distinct groups in Medina. The largest faction of the Ansars, the natives of the city, had staked their claim for the political headship and under the supervision of their leader Saad ibn Abada, had gathered at Saqifah Bani Saida, a suburb of Medina, to choose the course of action to realise their claim. The Muhajirun were divided in two groups; the larger one comprising the non-Hashmites was led by Abu Bakr and Umar and the members of the House of Muhammad, the Hashmites had an undisputed leader in Ali. It was Umar who moved quickly to quash the aspiration of the Ansars. He took Abu Bakr along to the meeting of the natives; both Abu Bakr and Umar addressed the gathering arguing that a Qureish had a better claim to the Caliphate of the Messenger of God than any local Muslim. Thereafter, Umar suddenly held the hand of Abu Bakr and vowed his allegiance. Most of the Ansars, as they were in awe of Umar, pledged the allegiance to Abu Bakr. This was a brilliant tactic as it not only ensured the homage of the largest group in favour of Abu Bakr but also isolated the Hashmites and their leader Ali.

Though Ali resisted pledging homage to the first Caliph for about six months, he finally gave in to uphold the unity of the *ummah*. The Shias criticism of Abu Bakr's nomination rests on two points. First, instead of making arrangements for the funeral of the Prophet the two senior companions, Abu Bakr and Umar, got busy in politicking and ensuring the protection of their own interests. Their actions smack of political ambitions and an intense craving for earthly power, Two, the Muslims in general and Abu Bakr and Umar in particular, had conveniently ignored the wish of the Prophet announced publicly at Ghadir Khumm that for all those who thought of him as their protector and guardian, Ali would be their protector and guardian after his death. For someone who intends to sit in judgment without bias it would be a tough task to disagree with the Shia arguments.

Considering Abu Bakr's seniority and his long and selfless association with the Prophet his choice as the first Caliph was not altogether askew. He was a conscientious and kind-hearted man who would always empathize with the destitute and the weak and would leave no stone unturned to help them. He apportioned his fortune for two things—one, to support the needy members of the *ummah* and two, to donate for the cause of Islam. It is reported that once when the funds were needed for the protection of Medina, Abu Bakr placed all his wealth before the Prophet and when the Messenger of God inquired whether he left anything for himself and his family Abu Bakr replied, "Allah and His Prophet."

After his nomination, Abu Bakr addressed the Muslims in these words: "Behold me charged with the cares of the government. I am not the best among you; I need all your advice and your help.

If I do well, support me; if I mistake counsel me. To tell you truth to a person commissioned to rule is faithful allegiance; to conceal it is treason. In my sight, the powerful and the weak are alike; and to both I wish to render justice. As I obey God and His Prophet, obey me; if I neglect the laws of God and the Prophet, I have no more right to your obedience."[19]

During his short term of Caliphate, Abu Bakr proved to be a laudable administrator and protector of the faith. The first arduous task Abu Bakr had to face on assuming the charge of the Caliphate was to deal with the rebellion and intimidating designs of various tribes that had threatened the very existence of Islam. In conformity with the pre-Islamic tradition, various tribes, on hearing the news of the death of the Prophet, refused to pay taxes (*zakat*) claiming that they were obliged to abide by the terms of the alliance only during the lifetime of the Prophet; with the death of Muhammad the alliance too came to an end and, therefore, they had no obligation to pay taxes. Besides, since they were till recently the idolaters and had flexible moral norms, they felt rather stifled because of the austere moral code of Islam. The escape route was shown by some shrewd and unscrupulous individuals who declared that they were the 'prophets' themselves. The most well-known in Muslim accounts is the name of Musaylimah ibn Habib. He was the chief of a powerful and one of the largest tribes, Banu Hanifa, which helped him secure the solid support of his tribesmen for promoting the claim of his 'prophet-hood'.[20] Thus, Abu Bakr, immediately after assuming the charge of the Caliphate, had to deal with two thorny problems. First he had to force the rebellious tribes to pay taxes and second, to suppress the fast-spreading iniquity of apostasy.

Abu Bakr met the dual challenge with astounding competence and swiftness. He systematically divided the Muslim army into eleven companies and put each one of it under the command of a skilful warrior. The strongest company was the one commanded by Khalid bin Walid. The strategy of Abu Bakr was first to suppress the rebellions in the areas that were closest to Medina. Thus began the Wars of Apostasy (*Ridda Wars*) within months of the death of the Prophet. The Muslim forces under various commanders routed the rebellious tribes in Bahrain, Oman, Hadramawt and Yeman where al-Aswad had claimed himself to be a 'prophet'.[21] The toughest was of course the Battle of Yamama waged against Musaylimah in which the Muslim forces were led by Khalid bin Walid. With a remarkable victory achieved by Khalid the Wars of Apostasy finally came to an end in 633. Islam was once again firmly established in Arabia.

The emergence of Islam and the remarkable display of brotherhood and unity by the ummah under the standard of the Sovereign Allah alarmed the Byzantine and the Persian, the two major empires neighbouring the Arab peninsula. They were planning to destroy the nascent *ummah* before it became too strong. Abu Bakr got wind of the militant designs of the adjoining empires. The confrontation began first with the Persians. A Muslim commander, Misnah ibn Haris, invaded some of the Arab towns of Iraq that were part of the Persian Empire and surprisingly subdued the armed forces of one of the two strongest empires of the time. The rich spoils of the war the pastoral Muslim warriors collected were something they had never imagined of. The booty stunned them. Ibn Haris reported to Abu Bakr about his astonishing victory and in return got the official sanction of the conquest of Persia. It was not purely a religious zeal, which is the preferred refrain of the Muslim chroniclers, which prompted the Muslim armies to take on the world's most powerful and advanced nations of the time. There was certainly an economic dimension to their conquests. The Persian Empire at the time was perhaps the mightiest because on many occasions it had subjugated its traditional rival the Byzantine Empire. The Persians had no feeling for the Arabs except contempt. They, therefore, could never imagine that the poorest, the dullest and the weakest people of the Arabian Peninsula could become a threat to their gigantic empire. Call it audaciousness or an error of judgment, the subsequent events proved that the Persians were awfully wrong.

For a methodical conquest of the Persian Empire, Abu Bakr took some level-headed decisions. First, he did not force every able-bodied Muslim to join the army. He appealed only to those who had the genuine commitment to fight for the mission of Allah to go in with the forces. Secondly, he appointed Khalid bin Walid the commander of the Muslim army. It must be underscored here that in the seminal years, the cause of Islam was competently served by the military genius of Khalid bin Walid. This natural warrior who had almost won the Battle of Uhud for the enemies of Islam became the sword of Islam after joining the Muslim brotherhood. The Prophet had assigned him the command of the Islamic army on quite a few occasions. Abu Bakr too entrusted him the similar responsibility against the Persians.

Khalid began the conquest of the Persian Empire in March 633, as the head of eighteen thousand soldiers and in two months he decisively defeated the Persians in four consecutive battles, Battle of Chains, Battle of River, Battle of Walaia and the Battle of Ullais. In the last week of May, the capital city of Iraq, Hira, too was conquered. In June, Khalid added the city of al-Anbar to the Islamic state and the following month vanquished the city of Ein ul-Tamr. With this almost the entire Euphrates region of Iraq had come under the sway of Islam. Then, Khalid was commanded by the Caliph to lead a reinforcement army to help another Muslim commander, Ayaz bin Ghanam, who was surrounded by the rebel tribes in northern Arabia. Khalid defeated the mutineers in the Battle of Daumat ul-Jandal in the last week of August 633. In the meantime, a huge Persian army had advanced to expel the Muslims from Iraq. This was a litmus test for Khalid to prove his military expertise. He did exactly that. He surprised the huge and well-armed army of the Persians by attacking it at night from three directions in a series of well synchronized attacks. He decisively defeated the Persians in the Battle of Muzieh, the Battle of Sanni and the Battle of Zumail. These setbacks almost ended the Persian suzerainty over Iraq. Khalid then moved on to eliminate the Persians from the southern and western parts of Iraq. In the Battle of Firaz fought in December 633, Khalid routed the united army of the Persian and Byzantian soldiers. Then he turned his attention to capture the Persian Capital Ctesiphon (Arabic Madain). However, before he could do it he was commanded by Abu Bakr to proceed to Syria to help the Muslim army against the Byzantines.

The threat from the Byzantine Empire was, in fact, sensed during the lifetime of the Prophet and to face the imminent danger he had also sent an army under the command of Usama, the son of Zaid. The army had marched from Medina on its way to Syria and put up a camp not far from the city when the news of the illness of the Prophet reached Usama. He called off the expedition and returned to Medina. Abu Bakr, on becoming the Caliph affirmed to accomplish what the Prophet had desired. He sent three companies, each comprising three thousand men under the separate commands of Amr bin Aas, Yazid bin abi-Sufyan, and Suhrabil bin Hasanah to invade Syria. The parting instructions he gave the three commanders were extremely humane and sensible. One can put them side by side the Geneva Convention and the agenda of the Greens. It is the finest argument against those who spread the canard that Islam is a violent religion. A part of the instructions is worth citing here:

> See that thou avoidest treachery. Depart not in any way from the right. Thou shalt mutilate none, neither shalt thou kill child or aged man, nor any woman. Injure not the date-palm, neither burn it with fire, and cut not down any tree wherein food for man or beast is. Slay not the flocks or herds of camels, saving for needful sustenance. You may eat the meat which the men of the land shall bring unto you in their vessels, making mention thereon of the name of the Lord. And the monks with shaven heads, if they submit, leave them unmolested.[22]

In the first encounter Yazid defeated Sergius, the Byzantine ruler of Palestine Heraclius, the Byzantine Emperor, on hearing the news of Sergius' defeat, dispatched a huge army under the command of his brother, Theodorus. It was at this point that Abu Bakr ordered Khalid bin Walid to rush to assist the Muslim forces on the Syrian front. Riding across an almost waterless Syrian desert for eighteen days, Khalid reached the outskirts of Damascus when the gigantic Byzantine army was about to execute its final assault to decimate the Muslim forces. The sudden arrival of Khalid at the rear of the Byzantine army and the heroic assault of the warriors under his command on a much powerful and larger force unnerved the Byzantines and they were totally routed. Thus began a series of Khalid's successful expeditions in Syria. He swiftly captured the strongholds of the Byzantines bordering Damascus and defeated the Christian army of the Ghassanids at Marj Rahit.[23] Thereafter, he reached Basra to assist the Muslim forces who were in a precarious position. Khalid's arrival on the scene turned a certain rout into a remarkable triumph. Here he met the forces that were under the command of Ubaida bin Jarrah and as per the instructions of the Caliph, assumed the command of a unified army of the Muslims.

In July 634, Khalid defeated a much larger Byzantine army in the Battle of Ainadayn. That left the city of Damascus vulnerable to the Muslims. Khalid moved towards Damascus. On the way he had to fight two more battles, the Battle of Yaqusa and the Battle of Maraj as Saffar; in both the battles the enemy forces were badly mauled. Finally Khalid besieged the oldest city of the world. It was during the siege of Damascus, which according to some accounts lasted for six months, Abu Bakr died and Umar assumed the charge of the Caliphate. So when Khalid conquered Damascus in September 634, Umar was at the helms of affairs.

In the Battle of Yamama, about six thousand Muslims had died and quite a few of them were those who had memorized the Quran. It created a difficult situation as the number of those who had committed the Quran to memory was drastically reduced. When Umar noticed the problem he informed Abu Bakr that the number of persons who had memorised the Quran would decline as the companions of the Prophet would gradually depart from the world. He, therefore, suggested that in order to preserve the Quran, an authentic version of it should be compiled in written form. Initially, Abu Bakr refused to undertake what the Prophet himself had not done. Nevertheless, on Umar's persistence, the Caliph agreed to undertake the project. He constituted a committee headed by Zaid bin Sabit, a scribe of the revealed verses. The committee devised a systematic and painstaking method for the compilation of the Holy Book. First, all the verses that were in possession of the companions were collected. Then after a scrupulous process of checking and counter-checking, the authenticity of each verse was established and then the verses were written down. Through this diligent method a single copy of the Quran was compiled and handed over to the Caliph. When Abu Bakar fell sick he had given this copy to Umar who later gave it to Hafsa, his daughter and the wife of the Prophet. It was on the basis of this copy that the standardized version of the Quran, was produced in the reign of Usman.[24]

Abu Bakr died on August 23, 634, after a brief illness. On his deathbed he dictated the testament to Usman nominating Umar as his successor. Though he was Caliph for barely two and a quarter years, he effectively guided the Muslim forces against the powerful Sassanid Empire of Persia and Byzantine Empire. Since he was the first Caliph, many institutions that came to be associated with a typical Islamic state were set up during his reign. For instance, the public exchequer of an Islamic state, *Bait-ul-Mal,* was established by him. Similarly, he instituted the crown pasture for the first time. It is also claimed in some accounts that he was the one who promoted *Ijtihad*.[25] He was a close friend of Muhammad and he was the first person outside the house of the Prophet who embraced Islam. After the conversion he remained selflessly devoted to the Prophet and the mission of Islam all through his life.

Since the Shias do not recognise the first three Caliphs as the legitimate successors of the Prophet, they criticise Abu Bakr for various reasons. Objectively speaking, two grievances appear to be genuine. The basic objection of the Shias is that he was installed as the Caliph by a joint conspiracy hatched against Ali by a larger group of the emigrants and the Ansars. Another grievance of the Shias is in respect with the property of Muhammad's daughter Fatima which Abu Bakr refused to restore to her and even doubted her testimony in the matter. It must be admitted that the post of the Caliph was essentially a political one. Shias confuse it with the spiritual position of Imamate. Ali should have been the natural choice not solely because he belonged to the house of the Prophet but he was also a great warrior as well as an intellectual. Nevertheless, the members of the house of the Prophet did not have the popular support. Though, no Caliph got elected democratically, as some of the Sunni ulama claim, the first two Caliphs at least had a wider acceptance among the residents of Medina than Ali. Therefore, the lapses on the part of Abu Bakr or later Umar in connection with the members of the house of Prophet were largely of a political nature. On account of them it is unfair to deride all the noble actions of Abu Bakr.

III

When Abu Bakr fell ill and had a premonition about his death he nominated Umar to succeed him as the Caliph and the choice was willingly approved by all the members of the *ummah* including the members belonging to the House of Muhammad. Umar was also an outstanding resident of Mecca, scion of a leading family of Banu Adi clan, a branch of the Qureish. The family had a distinction for its wide-ranging knowledge of genealogy. Umar's grandfather, Fuzail bin Abduluzza, was an important official of a department that looked after foreign affairs of *Khana-e-Kaaba*.[26] Umar too had expertise in the discipline of lineage besides being a master swordsman, a skilled wrestler and a reasonably moving speaker. He also had another merit that was extremely rare in seventh-century Arabia, i.e. the ability to read and write that he mastered at quite an early age. Like most of the Meccans, Umar too got engaged in business that made him travel to many foreign lands and endowed his personality with self-assurance.[27] He had a fiery temper and before converting to Islam was a vehement opponent of the Prophet and his monotheistic religion. His notoriety for the persecution of the Muslims was quite well-known.

Umar ibn al-Khattab was born in 583, about thirteen years after the birth of the Prophet, in the family of Adi ibn-Ka'b. When the Prophet began preaching among the residents of Mecca to renounce worshipping idols and accept the monotheistic faith of peace, Umar was twenty-seven. The mission of the Prophet infuriated him so much that he became an avowed enemy of all those who joined the ranks of Muhammad. It is reported that when his slave-girl, Lubniah[28] embraced the new faith he beat her so severely that she fell unconscious. Despite the fierce persecution of the neo-converts, the *ummah* was slowly growing. It was unacceptable to Umar. It is said that one day he drew his sword and set off with the intention of killing the Prophet. On the way he met a friend, Naim bin Abdullah,[29] who inquired why he looked so incensed and carrying a naked sword. Umar informed him about his intention. The friend advised him to go first to the house of his sister Fatima who along with her husband got converted to Islam. This was shocking news to him. Now he started towards Fatima's house in a furious rage with the intent to kill her and his brother-in-law. When he went up to the house he overheard some verses of the Quran that were being recited by his sister and her husband. The magic and the charm of the verses had a thrilling effect on his mind. He entered the house still carrying the naked sword. His sister and brother-in-law stopped reading and assumed that Umar would kill them. It is said that Fatima and her husband Said bin Zaid told Umar, "Yes, we have embraced Islam and believe in Allah and His Messenger. You can do whatever you like."[30] He asked his sister to recite again what she was reading. She did it. On hearing the sacred verses, Umar got intoxicated with spiritual ecstasy.

In a state of trance he went to the house where the Prophet was teaching the Muslims. He still held the naked sword that alarmed the handful of Muslims gathered over there. Nevertheless, they were pleasantly surprised when Umar kissed the hand of the Prophet and appealed to be taken into the brotherhood of the Muslims. According to traditions he was among the early converts: "He accepted Islam very early on, after forty other men and eleven women. Some say that it was after thirty-nine men and twenty-three women, and so some say, after forty-five men and eleven women. But it was only after he accepted Islam that Islam was shown openly in Mecca and the Muslims rejoiced in him."[31] No doubt Umar's conversion to Islam proved quite decisive for the mission of the Prophet. He was a man of courage and honour. His conversion to Islam was a huge setback to the Qureish for Umar was not the kind of person who would quietly suffer the persecution of the Muslims; now the enemies of Islam had to deal with substantial resistance. With Umar amongst their midst, the Muslims decided to say the prayers openly. On Umar's suggestion the small Muslim community offered the prayers within the precincts of the Kaaba. Besides being a brave man, Umar possessed a sharp mind that helped him appraise people and circumstances. He was an open, frank and honest person who would not mince his words expressing his views about someone or something. Once he joined the *ummah* he devoted himself totally to the Prophet and his mission. For his exceptional personal character, the Prophet gave him the title of *al-Farooq* (One who can distinguish between Truth and Deception).

When the Prophet permitted the believers to emigrate to Medina, Umar was in the second batch with twenty others who left Mecca. Nonetheless, being the kind of man he was, he did not conceal his emigration from anyone. According to Ali, "I don't know of anyone who didn't emigrate in secret except for 'Umar ibn al-Khattab; because when he wanted to emigrate he strapped on his sword, put his bow over his shoulder, carried his arrows in his hand, and came to Kaaba where the nobles of Quraysh were in the courtyard. He performed seven circuits, and then prayed two raka'at at the Station (of Ibrahim). Then he approached their circle one step at a time and said, 'What ugly faces! Whoever wishes to bereave his mother, orphan his children and widow his wife then let him meet me behind this valley.' Not one of them followed him."[32] He was an exceptionally brave man. As the subsequent events would reveal he played a crucial role in strengthening and expanding the Islamic state particularly after the death of the Prophet.

Abu Bakr and Umar were the principal advisors to the Prophet in Medina. Umar took part in almost all the battles that were fought during the Prophet's lifetime. In the Battle of Badr (624), the first Muslim who laid down his life was Maheja, a slave of Umar.[33] In the Battle of Uhud, when the Prophet got severely injured and fell into a trough, many companions were dispirited believing that the Messenger of Islam got killed. Some of them fled from the field, some stopped fighting while a few remained committed to the fight against the idolaters. About Umar, Shibli says, "...all traditions testify that despite being in a state of outrage, Hazrat Umar did not leave the battlefield and when he got the news that the Prophet was alive, he immediately rushed to care for the hallowed one."[34] Subsequently, Umar fearlessly subdued the Jewish tribe of Banu Nadir and in 627, he took part in the Battles of the Trench and Qurayza. In the Battle of Khaybar (628), he was very much in action. Likewise, he was with the Muslim army at the time of the Conquest of Mecca (630), Battle of Hunain and the siege of Taif. In 631, there were reports that the Byzantine army could attack Arabia. The Prophet got engaged in raising a suitable Muslim army and for the purpose he issued an appeal for donations. Umar donated half of whatever he possessed[35] and joined the army that had gone up to Tabuk under the command of the Prophet.

Umar played a key role in installing Abu Bakr as the first Caliph. Nevertheless, Sunni and Shia versions differ in respect with the fairness of strategy that Umar had resorted to in settling the contentious issue. There were three parties that were vying for the

Caliphate after the death of the Prophet. Ansars (literally helpers), the natives of the city of Medina wanted someone of their own to be the leader of the *ummah* and for this purpose they had organised a meeting at Saqifah, a suburb of Medina. Abu Bakr and Umar wished to nominate a Muhajir (the emigrant) as the Caliph. Therefore, when Umar got to know about the meeting of the Ansars, he proceeded to Saqifah and despite a hostile reception finally managed to convince a large section of the Ansars to accept Abu Bakr as the Caliph for the sake of the unity of the ummah.[36] The third party, the Hashmites, however, refused to accept Abu Bakr's Caliphate because they believed that it rightfully belonged to Ali. All the leading members of the House of Muhammad would regularly gather at the house of Fatima to discuss the course of action to challenge Abu Bakr's nomination. The Shia accounts suggest that Abu Bakr and Umar had used force to secure the allegiance of Ali and other Hashmites. Even though the expression 'use of force' sounds an overstatement, a Sunni source concedes that Umar made attempts to take the allegiance of the Hashmites by force but they stuck to their position. Therefore, Shibli on authorities of Ibn Abi Shibah and Allama Tabri states that Umar went to the house Fatima and called out, "O daughter of the Messenger of Allah! I swear in the name of God that all of us like you more than anyone. However, if people keep gathering in your house, then I, because of the presence of these people, will burn down the house."[37] Thus, all the accounts indicate two things: one, Umar played a pivotal role in the nomination of Abu Bakr and two, Ali did not pay homage to Abu Bakr willingly.

Umar was the principal advisor and secretary to Abu Bakr during his short-term Caliphate. When different tribes of Arabia refused to pay taxes, Abu Bakr decided to take military action against the rebels. Umar, initially had reservations about military operations against the rebellious tribes as he wanted to keep the Muslim-Arabian unity intact to confront a Byzantine or Persian invasion. Later, however, he accepted Abu Bakr's point of view and along with Khalid bin Walid, unreservedly took part in the Ridda wars. An incident that led to a difference of opinion between the Caliph and Umar relates to Khalid. Umar had advised Abu Bakr to recall Khalid from the front before the Battle of Yamama for according to Umar, Khalid had killed Malik ibn Nuwayrah, a rebel chief with the sole purpose of marrying his beautiful wife, Laila bint al-Minhal. It was Malik's brother who had misinformed Umar that Malik was a Muslim and an upright man; the fact was, he was not a Muslim and a state criminal. Abu Bakr refused to call Khalid back to the chagrin of Umar.

All accounts, Muslim as well as non-Muslim, acquiesce that Khalid bin Walid was a military genius whose role in Islamic expansion can hardly be exaggerated. Once he embraced Islam he remained completely devoted to the faith. When Umar took up the Caliphate, Khalid remained as loyal to him as he was to the Prophet and Abu Bakr. Under his command the Muslim forces gained remarkable successes in Iraq and Syria. His military exploits made him immensely popular throughout the Islamic empire. It was, therefore, quite shocking when Umar first removed him from the post of commander by placing him under the command of Ubaidah ibn al-Jarrah and ultimately, in 638, dismissed him from military service. The Caliph's decision was not palatable to many and people openly expressed their resentment against it in Medina. Some accounts imply that though Khalid was a cousin of Umar their correlation was far from amiable. The incident of Malik ibn Nuwayrah further exacerbated the already uptight rapport between the two. Many people in Medina, therefore, inferred that since Abu Bakr turned down Umar's advice regarding the ibn Nuwayrah's incident, Umar dealt with Khalid severely on becoming the Caliph.

Nevertheless, many Sunni accounts justify Umar's action on the ground that Khalid's unprecedented popularity could have led to idolisation of a man and thus undermined the cause of Islam. It is reported that Umar did not approve of Khalid's irregularities. Khalid would not submit the accounts to the office of the Caliph and even after Umar's directives to the effect, he refused to oblige. It was sheer defiance and thus Umar was justified in removing him from the position of commander-in-chief. Thereafter, the Caliph got the information that Khalid gifted ten thousand dirham to a poet. As a result, Umar wrote to Ubaidah ibn al-Jarrah that if Khalid had paid the amount from his own reserves he squandered the money and if he had paid it from the public exchequer then he was guilty of corruption. Thus, he was dismissed from military service. After the dismissal, Khalid reached Medina and having presented himself before the Caliph said, "Umar! God swear, you are unjust in my case. Umar asked, 'how did you get so much money?' Khalid replied, 'from the spoils of wars and I am prepared to hand over the amount that exceeds sixty thousand.' Then, Rs. twenty thousand were found in excess, which were deposited in *Bait-ul-Maal* (public exchequer). (Then) Hazrat Umar spoke to Khalid, 'Khalid! By God you are dear to me and I also respect you.' Thereafter, he wrote letters to all the officials of the empire that 'I did not dismiss Khalid because of corruption or antagonism but I had observed that people had started venerating him and, therefore, I thought it proper to dismiss him so that people should realise that it is God that makes everything happen."[38]

Umar's reign was a period of Islamic expansion. It was he who trounced great empires such as Byzantine and Persia and took the standard of Islam to Iraq, Iran, Egypt and Palestine. The Muslim army first defeated the Persian troops in a fierce battle at Qadisiyya. The Persians could never fully recover after this defeat and continued to lose grounds in subsequent battles. The decisive victory of the Muslims at Nihavand in 642 smashed the Persian resistance beyond recovery; the last Sassanid monarch fled to Khurasan where he was assassinated in 651.

Umar continued the offensive policy of Abu Bakr in respect of the Byzantine Empire. Under his Caliphate the Muslim troops had laid siege of Damascus and the city was comquered when Umar took charge of the Islamic state. For a short while the Byzantines forced the Muslims to retreat to Yarmuk. By this time Khalid was removed from the command of the army. The decisive Battle of Yarmuk was fought on August 20, 636, "on a hot day clouded by the wind-blown dust of one of the most torrid spots on earth and undoubtedly fixed upon by Arabian generalship. Before the terrific onslaught of the sons of the desert the efforts of the Byzantine troops, aided by chants and prayers by their priests and the presence of their crosses, proved of no avail."[39]

When Khalid had moved from the Iraqi front to Syria, he had given the charge of the conquered territories of the Persian Empire to a Bedouin commander, Musanna ibn Harisa. He was a brave soldier but he was not Khalid. Therefore, when the Persian attacked to push the Muslim forces out of Iraq he had almost lost the ground in the Battle of the Bridge. Somehow he later managed to push back the Persians but sensing his vulnerability, Umar appointed Saad bin Abi Waqqas the commander of the forces that were engaged in Iraq. Saad defeated Rustam, the administrator of the Persians in the Battle of Qadisiya in June 637. With this victory the entire fertile lowlands west of the Tigris (Dijlah) were within the reach of Muslim forces. The native Iraqis who were Christians by faith and Arabs by race actually greeted the conquerors because they were badly persecuted by their Zoroastrian masters for centuries. With the new masters they could at least relate to ethnically.

Saad moved towards Ctesiphon (Arabic Madain) the Persian capital of the province of Iraq and conquered it in June 637. The Muslim accounts suggest that the booty that was captured after the victory of Madain was worth nine billion dirhams.

The crucial victory of the Muslims at Yarmuk dealt a heavy blow to the Byzantines' military power and helped the Muslims occupy entire Syria and Palestine. The Muslim armies then marched towards northern Iraq and Armenia and finally laid a siege of Egypt. The conquest of Egypt commenced when Umar was in Jerusalem. Amr ibn al-Aas,[40] the commander of the Muslim forces in the area only had a casual authorisation from the Caliph for invading Egypt. In fact, Umar had commanded him to wait for his written order. Hitti cites the actual instruction quoting Yaqubi: "If my letter ordering thee to turn back from Egypt overtakes thee before entering any part of it then turn back; but if thou enter the land before the receipt of my letter, then proceed and solicit Allah's aid."[41] Umar on returning to Medina consulted with his trusted advisors who persuaded him against the conquest. Thus, the Caliph sent the message vetoing the campaign that reached Aas before he entered the territory of Egypt. Nonetheless, the geopolitical importance of the land of the Pharaohs and its agrarian wealth were too enticing for Aas to resist. He was well conversant with Egypt and its surroundings because before embracing Islam he had visited the country frequently as part of commercial caravans. So, he devised a way that could technically help him obey the command of the Caliph as well as execute his plan of conquering the grain producing country. He did not open the letter before he entered the territory of Egypt.

The first town that fell in January 640, to the advancing Muslims was Farama, a major military encampment for eastern Egypt. Next, Bilbis and other smaller settlements were captured. Then Aas, before besieging Babylon, sent for reinforcements that soon arrived under the command of Zubair bin al-Awwam. Now ten thousand Muslim soldiers had to take on twenty thousand well-trained Byzantine warriors. Aas attacked Ayn Shams, a nearby town and completely routed the Byzantines' resistance. Theodorus, the commander-in-chief of the Byzantine army took flight to Alexandria and Cyrus, the governor in charge sought refuge in the Babylon fortress. Then the siege began and got prolonged because Aas did not have the expertise in systematically demolishing the well-built walls of the stronghold. Cyrus fruitlessly tried to buy off the Muslim army offering huge wealth. Then he entered into negotiations. When Cyrus' envoys reached the Muslim camps they were astonished to see the simple and egalitarian lifestyle of their enemies. One of them observed and Hitti cites the account from Ibn Abd al-Hakam: "We have witnessed a people to each and every one of whom death is preferable to life, and humility to prominence, and to none of whom this world has the least attraction. They sit not except on the ground, and eat not but on their knees. Their leader (*emir*) is like unto one of them; the low cannot be distinguished from the high, nor the master from the slave."[42] Cyrus was in for a greater shock when he had to receive a black man, Ubadah ibn al-Samit as the head of the Muslim delegation. The Byzantines were offered the usual three choices, 'embrace Islam, pay tribute or let the sword decide.' Cyrus agreed to pay tribute.

According to the terms of the peace treaty signed in 641, the Byzantines handed over Egypt to the Muslims. Some of the terms of the peace treaty proved crucial as they were later incorporated in the Shariat. For instance the vanquished people were allowed to continue holding their lands as they came to be treated as the 'protected people' (*zimmis*) and in return they were required to pay jizya, the protection tax.

The properties of those who either fled or got killed were

declared state properties. Umar did not dismiss the local administrative authorities but appointed Muslim governors to check their functioning. He confined the Muslim soldiers to the cantonments to discourage their interaction with the native people. He started the practice of payment of regular salaries to the soldiers and allocated funds for the payment of pensions to the relatives of the Prophet. He unified all the areas that had come under the sway of Islam by introducing administrative reforms. He divided the huge territory under the Islamic rule into provinces and appointed a governor in each province to oversee the administration. It was perhaps for the first time in the Islamic state that separate departments, such as treasury, army, judiciary, police, public revenue and public works with well-defined powers and responsibilities were established.[43] Umar took a momentous decision to fix the Muslim calendar, the hegira, to the year of the Prophet's emigration from Mecca to Medina. Thus 1 A.H. corresponds to 622 C.E.

Nonetheless, the distinction of Umar in the history of Islam is not solely because of the conquests of foreign lands but his fame is due to the kind of rule he introduced which has few parallels in world history. It is reported that on taking charge of the Caliphate he addressed the people of Medina thus:

> ...O people, you have some rights on me which you can always claim. One of your rights is that if anyone of you comes to me with a claim, he should leave satisfied. Another of your rights is that you can demand that I take nothing unjustly from the revenues of the state. You can also demand that... I fortify your frontiers and do not put you into danger. It is also your right that if you go to battle I should look after your families as a father would while you are away. O people, remain conscious of God, forgive me my faults and help me in my task. Assist me in enforcing what is good and forbidding what is evil. Advise me regarding the obligations that have been imposed upon me by God...

His greatness lies in the fact that he abided by every word that he spoke in his maiden speech as the Caliph of the *ummah*. Though he was not elected on the principle of 'universal adult franchise' that is called the soul of modern democracies, his rule was truly democratic. True, the state that he ruled over was theocratic but the religious minorities, contrary to the false propaganda usually carried on by the Western critics and the Hindu fascists, enjoyed reasonable freedoms that did not have any parallel at that time. For instance, when Khalid bin Walid conquered Syria and subsequently signed a treaty with the leaders of the local populace he displayed remarkable tolerance in finalising the terms of the pact. He promised the local inhabitants security for their lives, property and churches. No Muslim, as per the treaty, could forcibly occupy the house of any local resident nor demolish any building. This tolerance was on display throughout Umar's reign. When the Byzantines agreed to surrender Jerusalem, Umar personally proceeded to take charge of the city. It is stated that Umar and his slave had only one camel between them on which each of them rode by turn.

At the time of entering Jerusalem it was the slave's turn to ride on the camel. "Though the slave offered his turn to the Khalifa, Hazrat Umar refused and remarked: 'The honour of Islam (i.e. being Muslim) is enough for all of us.' He entered Jerusalem holding the rope of the camel on which his slave rode. His clothes were dirty and there were several patches on them."[44] The residents of the city who were used to the sights of the splendid attire and elaborate rituals of the Byzantine and Persian rulers were rendered speechless. They were in for further astonishment when Umar disclosed the terms of the treaty that were quite reasonable and based on the principle of religious tolerance. A few terms of the pact were:

> This is the protection which the servant of God, 'Umar, the Ruler of the Believers has granted to the people of Eiliya [Jerusalem]. The protection is for their lives and properties, their churches and crosses, their sick and healthy and for all their coreligionists. Their churches shall not be used for habitation, nor shall they be demolished, nor shall any injury be done to them or to their compounds, or to their crosses, nor shall their properties be injured in any way. There shall be no compulsion for these people in the matter of religion, nor shall any of them suffer any injury on account of religion... Whatever is written herein is under the covenant of God and the responsibility of His Messenger, of the Caliphs and of the believers, and shall hold good as long as they pay jizya [the poll tax] imposed on them.

In the current world scenario that is plagued by the fanatical enmity between the Arab Muslims and the Jews and Christians, few would believe that it was Umar who allowed the Jews to enter, reside and practise their religion freely in the Holy Lands for the first time after a gap of 500 years.

Umar was a simple man whose integrity of character was legendary. There are countless instances that reveal that Umar was not only accessible to the common people but also accountable, as a Caliph, for all his actions. Shibli, on authority of Imam Razi's *Aasaar ud Dawal* quotes this incident:

> Once Hazrat Umar got on the pulpit and addressed the congregation, 'pay attention and submit.' His voice had not yet travelled to the last row that a man rose and shot back, '*la sam'an wa la ta'atan*', i.e. neither shall we listen nor shall we submit. Hazrat Umar asked, 'why not?' The man replied, 'Your share in the Yamani sheets of cloth that were distributed among the Muslims was not more than one. However, the dress that you wear now and which is made of those sheets would have certainly required more than a sheet. What right have you to get more than your share?' Hazrat Umar signalled his son Abdullah who got up and replied to the man who had raised the issue, 'I gave from my sheet the extra cloth that was required for the stitching of the dress.' After that the man said, 'all right, now we'll listen and submit as well,' and sat down.[45]

Such was the character of the Caliph Umar who was at the time ruling over Arabia, Iraq, Iran, Syria and Palestine. Additionally, the just mentioned episode indicates the kind of rights the common citizens enjoyed under his rule. Umar's Caliphate lasted for ten years (634-644). The last notable achievement of the second Caliph was the vital victory over the Sassanid Persians at the Battle of Nihavand that is known in the history as 'Conquest of the Conquests', which brought Iran, permanently under the sway of Islam. This illustrious Caliph whose reign was the best and extremely rewarding in the early history of Islam, regrettably met with a violent end. He was assassinated while leading the morning prayer. Quite a few sources suggest that it was a Persian conspiracy planned well in advance. The chief of the conspiracy was Hormuzan, the Commander-in-Chief of the Persian army before his capture by the victorious Muslim army. When he was brought to Medinah he pretended to have embraced Islam. The conversion was a sham and he only did it to save his life. The other conspirators included Kaab al-Ahbar, one of the advisors of Umar and before his pretentious conversion to Islam was a Jewish Rabbi, Jafinah, a Christian from Iraq and Piruzan, a slave of Mughira ibn Shuba, then governor of Busra. Piruzan was popularly known as Abu Lulu and it was he who had to actually assassinate Umar. Abu Lulu carried out his evil assignment within the precincts of Masjid-e-Nabavi; it is reported that he stabbed Umar seven times and later killed himself with the same dagger. Three days later, i.e. November 7, 644, Umar succumbed to his wounds. His testament is often cited as a model code for a civilised and just government. Consider a part of it:

> Be kind and generous to the Muhajirun and the Ansar. Those out of them who are good, be good to them; those who are bad overlook their lapses. Be good to the people of the conquered lands. They are the outer line of our defence; they are the target of the anger and distress of our enemies. They contribute to our revenues. They should be taxed only on their surplus wealth. Be gracious to the Bedouins as they are the backbone of the Arab nation. I instruct you to be good to the Zimmis for they are your responsibility. Do not tax them beyond their capacity. Ensure that they pay the jizya without undue inconvenience. Fear God, and in all that you do keep His pleasure in view. In the matter of people fear God, and in the matter of Allah do not be afraid of the people. With regard to the people, I enjoin upon you to administer justice with an even hand. See that all the legitimate requirements of the people are met. Be concerned for their welfare. Ensure the safety of their person and property. See that the frontiers of our domains are not violated. Take strong steps to guard the frontiers. In the matter of administration do not prefer the rich to the poor. Be hard against those who violate the law. Show them no mercy. Do not rest content till you have brought the miscreants to book. Treat all the people as equal. Be a pillar of strength for those who are weak and oppressed. Those who are strong but do wrong, make them pay for their wrong-doings. In the distribution of booty and other matters be above nepotism. Let no consideration of relationship or selfish interest weigh with you...

IV

On his deathbed Umar nominated an electoral committee comprising six members to choose the next Caliph. The members included: Abdur Rahman bin Awf, Saad ibn Abi Waqqas, Talha bin Ubaidullah, Usman bin Affan, Ali bin Abi Talib and Zubair bin al-Awwam. At this time, it was Ali who was most suited for the job. Moreover, Umar had hinted whom he wished to be his successor when, at the time of his journey to Jerusalem, he made Ali in charge of the administration at the *Dar ul Khilafa*. Nevertheless, Abd ur Rahman bin Awf who was acting as the moderator of the electoral committee acted injudiciously and influenced the opinion of the majority of the members in favour of Usman ibn Affan. This unfortunate decision, in reality, was the starting point of the great divide in the ummah and the emergence of two sects, the Shia, the party of Ali and the Sunnis, the faction that accepted the appointment of Usman. The members of the House of Muhammad were rightfully disappointed and angry with selection of Usman, a member of Banu Omayya, as the third Caliph. The subsequent imprudent actions of Usman further intensified the enmity between the two factions.

Usman bin Affan was born in Taif, a hill station near Mecca in c. 577, into a prosperous family that belonged to the Banu Umayyah clan of the Qureish. Usman had to look after the vast business of the family at an early age as his father, Affan, died when Usman was still young. On Abu Bakr's persuasion he got converted to Islam sometime in 611; thereafter he is reported to have dedicated a large part of his fortune for charity. The members of his clan fiercely disapproved his conversion and his wives refused to embrace Islam. He had no choice but to divorce them. Subsequently he married Ruqqayyah, the daughter of the Prophet.

In about 615, when the Prophet dispatched a delegation of the Muslims to Abyssinia (the present-day Ethiopia), Usman and his wife Ruqqayya were among the delegates. Two years later, on hearing the rumour that all the members of the Qureish had embraced Islam, Usman and Ruqqayya returned to Mecca only to find that it was only a rumour. All these years he was actively engaged in spreading his business. After Muhammad's emigration to Medina, Usman and Ruqayya too chose to leave Mecca. In 622, they joined the third batch of Muslims that emigrated from Mecca to Medina. The business activities in Medina were under the control of the Jews while the local Muslims, the Ansar, were usually peasants. Usman's wealth and business acumen helped his business empire to flourish and soon he became the richest man of Medina.

At the time when the Muslims were being enlisted to go and capture a caravan of the Qureish, Ruqqayya was seriously ill. Consequently, Usman was exempted to join the impending battle. When the Battle of Badr was being fought, Ruqayyah died. Thereafter, he married another daughter of the Prophet, Kulsum, and thus got the title of *Zul-Noorain* (The Possessor of Two Lights). Usman was among those *sahaba* (companions of the Prophet) who had fled from the Battle of Uhud that was fought in 625. It was for this reason that a verse in the Quran announces that all those who fled were absolved by God. In the Battle of the Trench (627), however, Usman was leading the Muslim forces in an assigned sector of Medina. He also participated in the campaigns against the Jews of Medina. Later he also fought in the Battles of Khaybar and Hunayn.

In 628, the Messenger of Allah left for Mecca to perform Hajj. The enemies of Islam, nevertheless, refused to allow entry to the Muslim party of pilgrims into the city of Mecca. The hostile attitude of the Qureish forced the Prophet to halt at a place known as Hudaybiyyah. Afterwards, the Prophet selected Usman to act as an emissary and negotiate with the Qureish. When Usman reached Mecca, the Qureish arrested him. The resultant delay in Usman's return convinced the Muslims of his murder. At this point the Prophet decided to act tough; he took the pledge from 1,400 Muslim soldiers that they would fight till their death to avenge the assassination of Usman. The pledge was taken under a tree and therefore, came to be known as the 'Pledge of the Tree'. The sheer determination of the Muslims to fight scared the Qureish and they immediately released Usman. Subsequently, the Qureish sent their emissary to settle the terms of the treaty which is referred to as the 'Treaty of Hudaybiyyah'. The Qureish put up with the terms of the treaty only for two years; as in 630 they refused the admission of the Muslims into Mecca, the Prophet decided to attack the city. The Muslim forces triumphed over the Qureish and the Messenger of Allah announced general amnesty for the residents of the city. Nonetheless, a few who were not granted amnesty included Abdullah ibn Saad, a foster brother of Usman. His mother appealed to Usman who approached the Prophet with a request for sparing the life of Abdullah. The Prophet acceded to the request. It was at this point that the members of Usman's family were converted to Islam. Kulsum, Usman's wife and the daughter of the Prophet died a few days after the victory of Mecca. A year later while he was in Mecca to perform Hajj, Usman married Saeed Fatima bint al-Walid, who belonged to a family of the Qureish.

During Abu Bakr's reign when the Ridda Wars were being fought, Usman did not participate in the actual fighting; he remained in Medina to assist the Caliph. When Umar was chosen as the second Caliph, Usman was the first person to affirm his commitment to him. Umar nominated him as a member of his advisory council. After the conquest of Jerusalem, when the Byzantine invited Umar to personally take charge of the city, Usman advised the Caliph not to undertake the journey. Nonetheless, Umar rejected his advice and went to Jerusalem to earn the amity of the Christians. In the time of a severe drought during Umar's Caliphate, Usman himself bought a huge quantity of food grains to be supplied to the poor sections of the Islamic state.

When Usman became the Caliph the Islamic realm extended in the west of Medina to Morocco, in the east to the northwest border of the Indian subcontinent and in the north to Armenia and Azerbaijan. Initially, he continued the administrative policies that were adopted by Abu Bakr and Umar. He too worked at expansion of the Islamic mission. He is credited to send the first emissary of Islam, Saad ibn Waqqas, to China in 650. Though the Emperor of the Tsang Dynasty, Gaozong, refused to embrace Islam, he allowed the Muslims to preach their faith in China and also permitted them to construct the first mosque in China at the capital city Changan in 651. In this way, Islam was introduced to the Chinese. During Usman's reign, Muslim envoys were also sent to Sri Lanka.

Usman had to vanquish rebellions in the provinces of Iran that had surfaced after the death of Umar. Practically, he had to recapture most of the provinces of the erstwhile Persian Empire. The Byzantine emperor, Constantine III, too resorted to offensive tactics to recapture the lost territories in Syria. Usman not only successfully repulsed the Byzantine offensive but also launched a series of attacks between 647 and 651, on various cities of the truncated empire that ultimately forced the new Byzantine emperor, Constans II, to plead for a truce. It was during the Caliphate of Usman that the first Islamic navy was put together that helped the Muslim forces to capture the island of Cyprus in 649. Soon after, other islands such as Crete and Rhodes were also added to the rapidly expanding Islamic state. Usman had made preparations to launch an attack on Constantinopole in 655 but before it could materialize he was murdered. Parts of North Africa, Nubia and coastal districts of Iberia had been vanquished; however, Usman's assassination and the consequent civil war in the Caliphate forced the Muslim armies to retreat from these African territories.

Usman's business acumen was useful in restructuring the economy as well as introducing new fiscal reforms in the Islamic empire. Umar had introduced the system of paying salaries to the public servants. However, the payments were meagre. Usman increased the salaries of the officials by twenty-five per cent. Regarding the agriculture lands in the conquered territories, Usman retained Umar's policy that the farmlands should not be distributed among the soldiers and that the local peasants, Muslim as well as zimmis should be allowed to continue agrarian activities. Nevertheless, he altered Umar's policy of complete ban on Muslims to deal in non-agricultural lands in conquered territories because, as a businessman, he thought it was detrimental to the growth of trade and commerce. In the tribal Arab society indigenous coins were a rarity. This was the situation till 651, when Usman struck, for the first time, the Islamic coins; the coins were in fact Persian dirhams on which Usman added the Arabic set phrase, *Bismillah* (In the name of Allah). It was the Ommayyad ruler, Abdul Malik, who issued the first original Islamic coins in 695.

Usman's fiscal reforms certainly made a section of the people more prosperous. The ever-expanding Islamic state coupled with the business-oriented policies of the Caliph enriched the public exchequer that encouraged Usman to undertake an ambitious project of building construction. Consequently, during his reign as many as five thousand new mosques were built all over the empire. Usman also renovated and enlarged the Masjid-e-Nabawi and Kaaba. Several secular buildings and facilities such as guest houses, markets, public wells, canals and ports were also constructed during this period. In view of the army's expansion, Usman added many more new garrisons for the soldiers and stables for the cavalry in different parts of the empire. The highlight of the third Caliphate was the compilation of the genuine version of the Quran, a sensitive task that was successfully accomplished by a committee of experts constituted by Usman in the last part of his reign.

Usman, however, changed Umar's policy of severity regarding public money. Umar was a simple man; except for a small allowance he would not accept any money for himself from the public exchequer. Moreover, he would neither accept gifts himself nor would he allow any member of his family to accept gifts from anyone. Though Usman being a rich man did not sanction any salary for himself, he would accept gifts. He also allowed other public officials and his family members to accept gifts. This was, obviously the initiation of a wrong policy that produced controversies and germinated suspicions about the accountability of government.

Another improper aspect of Usman's Caliphate was the widespread nepotism. He appointed his relatives and persons belonging to his clan to important positions justifying his actions on the ground that for better governance in a vast empire the Caliph could rely only on his kinsmen. This explanation obviously undermines the criterion of merit that ought to be considered while appointing people for public offices. This slip-up in administration lamentably led to the tribal distrusts and clannish rivalries that were firmly suppressed by the first two Caliphs. In the absence of an effective political apparatus, the intense protests unleashed by Usman's adversaries went unchecked. The starting point of the agitations was the appointment of Usman's kinsmen as the governors of Egypt, Basra, Syria and Kufa and later the issue of Ali's right to be the Caliph was taken up by the protestors. It further accentuated the differences between the Hashmites and the Umayyads. Commenting on the deteriorating situation a scholar observes:

> The weakness and nepotism of Usman brought to a head the resentment which had for some time been stirring obscurely among the Arab warriors. The Muslim traditions attribute the breakdown which occurred during his reign to the personal defects of Usman. But the causes lie far deeper and the guilt of Usman lay in his failure to recognize, control or remedy them.[46]

In response to the growing agitations, the Caliph consulted the *Majlis al Shura* (the cabinet), which advised him to investigate the charges of corruption and maladministration against the governors by sending representatives to the provinces. Usman did as advised. The emissaries submitted their reports absolving governors of all charges and further adding that the protests were the handiwork of a few disgruntled elements who had feelings of resentment, primarily because of personal reasons, against the governors. The representative who was assigned to investigate the causes of agitation in Egypt, Ammar ibn Yasir, nevertheless, did not return to Medina and later joined hands with Muhammad ibn Abi Bakr, who belonged to the Umayyad clan but because of his rearing in Ali's house was emotionally attached to the Hashmites; in Egypt he was the leader of the protestors who were espousing the issue of Ali's Caliphate.

On the eve of Hajj in 655, Usman commanded all the governors and other important public officials to be present in Mecca. He also made a general announcement all over the empire that people having justifiable complaints against his administration should submit their grievances to the Caliph at the time of Hajj. Consequently, the protestors came to Mecca in large numbers. Usman addressed the large gathering and as per the Sunni accounts, offered a comprehensive and agreeable explanation of the criticism levelled against himself and his administration. The protestors, in view of the huge support the Caliph could muster as a result of his convincing address, could not present their point of view. However, a year later, with the arrival of Muhammad ibn Abi Bakr in Medina, the struggle against Usman gained momentum.

The Caliph realised that the nerve centre of opposition was Egypt. He, therefore, sent for Abdullah ibn Saad, the governor of Egypt for consultation. While the governor was in Medina, Muhammad bin Abi Hazaifa, Usman's adopted son and the deputy of ibn Saad, captured the control of the province in a coup. Ibn Saad rushed back to Egypt but in the absence of adequate military power could not regain the control of the province. By the middle of 656, the provinces of Kufa and Basra too revolted and almost became independent. Then, started a series of delegations from the rebel provinces to Medina; the contingent of Egypt comprising one thousand delegates requested Ali to take charge of the Caliphate. Ali firmly refused the proposal. The delegation from Kufa wanted al-Zubair to be the next Caliph while the deputation from Basra offered the Caliphate to Talaha. Both the offers were turned down by the respective persons.

Nevertheless, Usman's opponents had succeeded in offsetting the opinion of a large section of the residents of Medina by offering alternatives to Usman. Barring the Umayyads the other people in the capital of the Islamic empire refused to take sides in the dispute over the Caliphate. The division among the residents of Medina emboldened the opponents first to lay siege to the house of the Caliph and ultimately assassinate him. Usman's funeral took place three days after the murder because of the continuance of the siege. Accounts differ whether Ali's permission was sought for the burial or not. Also there is a controversy whether Ali attended the funeral or if he preferred to skip it. It has also been reported that because the opponents of Usman did not allow his burial in *Jannat ul Baqi,* his body was ultimately buried in the Jewish cemetery that was located behind the revered graveyard. During the Umayyad's rule, the wall dividing *Jannat ul Baqi* from the Jewish cemetery was demolished.

V

The fourth Caliph, Abul Hasan Ali bin Abi Talib was the cousin and son-in-law of the Prophet. It has already been pointed out that in the eyes of the Shias he was the first legitimate Caliph and Imam. Ali's father was an uncle of the Prophet. Ali was born in c. 600, to Abu Talib ibn Abdul Muttalib and Fatima bin Asad. Abu Talib was one of the most respected residents of Mecca who had raised the Prophet of Islam. Thus, Muhammad and Ali were brought up in the same household. Most accounts, including Sunni ones, affirm that Ali was the first male who accepted Muhammad as the Apostle of God, when the Prophet stated that he was receiving divine revelations. When the Prophet migrated to Medina, Ali followed him after a short while. It was in Medina that the Prophet made known to him that God had ordered him to marry his daughter Fatima to Ali. Ali was extremely devoted to the Messenger of God and his mission. He participated in almost all the battles that were fought against the enemies of Islam during the lifetime of Muhammad.

An overwhelming majority of the Muslims irrespective of sectarian differences hold Ali in high esteem. He is revered for his bravery, knowledge, upright character, integrity, devotion to Islam, judiciousness, compassion, generosity and absolute loyalty to the Prophet of Allah. Though Ali possessed numerous qualities, the two virtues that counted most those days, viz. courage and erudition were combined in his persona. His bravery in personal combats and military leadership was renowned while his authority in matters of interpretation of the Quran, jurisprudence, eloquence and religious ideas was matchless. These rare qualities make him the most outstanding personality after Muhammad in the history of Islam. Ali was also appointed as one of the scribes to record the divine revelations. He also drafted the Treaty of Hudaibiya in 628. Two years later the Prophet assigned him the lofty job of reading out forty verses of the Quran in front of the large gathering of the pilgrims in Mecca that *inter alia* conveyed to the idolaters of Mecca that the peace terms agreed by the Muslims would be no more operative because of their violation by the polytheists.

His role in extending the mission of Islam is stupendous. On one occasion, the Prophet sent out Khalid bin Walid to Yemen on a proselytizing mission but he could hardly achieve any success despite having preached the message of Islam for six months. Accordingly, the Prophet assigned the job to Ali. On reaching Yemen, Ali, within days, by means of his persuasive lectures succeeded in converting the entire tribe of Hamdan. On hearing the news the Prophet had uttered, 'As-salam Ali Hamdan.' It was through his lectures, letters and actions that Ali instilled a compassionate image of Islam. No wonder that all the Sufi orders except Naqshbandiya, trace their descent through Ali to Muhammad. Therefore, the companions of the Prophet who were present at Medina, in the aftermath of the assassination of Usman, unanimously nominated Ali the fourth Caliph. Regrettably his reign was marred by clannish conflicts, intrigues and civil war that never allowed him to pay much attention to military expansion or administrative reforms.

Ali belonged to the family of the Prophet and for that reason he was a part of the household that was most respected among the Qureish of Mecca. Abu Talib, father of Ali, uncle of the Prophet and son of Abdul Muttalib, the grandfather of the Messenger of God, was the custodian of Kaaba while his mother, Fatima bint Asad too belonged to a respectable family of the Qureish. Traditions attest that it was the face of the Prophet that Ali saw first as a new born because the Prophet was the first person who lifted him in his hands. He was also named by the Prophet as Ali that literally means 'the magnificent one.' In fact, Muhammad, an orphan was first raised by his grandfather, Abdul Muttalib and after his death he was brought up in the household of Abu Talib till he married Khadija bint Khuwailid. Ali was born a couple of years after the marriage of Muhammad and when Abu Talib faced economic hurdles because of a large family, Muhammad took the responsibility of raising Ali when he was barely six years old.

Ali was about ten years old when Muhammad first received the divine revelation and according to popular traditions he was the first male to embrace Islam. The issue is unresolved as other sources name Zaid to be the first male to enter the fold of Islam. Moreover, it is also argued that Ali at the time was just a child so his conversion to Islam does not merit serious consideration. The significant point, however, is that both Shias and Sunnis refer to him with the honorific of *Karam Allah Wajihu*, which literally means 'the one whose face shows the favour of God' but implies that Ali was not guilty of taking part in any polytheistic ritual in the *jahiliya* and his first religious action was to submit to the sovereignty of Allah and accept Muhammad as His Messenger. Therefore, the general reliable opinion is that he has always been a monotheist and the issue of his embracing Islam is redundant. During the initial years of proselytizing when the Prophet had to face the taunts, contemptuous shouts and even persecution, it was Ali, a teenager, who firmly stood by the Apostle of God. In 614, the Prophet invited about forty members of the Hashmite clan to a formal meal and proposed to them that they should join with him to advance the mission of Islam. It was shocking that not a single member volunteered to assist the Prophet. On that occasion it was fourteen-year-old Ali who rose and pledged his services for the promotion of Muhammad's mission. Referring to such a noble and spirited commitment of a teenaged Ali, a famous Scottish writer and historian comments, "Nevertheless, it proved not a laughable thing; it was very serious thing! As for this young Ali, one cannot but like him. A noble minded creature, as he shows himself, now and always afterwards; full of affection and fiery daring."[47] In view of his steadfast devotion to the cause of Islam, the traditions suggest that the Prophet had declared Ali his brother, inheritor and vice-regent.

In 622, when Muhammad decided to emigrate to Medina and when his persecutors got wind of the plan they hatched a conspiracy to kill him at night. It was Ali who took the risk of his life by sleeping in the Prophet's bed and thus, impeded the design of the enemies of Islam. A tradition is cited that Allah has acknowledged the sacrifice of Ali in the following verse:

> And of mankind is he who would sell himself, seeking the pleasure of Allah; and Allah hath compassion on (His) bondmen.[48]

Ali migrated to Medina along with his mother, Fatima, the Prophet's daughter who was destined to be his wife later and two other female relatives. His age at the time was about 23. In Medina, Ali became the confidant of the Prophet not because he had married his beloved daughter but because he served as his secretary, a bearer of the banner of Islam in various battles and a courier of his messages and commands. Nevertheless, all through his life Ali remained a poor man as he never aspired to pursue worldly possessions. Despite being engaged in assisting the Prophet in his divine mission, Ali had to work as a drawer and carrrier of water to earn his livelihood. Fatima, his wife, had to grind corn to ease her husband's burden. They led an arduous life but remained extremely devoted to each other. It was their dispositions that ensured bliss in the domesticity. Despite the permission of polygamy, Ali did not take another wife during the lifetime of

Fatima who bore four children that included the famous grandsons of the Prophet, Hasan and Husain.

Ali took part in all the battles, except the expedition of Tabuk, that were fought during the Prophet's lifetime. He could not join the Muslim army that had set out for Tabuk because the Prophet had entrusted him the responsibility of the safety of the *Ahl-e-Bait* (members of the house of the Prophet) for which he had to stay behind in Medina. Ali emerged an outstanding combatant first in the Battle of Badr in which he had vanquished the renowned Umayyad warrior, Walid ibn Utba besides killing about thirty enemy soldiers. His sword, Zulfiqar (split into two cutting segments at the point), has been enduringly etched in the psyche of the Muslims as the most outstanding weapon ever wielded by a soldier of Islam. He proved his bravery by shielding the Prophet when he was exposed to danger in the Battle of Uhud. In the Battle of the Ditch his legendary valour was again on display when he killed the champion warrior of the Qureish, Amr ibn Abd al-Wud that proved significant in turning the tide in favour of the victory of the Muslim forces. He led the Muslim forces in the Battle of Khaybar and most accounts concur that it was Ali's sheer courage, sagacity and leadership that smashed the resistance and won the battle for Islam. The Jews had six strongholds in Khaybar out of which the Muslim forces had conquered five but the sixth one Qamus proved a tough nut because of the exceptional courage of its Jewish commander Marhab. The Prophet first handed over the command of the army of Islam to Abu Bakr. Despite the valiant attack, Abu Bakr could not subdue the Jewish stronghold. Then Umar led the Muslim forces who too had to retire because of the relentless resistance of the Jewish forces. The Prophet, then declared, "Tomorrow, I will hand over the banner of the Islamic army to such a person who is an impetuous warrior and not an absconder, he befriends God and His Apostle and is also befriended by them. God is sure to grant victory to him."[49] The next morning Ali was commanded by the Prophet to lead the Islamic army against the dogged challenge of the Jews. Ali first killed Haris, a huge and well-built man and brother of Marhab. The death of his brother incensed Marhab who then challenged Ali to single combat. Ali stepped forward to face the ferocious warrior. It was Marhab who made the first move attacking

Ali with his three-pronged lance which Ali deflected the thrust skilfully; then before Marhab could recover, Ali dealt him a blow with his sword that was so vigorous that it split Marhab's head into two and in a split second the mightiest Jewish commander was lying lifeless on the ground. Thereafter, the Muslim army took control of Qamus. Through the remarkable victory Ali earned for himself the title of Asadullah (Lion of God) that was conferred by the Prophet himself. In the Battle of Hunain it was Ali again who risked his life to save the Prophet.

A part of an address of the Prophet that he delivered to the Muslims while returning from his last Hajj in 632, at a place known as Ghadir Khumm is read differently by the Shias and the Sunnis. The part in question is:

> O people, I am a human being. I am about to receive a message from my Lord and I, in response to Allah's call, (would bid goodbye to you), but I am leaving among you two weighty things: the one being the Book of Allah in which there is right guidance and light, so hold fast to the Book of Allah and adhere to it. He exhorted (us) (to hold fast) to the Book of Allah and then said: The second are the members of my household. I remind you (of your duties) to the members of my family.

Having made these observations the Prophet called Ali by his side, held his hand and by raising it declared:

> For whomever I am a *Mawla* of, then Ali is his *Mawla*.[50]

The Arabic term *mawla* means a guardian, protector or custodian. Shias interpret it as a clear evidence of the Prophet's intention to pass on the temporal headship as well as religious guidance of the Muslims to Ali and argue that on that account he had the right to be the first Caliph and Imam of the ummah. On the contrary, the Sunnis interpret the comments as merely an expression of the Prophet's love and affection for Ali and that Ali was delegated the responsibility by Muhammad to take care of the members of the house of the Prophet upon his death. The different points of view led to an intense controversy after the death of the Prophet when Ali refused to pay homage to the first Caliph, Abu Bakr, for six months. The debatable issue ultimately led to the schism in the ummah that created the two sects of Islam.

Political animosity aside, the members of the house of Muhammad were not fairly taken care of by the prominent people who had control over political power. For instance, when Fatima who was dearest of all to Muhammad appealed to Abu Bakr to hand over her rightful landed properties of Fadak and Khaybar to her, the first Caliph turned it down saying that the Prophet had not bequeathed any property. This was a shocking ruling considering the fact that along with Fatima, Ali and Umme Ayman[51], counted among the most pious and honest persons, testified that the Prophet had granted the properties to Fatima Zahra. Abu Bakr asked her to call upon other witnesses. What inference can one draw from this ruling? Did the members of the house of Muhammad make a deceitful attempt to seize something which was not theirs? Obviously they could not commit any deceit. If so, then why are the Sunni accounts silent on Abu Bakr's conduct? The judgment of the first Caliph incensed Fatima so much that she never talked to him till her death. During Umar's reign, Ali reiterated his family's claim over the properties of Fadak and Khaybar but Umar too rejected the claim.

Given that the genuine concerns of Banu Hashim were not even considered by the system that had emerged after the death of Muhammad in 632, Ali withdrew from military service and undertook political affairs only if consulted. He neither joined any conquest nor did he enjoy any significant position of authority till 656, the year Usman was assassinated. During this long period of almost a quarter of a century he took to farming and public welfare. He dug numerous wells and laid out many gardens in the suburbs of Medina and dedicated them to the people. Another significant undertaking that he got engaged in was the compilation of the Quran that he did in six months after the death of the Prophet. The order of the Surahs (chapters) was different in Ali's version of the Holy Book from the standard version that got compiled during Usman's Caliphate. Though his version of the Quran was disallowed by the majority of the ummah, Ali did not contest the opinion of the majority and sincerely accepted the standard version.

All through Abu Bakr's reign, Ali kept himself apart from the affairs of the Muslim state. To the second Caliph, Umar, he pledged his allegiance and helped him carry out public activities. Umar had always valued the unbiased suggestions and worthwhile inputs that Ali made in managing the affairs of an emerging empire. It was on Ali's advice that Umar set the Islamic calendar. Umar had also nominated Ali to the electoral committee that was to choose the third Caliph. However, the composition of the committee was not in his favour. Saad bin Abi Waqqas and Abdur Rahman bin Awf were cousins and Usman, the contender to the Caliphate was Rahman's brother-in-law. Additionally, Rahman had the casting vote with the permission of Umar. Rahman offered the Caliphate to Ali with a rider that he would abide by the canons of the Quran, the policies of the Prophet and the standards set by the first two Caliphs. Ali's contention was that if the precedents established by the first two Caliphs were in tune with the Quran and Muhammad's examples he would naturally abide by them but if they differed he would not. This provided the opportunity to Rahman which he was looking for to cast his vote in favour of his brother-in-law. Ali was left with no choice but to pledge allegiance to Usman.

Usman's reign, as has been pointed out above, was afflicted by preferential treatment and nepotism. His kinsmen, in particular Marwan, usurped all the powers and would, on purpose, humiliate the earliest and most respected companions of the Prophets. Such a state of affairs had its repercussions and by 651, there appeared an open revolt against the unjust policies of the Caliph. At this time of the crisis, it was Ali who made attempts to steady the rapidly deteriorating political situation. He too did not agree with the partisan policies and had made it plain to Usman on several occasions but for him it was the survival of the Islamic state that was dearer. Therefore, when the rebels from the provinces arrived in Medina, Ali acted as the negotiator between them and the Caliph. Nevertheless, such a selfless act was misconstrued by some as Ali's passive approval of Usman's opposition.

After Usman's assassination there emerged three main candidates for the Caliphate, viz. Ali, Talhah and Zubair. However, as per an account when the rebels requested Ali to take charge of the Caliphate he turned it down saying that he would rather prefer to be an advisor. Then the rebels approached Talhah and Zubair who also refused to accept the offer. Then the rebels delivered an ultimatum to the residents of Medina that if they failed to elect a Caliph in a day's time the city would have to face dreadful consequences. So, a large gathering of the Muslims in the Mosque of the Prophet insisted that Ali should agree to be the chief of the ummah. Ali was circumspect in accepting the offer because the most vociferous group supporting his candidature was that of the rebels. Later, the prominent companions of the Prophet too requested him to honour the preference of the Muslims of Medina and thus, on June 16, 656, Ali became the fourth and the last of the *Rashidun* Caliphs. The prominent persons who pledged allegiance to Ali included Talhah and Zubair who later declared that they were forced to pay homage. It is perplexing how anyone could force the senior most companions of the Prophet in an open gathering of the Muslims to pledge allegiance against their will. Ali, however, maintained that they came forward to pledge allegiance on their own. The records also suggest that most of the kinsmen of Usman did not attend the meeting that elected Ali and, therefore, later they questioned the legitimacy of Ali's Caliphate.

On assuming the charge of the Caliphate, Ali issued orders to replace the provincial governors who were mostly the kinsmen of Usman by his own trusted people because he had to have control over a vast empire that was extended to Egypt in the west and Iran in the east. All the governors obeyed the command of the new Caliph except Muawiya I, the governor of Billad-ash-Sham (Levant) that included the present countries of Lebanon, Israel, Syria, Palestine, Jordan and Iraq. Ali had explained his purpose in replacing the governors to the people of Medina and they believed that he was not acting out of personal ill will but wanted to establish a transparent and judicious administration. Ali had also restored the state lands that were granted by Usman to people who were close to him. He proposed a decentralised administration and approved of distributing equal shares of taxes and spoils between the Muslims of the empire. This policy was passionately supported by most of the Muslims; the Ansars were particularly happy because earlier they were practically subordinated by the powerful Qureish. Most importantly he steered clear of the policy of nepotism and even refused to appoint his own brother, Aqeel ibn Abi Talib to any state position. He was a firm believer in the equality of all

Muslims and in state affairs he never discriminated against meritorious persons. Thus, very soon he could unite the people of diverse clans and ancestries who formed a coalition in support of Ali to help him establish a genuine Islamic rule based on the Quran and path shown by Muhammad. This coalition came to be known as *Shia Ali* or 'party of Ali.' These earlier supporters of Ali, however, should not be confused with the people who later professed to be Shias religiously; the members of Shia Ali supported Ali politically and not religiously.

Ali, nonetheless, had to deal with strong opposition to his rule. The most prominent opponents were Aisha, the wife of the Prophet, Talhah and Zubair. Their contention was that Ali failed in punishing the killers of Usman because he covertly sided with them and further they insisted that the killers of the third Caliph should be handed over to them so that they would kill them to avenge the assassination of Usman. They first met in Mecca and with an intention to augment their military force and resources went to Basra in Iraq. They succeeded in gaining control over Basra and later killed many people. Ali first commanded them to obey the laws of the state and reminded Talhah and Zubair of their pledges of allegiance to his Caliphate. At this point the two senior companions of the Prophet proclaimed that they never pledged allegiance to Ali willingly. Ali was left with no choice but to meet them in a battle. It was the first civil war in the history of Islam that was fought in the outskirts of Basra and popularly known as the Battle of the Camel (656) because Aisha joined the battle riding a camel. Ali defeated the opposition; Talhah and Zubair were killed and Aisha was arrested. Nonetheless, Ali treated her with the utmost respect and reverence due to a wife of the Prophet and made arrangements to send her to Medina with dignity and honour. Subsequently, Ali shifted the capital from Medina to Kufa in Iraq because it was a centrally located place.

Ali's troubles, however, did not end with the victory in the Battle of the Camel. Muawiya I persisted in refusing allegiance to Ali and avowed to avenge the murder of Usman. He consolidated his position in *Balad ash-Sham* and insisted that the areas under his rule should be treated as autonomous. Ali first made attempts to resolve the galling problem by negotiations. Muawiya, however, was determined to subvert Ali's Caliphate, which forced the Caliph to take military action against the defiant governor of Levant. The two armies faced each other at Siffin but the battle did not break out immediately. Ali made every effort to avoid another civil war and for that purpose he wrote several letters to Muawiya. Skirmishes along with talks continued for about a hundred days; at last the Battle of Siffin (657) commenced and after a week of fierce fighting the Caliph's forces had almost routed Muawiya's rebellious army in a night-combat known as *Laylat al-Harir* (the night of commotion). Seeing the imminent defeat, Muawiya, acting on the advice of Amr ibn Aas, commanded his soldiers to hoist the copies of the Quran on their spearheads. It was, in fact, a ploy to prevent the advancing forces and buy some time to somehow wriggle out of the desperate situation. Though Ali himself saw through the game, the majority of his forces, seeing the copies of the Quran on the spearheads, preferred to enter into negotiations. What followed in the name of arbitration to determine the legitimacy of Ali's Caliphate was a charade that damaged Ali's coalition which comprised all the members of the ummah and not just of a clan. A section of Ali's supporters were opposed to arbitration; they rebelled and deserted Ali only to form the first institutionalized sect of Islam, the Kharjites (deserters/schismatics). Later, Ali had to fight against them in the Battle of Nahrawan. Ali wanted to nominate Abdullah ibn Abbas or Malik al-Ashtar as his arbiter but since the whole affair was a deep-rooted conspiracy he was convinced to appoint Abu Musa Ashari who was, in fact, an opponent of Ali. Therefore, the arbitration did not result in anything that could help Ali strengthen his position; in reality, it was a stratagem to weaken the rule of the Caliph.

Thereafter, Muawiya and his agents launched a vilification campaign against Ali and his supporters that was followed, a year later, by ransacking and plundering the cities of Iraq. Since the conspirators spread their tentacles wide and deep, Ali's governors failed to check the marauding bullies of Muawiya and regrettably people too did not rise against the raiders. Encouraged by the successes in Iraq, Muawiya, within a year, rummaged through Egypt, Hejaz and Yeman. Though, the majority of Muslims deeply distrusted Muawiya, they strangely failed to rally behind Ali to counter the depraved ascendancy of Muawiya. Ali was a pious Muslim and valiant soldier of Islam and he had a vision of a rule that was too idealistic for the time. He never resorted to expediency and stratagem that are supposed to be often employed in dealing with political problems. One can gauge the kind of political order he intended to establish by going through the instructions he gave to Malik al-Ashtar while appointing him governor of Egypt. His instructions read:

> Infuse your heart with mercy, love and kindness for your subjects. Be not in face of them a voracious animal, counting them as easy prey, for they are of two kinds: either they are your brothers in religion or your equals in creation. Error catches them unaware, deficiencies overcome them, (evil deeds) are committed by them intentionally and by mistake. So grant them your pardon and your forgiveness to the same extent that you hope God will grant you His pardon and His forgiveness. For, you are above them, and he who appointed you is above you, and God is above him who appointed you. God has sought from you the fulfilment of their requirements and He is trying you with them.

Could a polity that claims to be based on rule of law, has pretensions to be democratic and announces itself to be the defender of liberty, equality and human rights be based on a better set of principles than the ones cited above? The only difference in a contemporary ideal, civilized and responsible constitution perhaps could be the absence of references to a divine entity. Nonetheless, we cannot lose sight of the constraints of time and space while assessing Islam and the related issues.

The Kharjites, the first well-established sect of Islam, were the sworn enemies of Ali. So, a member of the sect, Abdur Rahman ibn Muljam, on 19th of Ramzan, attacked Ali with a poison-coated sword; the year was 661. Two days later this extraordinary man whose dedication to Muhammad was beyond compare and who had been instrumental in firmly ascertaining a refined and humane version of Islam breathed his last. On his deathbed he advised his elder son, Hasan not to attack the members of the Kharjites, that was the usual practice at the time, but to inflict a similar injury to ibn Muljim as he did to him. Hasan did exactly what he was advised. Ali was also concerned that his enemies would ransack his grave. Therefore, he instructed his family members and friends to bury him secretly. It was only during the Abbasid reign, the sixth Shia Imam, Jafar as-Sadiq, revealed the tomb of Ali within the precincts of the Imam Ali Mosque in Najaf. According to another account, Ali's dead body was carried to Afghanistan and buried in the city of Mazar-e-Sharif within the confines of the famous Blue Mosque.

VI

In the appraisal of the institution of the Caliphate the principle that should always be the cardinal criterion is to discern its roots in the canons of the Quran and the path of Muhammad. It is for this reason that the first four Caliphs are known as the 'Rightly Guided Caliphs.' The Prophet had not established a political order; he brought a code of conduct that catered to the spiritual needs of the desert people more than addressing the demands of a cosmopolitan empire that emerged within a few years after his death. The distinctiveness of an Islamic State got gradually chiselled during the reign of the first four Caliphs. The Caliphate evolved on certain principles, all of which were never adhered to strictly; some of them were altogether abandoned or got mutated in accordance with the opinion of the Caliph. One invariable feature, nonetheless, was that the Caliphate strived to establish the sovereignty of God, which made it a theocracy. It is, therefore, unfair to evaluate the rule of the first four Caliphs applying the yardstick of a contemporary liberal-secular-democracy.

Most of the Sunni ulama assert that the Caliphate was in essence a true democracy as the government (read the Caliph) was nominated by the free choice of the people. This was not exactly the case. Sunni ulama, in order to emasculate Ali's claim to the Caliphate on account of his relation to the Prophet, fling the bogey of democratic principle at the faces of Shia scholars. An objective analysis of the methods through which all the four rightly guided Caliphs got nominated would reveal that they were not democratic. When the Prophet died there were three groups in Medina, viz. Banu Hashim led by Ali, Muhajirun whose prominent leaders were Abu Bakr and Umar and Ansars whose chief was Saad bin Abada. If the Caliph was to be elected on democratic principles then Abada should have been the choice of the people as Ansars were in a majority and immediately after the demise of the Prophet they had gathered at Saqifah Bani Saida to elect one of them as the Caliph. When Abu Bakr and Umar got to know about this they rushed to the place and restricted Ansars to exercise their democratic right on the plea that the Caliph had to be from the Muhajirun and from the tribe of the Qureish. Considering the political situation of the time it might have been a pragmatic move. However, it was not in conformity with democracy. Moreover, what happened to the ostensible value of equality among the Muslim brotherhood? Again, if the Caliph had to be chosen from amongst the Muhajirun and Qureish then the observation of the Prophet made at Ghadeer Khumm, i.e. "For whomever I am a *Mawla* of, then Ali is his *Mawla*", should have been given a consideration. Even if it was not a clear evidence of nomination of a successor, Ali had all the merits that could have qualified him to be the first choice among the Muhajirun. Instead his reluctance to pledge allegiance was construed to be an act of defiance. Umar, as per the reliable accounts, had said: "Our story is that when God called His Messenger to heavens then Ansars opposed us and gathered at Saqifah Bani Saida and Ali, Zubair and their companions opposed us and Muhajirin gathered round Abu Bakr."[52] Umar had also made attempts to force Ali to pay homage to Abu Bakr.[53]

The issue is not that Abu Bakr was a bad choice. During his short reign he had succeeded in consolidating the ummah and restored a semblance of order. Yet, the point remains that Abu Bakr's nomination was not based on the principle of democracy as the Sunni ulama[54] claim. Likewise, Umar too was not elected by the majority of the people. On his deathbed Abu Bakr had in fact dictated his will and testament to Usman nominating Umar as his successor. Although, he did confer with Abdur Rahman bin Awf, Talhah and Usman before nominating Umar, he did not even think of taking Ali into confidence. Bin Awf and Talhah had some reservations about Umar while Usman gave his absolute consent.[55] Significantly Ali did not delay in pledging allegiance to Umar. Indeed, Umar proved to be the most successful of the four rightly guided Caliphs and he possessed some exceptional qualities that helped establish a kind of functional democracy wherein the mightiest and the weakest were equal in the eyes of the law. Though the extremist Shia position does not recognize the first three

Caliphs, an objective and unbiased evaluation tells us that Abu Bakr and Umar did not fail in running the affairs of the state as per the canons of the Quran. The injustices done to Ali and other members of the house of Muhammad were perhaps the offshoots of political expediency but the first two Caliphs were certainly not guilty of fraudulence, personal aggrandisement or nepotism.

Nonetheless, the manner in which Usman was appointed and the policies he pursued thereafter were questionable. The composition of the electoral committee that Umar had constituted was heavily loaded against Ali. Three members out of the six, Saad bin Waqqas, Abdur Rahman bin Awf and Usman bin Affan were related to each other. Moreover, according to Umar's command, Abdur Rahman had the casting vote. What transpired, therefore, in the name of deliberations was nothing short of a farce. Ali had all the virtues and the requisite qualifications to be the leader of the ummah and yet his claim was ignored. The personal failings of Usman and certain dubious actions he took have already been commented upon and need not be repeated here. It must, however, be added that injustice to Ali, in the real sense, was done when Abdur Rahman bin Awf offered the Caliphate to Usman. The Shias might be erroneous in proclaiming that Ali had a divine right to be the Caliph right after the death of the Prophet but ignoring his candidature for the third time was definitely scandalous. Though Ali pledged allegiance to Usman as well as he did to the two Caliphs earlier, he did it more to maintain the unity of the Muslims rather than out of conviction. The cause of the schism of Muslims into two major sects is, therefore, embedded in the injustice done to a man who was very dear to the Messenger of God; who was the cousin of the Apostle of Allah and the husband of his beloved daughter Fatima. The painful reality is that the important perpetrators of discrimination against Ali were the close companions of the Prophet.

3

Transformation of Khilafat

During the period of the Caliphs the learned men of the Christians and the Jews were not only held in great esteem but were appointed to posts of great responsibility, and were promoted to the high ranking job in the government....He (Caliph Haroon Rasheed) never considered to which country a learned person belonged nor his faith and belief, but only his excellence in the field of learning.

– Dr. William Draper in 'History of Intellectual Development of Europe'

We have never heard about any attempt to compel Non-Muslim parties to adopt Islam or about any organized persecution aiming at exterminating Christianity. If the Caliphs had chosen one of these plans, they would have wiped out Christianity as easily as what happened to Islam during the reign of Ferdinand and Isabella in Spain; by the same method which Louis XIV followed to make Protestantism a creed whose followers were to be sentenced to death; or with the same ease of keeping the Jews away from Britain for a period of three hundred and fifty years.

– Thomas Arnold in 'The Call to Islam.'

I

The institution of Khilafat underwent drastic changes after the reign of the Rightly Guided Caliphs. The institution, first of all, lost its spiritual dimension and secondly, the minimal democratic facet that existed during the phase of the first four Caliphs albeit with quite a few restrictions was unabashedly discarded. In Islamic history the periodisation of different dynasties were usually named after either clans of the rulers or the persons who first established them. Despite the concurrence among most Muslim historians that the successive Muslim regimes that emerged after the Caliphate of Ali were not Caliphates in the real sense of the term, yet many historians preferred to call them Khilafat mainly to attach some kind of sanctity to those rules, a throwback from the chronicles that were produced during these regimes or somewhat later. Another reason may be to distinguish the Sunni Muslim regimes from the Shia dominions that emerged later.

The first dynasty that consolidated its power in the Islamic world after the assassination of Ali was that of the Umayyad, whose rule spanning from 661-750, is, as pointed out above, referred to as the Umayyad Caliphate. It was first of the four major Caliphates that came to be established since the rise of Islam. It was in reality a dynasty of the scions of Umayyad who, like most Quraish, originally belonged to the city of Mecca. Though, a member of the Umayyad family, Usman bin Affan had been chosen as the third Caliph, it was Muawiya bin Abi Sufiyan who had actually founded the Umayyad dynasty. It must be borne in mind that in contemporary Islam many scholars, including Sunnis, maintain that Muawiya's family, in particular, his father Abu Sufiyan bin Harb and his wife, Hind bint Utbah, were the deadliest enemies of Islam and they came into the Islamic fold only after the Conquest of Mecca. Nevertheless, in Sunni accounts, Abu Sufiyan and his progeny have room for the family of the Umayyad.

The family of the Umayyad and that of Prophet Muhammad had a common ancestor, Abd Manaf bin Qusai. The Prophet's family could be traced to Abd Manaf's son Hashim while the Umayyad descended from the other son, Abd Shams whose son was named Umayyad. The two families came to be considered two significant clans, Hashmites and Umayyads, of the city of Mecca belonging to the same tribe of Quraish. Despite the common ancestry, there was hardly any camaraderie between the two clans even prior to the rise of Islam. In the aftermath of the Battle of Badr, Abu Sufyan bin Harb emerged the leader of the Umayyads as other prominent persons of the clan were killed in the battle by the Muslims. With the determination of annihilating the Muslims he attacked Medina a year after the Battle of Badr. Though the marauding forces of Mecca under Abu Sufyan in what is known as the Battle of Uhud could not vanquish the forces of Madina in absolute terms, the Muslims suffered considerably as many Muslim warriors including Hamza bin Abdul Muttalib, the uncle of the Prophet, were killed in the battle.[1] All the same, five years after the mishap of Uhud, the Muslims under the command of the Prophet triumphed over the Meccans without any bloodshed. The Prophet announced a general amnesty for all following which Abu Sufyan and almost all the members of the Umayyad clan embraced Islam. Later some of the Umayyads had to play crucial role in the history of Islam.

After the assassination of Ali by a Kharjite in 661, the supporters of the Hashmites had chosen Hasan, the elder son of Ali to be the rightful Khalifa. However, Muawiya I, the son of Abu Sufyan, who had caused much bloodshed during the Caliphate of Ali had continued to assert his claim to the 'Caliphate' within the confines of Syria. Hasan, in order to avoid further shedding of Muslim blood, entered into a peace treaty and relinquished the Caliphate to Muawiyah I with exacting conditions that he would rule the realm of Islam with benevolence and in accordance with the teachings of the Quran, the sayings of the Prophet and the precedents laid down by the Rightly Guided Caliphs. One of the conditions of the treaty was that Muawiyah I would not convert the Caliphate into a dynasty by nominating his son after his death.[2] Nonetheless, it was Muawiyah I who had obliterated the institution of the Caliphate completely and introduced, for the first time in the world of Islam, the dynastic monarchy.[3] Thus, the purported Umayyad Caliphate that was in reality a dynastic rule was established in 661 in Syria and continued to rule over the newly emerging Islamic empire till 750.

Muawiyah I died in 680 and his son Yazid I became the second ruler of the Umayyad. The pious and upright Muslims opposed the succession of Yazid as they favoured Husain bin Ali to become the Caliph and revive the genuine institution of the Caliphate. This tussle led to the most unfortunate tragedy of Islamic history when Yazid I's forces mercilessly massacred Husain (the son of Ali, and the grandson of the Prophet) and all the supporters and male members of his family, numbering 72, at Karbala on October 10, 680 (10th Muharram, 61 AH). The only male surviving member of the family of Husain was Ali, the son of Husain who was down with fever on the day of the battle and was, therefore, captured alive by Yazid I's soldiers.

On Yazid's death his son Muawiya II became the ruler in 683. Though he remained in power for a few months, he was not acknowledged as Caliph outside the province of Syria. Within the province itself there were two main factions, the one represented by Bin al-Zubair and the other by Marwan striving for the position of the Caliph. Their tussle led to a battle fought at Marj Rahit in 684. The victory of the supporters of Marwan made him the Caliph. Nevertheless Marwan remained in power for barely a year. His death in 685 brought his son Abdul Malik to power who ruled the Islamic world for about two decades. In the initial years of his 'Caliphate', Malik had to deal with the rebellion in Kufa led by Al-Mukhtar, who wanted to help Muhammad bin Hanafiyyah, another son of Ali become the Caliph. The Umayyad troops routed the rebel forces in 691. Thereafter, within a year, Malik consolidated his power throughout the empire that was under Islam.

It was during the reign of Malik that the Dome of the Rock (*Qubbat as-Sakhrah*) was constructed in Jerusalem in 692. Abdul Malik died in 705 and was succeeded by his son Walid I. Walid was also interested in the construction of grand buildings. Masjid-e-Nabawi at Medina and Grand Mosque of Damascus (*Jâmia Bani Umayyad al-Kabîr*) were constructed during his reign. Hajjaj bin Yusuf, the ruthless military commander, who had served under Malik as well, was appointed the governor of Iraq during Walid's supremacy. Hajjaj bin Yusuf's name is etched in the history of Islam for his notoriety and brutality. It was he, acting as the agent of the Caliph Abdul Malik, contemptuously disregar ded the word of warning of the Prophet prohibiting bloodshed within the city of Mecca, particularly in the Sacred Mosque, had brutally beheaded Abdullah bin Zubair, the grandson of the Caliph Abu Bakr within the precincts of Kaaba. Another significant event of the rule of Walid, from the point of view of the people of the Indian subcontinent, was the conquest of Sindh and Punjab in 712, by Muhammad bin Qasim. Though the Muslim Arab traders had their settlements in Kerala even when the Prophet was alive, the conquest of Sind heralded the arrival of Muslim warriors as conquerors in North-Western India.

Walid's successor was his brother Suleyman who became the 'Caliph' in 715. He could rule for only two years during which he made an attempt to capture, though unsuccessfully, Constantinople, the capital of the Byzantine Empire. In 717, Suleyman's cousin, Umar bin Abdul Aziz, succeeded him. Most Islamic scholars concur that Abdul Aziz was the only one who could qualify to be a legitimate Caliph in the tradition of *Khulfa-e-Rashidun* because of his piety and administrative acumen. Nevertheless, his death three years after his accession, brought Yazid II, another son of Abdul Malik to power in 720. His reputation in Islamic history is that of an iconoclast because he had ordered the destruction of all Christian images within the realm of Islam. His reign was also marked by a major revolt in Iraq led by Yazid bin Muhallab, who was the governor of the province. However, the forces of Yazid II suppressed the rebellion in 721. The last son of Abdul Malik, Hisham became the ruler after the death of Yazid II, in 724. During his rule of two decades, he made serious attempts to override the Byzantine. First of all, he shifted his capital from Damascus to Resafa, a city that was close to the Byzantine border. Then he launched a series of attacks which could lead to some significant gains in Anatolia. However, his forces were defeated in the Battle of Akroinon in 740, that forced him to abandon his grand plan of conquering the Byzantine.

Hisham's death in 743 led to the proclamation of Walid II, the son of Yazid II as the Umayyad 'Caliph'. This hedonistic man remained in power for barely a few months and was killed in 744 by Yazid III, a son of Walid I, who had become the new ruler. He too died six months after assuming power. His death in 744, led to a conflict between the brother of Yazid III, who was nominated to succeed by the deceased ruler and Marwan II, the grandson of Marwan I. Ultimately it was Marwan II who emerged victorious and continued to hold power for the next six years. During his reign he had to deal with the revolts of the Kharjites in Iraq and Iran and a serious challenge to his 'Caliphate' from Ibrahim the Imam, the fourth in descent from Abbas, the youngest uncle of the Prophet. In his revolt Ibrahim was supported by Abu Muslim, the military commander in Khurasan. In the intervening time, Ibrahim the Imam was captured by the Umayyad forces. He died in prison in 747. Thus, the new claimant to the Caliphate was Abdullah, the brother of Ibrahim, on whose behalf Abu Muslim continued the military expeditions against Marwan II. Abu Muslim expelled the governor appointed by the Umayyad ruler from Khurasan and conquered Kufa in 749. On receiving the news of the fall of Kufa, Marwan II marched towards Iraq with a huge army but Abu Muslim's army defeated the Umayyad forces in the Battle of Zab in January 750. Marwan II fled back to Damascus, where he could not find many supporters. He was ultimately killed on the run in Egypt in August, the same year. By April, Damascus too fell. So, Marwan II proved to be the last 'Caliph' of the Umayyad.

The most striking characteristic of the Umayyad Caliphate was the repudiation of the pious, simple, and by and large, judicious governance that was acknowledged as the paramount attributes of the Rightly Guided Caliphs. The only exception to the rule was a short duration of three years of the reign of Umar bin Abdul Aziz who faithfully emulated the traditions of governance laid down by the *Khulfa-e-Rashidun* and for that reason he is often referred to as *Umar Sani* (Umar II). During this period the Caliphate was transformed into a dynastic monarchy with all the trappings of grandeur, luxury, self-indulgence and, of course, debauchery. Though this development was disgusting and almost a sacrilege from the point of orthodox Islam, from the standpoint of political theory the Umayyad Caliphs did release a Muslim dominated state, to a considerable extent, from the shackles of Islam. The Umayyad Caliphs in the mainstream history of Islam are usually remembered as the non-conformists who erroneously deviated from the path of governance laid down by their predecessors. Nevertheless, from the point of political theory they did the same thing that was done, quite a few centuries later, by Machiavelli, i.e. secularizing the discipline of politics. They also made a huge contribution in expanding the Islamic empire and putting into place a viable administrative structure to govern it. At the end of the Umayyads, the Caliphate was spread over a vast area that extended from India and the periphery of China in the east to the coastal areas of the Atlantic and North Africa in the west. One of the members of the Umayyads had also conquered Spain and established his rule there. The vast area of the Caliphate also brought the riches to the Caliphate that helped it become a formidable political force.

II

The succeeding Abbasids vandalized the tombs of the Umayyad rulers and killed every member of the Umayyad clan wherever they found them. The only member of the clan who could survive was Abdul Rahman, a grandson of Hisham. It was he who established a kingdom in Andalus (Spain) and declared it to be a revived 'Umayyad Caliphate'. The main argument of the Abbasid was that since they were in direct descent from Abbas bin Abdul Muttalib, the youngest uncle of the Prophet, they had a legitimate claim over the Caliphate that, they asserted, should have gone to the family of the Hashmites right from the beginning. This argument, no doubt, helped them procure the absolute support of most Arab clans in the initial phase of the 'Caliphate'. Additionally, the Abbasids solicited the support of the non-Arabs known as *mawali* (friends, also the non-Arab Muslims). The non-Arab population of the Muslim empire was treated shabbily, even if they were Muslims, by the Umayyads. The Abbasids treated them judiciously as a result of which the support base of the Abbasid 'Caliphs' was much larger than the Umayyads.

Abul Abbas Abdullah al-Saffah was the first Abbasid 'Caliph' assuming power in 750. He belonged to a branch of the Hashmites through Abbas, the uncle of the Prophet. That explains the title, Abbasids, given to the Caliphs who followed Abdullah. The Caliphate of Abdullah was established in the city of Kufa, which was declared as the new capital of the Caliphate. Though Abdullah ruled for only four years, he was successful in consolidating and rebuilding the Caliphate. Most importantly, he opted for a policy of all-inclusive governance, which was a radically progressive measure in the extremely clannish culture of the Arabs. The Jews, Christians, Iranians and even Chinese held important positions in the administration. He also adopted a policy to encourage education and business. Many Chinese were captured and made prisoners after the Battle of Talas (*Jang-e-Nahr-e-Talas*). The Abbasids learnt from these Chinese, the art of paper-making and subsequently, the first paper-mill was set up at Samarkand. Many Chinese were employed in the mill. His vision for an all-inclusive governance was also reflected in the reforms he brought about in the armed forces. During the Umayyad rule non-Muslims and non-Arabs were not recruited to the army but Abdullah started a healthy practice of opening the positions in the army for all irrespective of race or faith.

It is appropriate to mention here a few words about the entry of the Barmakids (*Baramikah*) in the court of the Abbasids. The family was originally from Balkh who converted to Islam with the Arab invasion of Iran when the Sasanian dynasty was in power. Most Muslim historians have recorded that the Barmakids were originally Zoroastrian priests before embracing Islam.[4] This is an erroneous view because they were Buddhists and the word *Baramikah* itself is derived from the Sanskrit term *pramukha*, meaning leader or chief administrator. The *Baramakahs* were the administrators of the Buddhist monastery in Balkh that was known as Navavihara (Navbahar in Persian) before they came in contact with Islam.[5] When the Abbasid Caliphate was established it was Khalid bin Barmak who came to occupy the position of importance under the first two Abbasid Caliphs, Abbas and Mansur. Slowly, he rose to the position of the vizier.[6]

His reforms helped him acquire wider acceptance. However, the Shias opposed his Caliphate for two reasons. First, Abdullah declared Sunni Islam as the official religion and second, his lineage was not from Ali. Their opposition, nevertheless, remained low-key during his four-year rule. Abdullah died of smallpox on June 10, 754, nominating his brother Abu Jafar Mansur as his successor.

The second Abbasid Caliph, Abu Jafar Al-Mansur's father "Muhammad was reputedly a great-grandson of Abbas bin Abd al-Muttalib, the youngest uncle of Muhammad; his mother, as described in the 14th-century Moroccan historical work *Rawd al-Qirtas* was one Sallama, 'a Berber woman' given to his father".[7]

The most significant thing that Mansur did was founding the city of Baghdad in 762 and shifting the capital of the Caliphate to the newly established city. He also took a few measures to consolidate his position. Though Abu Muslim was an able military general whose contribution in establishing the Abbasid Caliphate was momentous, he had started behaving as the independent ruler of Iran and Transoxiana. Therefore, in 755, on the orders of Mansur he was assassinated.

Mansur's reign is notable in Islamic history because it was he who truly launched a well planned movement for promoting literature, science and scholarship which later came to be known as the beginning of the Islamic Golden Age. His rule was marked by religious ethnic and racial tolerance as many Iranians and Turks were appointed to high offices in the Caliphate. It must be pointed out that the Iranian civilization was far superior to the Arabs and Mansur openly acknowledged this fact by ordering the translation of Persian literature into Arabic and encouraging the adoption of Iranian art, culture and scholarship. Thus, began a healthy communication between Iranian and Arab cultures.

During Mansur's rule many non-Arabs embraced Islam because reverting the policy of the Umayyad who would discourage conversion for collection of *jizya* (poll tax) from the non-Muslims, Mansur promoted the policy of conversion. This policy remained a constant throughout the Abbasid period. He also established peaceful and advantageous relations with China. In 756, he assisted the Chinese ruler in suppressing the An Shi Rebellion by sending four thousand troops. In return, the Arabs were benefited by learning many scientific ideas from the Chinese.[8]

Some sources claim that Mansur imprisoned and tortured two founders of the schools of jurisprudence of Sunni Islam, viz. Imam Abu Hanifa and Imam Malik. Nevertheless, other equally reliable sources assert that Mansur personally was not responsible for these unfortunate occurrences. In 775, he planned to go to Mecca to perform Hajj but he could not complete the journey; he died on the way. His son Mahdi succeeded him.

The third Abbasid Caliph Mahdi's real name was Abu Abdullah bin Abdullah al-Mansur but he was better known as al-Mahdi. The Barmakid family that enjoyed considerable influence in the Abbasid court as viziers became even more powerful under the rule of Mahdi. The third Caliph appointed Yahya, the son of Khalid bin Barmak and the Governor of Armenia as the tutor of his son who was to become the future Caliph famously known as Harun al-Rashid. It must, however, be acknowledged that the Barmakids worked sincerely and diligently to enrich the fortunes and augment the standing of the Abbasids.

Mahdi was in power for ten years Two notable events of his

reign were: one, he imprisoned his vizier, Yaqub bin Dawud who was, earlier, quite close to the Caliph; and two he brought about an official inquisition as a result of which many heretics (dualists/ *zindiqs*)[9] were executed. Nevertheless, despite the muted censure of orthodox Arab ulama, Mahdi himself was a patron of music and poetry. Many musicians and poets of the time were associated with his court. The reliable reports suggest that Mahdi was poisoned by one of his concubines in 785. Before his death he, however, had nominated his son Musa al-Hadi as his successor.

During Mahdi's reign, the city of Baghdad developed into a truly cosmopolitan metropolis. Many scholars, scientists and artists from Iran, Iraq, Syria, Afghanistan and Spain had settled in the city. The important fact was that many of these talented people were non-Muslims. In Mahdi's times, Baghdad had acquired the distinction of the world's largest city. His ten-year rule was remarkable from the point of view of administration too. He created quite a few departments dealing with the affairs of army, law and revenue. The discriminatory laws against the non-Arabs were rescinded. The first paper mill that was established in 751 played a significant role in the promotion of scholastic pursuits. In Baghdad the sale of paper increased manifold and huge book stores came about in the city.

Mahdi's eldest son, Abu Muhammad Musa al-Hadi was the fourth Caliph who assumed power in 785 but died a short while after in 786. In the tradition of his father, Hadi too continued to follow the forward-thinking, liberal policies because of which, though he ruled for a short period, he came to be known as 'the enlightened Caliph'.

During his short reign, he had to crush the rebellion of Husain bin Ali bin Hasan who had declared himself the Caliph in Medina. However, a cousin of Husain, Idris bin Abdullah had founded the kingdom of Idrisi in Morocco. Hadi had to deal with the Khajites as well who would revolt intermittently at different places in the Caliphate. Moreover, he had successfully repelled the invasion of the Byzantine and conquered chunks of the Byzantine territory. His death in 786, was also a matter of controversy. Some believed he died of an ulcer but other sources claimed that he was poisoned by his stepmother.[10] A significant move that he took before his death was moving the capital from Baghdad to Hadisa in North-West Iraq.

The fifth Abbasid Caliph Harun al-Rashid is perhaps the most well-known Caliph all across the world because his name was associated with many tales such as *The Arabian Nights,* and many anecdotes were linked to him. He became the Caliph in 786 and ruled over the Islamic world for almost a quarter of a century. He presided over the Islamic Golden Age, and contributed significantly to promote science, scholarship, culture and religious studies. He established the famous House of Wisdom (*Bait-ul-Hikmat*) in Baghdad that was actually a huge library with an attached scientific laboratory. On accession he had immediately moved the capital from Hadisa to Baghdad and later, in 796, shifted the seat of the Caliphate to Ar-Raqqa, in Syria.

Since Harun himself was a highly educated man, an able administrator and formidable military commander, his reputation as a legendary ruler travelled beyond the confines of the Caliphate. Quite a few rulers of the time sent delegations to his court to establish peaceful relations with the Abbasids. It is historically recorded that in 799, Harun sent a clock as a present to Charlemagne with a visiting Frankish delegation. The famous Charlemagne who had conquered almost the entire Western Europe and was the founder of the present-day France and Germany, was awestruck on receiving the clock and thought it to be a work of sorcery because of its sound and tricks that it displayed every hour.

Harun was born in the town of Rey which is close to present-day Tehran. He was the third son of the third Abbasid Caliph Mahdi. His mother Khayzuran was a Yemeni slave girl who had a great influence on Harun in the governance of the Caliphate. Besides his mother his Prime Minister, Yahya Barmakid and his sons were extremely influential in running the administration. Some sources suggest that the Barmakids remained powerful till the death of the Caliph's mother who died in 798. Thereafter the Barmakid had to face the wrath of Harun who thought they had become disrespectful and too powerful. He imprisoned Yahya and his sons and confiscated their properties. His son Mamun was born to an Iranian mistress the day he assumed power and a short while later, Amin was born to his properly wedded wife Zubaida who was a daughter of Mansur, the second Abbasid Caliph. Therefore, Amin because of his mother's ancestry was considered to be the rightful successor of Harun.

Despite the peak of the Islamic Golden Age his reign got to be known for, Harun had to face political opposition and unrest in different provinces. Syria, that had remained the capital of the Umayyad Caliphs would frequently witness unrest because many Arab tribes residing there were sympathetic to the Umayyads. For that reason, Harun had to shift his capital from Baghdad to Ar-Raqqa. The province of Egypt was also in turmoil because of lack of proper governance and high taxation. A branch of the Umayyad had already established in 755, a parallel centre of the Caliphate in Spain.[11]

Then the Idrisis[12] kingdom was founded in 788 in Morocco and the Aghlabids[13] established an emirate in Tunisia in 800. All these troubles could not weaken the basic authority of the Caliphate mainly because of the competent administrative acumen of Yahya Barmakid and his sons.[14] In 808, Harun went to suppress the rebellion of Raafe bin Lais in Transoxania but died there in 809. He was buried in Khurasan itself where in later years the city of Mashhad was to emerge. The city was so named because of the martyrdom of Imam Riza there in 818. The Shias disparage Harun because of the murder of the seventh Imam Musa bin Jafar.

In his lifetime Harun had virtually divided his Caliphate between his two sons, Mamun and Amin. Later another son Qasim was also awarded a part of it. This was not a very wise move because after his death it led to the outbreak of a civil war as all his sons were fighting to gain control of the entire Caliphate. The fate of the next Caliph was thus decided on the battlefield in 827, when Mamun ultimately triumphed.

As pointed out earlier, Harun's son Muhammad better known as Amin, got precedence over Mamun in the matter of succession because the former was born to Zubaida, an Arab woman and granddaughter of Mansur while the latter's mother was an Iranian concubine. Harun had divided the Caliphate between the two sons and advised them to honour the arrangement that he had made for them. He had called both the sons to Mecca during the Hajj and made them sign the pledge and his will within the precincts of the

Sacred Mosque. According to Harun's arrangement Amin was to succeed as the Caliph and Mamun would become the governor of Khurasan with complete autonomy. On Amin's death, Mamun was to assume the Caliphate.

This arrangement was not an astute stratagem to maintain peace between the two ambitious sons. Therefore, Amin soon after becoming the Caliph connived effectively to win over Mamun's financial agent in Rey and ordered Mamun to hand over the governorship to Musa (Amin's son) and return to Baghdad. Mamun who was, as almost all sources concur, far more intelligent, brave and competent administrator than Amin, acted swiftly. He dismissed his financial agent and disdainfully refused to acknowledge Amin's orders. Since Mamun's mother was Iranian, he had the solid backing of the people of Iran. Amin sent a large army under the command of Ali bin Isa to arrest Mamun. Mamun's forces were under the command of the astute general, Tahir bin Husain, who was Iranian by origin. He defeated the forces of the Caliph and killed Ali. Subsequently, Tahir conquered Ahwaz, Bahrain and parts of Arabia. In Iraq, Basra and Kufa declared loyalty to Mamun.

Finally, Tahir laid siege to Baghdad. Soon the forces of Mamun entered the capital of the Caliphate. Amin then agreed to hand over power to Mamun provided he was given safe passage out of Baghdad. Tahir agreed to consider Amin's request if he submitted his sceptre, seal and other insignias of the Caliphate. Amin attempted to flee by boat without surrendering the official motifs of the Caliphate. Tahir found out and executed him.

According to reliable reports, Amin was perhaps a bisexual and was sexually attracted to eunuchs.[15] It is also recorded that his mother would send slave women disguised as eunuchs to him, so that he would gradually become interested in women.[16] As a last ditch, Amin had requested his mother to settle the dispute of the Caliphate in his favour by prevailing over Mamun. Nevertheless, she refused and thus Mamun became the Caliph.

The seventh Abbasid Caliph, Abu Abbas Abdullah al-Mamun was born in 786 in Baghdad. By many historians he is regarded the best of all the Abbasid Caliphs though Harun Rashid's name is quite well-known since he figures, wrongly of course, in some of the stories of the *Arabian Nights.* Shibli Nomani, the reputed historian and religious scholar chose Mamun as the most distinguished Caliph in the long list of the Abbasids and wrote his biography in the *Heroes of Islam* series. Mamun made sincere and significant attempts to put an end to the Sunni-Shia conflict that had become the root-cause of disunity among the Muslims.

On becoming the Caliph, Mamun decided to make Merv, a city in today's Turkmenistan, the capital because of its proximity to Iran. His competent Iranian vizier Fazl served him devotedly. As part of the policy of uniting Sunnis and Shias, Mamun invited Ali Riza, the Shia Imam, and married his own daughter to him. He also declared Ali Riza as his successor after his death. This measure, however, neither convinced the Shias nor the Abbasids. The Shias thought of it as a ploy because Ali Reza was much older than Mamun and, therefore, there was hardly a possibility of him succeeding the reigning Caliph. The Abbasids were unhappy obviously because for them the legitimate heir of the Caliphate should be an Abbasid alone. An Abbasid prince, Ibrahim, son of the third Caliph Mahdi revolted and declared himself the Caliph in Baghdad. This made Mamun march towards Baghdad. During the course of his long journey his trusted vizier Fazl was assassinated in February 818. Shortly afterwards, Imam Ali Riza also died after a brief illness. The Shias insisted that he was poisoned by the Caliph. Having quelled the rebellion of Ibrahim, Mamun moved the capital back to Baghdad.

Mamun is acknowledged as the most gifted of all the Abbasid Caliphs not only because he was a judicious ruler and competent administrator; his reputation as the steadfast supporter of rationality, philosophy, scholarship and science is unparallel in the history of Islam. He initially made sincere efforts to do away with the sectarian schism in Islam. However, the political expediency compelled him to give up intervention directly in sectarian matters. Instead he decided to infuse rationality and enlightenment among Muslims that, he believed, would inevitably render all sectarian conflicts redundant.

He started supporting the thoughts of the Mutazilites because of their rational approach in interpreting religious issues. In 833, Mamun made Mutazilism, the official doctrine of the Caliphate, a strategy that was absolutely perfect to instil rationality and scientific temperament among the Muslims. However, it was opposed by the orthodox sections. It is, therefore, necessary to explain the basic arguments of the Mutazilites whose influence can be traced in the writings of the best Muslim minds including Syed Ahmed Khan. Considering the significance of the first rationalist movement in early Islam it is imperative to reflect on it briefly.

The Mutazilites were the earliest philosophers of Islam who made a forthright effort at the beginning of the second Islamic century to offer a rationalist interpretation of major Islamic positions without injuring the divinity of the faith. Though it began as a puritanical movement focusing mainly on the issue of 'creation of the Quran', it later ended as the first notable rationalistic pressure group which underlined the primacy of reason as a perfect value that could not be discounted in the reading of the Quran. The upholders of Mutazilism pointed out that the popular belief that the Quran was the uncreated word of God and eternal would actually go against the principle of the Divine Unity and thus destroy the foundation of Islam. The orthodox view is that the Quran, in its Arabic language, is in fact the exact replica of a divine original written on a *luh mahfooz* (guarded tablet) kept in paradise and that it is eternal. The Mutazilites argue that God is the Creator of everything and, therefore, He has also created the Quran; to call the Holy Book eternal is erroneous because nothing is eternal save God. This became a furious controversy when Mamun wrote a command to the governor of Baghdad, Ishaq bin Ibrahim, from the battlefront. The gist of the command was as follows: "Being the Caliph of Islam, I am duty bound to support and protect this faith. I have observed that the ignorant and common Muslims believe the Quran is as ancient as Allah and then claim that they are monotheist and truthful and the others are heretic and kafir. In fact quite a few verses of the Quran negate their faith.

"What is more, the support of the hypocrite and the greedy-for-power jurists has instigated them. Therefore, read out this command of mine before all the Qazis. Anyone who refuses to believe that the Quran is created, strike off his name from the list of the department (of Justice), and his testimony should be treated null and void."[17]

The ultimate objective of the Mutazilites was to transform an inflexible legalistic faith, which Islam had been driven down to by then, into a reasonable and more humanistic creed. Their efforts bore fruits when Abbasid Caliphs, in particular Mamun and his two successors, patronised the movement. Nevertheless, political patronage proved inadequate and fleeting as another Abbasid Caliph Mutawakkil in 848 adopted a hostile policy towards the rationalistic interpretation of Islam. It was a defining moment in the history of Islam as the suppression of Mutazilism denied Islamic civilization exploiting the gems of Greek and Hellenistic intellectual legacy that were later used to the hilt by the European Christians after the end of the Dark Ages. The consequences are conspicuous for all to see.

Let us consider why these earliest rationalists in the history of Islam came to be labelled as the Mutazilites and their movement Mutazilism. The term Mutazili is Arabic derived from the root word Mutazila meaning 'to secede', 'to withdraw' or 'to leave'. There is an anecdote that helps understand why the movement was so named. It is recounted that once a renowned Sufi scholar of his time, Hasan al-Basri was teaching his students in a mosque in Basra when a visitor approached him with a request to explicate his view on an issue of religious significance. He is believed to put the following poser to Hasan:

He first informed that people belonging to a particular sect[18], which believed that even a perpetrator of a grave sin, so long as he remained a believer, continued to be a Muslim and such a person would surely be forgiven by the Almighty. His poser was, what Hasan thought in the matter and what could be the appropriate position in the light of the teaching of Islam?

Since the issue was an intricate one, Hasan pondered over it for a while and before he could elucidate his opinion a student got up and pronounced that the perpetrator of a grave sin could neither be called a Muslim nor a non-Muslim.[19] His contention was that the sinner could not be considered a Muslim because he was guilty of a grave sin; however, he could not be called a non-Muslim because he continued to be a believer. According to the student, the perpetrator of a grave sin could be placed in an intermediate position, *manzilah bain al-manzilatain*. The impudence of the student took his teacher by surprise and he was left speechless. Then the student left the gathering along with some of his friends and went to another part of the mosque and began further explaining his position to his friends. Hasan's comment about the student was, *I'tazala 'anna* which means 'he got separated from us.' The name of the student was Wasil bin Ata,[20] who because he walked out of Hasan's class was called a Mutazili and the theological movement that he initiated later came to be known as Mutazilism. However, shortly after the commencement of the movement its proponents preferred to call themselves *Ahl al-Tawhid wa al-Adl,* that may be translated as the Advocates of Divine Unity and Justice, a label that never got wider currency in the historical accounts.

There is another explanation about the nomenclature of the movement according to which the term Mutazila got popular prevalence after the death of Hasan. Qatadah succeeded Hasan, however, a group led by Amr bin 'Ubaid refused to be part of Qatabah's class and thus they were called the Mutazilites. Nonetheless, most sources agree on one point that it was Wasil bin Ata who was the initiator of the movement. Wasil was an intellectual who was born in Madinah in 699 and died in 748. Before joining the circle of Imam Hasan al-Basri's pupils, Wasil was a student of abu-Hashim Abdullah but decided to leave him because he could not agree with his teacher on certain issues such as Imamat. Though he wrote quite a few books the prominent among them are three: *Kitab al-Manzilah bain al-Manzilain,* (A Treatise on the Intermediate Position), *Kitab al-Futya* (Technical Book?...), and *Kitab al-Tawhid* (A Book on the Unity of God).

As the founder of Mutazilism, Wasil's ideas comprise four cardinal points. First, he refused to accept the practice of assigning attributes to God. Second, he believed that man possessed the free-will to opt for good actions. Third, a believer who commits a grave sin can neither be called a believer nor an unbeliever but he occupies an intermediate position. Fourth, one of the opposing parties that were involved in the Battle of the Camel,[21] was not on the right path. And also one faction among the assassinators of the third Caliph, Osman and his allies was guilty of committing an error. In both the cases, however, he did not specify the offenders.

Issues such as whether the Quran is a creation of the Almighty and whether it is eternal, whether God has also created evil, whether everything is predestined for men or they possess free-will, whether the attributes of God that find expression in the Quran be taken literally or they should be interpreted allegorically are the major topics that have been discussed by the Mutazilites. It must be borne in mind that the Mutazilites were not the first to deliberate upon such issues; they were under scrutiny since the beginning thanks to the sectarian conflicts and interfaith polemics. It is, therefore, unfair to accuse Mutazilism, as most of the Sunni ulama do, that it has gratuitously brought into focus the issues that should have been better left untouched. Deliberations, arguments, counter-arguments and dissension are bound to take place among the adherents of a faith that is claimed to be closest to nature. Interestingly, even Mutazilism did not remain impervious to this all-pervading fact. It too went through dissent and conflict resulting in the emergence of two groups, the Basra School and the Baghdad School and the interaction between the two was far from amiable. In the aftermath of the Mongol invasions in the thirteenth century the Basra School ceased to exist. Despite the hostile standpoints of the orthodox ulama and intimidating policies adopted by the Muslim states in the late third century AH and thereafter towards Mutazilism, elements of the doctrine got absorbed in Shi'ism in Iran. Zaidis of Yemen too largely adhere to the spirit of the doctrine.

Most assessments of Mutazilism by the conservative Muslim ulama portray it as a movement that could damage the divine characteristic of Islam because its promoters heavily relied on the wisdom that got expressed in Greek philosophy and in the process undermined the core of Islam. An objective analysis of Mutazilite doctrine, however, reveals that such estimations are incorrect. The hostile stance towards Mutazilism could possibly be the offshoot of animosity that had always existed between various theological schools, which in the end split the religion of one God and one Book into more than 70 sects. The fact is that for the Mutazilites the divine truth that was revealed in the Quran had always been the driving force of their movement. Though they sought inspiration from Greek philosophy, it was not the mainstay of their reading of Islam. From the Greeks they primarily borrowed the point of view about cosmology.

The Universe, in the view of the Mutazilites comprises bodies that differ from each other in terms of qualities. Some bodies are animate while others are inanimate. Some are hot while others are cold; some are mobile while others are static and so on. The Mutazilites further expound that the qualities of the bodies change with the change in time and space. For instance, an inanimate body such as a stone turns into a mobile one when it rolls down a hill but goes back to its original quality of immobility when it reaches the foot of the hill. The same applies to a particular body turning from hot to cold and vice versa. In order to answer the differences between bodies, their qualities and the changes that take place in the same bodies with the change of time and space, the Mutazilites appear to rely on the Greek philosopher Leucippus and his student Democritus who in the fifth century BC had developed the theory of atomism.

Atomism is a speculative theory of Natural Philosophy that attempts to explain the mystery of the Universe, which according to the atomists comprises two opposite and indivisible bodies, viz. atoms and voids. Though very little is known about Leucippus, his student Democritus explains that atoms by their very nature are unchangeable and indivisible bodies while voids are nothing or the negation of bodies. When atoms coalesce with voids they form various masses that are popularly called natural phenomena. In view of this all objects in the universe are in fact composed of atoms.

Similarly, the Mutazilite theorists such as Dirar bin Amr (d. 815) and Abu al-Hudhayl (d. 841) who belonged to the Basra School affirm that all bodies are composed of atoms (*ajza*) which are isolated invisible bodies similar to mathematical points. They, however, have the faculty to combine with other items to form clusters. The only difference between Mutazilites' understanding of the universe and the Greek classical theory of atomism is in respect with void or the negation of body. Mutazilites claim that it is the will of God that helps atoms face up to various spiritual accidents (*arad*) that culminate into creation of various objects, while for the Greek atomists it is the combinations of atoms and voids that result into the formation of diverse objects.

It must be emphasized that later the Asharites who branched

out from Mutazilism also accepted the Mutazilites' position on cosmology. For instance, in the works of al-Ghazzali (1058-1111), the most prominent philosopher of the Asharite School, the Mutazilites' theory of atomism finds expression. Nevertheless, some other Islamic philosophers, in particular, those belonging to Spain disagree with the Mutazilites' views on cosmology. For instance, Averroes (Ibn Rushd, 1126-1198) entirely rejected it while writing a critique of al-Ghazali's notable work *Tahafut al-Falasifah* and approved of Aristotle's theory of cosmology.

Mutazilism as a theological doctrine postulates five precepts. The first is about *Tawhid* or Unity of God which is the most crucial tenet of Islam. Mutazilites vigorously assert in Divine Unity and elucidate that the Almighty is altogether a distinctive entity and any attempt to confuse it with a natural object, humans, animate or inanimate phenomena is a grave sin. It is because of the human inadequacies in terms of intellect and articulation that makes the task of conceptualization of God impossible.

A delicate issue that has always confronted Muslim theologians is that of explaining the divine attributes. Whether the attributes that are enshrined in the Quran are distinct from the Almighty or form the essence of God? The Mutazilites believe that the divine attributes are not distinct from the essence of God and that it is His omniscient essence that makes Him the knower of all things and for this He does not require a separate source. They insist that the literal interpretation of the anthropomorphic verses of the Quran that deal with the attributes of the Almighty must have a metaphorical reading so that it does not leave any possibility of divisibility of Divine Unity and this is exactly in conformation with the message of the Quran. Thus, unlike some theologians, the Mutazilites opt for an allegorical interpretations of the Quranic verses and the traditions (*ahadis*) pertaining to the Unity of God. Mutazilism maintains that God is the creator of the universe and all that is within it; He is omnipresent as He existed when there was nothing and would exist eternally; He is omnipotent for there are no barriers to His power and He does not have a form or organs nor does He need any such tool.

Another related issue is about human nature. Whether human nature will be different in the hereafter from what it is in this world?

The Mutazilites suppose that human nature will not change in life after death. This position takes apart the popular view that the people residing in paradise will see God. Logically arguing, the Mutazilites point out that it was impossible even for Prophet Moses to see God in this world. Since human nature is not going to be different in the hereafter, it will be impossible for any human being to see God with his own eyes. The Mutazilites underscore that God is not a material entity and for that reason He cannot be seen by human eyes.

The second precept of Mutazilism relate to the concept of *Adl Ilahi* or Divine Justice. In this context Mutazilites emphasize the power of reasoning that is bestowed on human beings by the Almighty so that they discriminate between good and evil. Congruent to it is the issue of free will of human beings, which empowers a person to opt for good actions and shun the evil ones. Nicholson says: "On this subject the Koran speaks with two voices. Muhammad was anything but a logically exact and consistent thinker. He was guided by the impulse of the moment, and neither he nor his hearers perceived, as later Muslims did, that the language of the Koran is often contradictory."[22] In support of his observation, Nicholson cites two verses of the Quran which contradict each other and also relate to the issue under consideration. The first verse: "*Every soul is in pledge* (with God) *for what it hath wrought.*" And the second: "*Whoso does good benefits himself, and whoso does evil does it against himself.*"[23]

In the first century of Islam these mutually contradictory verses led to an intense controversy between those who believed in predestination and claimed that God alone determined all human actions, good or evil and those who thought human beings possessed free will and God had nothing to do with evil actions of the people. The former were in overwhelming majority and the political authority of the day, the Umayyad government, too was on their side. Consequently, quite a few believers in the doctrine of human free will were put to death. The controversy, nevertheless, persisted and in Islamic literature it is referred to as the conflict between the *Qadarites* and *Jabrites*. The former believed in human power (*Qadar*) of free will that empowers man to determine his own action while the latter held the view that man was completely powerless and he acted only under the compulsion (*Jabr*) of God. The Mutazilites favoured the *Qadarites'* point of view.

It is, therefore, human free will that is at the root of good and evil. The Mutazilites assert that God does no evil nor does He motivate a person to do an evil act. This position is in tune with the Islamic concept of Divine Judgment when the evil doers will be punished depending on the gravity of their sins. The Mutazilites justly argue that if everything, including the sins of human beings, come about with the will of God then administering punishment to the sinners would become a meaningless exercise because a sinner would not be held guilty of acting as per the will of God. They also deny the concept of Divine Intercession for they believe that it negates the doctrine of Divine Justice. According to those who believe in the concept of Divine Intercession such as the Asharites, the Muslims who commit grave sins in the world may hope for God's help and a lesser punishment in the hereafter and that ultimately they will be taken out from hell and rewarded within a residence in paradise. The Mutazilites insist that Divine Justice will not favour any sinner and each one will be punished in accordance with the nature of his sin.

In the context Mutazilites had to settle the poser of human sufferings such as poverty, afflictions, diseases and so on. If God does no evil then how can such evils exist for which the sufferers can be blamed for exercising their free will? In response to this, the Mutazilites seek the answer in the Islamic concept of human suffering, which advocates that for some the worldly life is a test of their faith and endurance. Despite the hardships if they steadfastly stick to Islam they would be appropriately rewarded by God in the life hereafter.

Imagine a situation wherein all human beings are equally affluent and uniformly healthy. In such a scenario none can be tested in regard with qualities such as charity, compassion, generosity and so on. In fact, concepts like poverty and afflictions would have no meaning because they owe their relevance to the existence of affluence and health respectively. The Mutazilites claim that the inequalities that are beyond the purview of human free will to be eradicated are the essential segment of the Divine system wherein those who encounter poverty, diseases and natural calamities undergo a severe test. If they remain unwavering in matters of faith, they would be handsomely compensated on the Day of Judgment as the Quran proclaims: "Say: O bondman who believe! Observe your duty to your Lord. For those who do good in this world there is good, and Allah's earth is spacious. Verily the steadfast will be paid their wages without stint."[24]

Conversely, inequalities also put the wealthy and healthy under a severe trial. They have to use their good fortunes fairly by helping the poor, needy and weak and refrain from indulgence, debauchery and similar sins. If they fail in the test severe punishments await them in the life hereafter. The Quran says:

> He is who hath placed you as viceroys of the earth and hath exalted some of you in rank above others, that He may try you by (the test of) that which He hath given you. Lo! Thy Lord is swift in prosecution, and lo! He is Forgiving, Merciful.[25]

Mutazilism believes that the tests of the worldly lives are meant for adults and mentally stable people. Children and insane individuals are not subjected to the divine tests. It is true that children and the mentally unstable suffer in God's scheme of things; however, their actions would not be put to scrutiny. The Mutazilites, in fact, reaffirm that all believers would be suitably compensated and in particular children, even if their parents happen to be polytheists (*mushrikin*), are destined to go to Heaven for Allah decrees in the Quran:

> Say: Shall I seek another than Allah for Lord, when He is Lord of all things? Each soul earneth only on its own account, nor doth any laden bear another's load. Then unto your Lord is your return and He will tell ye that wherein you differed.[26]

The third precept of Mutazilism concerns the subject of Divine Promises and Threats (*al-Wa'da wa al-Wa'id*). The Mutazilites firmly believe that Allah's promises and threats that get expressed in the Quran are irrevocable. God will certainly recompense those who obey Him in entirety and do the good deeds as per His instructions. Likewise Allah will definitely punish those who defy Him and do things in contravention of His command. In fact, such a position should not have been contested by any believer. The Asharites, nonetheless, argue that the Mutazilites by calling Allah's promises and threats irrevocable have actually imposed an obligation on the Almighty to fulfil His promises and accomplish His threats. The Mutazilites counter that each word of the Quran is based on truth and so are the promises and threats. Breaking promises and not carrying out threats is a failing of human beings but not of Allah. In the context, Asharites seem to be on shaky ground. Their objection is just a crack to win a point in the theological dispute.

The fourth principle of the Mutazilites is, in point of fact, the issue that gave birth to the movement. In Arabic it is called *al-Manzilah bayna al-Manzilatayn* which may simply be explained as an intermediate position assigned to the believers guilty of perpetrating grave sins. The Mutazilites hold the view that Muslims guilty of committing grave sins and fail to repent for that in their lifetime cannot be designated either as non-believers or believers but occupy a position between the two extremes. Their argument is that a believer is one who does not deny the existence of God and being a Muslim he has also not associated any other deity with the Almighty. A believer who professes his belief in One God may go astray and commit sins; some of them may be grave. On this account, however, he does not become a *kafir* or a non-believer. Now the conventional Islamic belief is that the perpetrators of grave sins are bound to go to hell. Mutazilites do not question the belief. They, however, point out that hell is a hierarchical place wherein the sinners would be accommodated at different stations as per the nature of their sins. According to the Mutazilites believers guilty of grave sins, on account of their faith in the Almighty, would occupy the intermediate position in hell. In simple terms they would be awarded a lesser punishment.

The doctrine of the intermediate position as explained by Abdul Jabbar, a Mutazilite ideologue is that a believer who has committed rape or murder can neither be called a believer nor can he be a non-believer. He occupies an intermediate position that entitles him to marry a Muslim and after death get buried in Muslim graveyards. Thus, the Mutazilites have adopted a midway position between the Kharjites who consider the perpetrator of grave sins as *kafir* and the Murjites who do not express their position and leave the issue to the will of the Almighty.

The last principle of the Mutazilites' doctrine concerns the advocacy of good and prevention of evil. In Arabic it is known as *al-amr bil ma'ruf wa al-nahy 'an al munkar*. The Mutazilites make a distinction between the kinds of good. The first one is obligatory and the second is supererogatory doing something good beyond obligation. A *momin,* a devout Muslim, performs supererogatory good in addition to the obligatory good. In case of evil the Mutazilites argue that all evil actions must be shunned because there cannot be any kind of justification in committing an evil act. A Muslim, therefore, must strive not to commit any evil act himself and also be instrumental in prohibiting evil actions of others. In this context they make a reference to the word of God:

> And if two parties of believers fall to fighting, then make peace between them. And if one party of them doeth wrong to the other, fight ye that doeth wrong till it return unto the ordinance of Allah; then if it return, make peace between them justly, and act equitably. Lo! Allah loveth the equitable.[27]

It is, therefore, binding on a Muslim to avoid evil himself and also prohibit others to execute evil deeds. The Mutazilites, however, concede an exception to the rule. Their argument is that if prohibition of an evil might lead to widespread defiance and revolt, in short if it gives rise to more evil across society then prohibiting others doing evil might be avoided.

Though Mutazilism appeared in Iraq in the mid-eighth century during the Umayyad period, it flourished at the beginning of the next century. The political power had changed. It is widely acknowledged that the Abbasids, in particular, initially promoted intellectual activities and rewarded the creative minds and scientists. It was the commencement of the discoveries and intellectual awakening since the death of the Greek and Hellenistic scholastic traditions, roughly seven centuries prior to the European Renaissance. The Muslim intellectuals and masterminds first began offering varied examinations of Theology but soon traversed to other fields of knowledge and made luminous contributions to Mathematics, Law, Philosophy, Astronomy, Medicine and Natural Sciences. The geniuses such as Tabari, Razi, Majusi, Avicenna/Ibn Sina (Medicine) Kindi, Farabi (Philosophy), Battani, Biruni, Umar Khayyam, Khwarizmi (Mathematics/Astronomy), Jahiz (Chemistry) Yaqut (Geography), Tabari, Masudi (Historiography) et al. belong to the enlightened Abbasid period. While the Abbasid rulers were patronizing philosophy and scientific research their European contemporaries, in the words of Hitti, "Charlemagne and his lords, were reportedly dabbling in the art of writing their names."[28]

Mutazilism was a pre-Abbasid period movement but the strong winds of intellectualism and liberalism blowing across the Abbasid state at the beginning of the ninth century provided it the suitable environ to prosper. It was during this period that the Muslim intellectuals and scientists made the first significant attempts to explore the scholarly outputs of the Greek and Hellenistic civilizations that in Europe were either destroyed or dumped in a way so as not to be accessible to the people ever by the Holy Roman Empire. The Muslim intelligentsia did not only seek inspiration from the Hellenistic and Greek scholastic legacy but make the world aware of its existence. The Mutazilites found the opportunity to free Islam from the clutches of orthodox theologians. Their starting point was to advocate the supremacy of Reason in all human matters including religion. They could succeed in winning over prominent officials of the government to their side by their logical arguments that the Quran was a creation of God and that it could not be eternal because except God nothing was eternal.

Mamun himself had philosophical and rationalistic leanings and, therefore, promoted the fundamental principle of Mutazilism that religious texts should be in conformity with reason. Referring to al-Nadim's work *al-Fihrist,* Hitti observed "that Aristotle appeared to him (Mamun) in a dream and assured him that there was no real difference between reason and religious law. In pursuance of his policy, Mamun in 830 established in Baghdad his famous *Bayt al-Hikmah* (House of Wisdom), a combination of library, academy and translation bureau which in many respects proved the most important educational institution since the foundation of the Alexandrian Museum in the first half of the third century BC."[29]

Mamun not only became a staunch supporter of Mutazilism himself but almost made the rationalistic doctrine a state religion. In 827, he issued a decree that legitimized the Mutazilites' position of "creation (*khalq*) of the Quran" as an official article of faith and insisted that all Muslims should adhere to it. All government officials including the judges had to subscribe to the rationalistic principle. Subsequently, Mamun instituted an inquisitorial tribunal for the trial and conviction of those who were opposed to the belief of 'creation of the Quran.'

The masses as usual had been under the control of the orthodox ulama, the most prominent among them was Imam Ahmad bin Hanbal who fiercely opposed Mutazilism. Besides, the Asharites contested a couple of precepts of the Mutazilites by joining the popular resentment against the rationalistic doctrine. The founder of the Asharite School, Abu Hasan Ali al-Ashari was, in fact, a Mutazilite earlier who remained committed to rationalism for over forty years. With the change in the political climate caused by the death of Wasiq, Ashari, who was a student of a Mutazilite theologian, Abu Ali al-Jubbai, opted to attack Mutazilism as it was a politically correct move. The then reigning Caliph, Mutawakkil (847-861) neither inherited the intellectual and liberal propensity of his predecessors nor was he open-minded enough to tolerate a rationalistic doctrine, which the conservative and orthodox ulama and because of their sway, the commoners had dubbed as heresy.

Ashari began his revolt against Mutazilism by rejecting two of its tenets, viz. the concept of free will and the belief that God does no evil for human beings. In support of his refutation, Ashari posed a query to his teacher Jubbai as to what explanation would he offer when members of the same family end up at different destinations? He cited the cases of three brothers of whom the first one lived and died a believer; the second one, though born a believer, renounced the faith and died as a *kafir*, a non-believer; the third brother died in his infancy. In respect of the first brother there could be no argument against the position of the Mutazilites as a person who was born a believer and died a believer was bound to go to paradise. Nonetheless, Ashari asked his teacher what good God did in allowing the second brother to end up an infidel. Likewise, how could the death of the third brother in infancy be called a good action of the Almighty?

Although the examples cited by al-Ashari and the posers derived thereon were sheer polemics, the teacher, Jubbai, replied in accordance with the principles of Mutazilism. About the second brother the teacher said he would certainly go to hell as he chose to be an unbeliever. In the context the issue of God doing good for human beings could not arise as it pertained to human free will. Regarding the third brother, Jubbai reiterated the Mutazilites' belief that children, on account of their innocence, would not be sent to hell. Nevertheless, Ashari was not convinced or preferred to be in disagreement with his teacher to be in tune with the prevailing resentment against Mutazilism. He renounced the rationalist doctrine and later founded a new theological school that came to be designated after his name, Asharism. The new school conformed to certain ideas of Mutazilism such as the atomistic view of cosmology but asserted that reason should be subservient to revelation. This was nothing but neo-orthodoxy that found its finest exponent about a century later in Abu Hamid al-Ghazzali (1058-1111) who firmly established the orthodoxy of Sunni Islam that has survived till the present. For the Sunni Muslims the position of Ghazzali is so exalted that they say "if there could have been a prophet after Muhammad, Ghazzali would have been the man."[30]

It was not just the orthodox majority that pushed Mutazilism to obscurity; it was also the authoritarian manner in which its political patrons, in particular, Mamun promoted it that went heavily against it when the political scenario changed. Being rationalists they should have known better that political patronage for any theology or ideology ultimately leads to its downfall. True, the Mutazilites themselves were not responsible for the hounding, in most cases public flogging, of government officials including judges who refused to assent to the belief that 'the Quran was a creation of Allah'; it was an overenthusiastic Mamun's inquisition (*mihna*). Yet, in popular perception they were blamed for the excesses against their adversaries. Mamun's policy to declare Mutazilism a state religion proved counterproductive. It was ironical that a rationalist movement that was intrinsically supportive of freedom of thought became a tool of oppression in the hands of an overzealous and powerful benefactor. The leading lights of Mutazilism of the time should not only have distanced themselves from Mamun's inquisition policy, they should have publicly opposed it. For short-term gains they remained quiet and consequently a movement that could have changed the course of

Islamic history for the better suffered beyond revamp.

Mutazilism can best be described as a half-hearted attempt to make an established religion compatible with rationalism. The knowledge of Greek philosophy did inspire the Mutazilites to espouse an atomist view of cosmology. However, they could not go whole hog with Democritus to embrace a materialist interpretation of the universe. They preferred to underscore the Divine will that caused spiritual accidents to transform atoms into various bodies rather than accepting the concept of void, the negation of body, that found expression in the original Greek theory of atomism. Though their opinion that the Quran's reading should not be absolutely literal but allegorical was a courageous and proper idea, they failed to offer an allegorical explanation of the Hereafter. Also, their efforts to accentuate the Unity of God devoid of anthropomorphism, a result of certain Quranic verses that speak of the Divine attributes, could not convince the masses who expected to meet Allah face to face in paradise.

Their concept of God who can neither do evil nor cause human beings to carry out evil deeds is laudable that expounds a just and human-friendly conception of the Almighty. Nonetheless, they miserably failed to offer a truly rationalistic explanation concerning poverty. Their position that it is a deliberate strategy of God to make people face poverty or affluence to test them, of course, for diverse reasons is far from convincing. It is no different from the view of orthodox mullahs. As rationalists they failed to distinguish between primordial inequalities related to race, gender, physical prowess, geography, language, etc. and the man-made inequalities such as poverty affluence and so on. Poverty and affluence depend on the lack of money-oriented possessions or the presence of them respectively. It is quite apparent that money or the property rights are the creations of man and since the invention of agriculture the more powerful (mendicants, priests, sorcerers, physically strong) members of society had usurped all indices of power and thus rendered the vast majority powerless and poor. The Mutazilites failed to scrutinize the exploitative structure of society.

Despite the inadequacies, Mutazilism was the first significant rationalist movement that strived to close the gulf between religion and reason. Had it been allowed to prosper, the Muslim East would have reached the level of scientific and intellectual progress, which is the hallmark of the West today, almost a millennium ago. The movement of the Mutazilites, however, was not entirely a fiasco. Dialectically some of its elements got absorbed in Shi'ism of Iran and also gave birth to a few other liberal movements in Islam. For instance, the movement of *Ikhwan us Safa* was a logical offshoot of Mutazilism.[31] In India, Syed Ahmed Khan was greatly influenced by Mutazilism. The rationalist approach is clearly on display in his *Tafsir-ul-Quran,* an incomplete exegesis of the Holy Book, and for that reason it is not much talked about even among the scholars of the Aligarh Muslim University.

The orthodox Sunni ulama accused Mutazilas of promoting the ideas of a section of the Shias and Jahmites.[32] In response to opposition to his stand on the doctrine of the Mutazilites, Mamun decided to make it obligatory for all *qazis,* theologians and scholars to accept the Mutaliza doctrine as an article of faith. Since he was busy in the expedition against the Byzantines, he entrusted the task of seeking adherence to the doctrine to Ishaq bin Ibrahim. Thus began, what is known as the reign of *Mihna* (inquisition) in 833. The *Mihna* was a kind of test in which the *qazis,* theologians, jurists and scholars, in short the elites, were asked to declare their adherence to the doctrine that the Quran was the created word of God. If they refused then they would be imprisoned or even killed. This policy continued even after the reign of Mamun as his successors Mutasim and Wasiq faithfully implemented it. It was withdrawn by Muawakkil.

Mamun died on August 9, 833 near Tarsus, in south-central Turkey. He was succeeded by his brother Mutasim. Among all the Abbasid Caliphs, Mamun was known for forbearance and clemency. He would sometimes forgive even his deadliest enemies. For instance, he had forgiven Fazal bin Rabi who was the main provocateur behind all the battles that Mamun had to fight against Amin. He was exceptionally good in learning and literature and because of this interest would hold scholars and litterateurs in the highest regard. Qazi Yahya bin Aksam, who was a reputed scholar and man of letters of the time would always go together with the Caliph.

The eighth Abbasid Caliph, Abu Ishaq Muhammad bin Harun

Rashid better known by his royal title Mutasim was the half brother of Mamun. He succeeded Mamun because the dying Caliph willed so rather than nominating his son Abbas. Mamun's decision to bequeath the Caliphate to his half brother was the upshot of Mutasim's strong personality and leadership quality.[33] Mamun had appointed him the military commander and in that capacity he had raised a formidable regiment consisting solely of Turkish slave-soldiers known as *mamalik* or *ghilman*. The mamalik were answerable only to the Caliph and the military commander who happened to be Mutasim during Mamun's reign. Mamun came to depend exceedingly on the mamalik because of which they could become very powerful. The residents of Baghdad, mostly Arabs and Iranians were quite dejected because of the arrogance of the Turkish soldiers who would frequently humiliate and even beat anyone with impunity. When the situation turned critical because of repeated occurrences of violence and rioting, Mutasim established a new military encampment-cum-city Samara about 80 miles north of Baghdad and shifted the Turkish soldiers there. In course of time it became the capital of the Caliphate because Mutasim preferred to reside away from the common people surrounded by his trusted troops who were all Turkish and owed allegiance only to him.[34]

The ascension of Mutasim to the position of the Caliph was momentous from the point of view governance. Unlike his predecessors who maintained a manageable balance between people of different ethnicities, Arabs, Iranians and Turks, Mutasim mostly relied exclusively on the mamalik, the Turkish military regiment that he had created. Consequently the Caliphate turned into "a new regime that was militaristic and centred on the Turkish corps."[35] As a result of this development the Caliphate itself turned into an institution dependent on military power and instead of Arab people, other ethnicities, particularly the Turks, became a dominant segment of the Islamic world.

The increasing dominance of the Turks was naturally resented by most Iranians who were solely responsible for making Mamun the Caliph. So, Ujaif bin Anbasa, a Khurasani who had served Mamun faithfully got together with other disgruntled Iranian and Abbasid elites and hatched a conspiracy to kill Mutasim and appoint Mamun's son Abbas as the Caliph. Though Abbas was eager to become the Caliph, he did not favour the idea of killing Mutasim. His reluctance to approve the entire plot exposed the conspiracy. Abbas was arrested and about seventy conspirators were executed. The entire operation of arresting and executing was carried out by the mamalik and that further strengthened their position in the Caliphate.[36] Mutazilism continued to be the doctrine of the Caliphate as Mutasim genuinely respected Mamun's religious views. Mutazilism was, in fact, the first rationalist movement in Islam and Mamun by making it the official doctrine of the Islamic State, had made an attempt to create a progressive, almost secular and integrated Caliphate wherein all the warring sects of Islam could live harmoniously with each other and would also interact amicably with Christian, Jew, Zoroastrian and Chinese people. Nevertheless, the controversy over the created or eternal nature of the Quran, unnecessarily embroiled this progressive movement into a quagmire that could have been tactfully avoided by Mamun and his successors. The policy of mihna, gave a bad name to the official machinery that went overboard in procuring the consent of the ulama, qazis and theologians that gave the traditionalist scholars to harden their stand against the entire doctrine. During Mutasim's time the chief Qazi, Ahmad Bin Zuwad was too harsh in the enforcement of mihna and in the process became a dominant force of the Caliphate.[37] Mutasim died on January 5, 842 and was buried in Samara.

Abu Jafar Harun bin Mutasim popularly known as Wasiq, succeeded his father Mutasim as the Caliph on the day his father died. His mother, Qaratis, was Mutasim's Greek concubine.

His reign was marked by a number of rebellions that broke out in Baghdad, Syria and Palestine. The major reason for these revolts was the dominance of the Turkish regiment that was stationed at Samara and the Caliph could not take any decision that would not be approved by the Turkish commanders. The Arabs, in particular, resented the ever-increasing dominance of the Turks for, in their estimation, the people of Arab origin should have primacy in all the affairs of the Caliphate. In 844-45, Wasiq sent his Turkish general, Bugha Kabir to crush the revolt in Arabia. Bugha Khan quelled the revolt and arrested many people who were behind the unrest. The same Bugha Khan had to deal with a more organized rebellion by Nasr bin Malik. Bugha Khan successfully suppressed the planned revolt and arrested Nasr bin Malik. Wasiq beheaded the insurgent leader himself.

Wasiq had a scholastic bent of mind and besides scholars he also patronised artists. Wasiq himself was an accomplished musician. He had composed more than a hundred songs. He died on August 10, 847 after ruling for five years.

Jafar bin Muhammad, better known as Mutawakkil, was the tenth Abbasid Caliph. He was born in Samarra and succeeded his brother Wasiq and reigned for the next fourteen years. During his reign Muhammad bin Faraj Neshapuri gathered a band of faithful followers by proclaiming himself to be a prophet. Mutawakkil imprisoned Neshapuri and his prominent followers where they ultimately died in 850. Then the Armenians revolted. Mutawakkil sent Bugha Kabir to subdue them and peace returned to Armenia. The people of African origin known as Bujah in Egypt raised the banner of revolt by refusing to pay taxes. Mutawakkil successfully quelled that revolt as well.

The most notable event of Mutawwakil's reign was the end of mihna. He banned the practice of forcing the elites of the Caliphate to believe in the created characteristic of the Quran. However, he did not change the policy of reliance on Turkish soldiers and elites for the governance of the Caliphate. Ironically, on December 11, 861, Mutawakkil was assassinated by his Turkish guards. Some sources indicate that his son Muntasir had hatched the conspiracy to kill his father because he feared that Mutawakkil would not nominate him as heir. All accounts agree that Mutawakkil was the last of the Great Abbasid Caliphs.

The day Mutawakkil was assassinated Muntasir ascended the throne of the Caliphate obviously with the consent of the Turkish soldiers. Muhammad bin Mutasim bin Harun Rashid's mother, Hubshiah, was a Roman concubine. It was under the pressure of the Turkish faction, Muntasir had to remove his brothers from succession. He himself feared that his brothers could hatch a conspiracy against him for settling of scores with him for their father's assassination. Since he owed his Caliphate to the support of the Turks, they started controlling the affairs of governance.

Muntasir could not take any decision without consulting the Turkish commanders.

Muntasir had a few personal qualities. He was compassionate and gallant. Despite the Turkish regiment's control over the Caliphate, he took a bold decision of lifting all oppressive restrictions that were imposed on the Shias by his father Mutawakkil. On his order all the descendants of Ali started getting stipends from the government treasury.[38] He died without nominating a successor on June 7, 862, His reign lasted for only six months.

Since there was no heir the Turkish leaders formed a council that comprised three persons, Bugha Kabir, Bugha Saghir and Atamash, to select a new Caliph. After much deliberations they first considered to nominate Ahmad bin Mutasim. Nevertheless, they were informed by reliable sources that Ahmad was a very ambitious man and he would not be a puppet ruler. Bugha Kabir, in fact, preferred Ahmad bin Mutasim because of his overbearing personality arguing that with such a man at the helms of affairs would force all to remain within limits and this in turn would ensure unity among them. Bugha Saghir and Atamash, however, wanted a weaker person to be the Caliph so that they could rule by proxy. Thus, they ultimately chose Ahmad bin Muhammad who was the grandson of their real benefactor, Mutasim. Ahmad is better known by his regnal name, Mustain which means one who seeks the help of God.

The people of Baghdad and the non-Turkish military personnel were naturally dejected by the choice of the Caliph and the overall dominance of the Turks. Arabs, in particular, were very unhappy. So were the Iranians. Accordingly, all the disgruntled soldiers in collaboration with the people of Baghdad revolted against the newly appointed Caliph. The Turkish regiment ruthlessly crushed the revolt and made the Arabs and others realize that they were no more counted in matters of governance. The Turkish grandees also removed Ahmad bin Khateeb from the premiership and Atamash was appointed the Prime Minister.

Yahya bin Umar Zaidi representing the Alids drew together many of his supporters and took over Kufa. Mustain dispatched an army under the command of Hasan bin Ibrahim. Yahya's inexperienced militia met with a crushing defeat. Hasan decapitated Yahya's head and sent it to Samarra where it was hung up at the main gate. The people violently opposed the action, therefore, the Caliph sent it to Baghdad for its suspension from any of the city gates. The people of Baghdad too resisted the Caliph's evil intention. Finally it was buried.[39]

Bugha Kabir was right in believing that a domineering person as Caliph would ensure unity among the Turkish emirs. Prime Minister Atamash had become too powerful and amassed huge wealth in the process. Out of covetousness a Turkish emir Baaghar plotted to kill Mustain and his Turkish mentors, Bugha Kabir and Waseef. Nonetheless, Mustain got wind of the intrigue and Kabir and Waseef killed the plotter. Baaghar's supporters raised the banner of revolt in Samarra itself. Kabir and Waseef shifted the Caliph to Baghdad for security reasons. The Turkish soldiers brought Muatazz bin Mutawakkil out from the confinement and declared him the Caliph and his brother Moed as the heir apparent.

A bloody battle that followed decided the fate of the Caliphate. The supporters of Muatazz proved more powerful and finally at the beginning of 866, Mustain agreed to abdicate the Caliphate. As per the terms of the truce, Mustain was to live at Medina with a substantial pension. Nevertheless, he never got the opportunity to leave Baghdad. In the end, he was killed on October 17, 866, on the orders of the Caliph.

Mustain's campaigns against the Byzantine ended in disaster. In 863, about 8000 soldiers of the Caliph army were killed at the Battle of Lalakaon. Despite such heavy losses on the fronts of Armenia and Asia Minor, neither the Turkish emirs nor the Caliph did anything to upgrade the armed forces.

Abu Abdullah bin Mutawakkil better known by the regnal name of Muatazz was born in 847. So when the Turks made him the Caliph he was 19 and this made him the youngest man to become an Abbasid Caliph.[40] Muatazz's reign was plagued with factional conspiracies and internal dissension. The Caliph was just a pawn on the political chessboard. The major players were of course the Turks who had their base at Samarra where they resented the presence of the Berbers and Moors whom they would refer to as 'Westerners'. Most Arab and Iranian population was confined to Baghdad and they begrudged the dominance of the Turks over the Caliphate. The Caliph had to carry out whatever the Turkish commanders wanted him to do whether he hated to do it or not. On their instigation he killed the former Caliph and then two of his own brothers.

The financial condition of the Caliphate was also unsteady since a major portion of the revenue was purloined by the high ranking Turkish commanders. As a result, the administration could not even pay the soldiers properly. The fallout of such a state of affairs was obviously revolt. The people in Baghdad demanded that the name of the Caliph should not be referred to in the *khutbas* (sermons from the pulpit). The revolt that was confined to Baghdad was subdued after considerable loss of lives and property. A year later, however, most soldiers, Turkish, Arabs, African and Iranians, besieged the palace demanding immediate payments of their salaries. The Caliph was not in a position to pay because the treasury was empty. When the soldiers got to know about the Caliphate's ruined financial status, a soldier Salih bin Wasif kidnapped the personal secretaries of the Caliph. He begged the rebels for the release of his secretaries but they did not budge. Finally, Salih in alliance with another leader of the rebels, Musa, made the decision to throw out the Caliph. They carried out their plot in a brutal manner. First, Muatazz was mercilessly beaten within the palace, then he was dragged out and forced to sit in the scorching summer heat and finally he was confined to a dingy room without food and water. Three days later he died. The year was 869, which means this ill-fated Caliph was 22 years old at the time of his death.

When the Turkish commanders decided to appoint Muhammad Muhtadi bin Wasiq as the new Caliph, Muatazz was still alive in the dingy cell where he was locked up. When the Turks brought Muhtadi from Baghdad to Samarra and expressed their desire to swear their allegiance to him as the new Caliph, Muhtadi let them know that he would first like to see Muatazz. When the haggard Muatazz was brought before him, Muhtadi felt extremely sorry for him and petitioned for his return as Caliph. Muatuzz told him that the Turks would not accept his request and that was true. Muatazz was sent back to jail to die.

Muhtadi agreed to be Caliph only after Muatazz's death. He

was a pious, judicious and a devoted practising Muslim. For better governance of the Caliphate he chose Umar bin Abdul Aziz as his exemplar and accordingly he expelled the musicians and singing girls from the courts of nobles and banned wine and gambling. He would keep his court open for everyone and would deliver judgments with utmost integrity and sagacity. Following the example of the Caliph, soldiers and common people too turned righteous. Obviously, such policies were not approved by the Turkish commanders who were primarily concerned about their own empowerment. Consequently, they killed the Caliph in June 870, thus ending the reign of this sagacious Caliph within a year.

Ahmad Muatamid Ali was Mutawakkil's eldest surviving son. He was born in 844. The Turkish commanders released him from jail where he was confined during the reign of Muhtadi and appointed him as the 15th Abbasid Caliph on June 19, 870. Muatamid's reign spanned over 23 years but all through he remained a titular head. The Zanj Revolution[41] had become a serious threat for the Abbasid Caliphate. In order to suppress it the Turkish commanders allowed the Caliph to appoint his brother Abu Muhammad Talaha Muwaffaq as the commander of the armed forces. Though the move lessened the dominance of the Turks to some extent, it helped Muwaffaq seize almost all the powers of the Caliph. After a while, Muwaffaq delegated most of his powers to his son Muatazid as he did not have good health. Muatazid was admired by the people of Baghdad. Consequently, Muatamid never had the real authority. After the death of Muwaffaq, the Caliph was forced to remove his son Mufawwad as heir and appoint Muatazid as his successor. Consequently, Muatamid did what any titular head of a huge empire would do—he drank himself to death, He died in October 892.

Abul Abbas Ahmad bin Muwaffaq better known by his regnal name Muatazid was born either in 854 or 861. He got martial training under his father whom he served in many military campaigns including the Zanj Rebellion. Muatazid became the Caliph on the death of Muatamid in 892. According to an Orientalist Karl Vilhelm Zetterstéen, Muatazid "had inherited his father's gifts as a ruler and was distinguished alike for his economy and his military ability", becoming "one of the greatest of the Abbasids in spite of his strictness and cruelty".[42] He moved the capital back from Samarra to Baghdad and built many impressive buildings there. With his dynamism and capability he could restore some of the power that was the hallmark of the Abbasids during the reign of Harun and Mamun. He could also secure a few provinces that had become independent because of the debility of the central authority of the Caliphate. With a series of intensely fought campaigns he recaptured regions such as Jazira (present-day northwestern Iraq), Thughur (frontier zone between the Byzantine Empire and the Caliphate) and Jibal (western Iran), These successes, however, consumed the major portion of the economy and also gave rise to a powerful fiscal bureaucracy, which would devise ways and means to fleece people in the name of various taxes. Muatazid failed to revive the former grandeur of the Caliphate mainly because he ruled for less than a decade. Additionally sectarian conflicts was a major threat to the stability of the Caliphate. He died on April 5, 902 and became the first Abbasid Caliph to be buried within the city of Baghdad.

Abu Ahmad Ali bin Muatazid was born in 877 or 878. His mother was a Turkish slave-girl. He is better known in history by his regnal name Muktafi. He was not in Baghdad when his father died. On receiving the news, he at once rushed back to the Capital from Raqqah where he was commanding the forces. Thus, in 902 he became the Caliph and early enough he won over the hearts of the people by abolishing the secret torture cells. He, nevertheless, had to deal with internal uprisings and external threats.

The most critical uprising was that of the Qarmatians (Carmathians)[43] who were wreaking devastation in Iraq, Syria and Bahrain. First Muktafi dispatched a force of ten thousand troops under the command of his slave Abul Asghar but the rebels could not be subdued. Then, he personally led a huge force and after an exacting battle the Qarmatians could be suppressed. However, they were not completely decimated; they raised the banner of revolt again in later years too. The external threat to the Caliphate existed in the form of raids by the Byzantine Greeks. Muktafi, however succeeded in protecting the interests of the Caliphate and when he died in 908, the frontiers of the Caliphate were reasonably secure.

Muktafi had not nominated anyone as his successor. The vizier,

Abbas bin Hasan, after consultations with the nobles, therefore, made up his mind to appoint Abdullah bin Muatazz as the Caliph, Abdullah was a learned and judicious person. These qualities ultimately proved his undoing. Abul Hasan bin Furat the personal assistant of Abbas, advised him that appointing a sagacious and experienced person such as Abdullah would be disadvantageous to the vizier. An able Caliph would not let him misappropriate the Caliphate's funds. Abbas appreciated the advice and then nominated a 13-year-old Jafar bin Muatazid who later came to be known as Muqtadir. Though many nobles paid their allegiance to the teenager Caliph, some nobles, *qazis* and the commanders of the armed forces expressed their dissent. In view of this, Abbas wrote to Abdullah whether he would agree to be the Caliph. He replied that if the majority of the nobles and the commanders agreed to his name and if this did not lead to any bickering and bad blood, he would agree to the offer. Nonetheless, the vizier's real intention was to let Muqtadir continue as the Caliph and for that reason he did not act upon Abdullah's rejoinder. Consequently, the nobles who were supporters of Abdullah murdered the vizier and paid allegiance to Abdullah. On assuming power, Abdullah ordered Muqtadir to leave the capital within a day. The supporters of Muqtadir led by Abul Hasan bin Furat then broke into the palace at night with the intention of killing Abdullah. The Caliph somehow managed to flee. Next morning, the army slew all those who had paid allegiance to Abdullah. A short while later, Abdullah was also arrested and Muqtadir put him to death.[44]

Muqtadir was chosen to be the Caliph because he was just a boy and, therefore, could be easily controlled by those who wanted to rule by proxy. According to a scholar it was a baleful plan that had succeeded and as a result led to one of the "the most disastrous reigns in the whole of Abbasid history...a quarter of a century in which all of the work of (al-Muqtadir's) predecessors would be undone."[45] Muqtadir's mother, Shuab, emerged as the most powerful person of the Caliphate who did not have the faintest idea about politics or administration. She was only interested in amassing wealth and, therefore, would not allow any administrative order to be issued unless the party concerned paid a bribe to her. As a result, corruption was rampant and all the officials of the Caliphate were dishonest. The important positions in the Caliphate including that of the vizier could be acquired by paying huge bribes to the Caliph and his mother. Muqtadir's reign set in the depravity and dissipation in the Caliphate from which it never recovered. All the magnificence and high standing that were the hallmarks of the Abbasid Caliphate came to an end during the reign of Muqtadir that lasted for quarter of a century.

The corrupt internal administration had its impact on foreign affairs too. There were a series of clashes between the Caliphate forces and the Greeks in Asia Minor. The Greek forces always had an upper hand in these encounters causing heavy losses to the Caliphate. Then, the Muslims got some respite because of the Bulgarian conquest of the Byzantine. The Byzantine empress Zoe Karbonopsina decided to secure the eastern frontiers by making peace with the Caliphate so that she could focus on driving back the Bulgarians. Subsequently, Samal, a valiant slave of the Caliph led a successful onslaught against the Byzantine and pushed back the Roman forces to the interior of the Byzantine territory.

An extraordinary fact of Muqtadir reign was the appearance of a galaxy of exceptionally talented people who became internationally renowned because of their brilliant contributions to their respective areas of interest. Some of the most prominent names are: Ishaq bin Hunayn (d. 911), a physician and translator of Greek philosophical works into Arabic; ibn Fazlan, explorer; al Battani (d. 923), astronomer; Tabari (d. 923), historian and theologian; al-Razi (d. 930), a philosopher who had also exceptionally contributed to the fields of medicine and chemistry; al-Farabi (d. 950), chemist and philosopher; Abu Nasr Mansur (d. 1036), mathematician; Alhazen (d. 1040), mathematician; al-Biruni (d. 1048), mathematician, astronomer, physicist and chronicler; Omar Khayyám (d. 1123), poet, mathematician, and astronomer; and Mansur al-Hallaj, a mystic, poet and teacher of Sufism who was executed by Muqtadir because of his alleged 'sacrilege'.[46] Muqtadir was killed in the hideous struggle for power between Monis Muzaffar and Muhammad bin Yaqut. The former was the commander of the Caliph's army while the latter was a vizier. Since Muqtadir seemed to favour Yaqut, the soldiers under Muzaffar viciously murdered him after undressing him publicly on November 1, 932.

The nineteenth Abbasid Caliph Abu Mansur Muhammad, better known by his regnal name, Qahir-billah was born in 899. His mother was a Berber woman. Since Muqtadir had not nominated anyone as his successor, the nobles initially thought of appointing his son Abu Abbas Ahmad who was quite capable of being a Caliph. There were, nonetheless, two misgivings in the minds of the nobles about Abbas. One, they feared that he might punish those who were responsible for his father's brutal murder and two, Abbas's grandmother who enjoyed tremendous power and influence during Muqtadir's reign would again wield all the power. Accordingly, they concurred on the name of Muqtadir's brother, Abu Mansur Muhammad and granted him the title of Qahir-billah.

Qahir proved a ruthless and voracious ruler. He confiscated all the properties of the close relatives of Muqtadir. Then, he turned his attention to Muqtadir's mother and demanded that she should relinquish all the riches that she had accumulated during her son's reign. She said she had nothing. Qahir got her arrested and cruelly tortured her. When he failed to wheedle out a substantial amount of wealth from her, Qahir, in violation of the shariat confiscated all the endowments that she had bequeathed and sold them.

Qahir's viciousness could be gauged by the fact that he walled up alive his nephew only because he could be a claimant to the Caliphate. The worst part was that Qahir did not pay any attention to the administrative matters. His debauchery and profligacy severely affected the conditions of the Caliphate to such an extent that even his nobles were depressed. This state of affairs encouraged the former vizier Ibn Muqla to plan a coup against the Caliph. One night in 934, the plotters assaulted the palace when Qahir was inebriated. He was caught, blinded and thrown into prison. He was released from prison eleven years later only to die on the streets of Baghdad as a blind beggar.

The day Qahir was thrown into prison, the leading nobles, Ibn Muqla, Muhammad bin Yaqut and his brother, Muzaffar decided to appoint Abu Abbas Muhammad bin Muqtadir, who was in jail, the twentieth Abbasid Caliph. He adopted Raazi-billah as his regnal name and officially took up the charge of the Caliphate on April 23, 934.

Though Raazi reigned for seven years, he did not exert real powers which were seized by the nobles who made him the Caliph. Nevertheless, in a while the nobles developed distrust and suspicion about each other. Ibn Muqla complained against Muhammad bin Yaqut to the Caliph and got him and his brother Muzaffar arrested. Bin Yaqut died in jail, however, Ibn Muqla got Muzaffar released after getting a vow of allegiance from him. Raazi created a special post of *Emir-al-Umara* (Emir of the Emirs) and appointed Ibn Raiq, a competent but equally vicious man to the post. Early enough, Raiq hogged all the powers and became the de facto ruler.

There was no serious external threat to the Caliphate at least from the Byzantine thanks to the military competence of Ali bin Abdullah, a Hamdani prince popularly known as *Saif ud-Dawlah* (the Sword of the Nation) who had founded an almost autonomous emirate in northern Syria. The internal turmoil, however, had greatly damaged the central authority of the Caliphate. Most provinces had become independent and had stopped contributing revenue to the central exchequer. To exacerbate the already anarchic conditions, the followers of Imam Hanbal[47] had become so powerful that they had launched a kind of a Sunni inquisition. They would murder adherents of Shiaism wherever they found them.. They would force their way into the privacy of homes and would damage everything not permitted in their tenets. They, therefore, emptied vessels of wine, smashed musical instruments and severely punished the owners. In the streets of Baghdad their diktat reigned. They would publicly flog singers and adult men without beards. If a man and a woman were found together in the street, they would force both of them to prove that they were *mehram* (relatives among whom marriage is forbidden or spouses of each other). In case they failed, they would face the scourge. They had also prohibited the followers of Imam Shaafai from entering mosques. People appealed to the Caliph to restrain the activities of the Hanbalis. Responding to people's petition, Raazi addressed the following decree to the Hanbalis:

> Your activities in the name of Islam are absolutely disgraceful. How erroneous is your conviction that Allah's countenance is similar to that of your ill-omened and despicable faces! His hands, fingers, legs,

> palms, etc. are also like yours! Moreover, you also believe in His ascent on and descent from the skies. You pass sardonic against the excellent imams. You invite people to espouse your nonsensical ways and heresies which are neither supported by the Quran or ahadis. You decry the practice of visiting graves but yourselves gather at the grave of an ordinary man[48] and attribute to him the kind of miracles and marvels that could only be performed by the prophets and saints although that man neither belonged to the class of nobles nor was he a descendant of the Prophet.
>
> The truth is that Satan has crafted your actions propitious in your eyes. Now, Emir ul-Momineen has sworn that if you do not abstain from your erroneous faith and evil actions, the might of the sword will be against you. You will be killed and scattered and your dwellings will be charred.[49]

Personally Raazi had quite a few qualities. He was well educated and honest by nature. He was comfortable in the company of scholars. He also had a fascination for literature. He was a poet himself. Though the Caliphate had lost much of its grandeur and standing by the time he became the Caliph, he happened to be the last Abbasid Caliph who could have some role to play in administrative matters. After him all kinds of power were seized by *Emir al-Umra*, a post ironically created by Raazi himself. Raazi died on December 18, 940.

How insignificant, the position of the Caliph had become by now could be measured by the apathy shown by Bajkam, Emir al-Umra, on receiving the news of the death of the Caliph, Raazi. Bajkam was away from the capital but did not bother to return to Baghdad. Instead he went out on a hunting expedition. Nevertheless, he sent his secretary Abu Abdullah Kofi to the capital to appoint someone as the Caliph after consulting the nobles. Thus, for more than a week the Abbasid Caliphate was without a Caliph. The nobles ultimately chose Ibrahim bin Muqtadir as the new Caliph who was formally appointed with the regnal name of Muttaqi.

Bajkam was murdered during his hunting expedition by a group of Kurds. Baghdad was in turbulence again as quite a few nobles tried to grab the all-powerful position of Emir al-Umra. Muttaqi appointed Ibn Raiq to the post but the rival claimants could not be pacified. Sensing an imminent threat to their lives, the Caliph and Ibn Raiq took off to Mosul. The Hamdani chiefs of Mosul welcomed the Caliph and Emir al-Umra but shortly afterwards murdered Ibn Raiq. Now Nasir ud-Dawlah, the Hamdani prince got himself appointed to the coveted post of Emir al-Umra. Nonetheless, in time he realized that Baghdad was too dangerous a place to be in. He, therefore, returned to Mosul. Muttaqi then appointed a Turkish military commander, Tuzun as the new Emir al-Umra. Tuzun was an ill-mannered and gluttonous character. He blinded Mutaqqi and removed him from power on October 12, 944.

Tuzun then appointed Abdullah bin Muktafi who adopted Mustakafi Billah as his regnal name. The newly appointed Caliph had to deal with the threat from the Buwayhid dynasty. The dynasty was established by Ali bin Buya, who after conquering parts of Iran in 934 made Shiraz the capital of his domain. Ali's younger brother, Hasan also subjugated parts of Jibal and by 943 conquered Ray. It was the youngest brother, Ahmed who was knocking at the door of Baghdad when Mustakafi became the Caliph. The Mosul governor had also stopped paying tribute. Tuzun led a military expedition against the Hamdani rulers but the issue was ultimately settled peacefully.

Shortly after securing a peaceful settlement with Mosul, Tuzun died and one of his trusted generals, Abu Jafar was appointed Emir al-Umra. The situation in Baghdad, however, turned into anarchy. All kinds of supplies had stopped coming to the capital and people were starving. It has also been reported that after a while the people of Baghdad had no choice but to eat the meat of cats and dogs. Soon enough looting, pillaging and plundering followed and the unrest also spread to other parts of the Caliphate. At this time, Abu Jafar invited Nasir ud-Dawlah, the ruler of Mosul, to Baghdad and even offered to step down from the post of Emir al-Umra in his favour. The Hamdani governor was, however, engaged in repelling the conquest of Russia and for that reason could not pay attention to Jafar's request.

In these chaotic circumstances, Ahmad bin Buya conquered Baghdad that forced the Caliph and Emir al-Umra to flee for their lives. In time, nevertheless, the Caliph made peace with Ahmad by offering him the post of Emir al-Umra and conferring on him the title of Muiz ud-Dawlah. Ahmed, nonetheless, was not satisfied with the honours because in his estimation, the Caliph was a stooge of the Turks. Therefore, forty days after entering Baghdad, Ahmad blinded the Caliph and deposed him in January 946.

Thereafter, Ahmad Muiz ud-Dawlah, appointed Mustakafi's cousin, Fazal bin Muqtadir who was in hiding, the twenty-third Caliph of the Abbasid with the regnal name of Muti. All the powers remained in the hands of the Buwayhids and the Caliph was deprived of authority. Since the Buwayhids were Shias, Muiz ud-Dawlah commanded that all the shops and offices should remain closed on the 10th of Muharram, the day of the martyrdom of Husain. All the women should publicly mourn with untied hair. *Eid-e-Ghadir* (the day the Prophet had hinted Ali to be the *Mawla*— lord— of the Muslims after him) was enthusiastically celebrated. Since most people of the Caliphate were Sunnis, sectarian riots would break out frequently.

The residents of Baghdad continued to suffer because of the food shortage. The governors of various provinces were up in arms against Muiz ud-Dawlah. The Emir of Mosul, Nasir ud-Dawlah had been planning to take over affairs of the Caliphate in his hands but the frequent skirmishes with the Byzantine kept him stuck in the north. After Muiz ud-Dawlah's death his son Bakhtiyar succeeded him. The conditions during his reign deteriorated even further because he was a decadent and absolutely corrupt man. During his reign the Fatimids who had their sway in the Tunisian city of Mahadia since 921 captured Egypt and in 969 for the first time in the history of Islam declared a Shia Caliphate. Buwayhids themselves were Shias and ruled Baghdad for over a century but refrained from appointing a Shia as the Caliph as they feared a severe Sunni backlash across the Caliphate.

During Muti's reign, the Byzantine forces captured many border cities of the Caliphate and devastated them completely. Yet, the nobles and central military commanders did nothing to secure the north-western boundaries of the Caliphate. The Caliph was only a titular head and many of his nobles were thoroughly corrupt. Muti led the life of almost a recluse. He had to suffer a paralytic attack in 974 and consequently he was deposed by the Buwayhids on August 17.

The day Muti was deposed, Abul Fazal Abdul Karim bin Muqtadir was appointed Caliph with the approval of the Buwayhids with the regnal title of Taae. Though the twenty-fourth Abbasid Caliph's reign extended over more than 17 years, he hardly ruled for a day. He was completely under the command of the Buwayhids. During those 17 years five Buwayhids Emirs, viz. Bakhtiyar, Rukn ud-Dawlah, Samsaam ud-Dawlah, Sharf ud-Dawlah and Baha ud-Dawlah, controlled the affairs of the Caliphate.

The Fatimidds captured a few more regions as a result of which in addition to Egypt, Syria and Hejaz also came under their Caliphate and the name of the Abbasid Caliph was stopped from being recited in the *Khutba* (sermon delivered in congregational Friday and Eid prayers) in those provinces. The area of the Caliphate substantially shrunk as many Emirs ruling in far away provinces had become almost independent. The Buwayhids were interested only in amassing wealth thus, leaving the security of the frontiers to the petty chieftains who had become autonomous. Taae was deposed by Baha ud-Dawlah in 991.[50]

Abul Abbas Ahmad was the grandson of Muqtadir who was exiled from Baghdad during the reign of Taae. He was recalled by the Emirs of Baghdad after the deposition of Taae and appointed the Caliph on October 3, 991, with the regnal name of Qadir Billah. He remained the Caliph for more than forty years. Qadir's reign was characterized by huge political upheavals in the world of Islam. Quite a few new dynasties emerged on the ruins of the old ones and the area under the sway of Muslim rulers expanded. In the East, a new power, that of Mahmud of Ghazni appeared. Mahmud raided India as many as 17 times and accumulated immense wealth. He had become a serious threat to the Caliphate itself but his death caused conflicts within the Ghazni dynasty, which weakened it greatly.

Though Qadir did not have much say in the affairs of the Caliphate, the dominance of the Buwayhids by his time was considerably undermined. Qadir was also popular among the emirs because of his agreeable character. He was a scholar himself and preferred the companionship of learned people. He tried to diminish the Shia influence as much as he could and favoured the

Hanbali school in matters of jurisprudence. Qadir died at the age of 87 in 1031 and was succeeded by his son, Qaaim.

Abu Jafar bin Qadir was appointed the twenty-sixth Caliph of the Abbasids as per the will of his father. He adopted for himself the regnal name of Qaaim. He reigned for almost 45 years which were afflicted by violent conflicts, riots and rebellions. The Buwayhids had become powerless because of their internal conflicts and also because of the rise of the Seljuq (who were Turkish by origin) dynasty in Iran. The provinces of Syria and Armenia were annexed by the Seljuqs and thereafter they were planning to take Baghdad under their sway. Ultimately, the Seljuq ruler Tughrul Beg conquered Baghdad in 1055 and ended the rule of the Buwayhids. The Caliph acknowledged Tughrul as Sultan that heralded the dominance of the Seljuqis over the Caliphate. Qaaim died on April 2, 1075.

Abu Qasim Abdullah bin Muhammad, the grandson of Qaaim was appointed the twenty-seventh Caliph on the death of Qaaim by Seljuq Sultan Malik Shah. His regnal name was Muqtadi. His mother was an Armenian slave girl.[51] Muqtadi was a gallant man and was also interested in retrieving the lost glory of the Abbasids. He took some bold decisions such as closure of pleasure-houses, pigeon rearing and flying, gambling, etc. He also improved the water-supply system. His reign was marked by overall prosperity and abundance of food. Sultan Malik Shah was also a great warrior. He pushed back the Byzantine forces from the regions of the Caliphate that they had earlier annexed. He conquered Samarqand and punished other emirs of Iran who had stopped paying tribute to the Caliph.

The Seljuqs were fortunate to have a person like Abu Hasan Qawamuddin popularly known by his title Nizam ul-Mulk Tusi as their vizier. Since Nizam al-Mulk's contribution to the Seljuq empire and through it to the Caliphate was mammoth it is appropriate to have a look at his life and works. Abu Hasan bin Ali of Tus (April 10, 1018-October 14, 1092) was popularly known by his honorific title Nizamul al-Mulk. He was an acclaimed Iranian scholar who served as vizier in the court of the Seljuq Empire for twenty years. His father was a financial officer in the service of the Ghaznavids. Initially Ali Hasan served the Ghaznavids for a few years. He joined the service of the Seljuqs in 1043 and by 1059 was appointed as administrator of the province of Khorasan. In the power struggle that ensued among the Turkish princes after the death of Tughral Beg, Abu Ali Hasan sided with Alp Arsalan who ultimately became the Seljuq Sultan on April 27, 1064. Thus, Abu Ali Hasan was appointed as the vizier, a position he held during the reigns of Alp Arsalan and his successor Malik Shah I. Alp Arsalan conferred the honorific title of Nizam al-Mulk on Abu Ali Hasan. It was because of the effective administrative handling of Nizam al-Mulk that the Seljuq Sultans could completely concentrate on military expeditions. Nizam al-Mulk accompanied Alp Arsalan on quite a few military conquests such as campaigns of Byzantine Armenia, Caucasus and Georgia. Nizam al-Mulk successfully led a few military campaigns himself.

Alp Arsalan was assassinated in 1072 and was succeeded by his son Malik Shah I. It was the excellent military guidance of Nizam al-Mulk that helped Malik Shah to contain the Ghaznavids in Khorasan, defeat the Fatimids in Syria, conquer Georgia and enhance the reputation and prestige of the Abbasid Caliphs. Nizam al-Mulk's political aims included: a) creation of employment opportunities for the people in general and for the Turkish immigrants to Iran in particular; b) the enrichment of the power and grandeur of the Sultans; c) maintaining cordial relations between the Shias and the Sunnis and also among the members of the royal family; d) peaceful transformation of power from one Sultan to the other; and e) maintaining peaceful relations with the Abbasid Caliphs.

Nizam al-Mulk's reputation as a scholar, however, is far superior than his standing as an able administrator and valiant warrior. He established excellent educational institutions in many cities of the Islamic world including Baghdad, Isfahan, Nishapur, Basra, Mosul and Herat. These institutions came to be known as Nizamiyah schools after his name. These schools later served the models for the colleges and universities of Europe.

His magnum opus was a voluminous treatise on governance, *Siyasatnama* (The Book of Politics), which he wrote on the request of Malik Shah. It is considered to be an important source of understanding the politics, constitutions and governance of the nations ruled by monarchs. He also wrote another book *Dastur al-Wazarat* for the education and training of his son, Abul Fathe Fakhr al-Mulk. Shortly before his death when his rival courtiers were plotting against him he made a memorable speech in the court. An excerpt:

> Tell the Sultan, if you have not already realized that I am your co-equal in the work of ruling, then know that you have only attained to this power through my statesmanship and judgment. Does he not remember when his father was killed, and I assumed responsibility for the conduct of affairs and crushed the rebels who reared their heads, from his own family and from elsewhere? Tell him that the stability of that regal cap is bound up with this vizierial inkstand, and that the harmony of these two interests is the means of securing all objects sought after and the ultimate cause of all objects gained. If ever I close this inkstand, that royal power will topple.

Nizam al-Mulk was murdered while he was travelling from Isfahan to Baghdad on October 14, 1092. Most sources point out that he was killed by a *Hashshashin* on the order of Hassan-i-Sabbah near Nahavand.

Many historical records reveal that Nizam al-Mulk, Omar Khayyam and Hassan-i-Sabbah were childhood friends. In their youth, the three friends entered into a pact that if any one of them rose to a position of importance, he would help the other two friends to achieve some prominence. It was Nizam al-Mulk who was first appointed the vizier in the Seljuq court and as per the pact he offered his two friends significant positions in the royal court. Omar Khayyam whose reputation today is because of his poetry was, in fact, a great mathematician and therefore he declined the offer. Instead he asked for support in the pursuit of his scholastic activities. Nizam al-Mulk provided the necessary means and also constructed an observatory for Omar Khayyam. Hassan-i-Sabbah though he accepted the offer but was secretly hostile to Nizam al-Mulk out of jealousy. Later, Hassan captured the fortress of Alamut and established his band of Hashshashin (assassins).[52]

Sultan Malik Shah married one of his daughters to Muqtadi probably with the intention that the Seljuqs could appoint as Caliph if a son was born to his daughter. Though a son was indeed born but the mother left Baghdad with the new born and settled in

Isfahan. Thereafter, the relations of Malik Shah and the Caliph soured and the Sultan asked Muqtadi to step down and retire to Basra. Shortly afterwards, Sultan died and the retirement order of the Caliph could not be carried out. Somewhat later, Muqtadi also died in 1094.

Abul Abbas Ahmad, the son of Muqtadi succeeded as the Caliph with the regnal title of Mustazhir, He was born in 1078 and became the Caliph at the age of 16. Though he was a quite religious, generous and resolute character, he was powerless politically and did not have any role to play in the civil turmoil and external threats. The First Crusade in Syria came about in his reign. Another threat during his reign was the conquest of Baghdad by crusader Raymond IV of Toulouse who was defeated by the Caliphate forces near Tokat. Mustazhir, nonetheless did not play any role in these momentous issues. A significant rise in the population of Muslims across the globe was recorded during these times, which increased from 5 per cent at the beginning of the last decade of the eleventh century to 10 per cent by 1100.

The crusaders conquered Jerusalem in 1099 and massacred almost the entire population of the region. Though Jerusalem was part of the Seljuq Empire and thus was a part of the Caliphate, the Fatimid commander Emir Afzal bin Badr Jamali had captured it and when the crusader laid the siege of the city technically it was part of the Fatimid Caliphate. The crusaders declared Godfrey of Bouillon, the duke of Lower Lorraine (France) and the leader of the First Crusade, the king of Palestine. Godfrey, however, died a few months after his accession to the throne of Jerusalem. His brother Baldwin succeeded him.

The Muslims of the Caliphate were obviously in a state of shock. When they recovered from the initial jolt, they cried out for the blood of the Franks (The name with which Muslims in those days would refer to the crusaders). Surprisingly neither the Seljuq Sultan nor the Caliph showed any interest in challenging the Europeans. Therefore, in time the Europeans established their kingdoms in Antakya and Edessa as well. Thus, the followers of the two Semitic faiths were destined to fight bloody battles for the next two hundred years.

Mustazhir had named his son Abu Mansur Fazal to succeed him as Caliph. Therefore, Abu Mansur became the twenty-ninth

Abbasid Caliph on August 7, 1100 with the regnal title of Mustarshid. He made attempts to get independent of the control of the Seljuq Sultan, Mahmud II as he was involved in wars first with his uncle and then his brother in the East. He also ousted and imprisoned the Sultan-appointed vizier Ḥasan bin Ali. However, the Sultan appointed the son of Nizam al-Mulk Ahmad, the new vizier. In 1125, Mustarshid took the extreme decision of revolting against the Seljuq Sultan. Prior to it, he had removed Ahmad bin Nizam al-Mulk from the post of vizier and then sent an army to capture Wasit. The forces of the Caliph were defeated and Mustarshid was incarcerated within the palace.

The death of Sultan Mahmud led to the civil war because of warring claimants to the throne. Initially the name of Mahmud's son Dawood was recited in the *khutba* but the brother of the deceased Sultan Masud who was the Emir of Mosul and Azerbaijan staked his claim. In the consequent war, Dawood was defeated. This infuriated the patron of the Seljuq dynasty Sultan Sanjar who was the Emir of Rey. He defeated Masud and banished him to Ganja. Then he appointed Tughrul II, the Sultan who was another brother of the former Sultan. Nonetheless, Masud raised an army and with the support of Mustarshid overpowered Tughrul and regained the position of Sultan. By now, the Caliph had started taking independent decisions. Sultan Masud opposed it. Mustarshid deleted his name from the khutba and declared war against him. Masud defeated the army of the Caliph. Mustarshid was arrested within the four walls of the palace. He was killed by a *hasheeshin* on August 29, 1135.

On August 30, 1135, the son of Mustarshid, Abu Jafar Mansur was appointed the Caliph with the approval of the Sultan. His regnal name was Raashid. He had planned to avenge the humiliation of his father and for that reason he began plotting against Sultan Masud in collaboration with the nobles. He instigated Dawood, the son of Sultan Mahmud, against Masud. In response Masud started with his forces towards Baghdad. Consequently, the backers of the Caliph including Amad-ud-Din Zengi, the Emir of Mosul and the strongest supporter of the Caliph decided to leave Baghdad. In view of this Raashid too fled along with Zengi. On reaching Baghdad, Masud issued a fatwa from the jurists disqualifying Raashid from the Caliphate.

Abu Abdullah Husain bin Mustazhir was nominated the Caliph. Sultan Masud established a matrimonial alliance with him by marrying his sister Fatima to him. The disqualified Caliph Raashid made a desperate attempt to regain the Caliphate but failed. He was ultimately murdered in the region of Isfahan by the Hasheeshins. Muqtafi repelled quite a few onslaughts on Baghdad by different forces. On the death of Sultan Masud, however, his brother, Muhammad bin Mahmood who succeeded Masud, laid a siege of Baghdad. Nevertheless, he had to abandon the conquest of Baghdad because many nobles refused to join in a campaign against the Caliph. Moreover, Hamdan was under attack by Malik Shah. So, Muhammad proceeded towards Hamdan to quell the uprising. After dealing with Malik Shah, Sultan Muhammad returned to his seat of governance, Isfahan and subsequently died.

During Muqtafi's reign the second crusade got underway from Europe in 1145 that continued for the next four years. The primary reason for the commencement of the second crusade was the annexation of Edessa by the Zengi forces. Edessa was created as a country by Baldwin of Boulogne in 1098 after the first crusade. It was the Pope Eugene III who announced the second crusade. The main leaders were Louis VII of France and Conrad III of Germany. Many other European nobles too joined the huge army of the crusaders. Despite great preparedness and religious zeal the two armies of European monarchs were separately defeated by the forces of Seljuq Sultan in Anatolia. With great hardship the two monarchs Louis and Conrad with the remaining forces could reach Jerusalem and then joined in the conquest of Damascus. They were squarely defeated by the Muslim forces. Nonetheless, the Caliph and the Seljuq Sultan did not play any significant role in the victory against the crusaders. Muqtafi died on March 12, 1160 after being the Caliph for more than 24 years.

The thirty-second Caliph of the Abbasid was Abul Muzaffar Yusuf, the son of Muqtafii and his Roman wife Umme bin Taus. He adopted the name of Mustanjid as his regnal name. Arsalan Shah was the Seljuq Sultan during his reign though the grandeur and power of the Seljuq dynasty had deteriorated by the time. Another noteworthy highlight of Mustanjid's reign was that the

Fatimid Caliphate was finally put to an end after ruling independently from the Abbasid Caliphate for 260 years. It was Salahuddin Yusuf bin Ayyub, better known in the West as Saladin who decimated the Fatimids from Egypt. With this, the only Shia Caliphate came to an end. Though Salahuddin established the Ayyubi dynasty in Egypt, he accepted the spiritual superiority of the Abbasid Caliph. As a result, the Abbasid's Caliph's name was once again recited in the *khutba* in Syria as well as Egypt. Mustanjid did not rule very long as his death in 1170 ended his reign of a year and a month.

Abu Muhammad Hasan was the son of Mustanjid born to his Armenian slave woman Ghuzza. He was nominated the Caliph with the regnal title of Mustazi. His reign lasted for less than ten years between 1170 and 1180. Mustazi like his father could exercise his authority with a reasonable degree of independence in collaboration with his vizier. The renowned historian Abul Faraj bin Jawazi reported that Mustazi was a judicious and God-fearing Caliph. In order to give respite to people he reduced rates of taxation, built many schools and mosques. The most significant development of his reign was the complete decimation of the Fatimidd Caliphate from Egypt at the hands of Salahuddin who established the Ayyubi dynasty in the province and declared allegiance to the Abbasid Caliphate. Another notable incidence of Mustazi's times was the death of Nooruddin Mahmood bin Zengi, who was the master of Sultan Salahuddin and had shown exceptional courage and military dexterity during the crusade that had earned for him the title of *Mujahid-e-Azam* (the Great Warrior). Muslim chronicles mostly concur that after the Rightly Guided Caliphs and Umar bin Abdul Aziz, Mustazi was the best Caliph.

In order to gauge the grandeur and magnificence of the Caliphate at the time of Mustazi, an account of the traveller, Benjamin of Tudela who had visited the area at that time gives a glimpse. He wrote: "Two days from Akbara stands Bagdhad. The large metropolis of Calif Emir-al-Mumenin al Abassi Emir al-Mu'minin, of the family of their prophet, who is chief of the Mahomatan religion. All Mahomatan kings acknowledge him, and he holds the same dignity over them which the Pope enjoys over the Christians. The palace of the Calif at Baghdad is three miles in extent. It contains a large park filled with all sorts of trees, both useful and ornamental, and all kinds of beasts, as well as a pond of water carried thither from the river Tigris; and whenever the Calif desires to enjoy himself and to sport and carouse, birds, beasts and fishes are prepared for him and for his courtiers, whom he invites to his palace. This great Abasside is extremely friendly towards the Jews, many of his officers being of that nation; he understands all languages, is well versed in Mosaic law, and reads and writes the Hebrew tongue. He enjoys nothing but what he earns by the labour of his own hands, and therefore manufactures coverlets, which he stamps with his seal, and which his officers sell in the public market..."[53]

Abu Abbas Ahmad Nasiruddin bin Mustazi's mother, Zumurrud, was a Turkish concubine of Mustazi. He became the 34th Abbasid Caliph on March 30, 1180. By this time, the control of the Caliph over most provinces had not remained as secure as it was during the early Abassid Caliphs, though many independent rulers of these provinces would formally declare allegiance to the Caliph. It must, however, be mentioned that the ruler of Afghanistan, Gauri, was the contemporary of Nasir while the Slave dynasty existed in India.

Nasir made an earnest attempt to revive the past glory of the Caliphate and achieved moderate success. The military power, however, could not reach the earlier level. His most significant achievement was that he brought the entire Iraq and Iran under his control. By and large peace prevailed during his long reign of about 47 years but the Tartar menace was looming in the East. Quite a few historians hold Nasir accountable for entering into questionable and perilous secret dealings with the Tartar warrior Genghis Khan.

His reign also witnessed the rise of a youth organization, *Futuwwa,* whose members claimed to be virtuous, honest, peace-loving, generous and gentle. Nasir not only approved of the group but supported it in many ways. He himself established a Futuwwa in 1182, comprising militant youths who, for all practical purposes, acted like cavalries. This militant Futuwwa was involved in many sectarian conflicts. Nasir had turned the group into a part of his government by heading it himself.

At the beginning of his reign, Nasir made attempts to bring to an end the rule of the Seljuq in Iran. As a part of the strategy he instigated Alauddin Tekish who was the ruler of Khwarzim, to revolt against the Seljuq Sultan, Tughral III. Consequently, Tekish attacked the Seljuq forces and in the resultant battle Toghrul was killed. Nonetheless, the relations between the Caliph and Tekish soured because the Khwarzim ruler, enraged because of the insolence shown to him by Nasir's vizier, routed the Caliph's troops. In retaliation, the Caliph got a governor of Tekish killed by a member of the Hasheeshin. Later, the son of Tekish, Muhammad II, introduced a Shia Caliphate as a challenge to Nasir's spiritual position and had also planned to attack Baghdad. It was at this point of time, according to the accounts of quite a few historians that Nasir made a covert deal with Genghis Khan to pin down Muhammad II. Genghis Khan decimated not only the territories under the Khwarzim rule but many provinces of Central Asia. It was Genghis Khan's grandson, Halaku, who would ultimately put an end to the Abbasid Caliphate. Nasir suffered from paralysis and partial blindness and spent the last three years of his life afflicted with these disorders. His reign proved to be the longest among the Abbasid Caliphs.

Nasir nominated his son Abu Nasr Muhammad who became the Caliph with the regnal title of Zaahir on October 6, 1225. Though his reign lasted for barely nine months, he made attempts to root out corruption from the governance. He reduced the rate of taxation, restored the unjustly confiscated properties to the rightful owners and revitalized the army into a formidable fighting force. His death on July 10, 1226, ended the series of reforms that he intended to introduce in the Caliphate. Before his death, however, he had published a Code of Conduct for the ministers and officers of the Caliphate instructing them to be honest, judicious and non-corrupt in the performance of their duties.

Zaahir's son Abu Jafar Mansur acceded the Caliphate on July 11, 1226, with the regnal title of Mustansir. He continued the series of administrative reforms that were started by his father. He paid attention to improve the educational infrastructure and therefore, established a high-quality educational institution, *Madarsa-e-Mustansirya*. He improved transportation facilities by building a number of bridges and inns for travellers. His reign lasted for more than 16 years. He died on December 2, 1242.

Abu Ahmad Abdullah, the son of Mustansir succeeded as the thirty-seventh Caliph on December 6, 1242, with the regnal title of Mustasim and with his brutal murder (on orders of the Mongols, he was wrapped in a carpet and pounded to death), the Abbasid Caliphate came to an end. During his reign the threat of the Tartars to the Caliphate assumed menacing proportions as Tawali (Tolui) Khan, the son of Genghis got busy in his expansionist project. He had annexed the entire Iran but held back to attack Baghdad assuming that such an action would provoke the entire Islamic world against him.

A noteworthy action that Mustasim took during his reign was resisting the ascendancy of Shajar-e-Dur in Egypt during the Seventh Crusade. The chroniclers inform us that the Caliph conveyed to the noblemen in Egypt: "If you do not have men there tell us so we can send you men."[54] Nevertheless, Mustasim, rather the Abbasid Caliphate, had to face the worst challenge in the form of the dreadful forces of the Mongols that were about to attack Baghdad. Halaku (Hulagu) Khan, the son of Tawali Khan had already annexed the entire Transoxiana and Khorasan and had also sought the assistance of the Abbasid armed forces in 1256 to annihilate the Nizari Ismaili state of Alamut in Iran that was founded more than two centuries ago by Hasan bin Sabbah. Ironically, two years after seeking the assistance from the Caliphate army, Halaku invaded Baghdad.

The Muslim historians are divided on sectarian lines while probing the reasons for the Mongol invasion on the seat of Khilafat. Most Sunni sources point out that though the majority of Baghdad's residents were Sunni, the Shia population in the city at the time was considerable. It is argued that Shias had always been opposed to the Abbasid Caliphate. During Mustasim's reign, Sunni-Shia riots would frequently break out. Once, the Sunnis, with the tacit support of the son of the Caliph, Abu Bakar, attacked a Shia locality of Baghdad and killed many of its residents as well as plundered its properties. This incensed the Shia vizier of the Caliph, Ibn Alqami so much that he invited Halaku to invade Baghdad.[55] A Shia historian, Ibn Tabatabai Alvi, however, refutes this line of inquiry of the Sunni chroniclers by dubbing it as the invention of the anti-Shia historians.

In any case, Halaku invaded the Abbasid realm in 1258, that, by the time, had shrunk only to the provinces of Iraq and Syria. The forces of the Caliph were no match for the mammoth and terrifying army that was at the disposal of Halaku. Within ten days of laying the siege of Baghdad, the Mongols entered the city, killed almost all its residents and completely ransacked the city that was known as the most beautiful and advanced metropolis of the time. Mustasim appeared before Halaku and to pay homage, he presented a huge platter of the choicest precious stones. Halaku distributed them among his commanders. According to the account of *The Travels of Marco Polo,* when Halaku saw the huge treasury of the Caliphate he locked Mustasim within it without food and water and told him, "eat of thy treasure as much as thou wilt, since thou art so fond of it."[56] Abu Bakar bin Mustasim, the heir apparent, was hanged immediately in Baghdad itself. The Caliph, his other sons and eunuchs were chained and forced to march a few miles outside Baghdad. The accounts suggest that Halaku did not want to shed royal blood and for that reason Mustasim was wrapped in a carpet and crushed to death by horses. With the dreadful execution of Mustasim, the Abbasid Caliphate that existed for 524 years, was terminated.

If we make a brief assessment of the Abbasid Caliphate then the first point that comes to mind is that like its predecessor, the Umayyad Caliphate, was also established purely as a monarchical order. The title of the 'Caliph' used by the 37 Abbasid rulers and the assertion that all of them were in direct lineage of Prophet Muhammad's uncle was merely an attempt to camouflage their acquisitive streak and materialistic avarice. They adopted this stratagem right from the beginning because when the people swore allegiance to the first Abbasid Caliph, Safah then his spokesman declared from the pulpit that the Abbasid did not get hold of the Caliphate for hoarding of gold, silver and precious stones in magnificent palaces. The House of Abbas got the Caliphate when they witnessed that their rights were violated and the common Muslims were oppressed. The members of the House of Abbas now would govern the Islamic realm according to the guidance of the Quran and the course favoured by the Prophet.[57]

Most Muslim chroniclers find fault with the Abbasids because according to them many Caliphs could not contain the *outside* influence first of the Turkish military commanders and later of the Iranian military generals and administrative officials. This seems to be a strange logic for the promoters of a religion that was by all accounts meant to be the true faith for the entire mankind. It is also a distorted line of argument considering the fact that Islam highly recommends proselytization and once a person embraces Islam then he joins the *ummah* as an honourable and equal member of the brotherhood. By arguing that the power in the Abbasid Caliphate should have been restricted to the people of Arab descent alone, this school of Muslim historians fail to realize that they are arguing against the very spirit of Islam. Secondly, what harm was brought about by these ostensible *outsiders*? The well-known advances in the fields of art, architecture, philosophy, sciences, social sciences and even in Islamic history and theology were made mostly by the Iranians and those of non-Arab origin. Some staunch Sunni scholars such as Aslam Jairajpuri also blame the Shias for the downfall of the Abbasids. They question the very claim of the Alvids, the House of the Prophet, to the Caliphate and expediently suppress the fact that the Abbasids themselves justified their right to rule the *ummah* mainly on the ground of affiliation to the Prophet's uncle!

The reality is that the members of the House of Prophet or those who traced their lineage from Ali through his first wife Fatima, the daughter of the Prophet had always been imprisoned, persecuted and killed throughout the Abbasid Caliphate. First it was Muhammad bin Abdullah, known popularly by his title Nafs Zakiyah in Medina and his brother Ibrahim in Basra were suppressed by the second Abbasid Caliph Mansur. Then the successive Caliphs placed many discriminatory restrictions on the Shia Imams and their followers. For instance, when Husain bin Ali bin Hasan led a group of his supporters against the anti-Shia policies of the Caliphate, he was encircled and ultimately killed by the armed forces of the Caliph near Mecca. The two brothers of Nafs Zakiyah, Idris and Yahya succeeded in escaping from the horrifying carnage. Later Idrees founded the Idreesi rule in north Africa.

Yahya, however, was caught and imprisoned in Baghdad. Mamun, the most intelligent and enlightened Caliph of the Abbasids tried to placate the Shias by declaring the eighth Imam, Ali Raza, as his heir apparent though the Imam was older than the Caliph. On this count, the reaction of the Sunni populace was intensely hostile and the Sunni noblemen had even announced the dethronement of Mamun and appointment of his uncle Ibrahim as the Caliph. Mamun could manage with great difficulty to remain in power. The point to be noted is that the Shia-Sunni divide had always been a political schism and the pretention of most Muslim scholars about the monolithic structure of the *ummah* was a historical fallacy.

The Abbasid Caliphate perished for it had outlived its historicity and the justification for survival. The Mongol invasion was just an external factor to expose the internal fault lines of the Caliphate that obviously existed in a more than five-hundred-year old dynastic rule. The Mongol invasion of Baghdad was not an anti-Islamic mission as quite a few Muslim historians tend to argue. The subsequent developments proved that the Tartars contributed significantly to the glory of Islam after embracing the faith. The end of the Abbasids did not herald the end of the Islamic reign at that time. Andulus was under Islamic control, so were areas such as north Africa, Algiers, Tunis, Morocco, Egypt, Yemen, Faras and Nasiruddin Mahmud I was the Sultan of Delhi. Thus, we have to see the decline and fall of the Abbasid as an innate trait of the historical process. The Abbasid Caliphate was followed by the Ottoman Caliphate that survived for more than six centuries and during this long reign enriched the legacy of Islam in myriad ways.

III

In this brief historical survey of the Caliphate a mention must also be made of a Shia Ismaili Caliphate, known popularly as the Fatimid (Fatimidd) Khilafat that originated in north-west Africa and subsequently had its sway from the Red Sea in the east to the Atlantic Ocean in the west. At the peak of its power, the Fatimid Caliphate had under its control Egypt, Maghreb in north Africa, Sudan, Sicily, Hejaz and Levant (a geographical term that refers to the present-day countries of Syria, Lebanon, Jordan, Palestine and Israel). The Fatimid Caliphs claimed descent from the daughter of the Prophet, Fatima, the wife of the fourth Caliph, Ali. It was the eighth Shia Imam Abdullah Akbar who launched the Ismaili faction of Shiaism as he claimed his descent through his father, Imam Ismail from Fatima and Ali. Then he and the next two Imams, Ahmed and Husain, went underground to escape persecution but continued to guide their followers covertly. Abu Ahmed Ubaidullah was the eleventh Ismaili Caliph who started preaching the Ismaili theology openly as he got a firm base in north-west Africa.

Abu Muhammad Ubaidullah, claiming direct descent from the son of Imam Jafar Sadiq announced about 909 that he was the anticipated Imam Mehdi in Kutama, north-west Africa. Shortly afterwards his forces conquered Raqqada, the capital of Aghlabid. A decade later, Abu Muhammad made the Tunisian city Mahdia his capital. A few years afterwards when he annexed central Africa, the capital was shifted to Mansuriya near Kairouan in Tunisia. By this time he was strong enough to withstand the onslaught of the Abbasids and therefore, declared himself the Caliph with the title of Mehdi Billah. The emergence of another centre of the Caliphate gave confidence to the Emir of Andulus, Abdur Rehman Nasir, and five years later he too declared himself the Caliph. Thus, by 925, there came into existence three Caliphates that were sworn enemies of each other. This should be an eye-opener for those who still maintain that the abolition of the Ottoman Caliphate by Mustafa Kemal in 1924, was an un-Islamic act that destroyed the unanimity of the *ummah*! The fact remains that there was barely any unanimity or solidarity among Muslims after the demise of the Prophet.

After Mehdi's death his son Muhammad, the twelfth Imam succeeded his father as the second Fatimid Caliph with the title of Qaim Amar-allah. After becoming the Caliph, though Qaim never led any military expedition personally, his armed forces achieved notable victories in the Mediterranean and added Sicily and the Byzantine province of Calabria to the Caliphate. The third Fatimid Caliph, Abu Tahir Ismail succeeded his father, Qaim, in 946. During his reign he had to face a serious challenge to the Fatimid Caliphate in the form of Abu Yazid's revolt. He however valiantly suppressed it with the help of Berber Zirid. This victory encouraged him to take on the title of Mansur (triumphant). He also improved the administration and security of Sicily from where he had plans to invade Italy. He died in 953 by naming his son Abu Tamim Maad Muizzuddin as the Caliph.

In 969, during the reign of Muizzudin-illah (953–975), the fourth Fatimidd Caliph, Egypt was conquered and a few years later, Syria was added to the expanding territory of the Shia Caliphate. Muizuddin founded the city of *Qahira* (Cairo) that became not only the capital of the Fatimids but also a great centre of scholarship, research, art and culture in the Islamic world. The name of the city, Qahira signified planet Mars. The story goes like this: When Muizuddin planned to build a new capital city, he consulted an astrologer who suggested a particular time as the most auspicious for laying the foundation of the proposed city. As per the astrologer's instructions the foundation site was enclosed by fastening ropes with bells tied to them. The astrologer was supposed to jiggle the rope to cause the bells peal signifying the arrival of the auspicious moment and laying of the foundation. It so happened that a crow got entangled in the ropes and the bells started tolling. The engineers immediately laid the foundation. A short while later the astrologer came running to say that it was not the auspicious moment as planet Mars was just facing the site. Nothing, however, could be done as the foundation stone was already fixed. It was, therefore, decided to name the upcoming city after Mars as *Qahira*.[58] Muiziddin's greatest feat was the establishment of Jamia Azhar (University), named after Fatima whose epithet was *Az-zehra*. The University was started as a Madarsa attached to a mosque which in later years developed into one of the finest centres of research and learning. It is the oldest university of the world that has remained functional since its inception.

After the death of Muizuddin, his son Nizar bin Saad became the Caliph at the age of 21 with the title of Aziz Badin-allah. He further expanded the territory of the Caliphate. He was fortunate to have a competent and learned vizier in Yaqub bin Yusuf on whose advice Aziz took the necessary action to transform Jamia Azhar into an excellent centre of higher learning and research. During his time more than two lakhs books of various disciplines were added to the university library. After the death of Yaqub, Aziz took an astonishing decision by appointing a Christian, Bin Nistoras as his vizier who was succeeded by a Jew, Meshiya. A Western scholar informs us that Aziz had also sent missionaries to China for proselytization.[59] Aziz died on October 13, 1996 and was succeeded by his son Haakim ba-Amr-allah as Caliph.

At the time of the Caliphate's accession, Abu Mansur Haakim ba-Amr-allah was slightly more than eleven years old. Most Muslim chroniclers inform us that he was not mentally sound. It seems true when one takes into account some of the commands that he had issued. He had banned trading, selling, shopping activities during the day. Shops were ordered to remain open only during the night. As per his orders all the dogs in Cairo were killed. The slaughter of milch animals, in particular, cows and bulls was prohibited except for religious sacrifice. He ordered women not to venture out of their homes nor should they even steal a look out of windows. Women were disallowed to use bathhouses. Fishing was prohibited. Entry of donkeys into the capital was banned. In the beginning, he established many madarsas and appointed theologians and jurists to give instructions in those institutions. A few years later, however, he ordered the closure of all madarsas and executed all the teachers.[60]

Most Western historians too call Haakim a 'mad Caliph'. It could be partly because of his eccentrics and, to a certain extent, also because of his anti-Christianity policies that he adopted in the later phase of his Caliphate. His mother Syeda Aziza was Christian. Haakim's father, Aziz appointed her two brothers the patriarchs of Melkite Church. There are references about the appointment of one of her brothers as an envoy to Sicily.[61] Initially, Haakim too was favourable to Christians and appointed many of them to important posts. These Christian officials, according to a Muslim chronicler, turned biased towards Muslims. Subsequently, when the stories of discrimination against Muslims by his Christian officers reached Haakim he started persecuting Christians.[62] A Western scholar estimates Haakim thus: "His eccentric character, the inconsistencies and radical shifts in his conduct and policies, the extreme austerity of his personal life, the vindictive and sanguinary ruthlessness of his dealing with the highest officials of his government coupled with an obsession to suppress all signs of corruption and immorality in public life, his attempted annihilation of Christians and call for the systematic destruction of all Christian holy places in the Middle East culminating in the destruction of the most holy Church of the Resurrection in Jerusalem, his deification by a group of extremist Isma'li missionaries who became the forerunners and founders of the Druze religion, [which] all combine to contrast his reign sharply with that of any of his predecessors and successors and indeed of any Muslim ruler.... The question is to what extent his conduct can be explained as rationally motivated and conditioned by the circumstances rather than as the inscrutable workings of an insane mind."[63]

Nonetheless, a few scholars contest the majority view about Haakim being a man of unsound mind. For instance, a researcher argues: "His enemies called him the 'Mad Caliph' but he enhanced Cairo's reputation as a centre of civilization."[64] Likewise, another scholar says, "those distorted and hostile accounts, stating that the anti-Fatimidd tradition tried to make a real monster of this Caliph."[65]

Haakim, though controversial, is still a character of great consequence among the Fatimid Caliphs because the Nizari Muslims and Druze believe that he was the incarnation of God. It is reported that a Nizari (probably Ad-Darazi) wrote a book and presented it to Haakim. The book stated that the soul of God got transmitted first to Adam and later to Ali and finally to Haakim. Consequently, Haakim proclaimed that he was God incarnate and people should prostrate whenever they saw him or heard his name.[66]

His death/disappearance is also steeped in mystery. A few accounts suggest that on the night between February 12 and 13, 1021, he disappeared while on his regular night trip to Muqattam hills at a short distance from Cairo. The entire official machinery got involved to search him but in vain.[67] Other stories hint at his murder. As per one account, Haakim had accused her sister of sexual promiscuity and intended to execute her. She got wind of it and got him killed with the help of her slaves. Another narrative indicates that Haakim's heretical views and actions and particularly his assertion that he was God incarnate infuriated a pious person,

Bani Hasan, so much that he killed him at Muqattam hills and buried him there itself.[68]

Five days after Haakim's disappearance his sixteen-year-old son Abul Hasan Ali Zaahir was nominated the seventh Fatimid Caliph in 1021, under the regency of his sister, Sitt-al-Mulk. His regnal title was Aizazuddin-allah. Though personally he was a judicious man, he could not exercise power independently. His sister (who died in 1023) and later his vizier and a select coterie of courtiers had created so many restrictions that except for a few nobles no one could meet him. His reign was a difficult period for the people. Egypt and a few other provinces faced extreme famines and an epidemic of plague between 1023 and 1025. This led to anarchy across the Caliphate. Moreover, there were revolts in Palestine and Syria that could not be suppressed for almost five years.

Zaahir, however, made attempts to establish cordial relations with the Byzantine Empire and for that reason he lifted all the restrictions on his Christian subjects that were imposed by his father. He also ordered the reconstruction of the churches including the Church of Holy Sepulchre that were destroyed during Haakim's reign. Zaahir died of plague on June 13, 1036.

Zaahir's son Abu Tamim Maad was barely seven-years old when he was nominated to be the eighth Fatimid Caliph because of his father's death in 1036. His mother was an Abyssinian slave whom Zaahir bought from a Jewish merchant Abu Saeed Tastari. When Maad assumed the Caliphate with the title of Mustansir Billah, his mother invited her former master and made him the de facto ruler.[69] Mustansir has a distinction in Islamic history because he happened to be the only ruler who reigned for almost 60 years.[70]

A vizier of Mustansir, Badr Jamali had achieved prominence because of his military and administrative prowess. He was an Armenian of origin who was bought as a slave by the Fatimid nobleman Jamal-ud-Dawla. That explains why he came to be known as Jamali. When Mustansir sent him the epistle nominating him the emir of Syria, Jamali marched towards Cairo with a huge army. On entering the capital city, he killed all the Turkish nobles and confiscated their properties. Thereafter, Jamali reached Askandaria (Alexandria) and massacred all the opponents of

Mustanṣir. Besides these militant actions he helped the Caliph establish peace all across the Fatimid realm. He also devised schemes to support the peasants and improved the transport infrastructure to promote trade.

In his absence from Syria, a Turkmani commander Atsaz, established his rule there and a short while later arrived with his army on the outskirts of Cairo with the intention to conquer the entire Fatimid Caliphate. Jamali defeated him and brought Syria back under his control. In 1074, Mustansir appointed Jamali the Commander of the Caliphate armed forces because of which he became the de facto ruler. He died in Egypt in the year 1094. Jamali built quite a few magnificent buildings in Cairo and also rebuilt the city wall of the capital. A few days after Jamali's death, the Caliph too died on January 10, 1094. Though Mustansir's reign was the longest, he was not a judicious and competent ruler. It was because of Badr Jamali that the Caliphate managed to hold. Yet, Sicily that was under Muslim control since 872 was lost to the Normans under Roger I, in 1091.[71]

Mustansir's death led to a power struggle among his sons that ultimately caused a schism in the Ismaili Shiaism. The three sons of Mustansir, Nizar, Ahmed and Ismail disputed the succession. Though the eldest one, Nizar, was a competent claimant to the Caliphate, he did not have a good rapport with the Commander-in-Chief, Malik Afzal. Therefore, Afzal helped Abul Qasim Ahmed, the other son of Mustansir to take up the Caliphate. Qasim acquired for himself the title of Mustaali Billah and became the ninth Fatimid Caliph. Nizar fled and with the support of the governor of Alexandria, Nasruddaulah Aftagin made plans to invade Cairo. Afzal met the challenge of Nizar in the vicinity of Alexandria but was defeated by Nizar who later occupied the entire coastal region of the Caliphate. Afzal returned with a bigger force and laid siege of Alexandria. Finally Nizar and Aftagin surrendered; they were arrested and transferred to Cairo where both were hanged in 1097.[72]

Mustaali's Caliphate, nonetheless, was not unanimously accepted by all the Ismaili Shias. The defiance of the conventional practice of transferring the Imamate and Caliphate from one deceased Caliph to the eldest son was not approved by a sizable number of Ismailis in Syria and Persia where Nizar's supporters emerged as a new Ismaili sect known as Hashishin while the supporters of Mustaali constituted the Mustaali sect. It was during Mustaali's reign that the First Crusade commenced (1099) when the European forces annexed the region of Asia Minor.

Abu Ali Mansur succeeded his father as the 10th Fatimid Caliph with the title of Aemir Billah in 1101. He came to be recognized as the twentieth Imam of the Mustaali Ismaili sect. The Commander of the armed forces, Afzal continued to be the de facto ruler as he was during the reign of Mustaali. The year Aemir assumed power the Crusaders occupied Tyre and somewhat later also annexed Syria and Tripoli. The Crusaders continued annexing Fatimid territories in Asia Minor and Palestine for the first seven years of Aemir's reign. About 1120-21, on the orders of Aemir, the all powerful Commander Afzal was killed and all his properties that were huge were confiscated. The conflict between Nizaris and Mustaalis ultimately led to the assassination of the Caliph on October 7, 1130.

A power struggle appeared yet again over the succession after the assassination of Aemir. There are conflicting reports about the legal heir to the Caliphate after Aemir. Muslim historians such as Aslam Jairajpuri maintain that Aemir had no son. According to him though at the time of his murder his wife was pregnant, she later gave birth to a daughter and therefore Aemir's cousin Abdul Majeed assumed the Caliphate with the title of Haafizuddin-allah.[73] A Western scholar, however, quotes a Muslim chronicler Ibn Muyassar: "In Rabi al-awwal (of..524 AH) Qasim al-Tayyib, was born to al-Emir; ...Cairo was decorated. New suits of clothes were issued to the troops...at the 'aqiqa ceremony... in the presence of al-Emir...child was brought in, and Chief Qadi Ibn al-Muyassar was given the honour of holding it...the palace was filled with fruits and other sweets..."[74] This controversy led to a further schism even among the Mustaali Ismaili as the supporters of the two-year-old son of Aemir declared him the rightful Imam and the Caliph. Thus was born the Tayyibi sect to which the Bohras belong.

So far as historical continuity is concerned, Haafizuddin remained the Caliph till he died in 1149 at the age of 81. He was succeeded by his youngest son Abul Mansur Ismail with the regnal title of Zaafir-ba-Amrallah. He had no interest in the affairs of the

Caliphate as he spent most of his time in pleasure-seeking and depravity. Five years after becoming the Caliph, Zaafir was murdered by his vizier Abbas. The vizier then appointed the five-year-old son of Zaafir, Abu Qasim Isa as the Caliph with the title of Faaiz-ba-Nasrullah. The child-Caliph could never take the governing power in his hands as he died at the age of 11 in 1160. Then the vizier, Saleh Taae bi Razeek, appointed Abu Muhammad, a minor brother of Faaiz as the fourteenth Fatimid Caliph with the regnal title of Aaziduddin-illah. He happened to be the last Caliph of the Fatimid order who reigned between 1160 and 1171. By this time the Caliphate was at its nadir both in terms of wealth and military power. The Crusaders had established strong bases in Asia Minor and Palestine and they were waiting for an opportune time to pounce upon Egypt.

Then Shawar bin Majeer-al-Saadi, a subordinate officer of Nuruddin, the emir of Syria and the member of the Zengi (Zengid) family, somehow managed to become the vizier of Aazid in 1163 and achieved, to some extent, to streamline the administration of the Caliphate. Since he had the military backing of Zengi forces, Shawar repulsed the Crusaders' onslaughts on Egypt. The supporters of the former vizier, Saleh, under the leadership of Zargham made an attempt on the life of Shawar. They could kill only his son as Shawar managed to flee to Syria. Shawar's absence from Cairo encouraged the Crusaders to make successful incursions in Egypt. Shawar petitioned to Nuruddin Zengi to protect the Fatimid Caliphate that was about to be annihilated by the Crusaders. In response, Nuruddin dispatched a faction of his armed forces under the command of Asaduddin Shirkuh. A young nephew of Shirkuh by the name Yusuf Salahuddin, despite the lack of enthusiasm of his uncle, also joined the forces that were marching towards Egypt. He is the same person who later made a name as an invincible warrior in Islamic history by the name Salahuddin Ayyubi.

Shirkuh could take Egypt with minimal trouble. Zargham was killed and once again Shawar was appointed the vizier of the Fatimid Caliphate. Though Shawar agreed to pay a substantial amount as tribute to the Zengi ruler for his support to the Caliphate. Nuruddin Zengi, however, had planned to annex Egypt by removing the Fatimid Caliph. Through Shirkuh, this plan was conveyed to Zargham. Initially he concurred but later entered into a secret alliance with the Christian Kingdom of Jerusalem to get rid of Shirkuh and his forces from Egypt. The Christian forces reached Egypt to help the Caliphate forces under Shawar against the Zengi forces under Shirkuh. At this time, Nuruddin succeeded in completely driving out the Crusaders from Asia Minor and had designs to attack Palestine. This alarmed the Christian forces that were helping the Caliphate. Since they were to rush back to Palestine to defend their kingdom, they made an offer to Shirkuh, who was besieged in a fort, that his forces would not be attacked if he agreed to leave Egypt. Shirkuh accepted the offer and went back to Syria. He, however, had made up his mind to once again conquer Egypt and bring to an end the Fatimid Caliphate.

A few years later, Shirkuh convinced his mentor Nuruddin to let him make another attempt to take over Egypt. Nuruddin was not enthusiastic as he could not spare a large force for the Egyptian conquest. Yet, he allowed Shirkuh and his nephew Salahuddin to lead a force of barely two thousand soldiers. Shirkuh moved swiftly and occupied the northern part of Egypt. Shawar again appealed to the Kingdom of Palestine to come to his rescue. Though initially Shirkuh defeated the combined forces of Shawar and the Christians and also got control of Alexandria. Nonetheless in the later phase of the battle he was once again forced to leave Egypt. Then in his third attempt in 1169, Shirkuh conquered Egypt. Shawar was killed on the orders of the Aazid the Caliph as he was once again striving covertly to invite the Crusaders against Shirkuh. Thereafter, Aazid appointed Shirkuh as his vizier but a short while later he died on March 23, 1169. Aazid then appointed Salahuddin the vizier in place of his uncle. With the death of Aazid in 1171, the Fatimid Caliphate came to an end and a new dynasty, Ayyubi, was inaugurated in Egypt.

In most accounts of Sunni scholars we find a negative depiction of the Fatimid Caliphate.[75] Most Sunni theologians and jurists of the time did not even accept the claim of Ubaidullah Mehdi that he was a scion of the house of the Prophet through his daughter Fatima. The Abbasi Caliph, Qadir, even issued a manifesto in this regard that is known as the Baghdad Manifesto. It was a testimony given by almost all Sunni scholars of the time (it was issued in 1011) and also the *Asna-e-Ashri* (Shia Twellers) genealogists and jurists refuting the lineage assertion of Ubaidullah Mehdi from Fatima, the daughter of the Prophet. The manifesto stated that the founder of the Fatimid Caliphate originally descended from a Jew whose name was Ibn-al-Qaddah. Thus, the Baghdad manifesto, insisted that the Fatimid dynasty was established by an infidel. This hostility of the Abbasi rulers and the Sunni jurists and scholars towards the Fatimids is understandable because of the intense sectarian rivalry between various Muslim factions. Regarding, the Shia Twellers' opposition towards the Fatimids is concerned it is enough to say that they do not accept even the Abbasid Caliphs' lineage assertion to the house of the Prophet.

An objective assessment of the Fatimid Caliphate should not be based on the issue that whether its founder was really a scion of the house of the Prophet or not. It should be done on account of its administration, governance, the overall condition of the people during its sway, its contribution to the development of infrastructure, trade, science and technology, education, art, literature and architecture. From this viewpoint one can say that the Fatimids did extremely well compared with other political orders of the time. Egypt made the maximum progress because the Fatimids established a viable trade network involving many countries of the East and the West.

A remarkable feature of the Fatimid Caliphate was its tolerance towards people of other faiths. Besides protecting the rights of Sunni Muslims, the Fatimid Caliphs also extended full citizenship rights to Jews and Christians.[76] Berbers' contribution to the establishment of the Fatimid Caliphate particularly in the initial stage was considerable. On account of this their presence in military and administration was also substantial. Another notable quality of the Fatimid administration was its policy of recruitment. Most governments of the time both in the East and the West would recruit personnel for important positions on heredity or the membership of the ruling family. Fatimid Caliphs, on the other hand, introduced merit as the criterion for appointing important officials and this policy remained in force for almost two hundred years. The violation of the norm existed only during the last seventy years when the Caliphate itself was in a state of decline. Consequently, the important positions of the Caliphate were held not only by the Sunni Muslims but also by Christians and Jews. The Fatimids followed this policy even in appointing military personnel. Their armed forces were composed of Arabs, Turks, Berbers and even non-Muslim combatants.

Another area wherein the Fatimids' contribution is mammoth is the field of education and scholarship. It was not only the Al-Azhar University that they had established but had also set up many madarsas across the Caliphate to satiate people's thirst for knowledge and research. Intellectual ambience thrived in Egypt and other provinces of the Caliphate because of the government's patronage to education and research. They had also instituted many libraries stacked with valuable tomes of the times. The Al-Azhar had lakhs of books related to almost every discipline of knowledge. Fortunately, this priceless heritage of humanity has survived various political vicissitudes for centuries and is still catering to the needs of research scholars.[77] In the field of art the Fatimid potters matched the skill of Chinese artisans in making ceramic lusterware. Likewise, the glassware and metalwork artisans too had achieved excellence during the Fatimid reign. Fatimid architecture is also well known for its splendour and beauty. The building of Al-Azhar University and the Al-Haakim mosque located in Cairo are the best examples of the Fatimid architecture that had combined durability of the structure with exquisite design.

The decline of the Fatimid Caliphate began because of factionalism in the armed forces coupled with the successes of the Crusaders. As mentioned earlier, the Fatimid army was not ethnically a monolith construct. Initially the Berbers were the dominant segment of the army. In later years people of Turkish origin too constituted a strong faction. A third significant group also emerged in the form of black Africans. This led to factional rivalries and by 1020 the Berbers and the Turks formed an alliance to attack black Africans. This unsettled the unity of the army which is a primary requirement of a fighting force. By 1060 the army was not under the control of any central authority and a kind of civil war broke out between the Turks and the Africans.[78] The Berbers, by this time had perfected the role of fence sitters. They would always jump into the fray on the side of the winning faction. Though Badr Jamali could restore some order in the army and could also effectively ward off the external threat, his elevation to the position of vizier had greatly diminished the authority of the Caliph.

The internal schism among the Fatimids weakened their Imamet and ultimately the political power. The first dissent appeared after the demise of the eighteenth Caliph Mustansir and Mustaaili assumed power because the opponents claimed that the eldest son of the deceased Caliph Nizar was the rightful heir. Nizar was ultimately killed and Mustaaili's claim prevailed. Another schism was caused after the death of the twentieth Caliph, Aemir, who according to one group did not leave a male heir while the other faction claimed that his son, Tayyib Abi Qasim was born a short while after Aemir's death. The first group accepted the Imamet and the Caliphate of Aemir's cousin Hafiz whose ascension to the Caliphate won through. The external forces, in particular, the Zengis of Syria through their Ayyubi commanders ultimately brought to an end the Fatimid reign that was already on the verge of collapse.

IV

The most remarkable feature of the Osmani Khilafat (Ottoman Caliphate) was unlike the Abbasis and Fatimids, its rulers did not pretend to be scions of the lineage of the Prophet, his son-in-law Ali, his uncle Abbas or his daughter Fatima. Many of them did not even bother to use the honorific of 'the Caliph'. Ottoman ancestry originated from a warrior who was a kind of fortune hunter from Central Asia called Adghoze who settled in Asia Minor during the times of the Seljuqs. His progenies made a mark as courageous warriors in the Seljuqi armed forces and for that reason came to be known as the Ghazis (Muslim conquerors). When the Seljuq commander, Tughral Beg, occupied Baghdad in 1055, the mainstay of his army was a composite group comprising the Ghazis and Mamluks (slave soldiers).The occupation of Baghdad forced the Abbasid Caliph to recognize Tughral as the temporal head of Persia and Mesopotamia (roughly the area that includes present-day Iraq, Kuwait, north-eastern Syria, southeastern Turkey and southwestern Iran). Tughral Beg began purging the people of Arab origin from the administration and replacing them by Persians.

It was an extremely difficult task for the Persian administrators to make the Ghazis behave in accordance with the rules prescribed for the armed forces. The Ghazis, more often than not, would launch military expeditions on their own particularly against the Byzantine rulers and would also occupy the territory they had conquered. The Seljuq commanders had to make bases in and around Anatolia to keep the Ghazis under check. The second Seljuq Sultan, Alp Arsalan defeated the Byzantine army in 1071 and thus made the entire Anatolia vulnerable to the conquests of the Turks. Subsequently, the Sultanate of Rum (Islamic variant of Rome) came into existence with its capital in Konya, which later emerged as a powerful Turkish state.

In 1258, Halaku ransacked Baghdad and put an end to the Abbasid Caliphate and later conquered the Seljuq Sultanate too. However, the Sultanate of Rum survived the onslaught of the Mongols and when in the first quarter of the fourteenth century, the Mongol dominance withered away from the region, a new power emerged to have its sway in the area, the Ghazis who later came to be known as the Osmani (Ottoman) Turks. Osman was the name of a son of Artaghral, the emir of Rum who inherited the territory of Rum after the death of his father and ultimately established the Ottoman Sultanate. Osman was a great warrior king who established its dominance in the region because of an armed force that comprised the daredevil soldiers. He had to face quite a few attacks of the neighbouring Christian kingdoms but always came out victorious in those battles. Osman I assumed for himself the title of Sultan and chose Sogut (a town in present-day Turkey) as the capital of his expanding state. Byzantine rulers were alarmed because of the ever expanding territory of the Ottoman Sultanate. A huge army was, therefore, dispatched to overpower the Ottoman rule. Osman crushed the Christian attack. Subsequently. Osman sent a message to all the Christian rulers of the area that were technically under the Byzantine asking them to choose one of the options from the three that he offered 1) Embrace Islam; 2) Pay Jiziya or 3) Face war.[79]

Since many Christian rulers preferred the third option they had to face the armed forces of Osman under the command of his son

Orkhan that defeated the Christian forces in many battles and finally Bursa fell in 1326. The news of the annexation of Bursa reached Osman when he was on his deathbed.[80] He advised his son Orkhan in the last moments of his life: "Listen! You must always have the fear of Allah in your heart and justice should be your preference for it fortifies the foundation of the Sultanate. Be always compassionate for compassion is one of the attributes of Allah. In matters of rights treat strong and the weaker similarly. Implement Shariat and behave accordingly. If you behave as per my will then you will be counted among those defenders with whom Allah is pleased."[81]

Orkhan was not the eldest son of Osman. It was Allauddin Pasha. However, Pasha's inclination was towards piety, abstention and simplicity. In view of this Osman nominated Orkhan as his successor who was a fearless warrior.[82] Orkhan ruled between 1326 and 1359. He mostly concentrated on expansion of the territory and military reforms. He established a special wing of the army consisting only of the youths who got converted from Christianity to Islam. This wing of the army was directly under the command of Sultan and not answerable to any other authority. The main purpose of creation of this force was to keep them loyal only to the Sultan and aloof from other military commanders so that its soldiers should not get involved in conspiracies. This force was named *Bakichari,* which is known as *Ankashariyah* in Arabic. Orkhan ruled for almost thirty-four years during which he subjugated the entire Asia Minor. On 1354, he succeeded in establishing a base in Europe in the Gallipoli.

Murad I was the youngest son of Orkhan who succeeded as Sultan and he too continued the policy of expansion westward. His conquests in the region of Balkans[83] from 1362 to 1389 converted the Ottoman Sultanate into a transcontinental empire and by this time the Turkish Sultan had made the decision to declare himself the Caliph. In 1389 Murad's forces defeated the Serbian army commanded by Lazer in the Battle of Kosovo. Nevertheless, Murad died on the battlefield. There are two versions of Sultan's death. According to Western sources, both Sultan Murad I and Prince Lazar died on the battlefield. Though one of the Western chroniclers reported that Sultan Murad I was stabbed to death by a Serbian Milos Obilic at the beginning of the battle. The Muslim sources maintained that Murad I was assassinated after the end of the battle when he was attending the wounded soldiers.[84]

Sultan's eldest son Bayazid I had put on view tremendous courage in the battle of Kosovo and as a result was honoured with the title of Eldarum (lightning). The military commanders and the noblemen collectively decided to help Bayazid I succeed as Sultan on the battlefield itself. The problem was that his younger brother, Yaqub Chelpi, who too was a valiant warrior, was already nominated the heir apparent in the lifetime of Murad I. With the concurrence of the theologians and the noblemen, Bayazid I put Yaqub Chelpi to death to forestall any trouble in the future.[85] Bayazid added many significant territories to the Sultanate both in the East and the West. In 1390 he subjugated Aydin, Sauhan and Mentese in a single campaign. By 1395, both Bulgaria and Greece were parts of the Sultanate. Bayazid I also laid siege to Constantinople in 1394. In response the Byzantine emperor Manuel II Palaeologus appealed to the Christian rulers of Europe for a new Crusade against the Ottomans. This resulted in a failure. Thereafter the European forces under the leadership of the King of Hungary. Sigismund, marched against the forces of Bayazid I but were defeated in the Battle of Necropolis.

In 1402, Bayazid I had to face the humiliating defeat at the hands of Temur Lang (Tamerlane) in the Battle of Angura (Ankara). Bayazid was captured alive and died a year later in the captivity of Temur. The devastation caused by Temur's conquest created serious disorder in the entire Ottoman Sultanate. There were quite a few sons of Bayazid I who got engaged in a power struggle after their father's death. One of the sons, Suleyman who was the governor of Adrana declared himself the Sultan while another son, Musa announced himself the successor of Bayazid I in Barusa with the consent of Temur. A third son Eisa defeated Musa and announced his sovereignty. Another son Muhammad was ultimately successful in eliminating all his brothers and therefore crowned as the Sultan. He, nonetheless, had to fight various battles for survival as well as recapturing those areas that had seceded from the Sultanate taking advantage of the mayhem generated by the invasion of Temur. He was considerably successful in reclaiming the lost grandeur of the Sultanate. Sultan Muhammad I was a devout Muslim and it was during his reign that the practice of sending a huge sum annually for the upkeep of the holiest sites of Islam in the Arab peninsula was started.[86]

Muhammad I was succeeded by Sultan Murad II who was barely 18 at the time of taking over the affairs of the Sultanate. The first challenge that he had to face soon after his accession was to subdue his uncle, Mustafa Chelpi (Celebi) who was provoked by the Byzantine ruler Manuel II to put up his claim as the real Sultan. Mustafa could be defeated not before a lot of destruction that he had caused in the European provinces of the Sultanate. Now, the young Sultan made up his mind to teach a lesson to Manuel II who was behind the crisis that he had to face immediately after becoming Sultan. He reorganized his armed forces and the reformed army came to be known as Azeb. In 1421, Murad II laid siege to the capital of the Byzantine Empire, Constantinople. To wriggle out of the tight spot, the Byzantine ruler hatched another conspiracy. He joined hands with a few independent Anatolian rulers and goaded Mustafa, the younger brother of the Sultan, to rebel against the Sultan. Consequently, Murad had to call off the siege of the Constantinople to quell the rebellion of his 13-year-old brother. He defeated the rebel forces and to put an end to the constant troubles that the independent Anatolian states were causing to the Ottomans, Murad II permanently annexed those states, viz. Aydinids, Germyanids, Menteshe and Teke.

He then turned his attention to the European part of the Sultanate. In 1432 Venice gave up the belligerent posture against the Ottomans in the aftermath of the defeat at the second siege of Thessalonica. By the end of 1430, Murad's control over the Balkans was complete. In 1444, Murad defeated the Hungarian forces under the command of Janos Hunyadi. Following his victory over Hungary, Murad abdicated the throne in favour of his son Muhammad II but revolts in Asia Minor forced him to take back the affairs of the Sultanate in his hands. Having subdued the opposition in the Eastern provinces, in 1448 Murad crushed a coalition of Christian forces in the second Battle of Kosovo. Then in 1450 he laid siege to the Albanian castle of Kruje but at this time he fell ill and after a few months died.[87]

Muhammad II (Mehmet, the Turkish pronunciation) is known in Islamic and European history as Muhammad-e-Saani Fateh

(Mehmud II the Conquerer) mainly because as Ottoman Sultan at the age of 21 he conquered Constantinople (present-day Istanbul) and put an end to the Byzantine Empire. Prior to becoming the Sultan in 1451, Muhammad II had ruled about two years when his father Murad II had relinquished the throne in his favour.

When he permanently ascended the throne of the Ottoman Sultanate, Muhammad II concentrated on reforming and modernizing his armed forces, in particular, the navy with the intention of conquering the capital city of the Byzantine. Most Muslims believe that the conquest of Constantinople was preordained as per a prophecy of the Prophet (*Hadis*). According to the *hadis* which is included in the compilation of Bukhari and other books dealing with the traditions of the Prophet, the members of the first Muslim army that would invade the capital city of the Caesar (*Qaisar*, in Arabic) would be free of charge on the Day of Judgment. The Prophet is believed to have further added that the Muslims would certainly conquer Constantinople and the army that would take over the city would be a splendid one and its commander too would also be a marvellous person.[88] The Muslim forces invaded Constantinople nine times as per the reliable chroniclers. The first Muslim army was dispatched by Emir Muawiyah under the joint command of Sufiyan bin Awf and his son Yazid. The army included some prominent companions of the Prophet such as Abu Ayyub Ansari, Abada bin Samat, Abul Darda, Abdullah bin Umar, Abdullah bin Zubair, Abdullah bin Abbas et al. Abu Ayyub Ansari had died during the siege and therefore, was buried flanking the ramparts of the city. Thereafter, the second invasion took place during the reign of Suleyman Abdul Malik, third in the reign of Hishsham, fourth in the reign of Mehdi Abbasi, fifth when Haroon Rashid was the Caliph, sixth in the reign of Seljuq king Malik Shah and seventh in the reign of Bayazid Eldarum, the eighth one in the reign of Murad II and the ninth and the last one in 1453, when Muhammad II laid the siege of the city and conquered it.

The first action that Muhammad II took in his campaign to take over Constantinople was to send out, on April 22, 1453, his lighter warships to the Golden Horn's (a major waterway and the primary inlet of the Bosporus strait), northern shore. This heralded the siege of the capital city of the Byzantine. Fifty-seven days later Constantinople was conquered by the Ottoman forces on May 29, 1453. Muhammad II immediately shifted his capital from Adrianople to Constantinople that remained throughout the existence of the Ottoman Empire till 1920. It is reported that when Muhammad visited the ruins of the Palace of Caesars he narrated the famous couplet of Saadi Shirazi:

The spider weaves the curtains in the palace of the Caesars
The owl calls the watches in the towers of Afrasiab.[89]

The Byzantine emperor Constantine XI died on the battlefield. Muhammad II showed extraordinary magnanimity by appointing the nephews of the deceased emperor to high positions in the Ottoman administration. The eldest one was appointed the governor-general of the Balkans, another one became Admiral of the Ottoman navy and a third one was appointed the governor of the province of Gallipoli.[90] Subsequently, Muhammad conquered Morea, Bosnia and Trebizond in northeastern Anatolia. In 1480, the Ottoman armed forces under the command of the Grand Vizier Kadak (Gedik) Ahmed Pasha invaded Italy but could only conquer Otranto. After the death of Muhammad II, as a result of negotiations, the town of Otranto was restored to Italy in 1481.

In April 1481, Muhammad II fell sick while leading the army on a new expedition, A few days later, i.e. on May 3, 1481, he breathed his last and was buried within the precincts of the Fatih Mosque that he had built to commemorate the victory of Constantinople. He is remembered as the greatest among the Ottoman Sultans who had left a vast empire for his successors. Having Constantinople as the capital and control over vast territories in Eastern Europe, the Ottoman Empire had its sway for the next six centuries.

Muhammad II's successor was his eldest son Bayazid II. He could not add any new territory to the Ottoman Empire. The entire Balkans save Belgrade was already conquered by Muhammad II. His son made fresh attempts to take over Belgrade from Hungary but was not successful. A significant change that deserves mention was the Ottoman Sultan's preference to establish diplomatic relations with the European nations. It was Russia that first appointed its ambassador to the Ottoman Empire that helped

Russian businessmen to expand their trade. Subsequently, workable diplomatic relations were established with Rumania, Milano and others. During his thirty-two year rule Bayazid carried out the task of strengthening the Ottoman navy to match the best maritime forces of the time. It was during the reign of Bayazid II, that the serious crisis for the Muslim rule in Andulas got initiated. The last vestige of the Muslims there, the principality of Granada petitioned Bayazid II for support but he did not take any significant measures to help the Muslim state of Andulas. In 1512, there ensued a power struggle among the three sons of Bayazid II. The Sultan wanted the eldest one, Ahmad to succeed him but the military commanders favoured the other son Salim (Selim). Consequently, Bayazid II was forced to abdicate the throne and leave Constantinople. Shortly after that he died. Some chroniclers suspect foul play.

Salim I, had to subdue the revolt of his two brothers, Ahmad and Karuk, immediately after accession to the throne. Having defeated the rebel forces he killed both of them. Thereafter he invaded the bordering areas of Iran and massacred a large number of people primarily because they were Shias. He then put an end to the Mamluk Sultanate in Egypt as a result of which this prominent country of Africa was added to the Ottoman Sultanate. The Abbasid Caliphate had its nominal presence under the Mamluk dynasty in Egypt. The last titular Abbasid Caliph, Mutawakkil Aliullh, was in Egypt when it was annexed by Salim I. Aliullah handed over the symbolic possessions of the Caliphate, sword, standard and robe, to Salim I and since then the Caliphate was officially transferred to the Ottomans. He extended the Ottoman rule over Syria and Palestine as well and was also recognized as the guardian of the holiest places of Islam in Mecca and Medina. In the ninth year of his rule (1520) when he was preparing his maritime forces to attack the Rhodes Island (Greece) and the army for the expedition of Iran, he died on September 22, at the age of 55.

Suleyman I, the son of Salim I, became the Sultan in 1520 and reigned till 1566. This considerably long reign is referred to as the 'Golden Age' of the Ottomans not because of the longevity but because of his notable conquests and some extraordinary policies that had far-reaching consequences. For the Muslim chroniclers he is known as Suleyman I Qanuni (the law giver) because he comprehensively amended and codified the laws of the Ottoman Empire. For the Westerners he is Suleyman I, the Magnificent because of his complete domination over most of the Christian rulers of the time. He conquered Belgrade in 1521, the Rhodes island in 1522, killed the king of Hungary in 1526 at the Battle of Mohacs and took control of Buda on the Danube. Three years later he laid siege to Vienna, though failed to take it over. By 1530, the entire North African region was made part of the Ottoman Empire. In 1534, the Ottoman forces conquered Kurdistan and Mesopotamia that were under the control of Iran. When the Mughal emperor, Babur was in the process of consolidating his rule in India after defeating Ibrahim Lodhi in 1525, the Emir of Gujarat, Bahadur Shah appealed to the Ottoman Sultan for help to stop the advancement of the Portuguese who had taken control of the coastal areas of his province. Suleyman dispatched seventy warships from Egypt that first took control of Aden and later defeated the Portuguese by destroying their biggest military encampment at Diu.

Most historical accounts concur that Suleyman I was a down-to-earth ruler. His major policies had the mark of the diplomacy of the twentieth century. In 1536, for instance, he signed a pact with the ruler of France, Francis I, which helped the French get many concessions including favourable terms of trade. Though Palestine was a part of the Ottomans, Suleyman I, recognized France's right as the protector of the Christian holy places in that province. He died in 1566 while leading a military expedition against Hungary.

Before his death, Suleyman I was forced to get involved in the court intrigue contrived by his beautiful Russian wife Farhana who wanted her son Salim to be the Sultan after her husband's death. The grand vizier, Rustam Pasha, who was her son-in-law was also a part of the intrigue. Consequently, Suleyman I was decoyed to kill the heir apparent, Prince Mustafa who was very popular among the Ankashariya,. The heir apparent's murder incensed them and they demanded execution of the grand vizier. Suleyman I pacified them by dismissing Rustam Pasha from his post.[91] As a result of the intrigue, Salim II became the Ottoman Emperor on September 7, 1566 and remained in power for the next eight years. He was least suitable to head a huge empire like the Ottoman but he was lucky to have a competent and dexterous grand vizier in

Muhammad Pasha (Mehmed Sokollu). He managed the affairs of the Empire with a firm hand.

Muhammad Pasha first signed a treaty with Austria that brought Transylvania and Rumania under the subordination of the Ottomans. The pact with France was also renewed. In 1570, a treaty of friendship was also signed with Ivan IV of Russia. After a temporary setback regarding control of the Mediterranean Sea, the Ottomans regained control of the Mediterranean region in 1573. Thereafter, a short while before the demise of Salim II in 1574, the Ottoman forces also took back Tunisia from Spain that had annexed it two months earlier.

Salim II had six sons. The eldest one Murad succeeded his father as the Ottoman Emperor and immediately after accession to the throne he murdered his five brothers. The competent Grand Vizier Muhammad Pasha who had served Salim II continued to serve the Empire under Murad III as well until his assassination on October 11, 1579. The reign of Murad III was marked by a series of wars both on the Eastern and Western fronts of the Empire. In 1577, the Ottomans declared war against Iran that went on for the next 12 years only to be concluded by the Istanbul Treaty of 1590, which helped the Ottomans gain control over Tabrez and Sherwan. In order to protect its control over Morocco, the Ottoman forces had to defeat the Portuguese naval forces that had joined the rebel ruler Muhammad Mustansir. In the Western part, Rumania and Transylvania joined hands with Austria and Germany and declared their independence. The newly appointed Grand Vizier Sanan Pasha had a tough time to put down the rebellion. During Murad III's reign correspondence started between the Ottoman Emperor and the British Queen Elizabeth I. Some of these letters suggest that Murad III was keen to establish friendly relations with the British. He even mentioned that Islam and the Protestant faith had "much more in common than either did with Roman Catholicism, as both rejected the worship of idols".[92] The exchange of these letters ultimately led to military cooperation between the Ottomans and England with the purpose of containing the common enemy, Spain.[93] Murad III died in 1595.

Murad III was succeeded by Muhammad III as Ottoman Emperor on January 15, 1595 and ruled until his death on December

22, 1603. Having gained power he killed 19 of his brothers who were buried on the day of Murad III's burial.[94] Muhammad was the first Ottoman Sultan since Suleyman I to personally lead the forces in the battlefield. Under his leadership the Ottomans conquered Eger (a city in northern Hungary) in 1596 and ultimately defeated the joint forces of Habsburg and Transylvania at the Battle of Keresztes (a village in northern Hungary) which is known as the Battle of Haçova.[95] Thereafter he had to suppress the Jalili revolts in Anatolia. Taking advantage of the Ottomans' involvement in Hungary, the Iranian King Shah Abbas had recaptured Tabrez. Muhammad III dispatched the Ottoman army against Iran but before the start of the confrontation died in 1603 at the age of 38.

Ahmed I was the eldest son of Murad III who succeeded his father as Ottoman Emperor in 1603 and reigned until his death in 1617. It was during his reign that the Ottomans suffered significant losses both in Asia and Europe and the process of the decline of the Empire set in. In the war with Hungary, the Ottomans had suffered significantly and were forced to sign the Treaty of Zsitvatorok on November 11, 1606 that ended the fifteen-year war between the Ottomans and Hungary. The terms of the treaty, however, favoured the Christian nation of Europe. As per the pact, Austria recognized the sovereignty of Hungary and stopped paying annual tribute to the Ottomans. Similarly, the war with Iran resulted in the victory of Iran. According to the resultant pact, the Treaty of Nasuh Pasha signed in 1612, Iran got back the suzerainty over the entire Caucasus including the territories such as Azerbaijan and Georgia.

One commendable deed of Ahmed I was that he broke the tradition of fratricide. On becoming Sultan he made his brother Mustafa live peacefully with their grandmother Safiya Sultana. He was a good poet and used Bahti as his nom de plume. In the contemporary world, he is remembered for the construction of a grand and tasteful Sultan Ahmed Mosque, which is also called the Blue Mosque that was built between 1609 and 1616 at Istanbul. A year after the completion of the mosque Ahmed I died. His son, Osman, was barely 13-years old at the time of his death, so Ahmed I nominated his brother Mustafa I to succeed him.

Mustafa I was of unsound mind and, therefore, remained a

tool in the hands of the Grand Vizier and his mother, who as per their expediency, enthroned him twice first in 1617 for less than a year and second in 1622 for another year. After the nomination for the first time in 1618, the noblemen removed him in favour of Ahmed I's son Osman II. Three years later, the Ankashariya revolted against Osman II and in the ensuing mayhem, the Ottoman Emperor was assassinated. As a result, Mustafa I was again enthroned in 1622 and remained the Sultan for another year.[96] Mustafa's enthronement as the Sultan created a new principle of succession that the senior most male blood relative (not necessarily his son) of the deceased emperor could succeed him and this newly established practice was followed subsequently as well. Nonetheless, in the episode of Mustafa I and Osman II, the elite faction of the armed forces Ankashariya (Janissaries) could acquire tremendous power and subsequently they could enthrone the Sultan of their choice. Osman II was, in fact, trying to restrain the power of the Ankashariya that led them to revolt against him. The disorder at the capital of the Empire made available the opportunity for the governors of the provinces to declare their independence. Yusuf Pasha, the governor of Tripoli and Syria declared himself as independent ruler. Similarly, Abaza Pasha, the governor of Erzurum not only announced his self-government but also annexed Sewas and Angora. The eighteen months of disorder at the capital of the Empire finally brought in Kemankesh Pasha as the Grand Vizier who deposed Mustafa I and enthroned Murad IV, the third son of Ahmed I as the seventeenth Sultan of the Ottomans.[97]

Murad IV was fourteen years old at the time of his accession as the Ottoman Emperor and therefore in the early phase of his rule he was controlled by the Grand Vizier and his relatives. This was a period of complete chaos and most areas of the Empire were controlled by the local tyrants. Around 1632, Murad IV began asserting himself by subduing the tyrants and restoring the honour and majesty of the Emperor. The most significant event of the reign of Murad IV was the Ottomans' war with the Safavi Monarchy of Iran. Murad IV personally led the Ottoman forces against the Iranians that gave a boost to the morale of the Turkish soldiers. He was an accomplished wrestler and physically a very powerful man. The war with Iran that dragged on quite long (1623-1639) ultimately ended with the Ottomans having a slight edge over the Iranians. The Treaty of Zuhab signed between the two powers was also favourable to the Ottomans. According to the terms of the treaty Eastern Armenia, Eastern Georgia, Azerbaijan and Dagestan were given to Iran while Western Armenia, Western Georgia and entire Mesopotamia went to the Ottomans. The treaty established permanent peace between the Ottomans and the Iranians. This competent Sultan who could have completely restored the lost glory of the Ottomans had he lived longer but unfortunately he had cirrhosis that ultimately killed him in 1640 when he was just 27.[98]

Ibrahim Pasha was the only male member of the royal family who was alive when Murad IV died. His mental condition was questionable as in some accounts he is even mentioned as the insane Sultan. He was the son of Ahmad I and 25 years old when he was made the Sultan by the Grand Vizier and the noblemen of the Ottoman court. He remained the titular Sultan from 1640 to 1648. During the first four years of Ibrahim's reign, Kara Mustafa Pasha served as the Grand Vizier who competently upheld the peace and stability in the Empire. He signed a peace treaty with Austria in 1642. He also brought back the town of Azov under the suzerainty of the Ottomans by defeating the Ukrainian armed forces. During this period, Ibrahim Pasha also behaved reasonably well and even showed an interest in administrative matters.[99] However, the court conspiracies led to the murder of Kara Mustafa Pasha and Salih Pasha took over the charge of Grand Vizier. The connivers, nevertheless, continued scheming and looting the riches of the Empire. Salih Pasha was also murdered in 1647 and a year later, Sultan Ibrahim was arrested and the newly appointed Grand Vizier Ahmed Pasha was also publicly executed with the connivance of the corrupt ulama and the Ankashariya.[100]

Muhammad IV, the 6-year-old son of Ibrahim was enthroned as the Sultan of the Ottoman Empire and reigned from 1648 to 1687. His reign was a difficult one as the Empire had to deal with myriad problems. The court intrigues and domination of the Ankashariya had disrupted the administration and also provided the opportunity to the governors of the provinces to rebel. At this point in 1656, the mother of the Sultan invited 90-year-old Muhammad Pasha, a very competent and firm administrator known in Turkish history as Kopareli (Köprülü) to take charge as Grand Vizier.[101]

The competency and experience of Muhammad Pasha and his son Fazil Ahmed helped recover, to some extent, the prestige of the Empire. He disciplined the Ankashariya by executing quite a few of their bigheaded commanders. He also restructured the Ottoman naval forces and regained control of the Aegean Island from Venice and also conquered Crete. Under Muhammad Pasha's guidance the Ottomans got successes against Transylvania and Poland. The death of Muhammad Pasha brought Kara Mustafa to the position of Grand Vizier who could not handle the overall administration and command of the armed forces efficiently. He led the Ottoman army through Hungary and laid siege to Vienna. In the consequential Battle of Vienna, the Ottoman forces were squarely defeated by the Polish army and the troops of the Holy League allies commanded by the Polish King John III Sobieski. This victory of the Christian nations over the Ottomans was passionately celebrated across Europe and along with Vienna, Malta, Russia and most significantly the Papal authority jointly known as the Holy League avowed to throw out the Ottomans from Europe. The Ottoman Empire now faced a serious crisis because of internal disturbances and the open defiance of the Ankashariya. On November 8, 1687, Muhammad IV was deposed and imprisoned and his brother Suleyman II was made the Sultan.

Suleyman II ruled from 1687 to 1691. The decline of the Empire continued as immediately after the enthronement of Suleyman the Ottomans suffered another defeat in the Second Battle of Mohacs against the army of the Roman Emperor Leopold I. Thereafter the Ottomans also suffered heavily in their Crimean campaigns. Nevertheless, the Ottomans repulsed the Austrian forces that were advancing into Serbia. Suleyman II died in 1691 and was succeeded by his brother Ahmed II.

Ahmed II could do nothing notable during his four-year rule from 1691 to 1695. He had left the administration as well as the command of the armed forces in the hands of his Grand Vizier Fazil Mustafa Pasha. The Grand Vizier achieved a major victory at Belgrade, which rekindled the hope that the fortunes of the Empire could be overturned. Nevertheless, a short while later the Ottomans suffered a crushing defeat at a battle fought in the northwest of Belgrade. In 1692, the Habsburg (Austrian Royal House) commander also defeated the Ottomans at Varad (Oradea, Rumania) and thus the Ottomans were expelled from this seat of their governor which they had held continuously since 1660.

Ahmed II was succeeded by Mustafa II in 1695 and reigned as the Ottoman Sultan till 1703. During his reign the process of the Empire's decline was accelerated and the Ottomans could never recover their lost grandeur and glory afterwards. The Holy League conquered many territories of Europe that were under Ottoman rule. This provoked Mustafa II to personally lead the army to recapture the lost territories. Initially he achieved some notable successes. On September 18, 1695, the Venitian navy was destroyed by the Ottomans and a few days later the Habsburg forces were defeated. In the intervening time, the Russian advance towards the fortress of Azov was also successfully driven back. However, in August 1696, the Russians captured the fortress because the real Ottoman forces were engaged at the battles of Ulas and Cenel where they defeated the troops of the Habsburg. This helped the Ottomans to recapture Belgrade. About a year later in June 1697, the Ottoman army under the command of Mustafa II suffered a severe defeat at the hands of the forces of the Holy League. In 1699, the Ottoman Sultan was compelled to sign the Treaty of Kalowitz that dispossessed the Ottoman Empire of Hungary, Transylvania, Ukraine, Azov and island of Morea. Consequently, the Ankashariya deposed Mustafa II and enthroned his brother Ahmed III.

Ahmed III ruled for twenty-seven years from 1703 to 1730. He managed to salvage the fortress of Azov and Morea and also conquered a part of Iran. However, he could not get back the territories in the Balkans that were ceded to the Hasburgs. Nonetheless, he was successful in improving the finances of the empire through well-organized revenue administration. He was also a patron of the arts and through a command allowed the setting up of a printing press in Istanbul against the will of the orthodox ulama.[102]

Ahmed III was deposed on September 28, 1730 by the Ankashariya and the leader Batrona Khalil (Patrona Halil) enthroned Mustafa II's son Mehmud I. Despite Mehmud's coronation, the power remained in the hands of Ankashariya's leader Khalil. Ultimately, the Emir of Crimea helped the Grand Vizier to restore the sovereignty of Mehmud I. Thus, Khalil was put to death along with his seven thousand supporters who were of Greek origin. Mehmud's I's reign was marked by wars with Iran, Austria and Russia. During this period, Nadir Shah had seized power in Iran. He invaded Baghdad and Mosul and defeated the Ottoman forces, it was followed by a peace treaty that was signed on September 24, 1736 according to which the two powers agreed to respect the boundaries that existed during the reign of Murad IV.[103] When the Ottomans were engaged in the war with Nadir Shah, the combined forces of Russia and Austria invaded the Ottomans on the western front but the Ottomans defeated the invaders and could take back Belgrade as well. The peace treaty followed that dispossessed Austria of Belgrade and Russia of Azov. Nadir Shah invaded Baghdad again and trounced the Ottoman forces. He, nevertheless, recognized Mehmud I as the Caliph and for that reason requested the Ottoman Sultan that the Jafri faith should be accepted as the fifth faith of Islam and as there were four *Musalley* (prayer quarters) within the precincts of Kaaba, a fifth one for the Jafri faith should also be added. However, this request was turned down.[104] Mehmud I died in 1754.

Osman III was the son of Mustafa II who was the Ottoman Sultan for a brief period from 1754 to 1757. Nothing significant came about during his reign except for a few incidences of fire in the capital. He was very superstitious and by far would not rely on any one. His three-year reign saw the change of Grand Vizier seven times. He died on October 30, 1757.[105]

Mustafa III, the son of Sultan Ahmed III was enthroned after the death of Osman III. His reign lasted from 1757 to 1774. Mustafa III had foresight and for that reason he realized the significance of modern science and technology. He made genuine efforts to modernize the administration and the armed forces despite the embittered opposition of the conservative ulama and Ankashariya. He sought the services of foreign experts to modernize the Ottoman infantry and artillery. He also opened schools, colleges and academies for imparting modern sciences and military education. By his time, the Ottoman Empire was so much in decline that

Mustafa III's modernization project could not have much impact. He was realistic enough to assess the weakness of the Ottomans' military power and, therefore, he did not undertake any military conquest particularly against the European powers. However, when Catherine II of Russia annexed Crimea and had plans for further incursions into the Ottoman territories, Mustafa III declared war against Russia. However, his death on January 21, 1774, did not give him the opportunity to guide the campaign against Russia.

Abdul Hamid I succeeded Mustafa III as the Ottoman Sultan. He was the son of Sultan Ahmed III and reigned between 1774 and 1789. He took charge of the Ottoman Empire at a time when it was passing through the worst financial crisis. Despite this the Ottomans had to fight against the Russians as Abdul Hamid's predecessor Sultan Mustafa III had declared war against the advancing troops of Catherine II. The outcome of the war was a foregone conclusion as the Ottoman army was completely routed and was forced to sign the unfair Treaty of Küçük Kaynarca, on July 21, 1774. According to the terms of the treaty all the disputed territories including Azov were ceded to Russia and Crimea was declared an independent nation.

In the aftermath of the humiliating defeat against Russia, Abdul Hamid I got engaged in reforming the Ottoman army. In order to modernize the armed forces he established an Imperial Engineering School.[106] He succeeded in suppressing the revolts in Syria and Egypt and also pushed out the Iranian forces that had occupied Basra. The Russian expansionist programme in Eastern Europe did not stop even after the Treaty of Küçük Kaynarca. As a result, the Ottomans had to fight another war with Russia in 1787. In the initial phase of the war the Ottomans withstood the Russian onslaught but on December 6, 1788 Ochakov (Özü in Turkish, a small town in southern Ukraine) fell to Russia and the triumphant massacred all its residents. This shocking tragedy disquieted Abdul Hamid I so much that within four months he died.

Salim III, the son of Sultan Mustafa III ascended the throne after the death of Abdul Hamid I and ruled the Ottoman Empire from 1789 to 1807. He was an innovative and earnest Sultan who made sincere efforts to modernize law, administration and the armed forces. He was also a pragmatic ruler and for that reason he established diplomatic relations with many of his European neighbours. Initially he faced difficulties in making peace with the European nations because all the Christian nations had a deep-seated prejudice against Islam.[107] However, Salim III's sincerity overcame the prejudices against the Muslims and the Ottoman Empire established diplomatic relations with Britain, France, Russia and Austria.

Despite wars with Russia, Austria and Napoleon's invasion of Egypt and Syria, Salim III could not only keep up peace and order across the empire but also put the empire on a modern and progressive course. He paid full attention to reforms in the armed forces and hired the services of foreign experts to train Ottomans' newly created military wing called the *Nizam-e-Jadid* (the new order). This wing was Ottomans' new infantry corps methodically trained and equipped with the latest weapons that could match the best available to the European forces. It was instituted in 1797, and most of its recruits were youths belonging to the Turkish peasantry. It emerged as the most effective section of the Ottoman armed forces. Ankashariya, the traditionally dominant arm of the military obviously resented the *Nizam-e-Jadid* because it threatened their supremacy. Additionally, the orthodox ulama were also opposed to most of the European-modelled reforms that Salim III had brought about. They believed that the European style of military training and modern scientific education would rob the Ottomans of their Islamic traditions. Thus, the Ankashariya and the orthodox ulama formed a nexus against the foresighted Sultan and deposed him in 1806 and enthroned Mustafa IV after getting an assurance from him that he would cancel all the reforms that Salim III had brought about. Therefore, within a year, *Nizam-e-Jadid* was taken apart, the foreign experts were expelled, the diplomatic relations established with a few European nations were severed and Salim III was murdered.[108]

Mustafa IV who succeeded Salim III was the son of Abdul Hamid I. He was reluctant to ascend the throne because two worthier claimants of the throne, the deposed emperor Salim III and his brother Mehmud were alive. He ordered that both the claimants should be murdered first. When his supporters reported that both were murdered he took charge of the Empire.

Nonetheless, Mehmud survived the attempt on his life by hiding in a bath furnace.[109] Mustafa could barely rule for a year during which the Ankashariya indulged in a series of rioting and looting. They killed anyone whom they suspected a supporter of reforms that were introduced by Salim III. In these troubled times five Afendi (Efendi) brothers, known as *Yaran-e-Ruschaq* (Companions of Rusçuk, a city in Bulgaria). Tahseen, Bhij, Raamiz, Rafiq and Ghalib persuaded an upright military commander, Alemdar (standard bearer) Mustafa Pasha, stationed at the time in Ukraine and who was also a supporter of the reforms, to lead the people in getting rid of Mustafa IV. He managed to draw together a sizable army that attacked the palace, deposed Mustafa IV and enthroned his brother Mehmud.[110]

Mehmud II ruled from 1808 till his death in 1839. He appointed Alemdar Mustafa Pasha who helped the Sultan to undertake many reforms in administration, military and financial institutions. The most significant of the military reforms was the abolition, in 1826, of the self-serving and orthodox segment of the armed forces, viz. the Ankashariya. This smoothened the pace of reforms. The entire military was then restructured after the European model of the armed forces. Hereafter, most of those recruited as soldiers were from Turkey and Asia Minor. The reform project known as *Tanzimiyat* also introduced an element of accountability in governance as Mehmud II created a *Majlis-e-Vukla* (House of Counsellors).[111] This proved a very significant move as it ultimately led Turkey to become a modern democratic polity. These changes also included the adoption of the European style structuring of public institutions, land reform, architecture and most notably clothing.

In the initial phase of Mehmud II's reign, the Ottomans had to deal with the internal disturbances in the Arab peninsula as Abdullah bin Saud had established the so-called First Saudi State in 1814. Abdullah bin Saud had completely banned the entry of Muslims from the Ottoman Empire to visit the holy cities of Mecca and Medina. Enthused by Sheikh Muhammad Abdul Wahab's censorious and extremely rigid Salafism, Abdullah bin Saud and his followers had also vandalized the tombs of Ali bin Abi Talib and his two sons Imam Hasan and Imam Hussain. This insurgency was suppressed in 1818 and the holiest sites of Islam were again brought under the Ottoman control. Abdullah bin Saud and two of his staunch followers were publicly beheaded.[112] On the western front, however, the Ottomans lost control of almost all the European territories that had been under its suzerainty for centuries. Greece emerged as an independent nation after the revolution of 1821. In 1827, the three European powers, viz. Britain, France and Russia joined hands against the Ottomans and their combined maritime forces attacked and defeated the Ottoman navy. This defeat forced Mehmud II to recognize the independent state of Greece in 1832. The province of Algeria was annexed by France in 1830. The Ottoman-Persian War 1821-1823 resulted in the complete rout of Mehmud II's forces. The series of losses practically left the Empire truncated having control over only the Asian and African provinces. Mehmud II died of tuberculosis.

Abdul Majeed I (Abdülmecid I in Turkish) was the son of Mehmud II who succeeded his father on July 2, 1839. He reigned at a time when the nationalist movements had begun in quite a few provinces that were under the control of the Ottomans. He tried to suppress them but could not achieve much success. The first rebellion that he had to deal was that of Egypt. The governor of the province, Muhammad Ali Pasha, had almost become an independent ruler of Egypt and had also taken control of the Empire's naval forces. Abdul Majeed could resolve only through diplomatic means. The signing of the Convention of London in 1840 could nominally restore the Ottoman control over Egypt but Muhammad Ali Pasha continued to be the governor with nearly self-ruling powers.[113] The Ottomans were a part of an alliance of France, the United Kingdom, and Sardinia that successfully fought the Crimean War of 1856 in which Russia was defeated. The Treaty of Paris that was signed on March 30, 1856 restored to the Ottoman Empire almost all the Ottoman territories that the Russians were in possession. Nonetheless, Abdul Majeed I's endeavour to take back the lost territories in the Balkans was not successful and in 1861, he was forced to agree to the dominance of France over Lebanon. The Congress of Paris of 1856 officially included the Ottoman Empire as part of the European comity of nations.

Abdul Majeed I continued the process of reforms that was

undertaken by his father. The most remarkable feat that he attempted to implement after 1856 in an overwhelmingly Muslim Empire was to announce complete equality of the residents of the Empire irrespective of race, religion or language. This was perhaps for the first time that a Muslim state that also claimed to be the Caliphate, made available the equal social, economic and civil rights to non-Muslims along with the Muslim population. As expected this judicious set of reforms was bitterly opposed by the Muslim political elite and the regressive ulama. He also issued a command according to which the wearing of the traditional turban was banned and the use of the fez was encouraged. A number of conspiracies were also hatched to assassinate the Sultan. Nevertheless, like his father, Abdul Majeed I too died of tuberculosis at the age of 39 on June 25, 1861. The following are the most significant reforms that were brought about by Abdul Majeed I:

1) Introduction of the first Ottoman paper banknotes (1840)
2) Reorganization of the army, including the introduction of conscription (1842–1844)
3) Adoption of an Ottoman national anthem and Ottoman national flag (1844)
4) Reorganization of the finance system according to the French model
5) Reorganization of the Civil and Criminal Code according to the French model
6) Reorganization of the court system, establishing a system of civil and criminal courts with both European and Ottoman judges.
7) Establishment of the *Meclis-i Maarif-i Umumiye* (1845) which was the prototype of the First Ottoman Parliament (1876)
8) Institution of a council of public instruction (1846)
9) Creation of the Ministry of Education
10) Plans to send humanitarian aid of £10,000 (£24.83 million in 2013) to Ireland during its Great Famine, but later reduced to £1000 (£2.483 million in 2013) at the insistence of British diplomats.
11) Plans to abolish slave markets (1847)

12) Plans to build a Protestant chapel (1847)
13) Establishment of modern universities and academies (1848)
14) Establishment of an Ottoman school in Paris
15) Abolition of an unfairly imposed capitation tax which imposed higher tariffs on non-Muslims (1856)
16) Non-Muslims were allowed to become soldiers in the Ottoman army (1856)
17) Various provisions for the better administration of the public service and for the advancement of commerce
18) New land laws confirming the right of ownership (1858)
19) Decriminalization of homosexuality (1858)[114]

Abdul Aziz who succeeded Abdul Majeed I was the son of Sultan Mehmud II. Aziz took over on June 25, 1861 and reigned until May 30, 1876. He continued the process of modernizing Ottoman society with the same zeal that was displayed by Abdul Majeed I. He set up the new administrative districts across the Empire and also instituted a Council of State in 1868. The French model was followed for restructuring the modern education system and upgradation of Istanbul University in 1861.

He also concentrated on maintaining peaceful relations with major West European powers. As part of accomplishing this objective he visited Britain and some other West European countries. He happened to be the first Ottoman Sultan to do this. Queen Victoria of United Kingdom made him the Knight of the Garter in 1867. The same year he formally recognized the hereditary right of Muhammad Ali Pasha to be the *Khedive* (Viceroy) of Egypt and Sudan which made the provinces autonomous provinces under the nominal linkage with the Ottoman Empire. The financial situation of the Empire was far from satisfactory and the burden of foreign loans was the major burden on the Ottoman economy. Added to this there was rampant corruption in the administration. The Suez Canal was opened in 1869. Great Britain, in order to have its control over the Suez Canal, occupied Egypt and Sudan on the pretext of helping the Egyptian government suppress the Urabi Revolt.[115] Moreover, Cyprus also exercised greater autonomy and nominally remained an Ottoman territory until the outbreak of the First World War. When France that was Abdul Aziz's model European state was defeated by the North German Confederation in the Franco-Prussian War (1870-1871), the Ottoman Sultan made efforts to cultivate friendly relations with Russia to hold on to his presence in the volatile Balkans.[116] Though there were many reasons that posed severe challenges to the Ottoman Empire, the precarious financial condition coupled with an acute drought in 1873, which provoked his ministers, Rushdi Pasha, Husain Awni Pasha and Hasan Khairullah Efendi, to depose Abdul Aziz on May 30, 1876. A few days later he had allegedly committed suicide.[117]

The son of Sultan Abdul Majeed I, Murad V succeeded Abdul Aziz on May 30, 1876 and 93 days later, i.e. on August 31 was deposed. Murad V deeply absorbed himself in everything French be it administration, military, education or culture. This was one of the factors that led to his dethronement though the reason alluded to was his unsound mental condition.[118] He was a highly cultured and educated person who was a passionate votary of equality of all human beings. His opponents had spread trumped up stories about his abnormal behaviour that have been reported in the accounts of Muslim chroniclers. For instance, Aslam Jairajpuri writes: "Sometimes he would hug his personal servant or jump into the swimming pool with complete clothes on or sometimes would jump out from a window and run away."[119] The sustained campaign against him by his opponents could not allow him to introduce a modern and progressive constitution that he had intended to do. The instability caused by Murad V's dismissal encouraged Alexander II of Russia to declare war against the Ottomans that led to devastating consequences for the Empire. After dethronement, Murad lived almost like a prisoner in the royal palace and died on August 29, 1904.

The thirty-fourth Ottoman Sultan Abdul Hamid II was the son of Abdul Majeed I who ruled between 1876 and 1908. He was the last Sultan who could exercise absolute powers. At the time of his accession it was expected that he would introduce progressive and democratic reforms to transform the Empire into a civilized and responsible political power. On the contrary, within two years after taking charge, he suspended the constitution and parliament and became an autocratic ruler. Abdul Hamid II was severely criticized across Europe and also within the Empire because of the Ottomans' war with Serbia and Montenegro and the ruthlessness with which he suppressed the Bulgarian revolt. Russia declared war against the Ottomans on April 24, 1877. No European power made a common cause with the Ottomans though the British Empire had reasons to be worried about the Russian policy of expansionism. Fighting against the mighty Russians on its own was a daunting task for the Ottoman army. The result of the war was, therefore, on expected lines. The Russian forces inflicted heavy losses on the Ottoman army and concluded the war in their favour in February 1878. The peace came in the form of the Treaty of San Stefano that was full of harsh terms against the Ottomans. The Ottoman Empire was to award independence to Romania, Serbia and Montenegro. It was forced to concede autonomy to Bulgaria and introduce people-friendly reforms in Bosnia and Herzegovina. The Ottoman Sultan was coerced to relinquish Dobrudzha to Romania and Armenia to Russia. After such a humiliating defeat he made a decision to do away with the posturing of constitutionalism. After suspending the constitution and parliament in February 1878, Abdul Hamid ruled the Ottoman Empire as a despot for the next three decades.[120]

The terms of the Treaty of San Stefano alarmed the British Empire and Austria because of too many concessions that were given to Russia. In order to attain a balance of power among the European nations, a conference was held at Berlin under the chairmanship of German Chancellor Otto von Bismarck. It opened on June 13, 1878 and after hectic deliberations for a month many significant decisions were taken that *inter alia* included restoration of Armenia to the Ottoman Empire with a rider that the Sultan would introduce constitutional reforms in the province. Abdul Hamid II did not take the trouble to abide by the decision reached at the Berlin Conference. Consequently, the Armenians began their agitation around 1890 demanding reforms. In order to offset Armenian agitations, the Sultan empowered the Kurdish people of the province by conferring on them the semi-official status. This move deteriorated the situation further because the Kurds, in alliance with the Turkmani people, were already ill-treating the Armenians. The alliance of Kurds and Turkmanis was known as *Hamidiye Alaylari* (Hamidian Regiments) that would frequently attack the Armenians and confiscate their properties.[121] In order to counter the hooliganism of the Hamidian Regiments (HR), the Armenians formed their militant organization, the Armenian Revolutionary Federation (ARF). As a result the violent clashes between the HR and the ARF turned into routine phenomena. Sultan Abdul Hamid used excessive force, mostly against the Armenians, to suppress the unrest. Consequently, it is reported that about 300,000 Armenians were massacred in a few years. When the news of the ghastly occurrences travelled to Europe and the USA, Sultan Hamid was attacked in the worst terms in the international media. He was referred to as the 'Bloody Sultan'.[122] On July 21, 1905, the ARF made an assassination attempt on Abdul Hamid when he was to make a public appearance. The attempt, however, failed as he was late to the venue by a minute and the car bomb went off on the pre-set time killing 26 innocent people. In the aftermath of the Armenian massacre the Western powers, nonetheless, adopted a stern approach towards the Ottoman Empire.[123]

The emergence of a revolutionary group, the Young Turks, needs our attention as it ultimately caused the removal of Abdul Hamid II and also brought about momentous changes that changed the fate of the Ottomans. Young Turks were opposed to the conservative and autocratic rule of Abdul Hamid II and demanded socio-political reforms conducive to the changing times. Apart from a faction of the army, there were two ideological groups that constituted the Young Turks. There were liberals, most of whom belonged to the upper strata of Turkish society. They desired a liberal government that would encourage free market economy. They also favoured guaranteeing of autonomy to the religious and ethnic minorities of the Ottoman Empire. The other faction was composed of people who mostly belonged to the lower classes who aspired to preserve the Empire and were known as the Unionists. Their major demand was the establishment of a secular government. Though both factions demanded the restoration of the Constitution of 1876, their ideological differences remained intact.

The immediate cause of the Young Turk Revolution was the Anglo-Russian Convention of 1907, according to which the two powers were planning to control Persia which was the eastern front of the Ottoman Empire. The two European powers had also planned to eliminate the Ottomans from the Balkans and divide the region between themselves. In response the Ottoman army stationed in the Balkans raised the banner of revolt against Abdul Hamid II. Niyazi Buk and Anwar Buk[124] were the military commanders who led the revolt in July 1908 against the Sultan and demanded a constitutional government based on the Constitution of 1876. Initially Abdul Hamid II tried to suppress the uprising but the popularity of the revolutionaries among the people who had raised the slogan of *Ottomanism* did not leave any other course for the Sultan except accede to the major demands of the Young Turks. Abdul Hamid II restored the Constitution of 1876 on July 24, 1908 and thereafter the revolutionaries forced him to surrender all the powers.[125]

In the ensuing general elections held in 1908, the Committee of Union Progress got a majority in the Union Legislature and the session of the Senate of the Ottoman Empire was convened after a gap of 30 years on December 17, 1908. Abdul Hamid II, whose powers were drastically curtailed, made covert attempts to defeat the revolution by inciting a section of the army to demand implementation of *Shariat* in place of secular laws. The majority of the armed forces favoured the revolution and therefore, the reformist leaders removed Abdul Hamid II and put him under house arrest. He died in captivity on February 11, 1918.[126]

Abdul Hamid II was succeeded by his brother Muhammad Rishad who became the constitutional monarch of the Ottoman Empire with the regnal name of Muhammad V. Like many heirs of the throne before him, Muhammad Rishad was kept in custody in the royal palace for 30 years, nine of them he spent in solitary confinement. During this period he studied classical Persian literature and composed poems. He was a reputed poet. His titular monarchy commenced on April 27, 1909. Since the financial and military position of the Ottomans was shaky and taking advantage of this, Italy annexed the large territory of Tripoli. Thereafter, the Ottoman forces got engaged in a war in the Balkans against Bulgaria and Serbia. A short while later, Greece also declared war against the Ottomans. At many places in the Balkans the victorious Christian powers brutally massacred the Muslim population.

It was during these difficult times that a delegation of the Indian

Muslims led by the prominent Congress leader, Dr. Mukhtar Ahmed Ansari visited the Ottoman Empire under the auspices of the Red Crescent. Shoeb Qureishi, Abdur Rehman Siddiqui, Khailquzzaman Chaudhari were part of the 35-member delegation. Maulana Mohamed Ali mainly raised the funds for this delegation. Since it was essentially a medical mission, it performed the duties of tending the wounded soldiers of the Ottoman armed forces for eight months and returned to India in September 1913.[127]

The most significant event of the reign of Muhammad V was the Ottoman Empire's decision to join the Central Powers along with Germany and Austria in the First World War that was declared on November 11, 1914.[128] Interestingly, Muhammad V joined the war declaring a *jihad* in the capacity of the Caliph against the Entente Powers consisting mainly of Britain, France and Italy. Historically speaking it was the last jihad declared by a Caliph because hereafter the Caliphate was abolished in 1924. Muhammad V's death on July 3, 1918, just about four months before the end of the First World War, spared him the agony of the defeat of the Central Powers and with that dissolution of the Ottoman Empire.

Muhammad Vahiduddin (Turkish: Mehmed Vahideddin) was the brother of Muhammad V. He was the thirty-sixth and the last Ottoman Sultan with the regnal name of Muhammad VI who reigned between 1918 and 1922. His accession took place at a time when the Ottoman Empire found itself on the side of the vanquished Central Powers after the conclusion of the First World War and most territories of the Empire were about to be distributed among the Entente Powers. A short while before the enthronement of Muhammad VI, the Bolshevik Revolution was brought about in Russia, which was to be rewarded with a large chunk of Ottoman territory. In the post-Bolshevik Revolution period the USA joined the war on the side of the Entente Powers that sped up the defeat of the Central Powers and that came to an end on August 10, 1918.

At the post-War San Remo Conference held in Italy between April 19 and 26, 1920, was attended by the representatives of four main members of the Entente (Allied) Powers, viz. Britain, France, Italy and Japan. Among a bunch of resolutions passed at the conference was the one pertaining to the allocation of the former Ottoman territories of the Middle East under the Mandate System of the League of Nations. Prior to this the Allied forces had entered Constantinople and gradually the victorious forces started taking over the government institutions under their control. Muhammad VI had made an attempt to initiate peace negotiations with the British and he had also sent off a delegation to the Paris Conference held in June 1919. Since the Conference was focused on finalizing the peace terms with Germany that got expressed in the Treaty of Versailles, the issue of Ottomans was not taken for deliberation. The Allied had recognized the Greeks' claim over southern Albania, Thrace, western Anatolia and even Constantinople. Consequently, with the backing of the British, the Greek forces got control of the Smyrna port on June 15, 1918 and thereafter began taking control of the hinterland of Turkey.

In a series of peace treaties after the First World War, the Treaty of Sèvres was about the division of the Ottoman territories among the Allied Powers. In fact, France, Britain and Italy had secretly decided to divide the Ottoman territories as early as 1915 and the day they signed the Treaty of Versailles with Germany they had also signed a secret Tripartite Agreement to seal their mutual interests.[129] The Treaty of Sèvres was an open expression of their secret yearning that they were harbouring for long. The Treaty of Sèvres was signed on August 10, 1920 and immediately from then on began the division of the Ottoman territories among the Allied Powers that ultimately exterminated the Ottoman Empire. It not only deprived the Turks of the non-Turkish territories of their Empire but also snatched from them a large part of the Turkish territory as well. The Eastern Mediterranean lands were seized including Palestine and Syria that were given to Britain and France under the Mandate system.[130] The terms of the Treaty of Sèvres were so harsh that in comparison the Treaty of Versailles came across as a mellifluous charter. It was the culmination of Britain's secret craving to annihilate the Ottoman Empire from the face of the earth. The Kingdom of Hejaz, (the present Kingdom of Saudi Arabia) was recognized as an independent state though the British authority over it remained intact. Similarly Armenia was also acknowledged as an autonomous state.

The cruel terms of the Treaty of Sèvres served as the stimulus that was needed to stir the Turks out of the stupor of humiliation and defeat they had plummeted into. The nationalist movement was launched under the leadership of Mustafa Kemal Pasha. Though Kemal was a military commander, the nationalist Turks who had joined his resistance force did not have either the financial resources or enough weapons to drive the British, French and Greek forces out of their territories. It was sheer patriotism and national honour that enthused them to take on their powerful adversaries. Under the leadership of Kemal the Turks first defeated the French forces who had annexed Syria and south-eastern Anatolia. This was an outstanding victory in an extraordinary struggle the Turks were engaged in. The entire world of Islam was emotionally involved with the Turks. Nonetheless, Sultan Muhammad VI who was also the Caliph, under the British pressure declared Kemal Pasha and his supporters mutineers and confiscated their properties. He also awarded Mustafa Kemal Pasha, Fawwad Pasha, Dr. Adnan Buk, Rauf Pasha et al. the death penalty in absentia.

At this point Kemal Pasha signed a Unity Pact with Bolshevik Russia on March 21, 1921. Subsequently, Kemal could raise a resistance force of 2,00,000 dedicated freedom fighters and launched the attack against the Greeks who had taken possession of a large part of the Turkish territory. Kemal Pasha's soldiers fought with so much passion and patriotic fervour that the Greek army comprising 3,00,000 combatants with superior weapons was almost annihilated.[131] In view of the incredible and absolute victory of the Turkish forces led by Kemal Pasha, the Allied forces that were stationed at Constantinople promised to leave the Turkish territory and revise the peace terms. Accordingly, negotiations began at the Conference of Lausanne that opened on November 20, 1922. The representatives of Britain, France, Italy and Turkey participated in the deliberations. Turkey's representatives were Ismat Pasha, Riza Nur and the Jewish Rabbi Nahum. Lord Curzon, the British Foreign Secretary acted as the coordinator of the conference. The conference lasted for eleven weeks and concluded on June 4, 1923.[132] Turkey on its part accepted the British and French Mandate on Palestine and Syria respectively and the Allied representatives in return acknowledged the sovereignty of the Turks over Constantinople, Thrace, Anatolia and Asia Minor. Additionally all the sanctions imposed on Turkey were also rescinded. The Allied forces left

Constantinople on October 23, 1923.

Prior to this, on November 1, 1922, the Turkish Grand National Assembly had abolished the Sultanate and expelled Muhammad VI from Constantinople. On November 17 he left for Malta on a British warship. Two days later, Muhammad VI's first cousin Abdul Majeed II was elected the Caliph. Nevertheless, the nationalist leaders of Turkey soon realized that from the legal point of view, continuation of the Caliphate implied existence of two centres of power. Therefore, Abdul Majeed II was dismissed and in 1924, the Turkish Grand Assembly abolished the institution of the Caliphate. Until his death on May 16, 1926, in Sanremo (Italy), Abdul Majeed II was receiving a substantial annual retirement fund from the Nizam of Hyderabad.[133]

The Ottomans reigned for more than six centuries during which 37 Sultans ruled over the Empire, the territory of which kept varying at different stages of history. Speaking from the purely Islamic point of view, the first nine Ottoman rulers were Sultans and the rest till the last one, Abdul Majeed II were in addition to Sultans also the Caliphs.[134] The Ottomans were in control of the region around the Mediterranean basin because of which they had an advantageous position of lording over the Eastern and Western territories in Asia and Europe. The long reign spanning over six centuries could be broadly divided into two. First was the period of rise, expansion and prosperity and second was the beginning of decline and ultimate fall. Beginning from the founder of the great dynasty, Osman I in 1281 to the reign of Muhammad III that ended in 1603 was the period of the Ottomans' emergence, expansionism, prosperity, progress and grandeur. Though religious orthodoxy impeded the pace of progress and technology even during the first phase and its disasterous consequences could be noticed only in the second. For instance, the Ottomans lagged behind Europe mainly because of banishing emerging techonology such as the printing press for more than three centuries under the pressure of orthodox mullahs. While Christian Europe hugely benefited by the spread of new ideas and scientific research made easier by the printing of books, the Muslim world under the Ottomans failed to reap the benefits of emerging techonology because of the unwarranted interference by the mullahs in political and social spheres. With the inauguration of the reign of Ahmed I in December 1603, the rot got set that first led to stagnation and subsequently to defeats, losses, humiliation, decline and finally the annihilation of the Sultanate as well as the Caliphate with the dismissal and expulsion of Abdul Majeed II in 1924. In the reign of Bayazid I between 1389 and 1402, Taimur Lang (Tamerlane) had inflicted a severe blow to the Ottomans at the beginning of the fifteenth century that had subsequently divided the Ottoman Empire into three pieces, ruled by three Ottoman princes. At that point of time it appeared that the dynasty established by Osman I would not recover but the victory of Muhammad I over other claimants to the Ottoman throne rapidly restored the magnificence of the Empire.

The Ottomans had not only conquered most of the regions that previously were part of the Abbasid Caliphate in the East but also annexed the major part of the Balkans in Europe. The most significant event of the long reign of the Ottomans was the invasion of the capital of the Eastern Roman (Byzantine) Empire by a twenty-one year-old Ottoman Sultan, Muhammad II, who laid the siege to the famous city on April 6, 1453 and defeated the last Byzantine Emperor, Constantine XI, on May 29, 1453. Subsequently the Ottomans kept advancing westward and Suleyman the Great had even besieged Vienna in Central Europe. At their peak because of their capable infantry, experienced military commanders and formidable naval force, the Ottoman was not only the largest but also the most powerful Empire of the time. In 1583, when the grand armada of Spain was making plans to invade Britain, Queen Elizabeth sent out her emissary William Harborne to Constantinople with a request to the Grand Vizier of Sultan Murad III to help her country against the *Catholic Kuffar* (infidels) of Spain. Similarly, French monarch, Francis I, too had implored for help twice from Suleyman the Great, against Germany and Austria and on both occasions the Ottoman emperor had obliged.[135]

On the issue of Khilafat, the Ottomans though were aware of the religious significance of the institution and they also venerated it, most Sultans did not give much consideration to its temporal aspect, except invoking the title in times of difficulties to take advantage of the religious sentiments of the people of the Muslim world. For example, Sultan Mehmud had called upon his position as a Caliph by raising the ensign of the Prophet to suppress the revolt of the Ankashariya.[136] Since the Ottomans were the followers of the Hanafi school of Sunni jurisprudence, their Caliphate remained confined to the areas where Muslims subscribed to the Hanafi school. For the Shias and even for the non-Hanafi followers of the Sunnis, for instance, Malikis, the Ottoman Caliphate did not have any appeal. A tradition that had been in existence since the beginning that the Caliph or one of his representatives would lead the Muslim congregation at the time of Hajj was not adhered to by the Ottoman Caliphs. It showed their indifference to the ideas of universality or unity of the Muslim *ummah* or Pan-Islamism to which the Muslim activists from South Asia such as Jamaluddin Afghani and later Mohamed Ali Jauhar and his colleagues of the Khilafat Movement were committed to. This was perhaps one factor that was not completely gauged by the Pan-Islamists and Khilafatists from India and, therefore, they were hugely disappointed when the institution of the Caliphate was done away with by a modern democratic republic of Turkey in 1924. Many of them blamed it on the atheism of Mustafa Kemal Pasha while ignoring the rising tide of nationalism of popular governments in the Muslim-dominated countries. The institutions of Khilafat as well as absolute monarchy had outlived their relevance by the turn of the twentieth century and among the Muslim-dominated countries it was the people of Turkey who realised it first.

4

Khilafat Movement

To the Mussalmans swaraj means, as it must mean, India's ability to deal effectively with the Khilafat question. The Muslims of India are not to become impotent witnesses of the extinction of Turkey in Europe waters...in my humble opinion, attainment of swaraj is the quickest method of righting the Khilafat wrong. Hence, it is that for me the solution of the Khilafat question is the attainment of swaraj and vice versa.

– M.K. Gandhi

The Khilafat Movement was a foolish action, a lifeless lobby that had no correlation with Indian Muslims.

– Sir Muhammad Iqbal

I

Political consciousness among the large section of Muslims in India developed much later than among the Hindus mainly because of the hostile response of the elite of the community to Western civilization and modern education. The instantaneous reason for this was the decline of the Mughal Empire for which the Muslims held the British responsible. The Muslim ulama and the members of the aristocracy not only believed in the restoration of Muslim political power in India but also made desperate attempts to retrieve the lost glory. The Wahabi Movement[1] is a case in point. Secondly, the loss of political power had rattled the Muslim elites so much that they could not even visualize a proper course of action for the community to shape an adequately respectable position for the Muslims in the changed circumstances. Unlike Hinduism, Islam is an organized and much politicized religion. It was, therefore, not an easy task for the Muslim elites to devise an adaptable socio-political strategy to engage with the new political masters of India. The frightening prospect of living without political power was agitating the minds of the ulama because they or their forerunners had never faced such a thorny situation in the entire history of Muslim rule in India. Therefore, while the Hinduism were making concerted efforts to reform Hindu along scientific and rational lines and seizing every possible opportunity to acquire modern education, the Muslim elite were living in a fool's paradise cherishing a fantasy of revival of Muslim political dominance.

It took a blood-spattered uprising of 1857 to shatter their delusion and stir them out of the self-imposed stupor. By the time Syed Ahmed Khan (1817-1898) began his Aligarh Movement[2], the Muslims were already half a century behind in the race for the reforms in religion and acquisition of modern education. Though the project of religious reforms in Islam did not even take off, the Muslim elite, thanks largely to the stupendous efforts of Khan, gradually realized the significance of modern, scientific education. The disparity between Hindus and Muslims, however, in respect of education, a corollary of Muslim resistance to everything that was remotely Western, keeps persisting till today. The trajectory of Muslim social reform, though a later development, was similar to that of the Hindu reform movement. While the Aligarh Movement represented a modern, scientific and enlightened approach, a la Rammohan Rai's Brahmo Samaj, the Deoband Movement[3] of Maulana Qasim Nanotavi was a revivalist move like its Hindu counterpart, the Arya Samaj. The significant point, however, is that getting hold of modern, scientific education or its condemnation proved to be the starting point for the surfacing of political awareness both among the Hindus and Muslims. By the time the Khilafat became a political issue in India, the Aligarh and Deoband movements had produced many leaders who were capable of campaigning for the Muslim interests.

The first organized 'political' expression of Indians came into view in 1885 in the form of the Indian National Congress (INC). It was meant to be a nationalist forum of all Indians as its first President Womesh Chunder Bennerjee was a Christian, the second one, Dadabhai Naoroji was a Parsi and the third one, Badruddin

Tyabji was a Muslim. To begin with, the INC was an organization comprising the privileged section of Indians, most of whom had the advantage of modern British education. There were only two Muslims, Badruddin Tyabji and Camruddin Rahimtulla M. Sayani among the 72 delegates who atended the first session of the Congress in Bombay. The foremost reasons for Muslim apathy towards INC included its initial pro-British stance. In fact, it was a Scotsman, Allan Octavian Hume, who had motivated the educated Indians to establish an organization of their own as an interest group and it was with the approval of the Viceroy, Lord Dufferin, that the first session of the INC was held. The prime objective of the INC in its formative years was to seek a greater share in government jobs for the educated Indians. At that time the percentage of Muslims having modern English education was very low and despite Syed Ahmed Khan's valiant efforts, the overwhelming majority of the Muslims had remained violently opposed to the acquisition of modern, scientific education. For them, therefore, there was hardly any appeal in the objectives of the INC. All the same, the detractors of Syed Ahmed Khan argue that the negligible presence of the Muslims in the INC was because of his advice to the community to shun it. The critics also argue that such an attitude towards the INC infused a separatist tendency in the minds of the Muslims that ultimately resulted in the partition of the country. The Congress leaders never forgave and forgot Syed Ahmed Khan for it. Taking a cue from the Congress, the Hindu Right (that is always on the lookout to grab any opportunity to denigrate a Muslim cause or a Muslim leader) also joined the anti-Khan chorus. It was expected from the clear-headed leaders of the Congress that they should have analysed Khan's stance contextually with a dispassionate approach.

Syed Ahmed Khan did advise Muslims to shun the INC; however, his counsel was not the offshoot of any communal streak or separatism. At a time when he was struggling really hard to persuade Muslims to seek modern, scientific education so that they could also get benefits of opportunities made available by the British rule, he did not want the Muslims to get entangled in politics and lose motivation for educational development. The second reason that forced Khan to keep the Muslims aloof from the Congress was that he was sceptical about the success of the democratic form of government in India. He was of the opinion that since Indians were divided on the bases of religion, caste, language and culture, so a united national struggle that the INC was claiming to lead would not be successful and that a democratic form of government would not be established in India. Furthermore, he could not foresee that India would get rid of the British rule in the near future. He obviously erred on this count but he did not label the INC as a Hindu outfit. Also he did not encourage Muslim separatism, as many critics accuse him of. Syed Ahmed Khan's political ideas are devoid of communalism, Islamic revivalism or pan-Islamism. He was neither an enemy of the Congress nor hostile towards Hindus. In the words of R.C. Mujamdar, "Sir Syed was not so much anti-Hindu as he was pro-Muslim... It was not that he loved Hindus less but he loved the Muslims more."[4]

Separatist tendencies among the Muslim political elite (mostly the landed gentry of Northern India and the business classes of Bombay Province) emerged with the inception of the Muslim League in 1906, eight years after the death of Syed Ahmed Khan. It is incongruous to note that an organization, the Muhammadan Educational Conference, that Khan had established in 1886 with a rider that it would not take part in politics was itself converted into a political party. The annual session of the Muhammadan Educational Conference in 1906, was held at Dhaka where in the presence of more than 3000 delegates, the proviso dealing with a ban on politcal activities was removed by Muslim leaders like Nawab Sir Khwaja Salimullah, Ameer Ali, Sir Mian Muhammad Shafi, Sir Agha Khan III and others and transformed into a political party, the All India Muslim League. In the initial phase the key objectives of the Muslim League were to define and protect the civil rights of the community and secure the interests of the upper and gentry class of Indian Muslims. The formation of a political organization exclusively for the Muslims was obviously a setback to a united nationalist front that the INC was supposed to be. Though the League remained an elitist organization lacking a mass base, its very existence gave rise to fissiparous and communal tendencies.

With the intention of putting an end to the increasing state of distrust and hostility between the Hindus and Muslims, a commendable attempt was made in 1916 jointly by the leaders of the INC and the League with the signing of the Lucknow Pact. A few months before the actual signing of the Pact, the prominent leaders of the INC and the League convened the annual sessions of their respective organizations at Bombay in December 1915, and thus, could get the opportunity to interact with each other at one place for the first time. Subsequently, the members of the Imperial Legislative Council belonging to both the organizations submitted in October 1916, a joint memorandum to the Viceroy pertaining to the constitutional reforms. The British attitude towards the memorandum was far from encouraging. It, therefore, forced the leaders of the INC and the League to reiterate their suggestions regarding the future reforms in a joint meeting at Calcutta in Novemebr 1916. Thereafter, M.A. Jinnah, who at the time was a member of both the INC and the League because in those days there was no ban on dual membership, made a historic effort to convince the leaders of the two leading political organizations of the country to enter into a joint pact to put pressure on the British authorities to let Indians have a greater say in running the affairs of their own country. Jinnah's efforts got translated into the famous Lucknow Pact jointly entered into by the INC and the League in December 1916. It was because of this extraordinary feat, Sarojini Naidu gave Jinnah the title of "Ambassador of Hindu-Muslim Unity".

The main features of the Pact inter alia included: 1) There shall be self-government in India; 2) The number of Muslims in the provincial legislatures should be laid down province by province; 3) Muslims should be given one-third representation in the Central Government; 4) There should be separate electorates for all communities until they ask for a joint electorate; and 5) Half of the members of the Imperial Legislative Council must be Indians.[5] These were, therefore, the salient incidences of Muslim politics in India prior to the start of the Khilafat Movement.

A reference must also be made to another Muslim organization that was incepted the same year the Khilafat agitation was officially launched. Jamiat al-Ulama-e-Hind was established in 1919 by the leading Islamic scholars of the time such as Maulana Mehmood Hasan, Maulana Syed Hussain Ahmad Madani, Maulana Ahmed

Saeed Dehlvi, Mufti Kifayatullah Dehlavi, Mufti Muhammad Naeem Ludhianvi, Maulana Ahmad Ali Lahori, Maulana Bashir Ahmad Bhatta, Maulana Syed Gul Badsha, Maulana Hifzur Rehman Seoharvi and Maulana Abdul Bari Firangi Mehli. Though the ulama associated with the Jamiat were essentially men of religion, they chose for themselves the task to guide the Muslim community in political matters too. Mufti Kifayatullah while presiding over the Amritsar convention of the Jamiat in 1919, explained the need for a separate association of the ulama "through which they could speak with a united, authoritative voice, thus increasing their influence in the community. The divines remained wary of subordinating themselves to the Westernized Leaguers."[6]

The prime objectives of the Jamiat that were spelled out in the Amritsar meeting itself included providing leadership according to Islamic law in all matters concerning the Muslims, establishing fruitful contacts with the rest of the Islamic world, and promoting an amicable relationship with the non-Muslims of India. Along with these lasting aims the Jamiat in 1919, also addressed a specific issue that was troubling the Muslim political elite at the time, i.e. the issue of Khilafat. Though the resolution pertaining to the Khilafat issue was vaguely drafted, it did urge the government to pay attention to the Khilafat issue without delay or "the government will have great difficulties."[7] In this respect, the Jamiat's approach concurred with that of the Khilafat Movement. The only difference that could be pointed out was that the Central Khilafat Committee (CKC) focused mainly on protection of the institution of Khilafat while the Jamiat took upon itself the task of guiding the Muslims in all matters, political and non-political in the light of the teachings of Islam. A sensible characteristic of the Jamiat has always been its advocacy of nationalism. It, in fact, justified the concept of nationalism in the light of Islamic tenets and it was for this reason that in later years the many ulama associated with it strongly opposed the movement for Pakistan. In independent India the Jamiat maintains that the Muslims have entered into a mutual agreement with the non-Muslims and that agreement is the Constitution of India. They find a parrallel in the early Islamic history of such a mutual agreement that was signed between the Muslims and the Jews of Medina.[8]

II

Ottoman Turkey had entered the First World War (1914-1918) as an ally of the Central Powers and at the conclusion of the war found itself on the side of the vanquished nations. It was an earth-shattering event in the history of Islam because the Sultan of Turkey was also the Caliph, though merely titular, of all the Muslim nations of the world. The Armistice of October 1918, the Treaty of Versailles of 1919 and the occupation of Istanbul by the Allied forces, made the position of the Caliph extremely indeterminate and the very existence of the Ottoman Empire was in doubt. The defeat and the subsequent developments stunned the Muslims across the world. Indian Muslims, in particular, were too concerned about the fate of the holiest sites of Islam, viz. Mecca and Medina that were till then the part of the Ottoman Empire. They feared that Britain and its allied powers could enter the sacrosanct area of Hejaz, which was out of bounds for the non-Muslims, and desecrate the Kaaba at Mecca and Mosque of the Prophet at Medina. For the devout Muslims it was something that they had not envisaged in their wildest nightmares. At the end of the war, however, they had to face this agonizing possibility.

In order to take some immediate and appropriate action to save the holiest sites of Islam from desecration at the hands of the 'infidels', the Muslims of Bombay (now Mumbai) took the initiative to organize a protest meeting. It is a historical fact that must be underscored in no uncertain terms because almost all the historical accounts of the Khilafat Movement in India though refer to the Bombay protest meet chronologically as the first one but do not acknowledge the verity that the Muslims of Bombay had taken the initiative and that the Khilafat Movement was born in Bombay. The first protest meet to save the Khilafat was held on March 19, 1919, at Khadak (Dongri). A crowd of more than fifteen thousand Muslims of the city belonging to different walks of life, businessmen, educationists, lawyers, doctors, theologians, journalists and workers, participated fervently in the proceedings of the meet giving expression to their anguish and sense of helplessness in the face of, what they perceived, the worst scenario in the history of Islam. The major decision that was taken in the meet was to establish the Bombay Khilafat Committee under the chairmanship of Mian Muhammad Haji Jan Muhammad Chhotani[9] (1873-1932). The names of other members of the proposed committee were also finalized that included persons belonging to both sects, Sunni and Shia, of Islam.

As a first step the Bombay Khilafat Committee passed a resolution to submit an appeal to the Viceroy of India expressing concerns of the Muslims of India regarding the Khilafat and the protection of the sanctity of the holiest shrines of Islam. Mr. Chhotani, who was entrusted the task of submitting the appeal, was squarely rebuffed by the Viceroy who contemptuously threw out the appeal of the Muslims. Consequently, the Bomabay Khilafat Committee held another meeting on July 5, 1919 in which it was resolved to enlarge the area of its activities and for that purpose it made a decision to establish branches of the Committee in all the major cities of British India. Initially the main objectives of the Committee were two: first to impress upon the British to allow the Caliph to retain the temporal powers and two, to ensure the continuation of the Caliph's sovereignty over Mecca, Medina and Jerusalem.

Many scholars insist that the Khilafat Movement was the first organized expression of pan-Islamism of the Muslims of British India.[10] It is also argued that the ever-growing Hindu political ascendancy forced the Muslims to appeal to the supranational character of their faith to try to find some emotional solace in a desperate situation the *ummah* was confronted with in India and abroad. This seems to be a reasonable argument but beyond seeking emotional solace a pan-Islamic movement could hardly help the Muslims of India in tangible terms. Secondly, as has been mentioned above, the Khilafat Movement was initiated by the Muslims of Bomabay and most of them belonged to the trading communities of Kutchi, Khoja and Halai Memon. Though they were financially well-heeled, they lacked the intellectual aptitude to invent an ideological category for their initiative. Many of those who attended the first meeting of the Khilafat Movement were loyal citizens of the British Raj; they did not have any supranational loyalty. They were rattled mainly because of the impending threat of desecration to the holiest Islamic shrines located in the Arab peninsula. In later years when the Movement came to be dominated by north Indian Muslims and many of them, like the Ali brothers, Maulana Shaukat Ali[11] (1873-1939) and Mohamed Ali[12] (1878-1931), were the products of Aligarh's M.A.O. College, the discourse of pan-Islamism was started, not by all, but a few prominent leaders of the Movement.

Another point that needs a serious consideration is that the Movement, like all movements in those days, was directed by the Muslim elites and the masses were used for the show of strength in public meetings. Now, the Muslim elites were also not a monolith in ideological terms. Besides, the dominant faction of the Ali brothers, there were nationalist Muslims in sizable number who were part of the freedom struggle of the Congress. With Gandhi, the prominent Muslim Congress leaders did become part of the Khilafat Movement too but they obviously did not have any pan-Islamic aspirations. The involvement of the Congress in the Khilafat agitation inspired lakhs of Hindus to campaign for a Muslim cause bestowed a nationalist characteristic to the Khilafat Movement. Though it lasted for barely two years, the period between 1919-1921, during which the twin agitations of Non-cooperation and the Khilafat were concurrently kept going, was the pinnacle of true nationalism and Hindu-Muslim unity.

On the call issued by the Muslim League Council, more than four hundred delegates from different parts of India attended the All India Muslim Conference held at Lucknow in September 1919. Among its convenors there were prominent Muslim leaders like Sir Ibrahim Harun Khan Jafar of Poona, Sayyid Zahur Ahmed of Lucknow, Nawab Sir Zulfiqar Ali Khan from Punjab, Sir Fazilbhai Currimbhai of Bombay, Seth Haji Abdullah Harun of Karachi, Fazlul Haq of Calcutta, Dr. M.A. Ansari and Hakim Ajmal Khan of Delhi, Syed Raza Ali, a leading Shia barrister from UP and many others. It must be noted that the Raja of Mahmudabad was also present at the Conference and till then was also a supporter of the Khilafat agitation. He wanted Harun Khan Jafar to preside over the Conference while Maulana Salamatullah of Firangi Mahal and Hasrat Mohani asserted that Maulana Abdul Bari of Firangi Mahal should be the president. After much haggling a compromise was reached that Bari would preside over the morning session and Jafar would be the president of the afternoon session. Secondly, the Raja of Mahmudabad favoured a conciliatory approach involving submission of a petition to the government about the Khilafat issue, whereas the group led by Bari insisted on an agitational approach. This caused a serious rift between the two factions. Flustered by the disagreeable developments, the Raja of Mahmudabad decided to dissociate himself from the activities of the Khilafat Committee.[13]

In addition to 400 delegates representing almost every part of British India, thousands of people were in the audiences. The Conference passed quite a few resolutions including the one that appealed to the British Empire to uphold the religious position of the Turkish Sultan who was also the Caliph and let him exercise his temporal powers. Another resolution pertained to disapproval of severance of Syria, Palestine and Mesopotamia (present-day Iraq) from the Ottoman Empire. Besides sending the resolution to the Crown a copy of it was also mailed to the British Prime Minister. In order to express their grief and apprehensions it was also decided that the Indian Muslims would observe 'The All India Khilafat Day' (*Kul-Hind Yaum-e- Khilafat*) on October 17, 1919. It was at the Conference that the Bombay Khilafat Committee was christened as the Central Khulafat Committee which was sometimes also referred to as the All India Khilafat Committee, with Bombay as the headquarters. Thereafter, a chain of Khilafat Committees materialized in various provinces. The Conference also elected Mian Muhammad Jan Muhammad Chhotani as the President and, in absentia, Maulana Shaukat Ali as the General Secretary of the Central Khulafat Committee.[14]

The first meeting of the Central Khilafat Committee (CKC) was held between November 21 and 23, 1919, at Delhi. Gandhi's participation in the meeting made it one of the most significant events of India's freedom struggle. The support of Gandhi and later of the entire leadership of the Indian National Congress to the Khilafat Movement made it one of the strongest protest campaigns against the British Raj. Nonetheless, the alliance of the two differing schools of thought was not without controversy. For instance, Mohamed Ali Jinnah who was then with the Congress objected to the alliance on the ground that the Khilafat was purely a religious issue and a secular-nationalist movement like the Indian National

Congress had no justification to put it on its agenda. However, both Gandhi and the leaders of the Khilafat Movement had their respective rationale to join with each other. For Gandhi, it was a godsend opportunity to involve the lot of the Muslims in the freedom struggle and make the Indian National Congress a truly all-inclusive nationalist movement, which it was not till then because of Muslim separatism. For the Khilafat leaders it provided a possibility of strengthening their movement by involving a nationalist organization like the Congress.

Gandhi had, in fact, lent his support to the Khilafat Movement prior to attending the first meeting of the CKC. He had issued an appeal to the Congressmen and the Hindus to team up with the Khilafat agitators in observing 'The All India Khilafat Day' on October 17, 1919. The Khilafat Day met with extraordinary success as the history of the freedom struggle had not witnessed such a public display of Hindu-Muslim unity before. The strike was almost total across the country; both Hindus and Muslims observed a fast on the day and many of them were seen engaged in prayers. Markets, schools, colleges and courts were closed. Gandhi addressed a huge gathering in Bombay. In Madras, a crowd of about 20,000 comprising Hindus and Muslims gathered on the beach and peacefuly observed the Khilafat Day. In Calcutta, Fazlul Haq addressed a massive gathering. The Khilafat Day was successfully observed in other parts of Bengal as well. The biggest crowd, however, gathered in a protest meeting in Delhi. More than 50,000 people were present in the audiences that were addressed by Dr. M.A. Ansari, Swami Shradhanand, Mufti Kifayatullah and Asaf Ali (Secretary of the Delhi Khilafat Committee).[15] Besides the Ali brothers Maulana Abul Kalam Azad, Hakim Ajmal Khan and Hasrat Mohani were also active members of the movement. In order to transform an essentially religious movement into a truly broad-based national struggle against British imperialism, Gandhi linked it up with the Jallianwala Bagh tragedy and made it a part of the overall Non-Cooperation Movement. This was a master-stroke to attain the objective that was so dear to the Mahatma, the Hindu-Muslim unity. Gandhi's strategy brought in the desired result as almost all Indians, Hindus, Muslims and Sikhs turned into a monolith nation, perhaps for the first time, against the British.

The most significant resolution that was passed in the first meeting of CKC held in Delhi was to send a delegation[16] to meet the British Prime Minister, Lloyd George and submit to him a petition to address the grievances of the Muslims that emanated from the British policy towards the vanquished Ottoman Empire. The other resolution included a boycott of peace celebration that the government had planned after the conclusion of the First World War, an appeal to all Indian Muslims to adopt a policy of 'Non-cooperation' towards the government and another one, which was moved by Hasrat Mohani, was about 'progressive boycott of European goods'. Mohani's resolution generated heated debate because Gandhi, Seth Chhotani and other businessmen present did not favour it. Despite controversy the resolution was passed. It was, undoubtedly, a setback to the group of Bombay-based Khilafatists, most of whom were businessmen and for that reason did not favour a thoroughly confrontationist strategy to take on the government on the Khilafat issue. The Delhi-UP group was dominated mostly by those who favoured direct confrontation with the British on the issue. They were also planning to shift the headquarters of CKC from Mumbai to either Delhi or Lucknow. Though, they could not succeed on this count in the Delhi Conference, they did not abandon the plan.

Later, presiding over a Hindu-Muslim Unity Conference, Gandhi declared that the British Government had not only rejected the demands of the Muslims but also failed to take any cognizable action against General Dyer, the butcher of Jallianwala Bagh. The other prominent Hindu leaders present at the meeting were Swami Shradhanand, Jawaharlal Nehru and Pandit Madan Mohan Malviya. The widespread rumour at the time was that the Hindu leaders had reached an understanding with the Muslims according to which the Muslims agreed to stop slaughtering cows if the Congress supported the cause of Khilafat. Nonetheless, Gandhi asserted that the Congress support to the Khilafat cause was because the Muslims were justified in their protest. In his opinion the Hindu-Muslim solidarity was the healthy campaign for a nationalist cause. Nevertheless, Gandhi advised Indians to wait for the outcome of the meeting between the members of the CKC and the British Prime Minister and in case no concrete assurance was given by the British, the Congress and the CKC would jointly launch the Non-Cooperation Movement.[17]

The ulama were also in the forefront against the British on the issue of Khilafat. A mention must be made of Maulana Abdul Bari of Firangi Mahal, Lucknow who had convinced all the ulama of India, irrespective of sect, to sign an edict (*fatwa*) declaring the Sultan of Turkey as the legitimate Caliph of the Muslims of the world. The fatwa also stated that anyone challenging the Caliph would be opposed tooth and nail even if he was a descendant of the family of the Prophet. The inclusion of this expression was thought to be necessary because the British had suggested appointing Sharif Hussain as the Sultan and the Caliph in place of Sultan Abdul Hameed of Turkey. The other ulama too got themselves involved in the anti-British agitation. Mufti Kifayatullah announced, on November 25, 1919, the establishment of an organization of the ulama of India, the Jamiat-al-Ulama-e-Hind. He also declared that Hindu-Muslim unity was the treasured principle of the Jamiat. Mufti Kifayatullah announced that a meeting of the Jamiat would be held in the last week of December, 1919, in Amritsar, the venue where both the Congress and the Muslim League were to hold their respective sessions. The Jamiat had also announced to join the Non-Cooperation Movement.

A meeting of the Bombay Khilafat Committee was hurriedly convened on December 22, 1919 in the office of Muhammad Ali Khan. The details of that are as follows:

> The members who attended the meeting were: 1) Mian Mohamad Jan Mohamed Chhotani; 2) Mirza Ali Mohamed Khan, Solicitor; 3) Honourable Mr. Sheriff Devji Kanji; 4) Ahmed Haji Sidik Khatri; 5)Badruddin Abdulla Koor; 6) Moulvi Abdul Rauf; 7) Hakim Abu Yusuf Isphani; 8) Rafai; 9) Khan Bahadur Mahomedali of Taher and Company; 10) Mohamed Abba Juma; and 11) R. M. Chinoy. The issues that were discussed inter alia included the suggestions made in the Delhi Conference, viz. the boycott of British goods and Non-cooperation with the government. All members present with the exception of Koor and Rauf opposed the suggestions. It was ultimately decided to appoint a sub-committee to draft a reply to the CKC stating that its resolution passed at the Delhi Conference was neither feasible nor workable. The reply was to be presented before the CKC Conference that was to be held at Amritsar. The sub-committee

consisted of: 1) Chhotani; 2) Sheriff; 3) Faiz Tayabji; 4) Hadi Tayabji; 5) Khatri; 6) Rauf; 7) Isphani; 8) Haji Ismail Haji Muhammad; 9) Oomar Sobhani; and 10) Khan Bahadur Muhammadali of Taher and Company

When these crucial actions were underway, the Ali Brothers were serving a two-year term in jail for anti-British activities. They came out of jail just in time to go to Amritsar. A meeting of the CKC was, therefore, held in Amritsar. Maulana Shaukat Ali presided over the session attended by thousands that included all the prominent leaders of the time such as Gandhi, Motilal Nehru, Dr. Ansari, Hakim Ajmal Khan, Abdul Bari, Swami Shradhanand, Zafar Ali Khan, Pandit Malviya, Sayyid Husain et al. The CKC passed a resolution stating that if the British imposed un-Islamic peace terms on Turkey, the Muslims would be obliged to defend their faith. The vague manner in which the resolution was drafted was intentional because the Bombay-based Khilafatists would not have approved mention of any aggressive strategy for the defence of Islam. Moreover, in order to accommodate the Bombay pacifists, no resolution about economic boycott of European goods or adoption of the non-cooperative line of action was even moved. A decision was taken to obtain permission of the Viceroy to send delegations to England and America to explain Muslims'concerns about Khilafat. It was also resolved to send a delegation to Constantinople to pay respect to the Caliph. Then there were resolutions pertaining to reinforce the CKC. It was unanimously resolved to raise Rs. ten lakhs as 'Khilafat Fund' and to frame a constitution of the CKC. There was a general agreement on involving all the Muslims of India by opening branches of the Khilafat Committee in as many cities and towns as possible. Thereafter, the Ali brothers embarked on a tour of India spreading the message of Hindu-Muslim unity and appealing for donations to the Khilafat Fund. It was during these tours that the Ali brothers had emerged as the most popular icons of the Khilafat agitation. It must also be acknowledged that it was because of the activism of the Ali brothers that the Muslim masses, the least politically motivated segment of Indian society, got involved in Khilafat as well as Non-Cooperation agitations.

Mohamed Ali also drafted a petition addressed to the Viceroy of India imploring: to let the holy places of Islam under Muslim control; the sanctity of the position of the Caliph be honoured; and an ill reputed person like Sharif Hussain[18] should not be nominated to be the Caliph. The petition was signed by prominent leaders of the Congress and the CKC. Dr. M.A. Ansari submitted the petition to the Viceroy on January 19, 1920.

Having met the Viceroy, Mohamed Ali went to London as the leader of a delegation. His main objective was to put forward the issue of Khilafat before the British Prime Minister Lloyd George. The delegation comprised persons such as the renowned Islamic scholar, Maulana Syed Sulaman Nadvi, Syed Husain who had recently resigned from the editorship of the Allahabad-based paper, *Independent*, because of policy differences with Motilal Nehru, the owner of the paper. A close friend of Mohamed Ali, Hasan Muhammad Hayat was also part of the delegation in the capacity of his secretary. The composition of the group reflected the growing dominance of the north Indian Khilafatists, because there was no delegate from Bombay, the birthplace of the Khilafat agitation. The delegates met the Prime Minister on March 17, 1920. The Prime Minister haughtily informed the delegation that the British government would not allow the Turkish Caliph to rule over the Arab lands and that the Arabs would be given independence when they, in the estimation of the British, would be fully prepared for it. The discourteous response of the Prime Minister dismayed the members of the delegation.[19]

The delegates extended their stay lodging in a plush London hotel, undertaking journeys to Paris to meet journalists and diplomats, giving interviews to enlighten Europeans about the religious significance of the Caliphate for the Muslims. They also interacted with the delegates of the Peace Conference and went to Rome to meet the Pope and let him understand the religious magnitude of the Khilafat agitation. During this extended tour, Mohamed Ali cabled Chhotani requesting for more money that was needed for 'propaganda purposes'. Through a series of speeches, newspaper articles and interviews they made a frantic attempt to influence British and European people in favour of the Turkish Caliph who was the symbol of religious and emotional unity of the Muslims of the world. However, on all these activities, "they spent a great deal of money on travel, hotels, entertainment, and also contributed generously to the Red Crescent Fund for Turkish relief."[20]

The Khilafat leaders sent a medical team to Turkey led by Dr. M.A. Ansari with a message that Indian Muslims would always endeavour to protect the interests of Turkey and the Caliph. At a conference held in Bombay in February 1920, the Constitution of the Central Khilafat Committee was unanimously passed. The salient objectives of the CKC were described thus: 1) Central Khilafat Committee is to be depicted as the 'Centre of the Muslims of the world'; 2) the Arab peninsula where the holiest places of Islam are located must be proteced from non-Muslim control; 3) All possible efforts should be made to make India independent; and 4) (the CKC) should work for the religious, social, economic and educational welfare of Indian Muslims. The Constitution distinctly stated that the branches of the CKC should be established in all the provinces of India. It further explained the procedure of: a) electing the members of the executive committee; b) the nomination of fund collectors; c) selection of volunteers; and d) the method to finalize the delegates for the annual session of the CKC.

Nevertheless, a factional tussle was also on between the north Indian group led by the Ali brothers' mentor Abdul Bari and other Maulanas from Delhi, UP, Bihar, Bengal and Sindh (known as *Pirs*) on one side and the businessmen of Bombay led by Seth Chhotani on the other side. The internal strife led to a direct confrontation between the two factions in the February meeting. The contentious issue was Muslims serving in the army of the British. Maulana Abdul Bari, Maulana Azad Subhani of Kanpur, Maulana Daud Ghaznavi of Amritsar and a number of Pirs from Sindh insisted that the Muslims should leave the army because the British were likely to deploy them on some front to fight their Muslim brethren.The Maulanas also suggested to circulate a fatwa underscoring the provision of the Shariat banning such a service. The group comprising Seth Chhotani, G.M. Bhurgiri of Hyderabad (Sindh), Sir Fazilbhai Currimbhai of Bombay and Mirza Ali Muhammad Khan, a Bombay solicitor fiercely opposed the Ulama's proposal because of its illegality. Thus, the tussle turned into a conflict between the Shariat and the constitutional law of British India. Though the ulama exploited the majority of the members emotionally to pass their proposal, they could not afford to displease the Bombay businessmen for they needed their money. Consequently, the proposal was not put to vote.[21]

The passage of the Constitution of the CKC, was followed by conferences that were held at provincial levels. In the last week of February, 1920, the Bengal Khilafat Committee held its conference which was chaired by a young and upcoming freedom fighter, Maulana Abul Kalam Azad. In his well-expressed speech, Azad eruditely analysed the religious significance of Khilafat in the light of the Quran and ahadis and also spoke about the challenges that the institution was facing. It must be noted that Azad's view of Khilafat emphasized the religious as well as temporal powers of the Caliph. Though it was a correct reading of the institution of Khilafat historically, the ulama and activists of the Khilafat movement did not lay much emphasis on the temporal role of the Caliph. They were primarily concerned about protecting the religious position of the Turkish Caliph.[22] He also spoke at length about the Indian political situation. He justified the Muslims' demand regarding the continuation of the institution of the Caliphate and the protection of the holy places of Mecca and Medina from defilement.

The insensitive policy that the British had adopted regarding the Muslim concerns about Khilafat, forced the CKC to give another call for celebration of 'Khilafat Day' on March 19, 1920. Gandhi supported the call for a strike on March 19 but cautioned against violence and also disagreed with the programme of boycott of foreign goods because, in his view, it would be implacable and counter-productive. The prominent opponents of the observation of 'Khilafat Day' included M.A. Jinnah. The Bombay group of businessmen were also hesitant to go along with the resolution, which they felt was passed without taking into account their opinion. Prior to Khilafat Day, which was to be a day of complete strike, the Bombay businessmen called a consultative meeting of Hindu and Muslim leaders in Bombay. Maulana Abdul Bari, Shaukat Ali and Maulana Azad expressed disapproval of such a move. They argued that the time had come for non-cooperation with the British Raj. Consequently, most Indian shops and establishments remained closed on the day and Hindus and Muslim observed the day by offering prayers and peaceful public meetings. In Lucknow, special prayers were offered in the mosques in which the Shias who constituted a significant portion of the population of the city also participated passionately. This was indicative of complete unity of the Muslims on the question of Khilafat.

The Provincial Khilafat Committee of UP held its session in Meerut that was held between March 21 and 23, 1920. It was significant because it officially took the issue of non-cooperation for serious consideration. Though, the strategy of non-coperation got mentioned by many leaders at different meetings it was not passed as a resolution by the Khilafat Committee. The ulama belonging to the Jamiat were present at the session in large numbers. Besides Abdul Bari, Ahmed Sayeed of Delhi, Abdul Majid Badauni and Azad Subhani of Kanpur were also present. Also present was Maulana Habibur Rahman Usmani of Deoband seminary. He was nominated to preside over the session. Gandhi attended the session and linked the issue of Khilafat with that of the Jallianwala Bagh massacre as obtrusive examples of the British government's subjugation and brutality. In protest against British oppressive policies he announced the launching of the Non-cooperation Movement. He appealed to the Indians to: "1) Renunciation of titles; 2) Resignation from government service; 3) Resignation from the police and the military; and 4) Non-payment of taxes."[23]

A short while after the Meerut session, the Allied Powers forced Turkey to sign a treaty at the famous porcelain factory in Sevres, France. The Treaty's endorsement by Turkey on August 10, 1920, exemplified the end of the Ottoman Empire and with it the beginning of the end of the institution of the Caliphate. It is, therefore, appropriate to enumerate here the main provisions of the Treaty of Sevres to show how a document signed under daunting circumstances annihilated a nine hundred-year-old empire that had none but one parallel in the history of the world. The Allied Powers vindictively laid down extremely harsh conditions in the Treaty to seek retribution for the crushing defeat they met at the hands of the Turks in the Gallipoli campaign. It was, for that reason, Turkey was forced to renounce its control over non-Turkish lands. As per the terms of the Treaty, the Ottoman Empire's areas east to the Mediterranean were divided between Britain and France.

The Arab Peninsula with which the Muslims across the world were emotionally attached because of its significance as the birthplace of Islam and the location therein of the holiest sites of Mecca and Medina, was also seized by the Allied Powers which recognized the marionette contraption which they had installed during the course of the war by giving it the grandiose name of the Kingdom of Hejaz. Similarly, Turkey also lost Armenia which was declared an independent state. Turkey's loss was not merely in terms of territories; it also lost the control of its own finances to the Allies. As per the Treaty, the Allies were empowered to control and supervise the national budget and fiscal laws of Turkey. The Ottoman Bank too was taken over by the Allies. It was hardly surprising that the Allies put several military restrictions on Turkey. It could not maintain an army exceeding more than 50, 700 men and its navy was not allowed to possess more than seven sloops and six torpedo boats. So far as the air force was concerned, Turkey was prohibited to have it at all.[24]

The Hindu-Muslim camaraderie was further consolidated as a result of the publication of the Hunter Commission Report on the Jallianwala massacre and Turkish peace terms. The Hunter Commission Report was thoroughly criticized by Indians as an insensitive attempt to add insult to injury. Absolving Dyer of all charges of mass murder was a cruel joke, an exercise to play on the emotions of the hapless Indians. Also, the unjust terms of the peace agreement with Turkey enormously devastated the Muslims and the Raj was aware of this. In order to placate the agony of the Muslims, the Viceroy issued a statement that though the peace terms were not agreeable to most Muslims, the government was hopeful that they would not show any disloyalty towards the British. However, the anti-British sentiments among Indians were palpable that catapulted Gandhi and the Khilafat leaders to the peak of popularity. It was at this time that Gandhi linked the two issues—Khilafat and Jallianwala Bagh massacre—as examples of British cruelty and vengefulness and made them the major grounds for the Non-cooperation Movement. On May 12, 1920. A session of the CKC was held in Bomabay wherein Gandhi and Maulana Shaukat Ali appealed to all the members to support the launching of the Non-cooperation Movement. Some of the Congress leaders such as Motilal Nehru, C.R. Das and quite a few Muslim members of the Khilafat had reservations about the Non-cooperation Movement on the grounds of its unconstitutionality. Nonetheless, most Hindus and Muslims joined passionately the anti-British stir.

The Bombay businessmen too had objected to the call for resignation from the police and military service that was a part of the agenda of the Non-cooperation stir. They moved a proposal to delete it from the programme. Their effort, however, failed and consequently most Bombay businessmen resigned from the membership of the Committee.[25] Seth Chhotani, who was the president, on the other hand, decided to stay on and abide by the decisions taken by the CKC. Surprisingly, Gandhi who was earlier not certain about most of the Khilafatists' commitment to non-violence, decided ultimately to part ways with the moderate group of businessmen and supported the confrontationist strategy of Abdul Bari and Shaukat Ali. He, nevertheless, emphasized that during the Non-cooperation stir both Hindus and Muslims must not forsake the path of non-violence. Shaukat Ali assured Gandhi that the Muslims would not walk out on the policy of non-violence.

Consequently, in June 1920, another session of the CKC was convened at Allahabad to iron out differences among the members of the Congress and Khilafat Committee with respect to the Non-cooperation Movement. Annie Besant, was totally opposed to the non-coperation agitation. Motilal Nehru and C.R. Das and Pandit Malviya were sceptical about its efficacy while B.G. Tilak was also not certain about its success. Lala Lajpat Rai though he assured Gandhi of his support, did not approve of all the measures of the agitation. The cold response to Non-cooperation of some of the prominent members of the Congress saddened Gandhi. He was embarrassed to find out that he could not ensure complete support of the Congress to his Muslim friends. The Khilafatists themselves were divided on certain issues. Abdul Bari almost called Gandhi a betrayer. He along with the group of Pirs from Sindh advocated to start Non-coperation with or without Congress support while Saiyyid Zahur Ahmed, Raza Ali and Fazlul Haq suggested that to begin with Indians should only return their titles and the rest of the non-copertation agenda should be deferred temporarily. Shaukat Ali, Dr. Ansari and Ajmal Khan adopted an obscure middle stance. Surprisingly, Abul Kalam Azad was conspicuous by his absence. Perceptibly, it was resolved that the final decision would be taken at the Calcutta session that was to be held in September, 1920.

The situation among the members of the CKC was not significantly different. A few leaders did not favour the Non-cooperation Movement but an overwhelming majority supported Gandhi's suggestion. Therefore, the CKC passed the resolution to join the Non-Cooperation Movement under Gandhi's leadership. As a first step of protest the leaders of the Khilafat Committee decided to launch the Non-cooperation Movement on August 1, 1920. The Congress leaders had requested Gandhi not to launch the movement till the Congress session that was to be held in September at Calcutta. Nonetheless, Gandhi decided to go along with the date finalized by the Khilafat leaders. He observed: "When one has unshakable faith in a particular policy or action, it would be folly to wait for the Congress announcement...I dare not ask [my Muslim countrymen] to wait for any verdict but the verdict of their own conscience."[26]

Subsequently, Gandhi and Maulana Shaukat Ali toured the entire country asking people to shun cooperation with the British government. Their tour was enormously successful in the sense that wherever they went people, Hindus, Muslims and Sikhs thronged in large numbers to express solidarity with their cause. It was a defining moment in the history of the freedom struggle because prior to this, and sadly even afterwards, India could not witness the moving scenes of Hindu-Muslim camaraderie. The overwhelming public response to the Khilafat and Non-cooperation movements gave tremendous confidence to Gandhi and the Khilafat leaders and as per their agenda they began egging people on to return the titles conferred by the foreign rulers, shun state-run schools and colleges and establish their own educational institutions. Gandhi had also appealed to the lawyers to eschew the courts. Gandhi and the Khilafat leaders jointly urged the people not to participate in any way in the elections to provincial legislatures and municipal councils. In a nutshell, the people were counselled to stay away from all the activities that were carried out by the government.

The day, August 1, 1920, the twin agitations, Khilafat and the Non-cooperation movements were launched under the leadership of Gandhi, was also the day B.G. Tilak died. It impelled the agitators to take on, as a mark of respect to the departed freedom fighter, his legendary slogan—'Swaraj is my birth right'— as one of the catchphrases of their movements too. Though the Indian National Congress had not taken a decision either to support or reject the call of Non-cooperation, the provincial Congress committees had chosen to go along with the call of Gandhi. The provinces that took the lead in this regard were Bombay, Bihar and Punjab. What was significant was that despite C.R. Das's ambiguous stand on Non-cooperation, the Bengal Congress Committee made the decision to follow Gandhi's programme.

Around this time, Maulana Mohamed Ali returned from London and completely devoted himself to work under Gandhi's leadership since the cause that was very close to his heart, i.e. continuity of the Caliphate was very much a part of the ongoing agitation. Mohamed Ali was a fiery and imposing orater both in Urdu and English. His passionate speeches stirred the people of India to challenge the foreign rulers. Mohamed Ali, in particular, appealed to the Muslims to join hands with the Hindus in order to expel the British from India. At this point, the objective of India's independence became an integral part of the Khilafat Movement.

A special session of the INC was held at Calcutta to consider the Non-coopertion Movement that had already begun on August 1. Though the majority of the delegates approved Gandhi's programme, the opinions of some of the prominent members were at variance with the majority point of view. Lala Lajpat Rai was far from being enthusiastic to join the agitation. Other distinguished leaders such as Pandit Motilal Nehru, C. R. Das and Madan Mohan Malviya were opposed to the boycott of courts and provincial councils. M.A. Jinnah and Annie Besant were against the entire agitation. With the exception of Jinnah all the prominent Muslim members like Hakim Ajmal Khan, M.A. Ansari, Maulana Azad, Maulana Shaukat Ali, Mazharul Haq et al. stood behind Gandhi like a rock. This helped Gandhi to get the resolution passed in the Subject Committee though with a thin majority. The resolution got 138 votes in favour and 135 against it. In the open session though the Non-cooperation resolution was ratified with 1855 votes against 873. Nonetheless, the opponents of the Movement were hardly convinced because, in their estimation it would harm the interests of India. Lajpat Rai, who presided over the special session was not very enthusiastic about starting the Non-cooperation agitation but to make up for his lukewarm position he congratulated Muslims who used the real nationalist platform of the Congress to get approval for the Khilafat Movement. He acknowledged that the Muslims were the first to start the non-coperation and they had now the support of the Congress. "Lajpat Rai thus tried to smooth over any hard feelings as diplomatically as possible."[27]

Mohamed Ali reached Bombay on October 4, 1920 to invite Gandhi and his elder brother Maulana Shaukat Ali to Aligarh. That time M.A.O. College established by Syed Ahmed Khan was in the process of being converted into a complete university. It was, therefore, a loyal institution to the Raj. Mohamed Ali was particularly interested to take to pieces the loyal credentials of the A.M.O. College, which was his alma mater. Gandhi and the Ali brothers reached Aligarh on October 12 and without delay addressed the gathering comprising students, teachers and the trustees. They petitioned them all to join the Non-coperation and the Khilafat movements. They particularly appealed to the trustees to renounce taking government grants and convert the college into a truly nationalist institution. The trustees explained their position that they would better close down the college rather than acceding the demands of Gandhi and the Ali brothers. A section of the students, nonetheless, was eager to back the agitation.

Consequently, Gandhi and the Ali brothers decided to establish a truly nationalist institution that would cater to the needs of the youths who were opposed to the British rule. Thus, was born Jamia Millia Islamia, a parallel educational institute of the nationalists. The new college was inaugurated in the Aligarh College mosque by Maulana Mahmudul Hasan. In his speech Hasan stressed the point that non-coperation was a religious duty of all the Muslims. Therefore, the Muslim students should join it without hesitation.

They should listen to their conscience and should not follow the advice of their parents that might be against Non-cooperation. He suggested that Jamia Millia Islamia should adopt a curriculum that should be an amalgation of English education and religious education.[28]

Mahmudul Hasan, who had just returned from Malta, also known by the honorific Sheik-ul-Hind, was a Deobandi scholar who took part in the anti-British struggle. Having completed his education from Darul Uloom Deoband, Hasan joined it as a teacher in 1874. When the First World War broke out and Turkey, the seat of the Caliphate, joined the Axis Powers, Hasan became active to throw out the British from India. He chose the option of armed revolution and got engaged in encouraging his students to strike at the British Empire both in India and abroad. Quite a few students welcomed his suggestion and he sent some of them outside India to plan armed revolution against the British empire. Prominent among them were Maulana Ubaidullah Sindhi and Maulana Mohammad Mian Mansoor Ansari who were sent off to Kabul and the North-Western Frontier Province respectively to recruit foot soldiers to fight against the British. Hasan himself went to Hejaz to explore the possibility of setting up a military front with the Turkish support. He could get some kind of assurance in this regard from the Turkish Governor of Hejaz, Ghalib Pasha. The entire venture, which was audacious to say the least, was codenamed as the Silk Letter Conspiracy. The British intelligence agencies soon unearthed the plan and Hasan was arrested in Hejaz and imprisoned in Malta. After his release in 1920, he had reached Aligarh.

Jamia Millia was started first as a college and Mohamed Ali was appointed its first Principal. In the year of its inception Jamia was hardly an educational institution because the political climate under which it was born persisted for long. Mohamed Ali's lectures that were supposed to be on History and English were not academic orations but politico-religious speeches to motivate students to support Non-cooperation. However, Jamia played a significant role in mobilizing student support to Non-cooperation and the Khilafat agitations.[29] Later, when Jamia got the status of a deemed university, Zakir Husain was appointed the Vice-Chancellor of Jamia Millia Islamia who really worked hard to build up the nascent institute which was established not only without a government grant but also to oppose the British rule. It soon turned into a focal point of the nationalists who were associated with the Khilafat Movement. People like Dr. M.A. Ansari, who also served as the Vice-Chancellor, Khwaja Abdul Majeed, Hakim Ajmal Khan, Abid Hussain and Mohammad Mujib put in huge and self-sacrificing efforts to nurture the institution in the formative phase. In a sense, Jamia Millia Islamia is an offshoot of the Khilafat Movement. It must, however, be put on record that most students who joined the Non-cooperation and the Khilafat movements from Jamia and Aligarh colleges were Muslims; non-Muslim students were few and far between despite Gandhi's call.

The twin movements also got the crucial support of the ulama thanks to the enormous efforts by Maulana Mahmudul Hasan. Almost all the ulama throughout the subcontinent passionately advanced the cause of Non-coperation and Khilafat movements. Hasan appealed to the Muslim masses that it was obligatory for each Muslim to sacrifice everything for the cause of freeing India from the British. Maulana Abdul Bari also made similar pronouncements. He declared that anyone who cooperated with the infidels of the government would himself become an infidel. He also tried to secure the approval of a fatwa supporting Non-cooperation. The fatwa spelled that any kind of cooperation with the people who were hostile to Islam was prohibited under Shariat. Maulana Azad devoted himself to mobilize the support of the students for the twin movements. Maulana Shaukat Ali carried Gandhi's message to the common Muslims and appealed to them to follow the path shown by the Mahatma. For the entire year of 1920, Shaukat Ali travelled the length and breadth of the country with Gandhi. The two leaders were warnley welcomed wherever they went. Following their call many lawyers boycotted the courts, teachers and petty officers resigned from government services, the prominent people returned the titles conferred on them by the British, students left government owned educational institutions and many parents stopped sending their children to state-run educational schools and colleges. It was an astonishing phase of the freedom struggle when there seemed to be complete unanimity between the Hindus and Muslims.

The annual session of the Congress was held in the last week of December 1920 at Nagpur. Though a few delegates, including Jinnah, opposed the twin agitation of Non-cooperation and Khilafat, the overwhelming majority endorsed it. It was a momentous moment in the political career of Jinnah. The mammoth support that Gandhi got on the issue of Non-cooperation and Khilafat disrupted him so much that he left the Congress permanently. Once the resolution of Non-cooperation was passed at the Nagpur session, the ongoing agitation that was mostly confined to the urban centres spread to rural areas as well. Consequently the menial workers and the landless paeasants too joined the agitation and refused to cooperate with the landowning classes who had always been the stooges of the British. Along with Gandhi, the Ali brothers too bacame the cult figures all across the country.

As expected the repression by the government started with vengeance. The authorities first started arresting the editors of Urdu newspapers and periodicals because they were in the forfront in encouraging the non-cooperators and deriding the British. In October, 1920, Zafar Ali Khan, the editor of the Lahore-based daily *Zamindar*, was arrested on the charge of inciting people to violence against the authorities. Zafar ul Mulk the editor of *an-Nazir*, Lucknow, was convicted for seditious writings. Likewise, Tajuddin, editor of *Taj*, Jabalpur and *Khilafat* of Delhi was also put behind bars. Other prominent Urdu journalists who were asked to pay haeavy security deposits included Qazi Abdul Ghaffar of *Subah* (Delhi), Akram Khan of *Muhammadi* (Calcutta) and Habib Shah of *Siyasat* (Lahore). Also Asaf Ali, the secretary of the Delhi Khilafat Committee was warned for his activism about the Khilafat issue.[30]

It is pertinent here to say a few words about a remarkable woman, Bi Amma, who was perhaps the first Muslim woman to join the Indian freedom struggle. Born as Abadi Bano about 1850 in a respectable Muslim family of the native state of Rampur, Bi Amma played a substantial role in bringing up her five sons as unfaltering nationalists. Two of them, Shaukat Ali and Mohamed Ali ultimately became most prominent figures of the Khilafat Movement. Though herself illiterate, Bi Amma was intelligent enough to recognize the significance of modern education, in particular, for the Muslims of the subcontinent. She became a widow when she was not even 30, she did not abandon her resolve to give the best possible education to her children. She had to face many obstacles in implementing her plan to help her children get modern education. Besides financial constraints she had to face the fierce opposition of her family members. She defied all opposition and pawned her jewellery to finance her children's education in an English medium school and Aligarh College. Mohamed Ali was even sent to Oxford.

In the Muslim League session of 1917 held at Calcutta when her famous sons Shaukat and Mohamed were in jail she delivered a stirring speech that enthused Muslims across the subcontinent. Initially she appeared in burqa to address the meetings but later discarded it. Like any freedom fighter she constantly travelled goading people to join the Non-cooperation and Khilafat agitations. The moment she appeared on the stage to address any meeting the assembled crowd would shout two lines of a couplet that had in fact become a slogan of the Khilafat Movement—*Boli Amma Mohammad Ali ki/Jaan Beta Khilafat pe de do.* It is not known who had composed the couplet but it is counted among the most popular verses of Urdu. The failure of the Khilafat Movement distressed her a lot and about a year after it she died on November 13, 1924.

The intensity of anti-British feelings and the popularity of the twin-pronged agitation led by Gandhi and the Ali brothers unsettled the government so much that it started using force to suppress the popular demonstrations. It worsened the situation further as people refused to be cowed down. The use of force against the peaceful agitators resulted in loss of many lives in all the provinces of India. The unprecedented Hindu-Muslim unity demonstrated during this period frightened the foreign rulers who had thought that their strategy of 'divide and rule' would never fail in India. The schemers par excellence as they were, the British rulers, in addition to use of force, conspired in myriad ways to break Hindu-Muslim unity in repressive ways. Gandhi had strictly instructed his followers not to resort to violence under any condition. The Ali brothers advised their supporters not to react violently against government provocations. Despite these warnings, the agents of the government succeeded in dividing the agitators on communal lines because of which riots broke out in many towns. In order to bring the situation under control Mohamed Ali got into action. He toured the affected places and beseeched the people to maintain strict discipline and never renounce the path of non-violence.

Gandhi expressed his dismay over the divisive designs of the government and the agitators' violation of discipline in the Congrss meetings. In the Nagpur session of the Congress, held in December 1920, Gandhi was in complete control of the affairs of the organization. All opponents to the programme of Non-cooperation were rendered irrelevant. For instance, C.R. Das, the leader of the Bengal delegation and earlier a critic of Gandhi, moved the Non-cooperation resolution himself in the Nagpur session. M.A. Jinnah, nevertheless, remained steadfast in his opposition to Non-cooperation as well as Khilafat. When he realized that an overwhelming majority of the delegates in the session was behind Gandhi on the issue of Non-cooperation, he resigned from the Congress irreversibly. It was in this session that a Working Committee of the All-India Congress was instituted that was to have a stregth of three hundred members. Gandhi grandly declared that India would achieve Swaraj within a year.[31]

A short while after the Nagpur session a resolution was passed for the collection of funds to sustain the agitation. Gandhi called it the *Tilak Swaraj Fund*. Furthermore, an appeal was made to the Indian soldiers to abandon the military (the call was Mohamed Ali's idea though Gandhi did not endorse it) and the peasants were asked not to pay revenue. Gandhi, however, cautioned that under no circumstances should the principle of non-violence be forgotten. The drive for the collection of funds met with tremendous success as all sections of society, right from menial workers to the capitalists contributed voluntarily to the *Tilak Swaraj Fund*. By July 1, 1921, the last day of the collection of fund, more than a crore rupees were collected that was a huge amount in those days. The provinces that contributed generously to the fund included Bombay (Rs. 37.5 lakhs), Bengal (Rs. 25 lakhs), Gujarat (Rs. 15 lakhs) and the remaining amount was collected from other provinces. It was during this time that the popularization of the spinning wheel, Gandhi's pet project, caught the imagination of the people as this basic device of spinning reached countless towns and villages. The spinning wheel was a part of the overall programme of boycott of British goods. In the opinion of Gandhi, the spinning wheel epitomized the economic self-reliability of Indians.

In addition to the *Tilak Swaraj Fund,* the Ali brothers also collected donations for a separate *Khilafat Fund.* The Ali brothers had been engaged in raising funds for socio-political and religious causes of the Muslims. Earlier they had raised funds for Jamia Millia, Turkish relief, Anjuman-e-Khuddam-e-Kaaba and the Red Crescent. Now, collecting for the *Khilafat Fund* seemed to be a justifiable step by most supporters of the Khilafat. However, the collection of money for a separate fund sowed the seed of disunity between the Congress and the Khilafat leaders. The major contributors to these funds were mostly the businessmen of Bombay, many of whom like Seth Chhotani, Omar Sobani, Fazil Bhai, Karim Bhai and Haji Abdullah Haroon were also members of the Bombay Khilafat Committee. The Ali brothers trained volunteers to travel the length and breadth of the country and collect money by approaching people not only in big cities but also from small towns and villages. Small tea stall owners were asked to donate a day's profit every week to the *Khilafat Fund.* Furthermore, donations were also collected by selling Khilafat receipts in the denominations of one, five and ten rupees. Muslim women volunteers inspired by Bi Amma also got engaged in collecting money as well as gold and silver ornaments from middle class Muslim households of Northern India. The worst aspect of such a style of fund raising was lack of accountability.

After a year of active fund raising all across India, common Khilafatists expressed their misgivings about lack of transparency in the entire campaign of collection of funds. The Bombay businessmen who were the major donors were also wary of perpetual demands for money by the leaders of the Khlafat Committee. Though the demand for auditing the Khilafat Fund regularly was always expressed by ordinary members at meetings and the press, the top leaders did not pay much attention. When the criticism on the issue became louder, Shaukat Ali stated in March 1920, that the audited statement of the Khilafat Fund would soon be made public. However, nothing was done. Finally, the CKC appointed auditors to examine the accounts of the Khilafat Fund.

Many supporters of the Khilafat movement were taken aback when the expenditure of the Khilafat delegation to Europe was made public. Mohamed Ali and his colleagues had spent a huge amount by staying in plush hotels and travelling first class across Europe and justified it by saying that such an exorbitant amount of money was spent on 'propaganda'. It was true that the Khilafat delegation donated a considerable amount to the Red Crescent and some of the expenditure on propaganda was also justified but the common Khilafatists were not entirely satisfied by such justifications. Many fund raisers stopped collecting for the Khilafat Fund as the whole campaign was somewhat discredited in the eyes of the people. As a way out, at the beginning of 1921, the CKC started collecting money for another cause known as the Angora (Ankara) Fund.[32] The money collected for the Angora Fund was to be sent to the government of Mustafa Kemal Pasha who was valiantly engaged in the war with Greece over Smyrna (Izmir).[33]

By giving a new name to the exercise of fundraising, the Ali brothers succeeded in diverting the attention of the people from the mismanagement of the Khilafat Fund. Supporting Mustafa Kemal was another emotional issue for the Muslims and as expected donations started pouring in. Later the CKC tried to remove the aspersions cast on the Khilafat leaders, in particular, Mohamed Ali, by making public the accounts statement of the year 1920. The statements of the year 1921, nevertheless, were never published probably because the auditors refused to sign them because of the unaccounted excessive expenditure of Rs. two and a half lakhs during the European sojourn of the Khilafat delegates. This left suspicion lingering around the Khilafat Fund and in the process the image of the Ali brothers got a beating from which they never recovered completely.[34]

Besides Mohamed Ali's hyper-emotional nature also created a rift with the Congress. While addressing a huge gathering on the beach of Madras speaking about the loyalty of Muslims towards their motherland, Mohamed Ali went overboard and said that if any country attacked India with the intention of overpowering it, it would be the religious duty of the Muslims serving in the army to fiercely resist, even lay down their lives defending their country. On the other hand if a Muslim country, for instance Afghanistan, invaded India to defeat the British, it would be the duty of Muslim soldiers to join the invaders and help them vanquish the Indian army. This indiscretion shocked the Hindu audiences. The vision of Muslim soldiers of the Indian army joining hands with the forces of Afghanistan was frightening as, for many Hindus, it meant the revival of Muslim rule. Pandit Madan Mohan Malviya was quick enough to complain against Mohamed Ali citing his speech. Though Gandhi himself was perturbed by many statements of Mohamed Ali that were put across with a streak of violence, he could not admonish the Ali brothers at the time.

When the Non-cooperation movement was at the peak of popularity, Gandhi, therefore, attempted to justify Mohamed Ali in an article published in the issue of *Young India,* dated May 8, 1921. He wrote that in case Afghanistan invaded India to free it from the slavery of the British, he would also help the Afghans and ask Indians not to support the British. However, "he would not raise levies for the emir; that would be against his creed of non-violence." He rationalized by saying that this was probably what Mohamed Ali really meant.[35]

A meeting between Gandhi and the new Viceroy, Lord Reading took place in mid May 1921. The Viceroy broached the issue of the Ali brothers' pronouncements inciting people to violence. Gandhi refused to believe him. The Viceroy then showed him the selected portions of the Ali brothers' various speeches. Gandhi argued that such selective excerpts could be construed objectionable in isolation but if they were read contextually then they would not be provocation to violence. He, however, promised the viceroy that he would advise the Ali brothers not to make intemperate pronouncements in future. Gandhi met the Ali brothers after his meeting with the Viceroy. A short while later the Ali brothers' apology appeared in the press:

> Friends have drawn our attention to certain speeches of ours which in their opinion have a tendency to incite to violence, and we never imagined that any passages in our speeches were capable of bearing the interpretation put upon them. But we recognize the force of our friends' argument...We, therefore, ...express our regret for the unnecessary heat of some of the passages in these speeches, and we give our public assurance and promise to all who may require it that

> so long as we are associated with the movement of Non-cooperation, we shall not directly or indirectly advocate violence...

The reaction of the people and the press was very hostile. Their supporters and the pro-Khilafat journalists accused the Ali brothers of cowardice. Then, the government vexed the situation further by issuing a statement saying that though the authorities had decided to file criminal charges against the Ali brothers because of their utterances, "it was urged on the government that their immediate object could be obtained" without taking criminal action against them.[36]

The Ali brothers tried very hard to explain to their supporters that they did not issue the apology on the government's prompting and added that they had apologised to their countrymen and not the government. They were also unhappy with Gandhi for not hinting that he was giving them advice to apologise after discussing the matter with the Viceroy. Gandhi on his part explained that he advised the Ali brothers to apologise only to keep his movement untarnished and further added : "No non-cooperator can afford to go to prison on a false issue, certainly not on a denial of his faith, i.e. non-violence."[37] In the eyes of many of their supporters, however, the Ali brothers lost their image of 'fearless soldiers of Islam who could challenge even the mightiest British for defending their faith'. The loss of face was indeed very painful for both the brothers. The ordinary volunteers, in particular, Muslim agitators were, however, disappointed by the apology and many of them blamed Gandhi for this regrettable turn of events. Though Mohamed Ali still had complete faith in Gandhi's leadership, many Congress leaders thought that the Mahatma failed to see through the subtle machinations of the Viceroy. It was indeed a plot of the government to split the Congress and Khilafat leaders because the report that the Viceroy sent to the Secretary of State after his meeting with Gandhi squarely held Mohamed Ali responsible for all the violent incidents that had taken place. Mohamed Ali was also labelled as the principal link between the Hindus and the Muslims. This was a deliberate attempt to create a difference of opinion between the two stalwarts of the agitation that had unsettled the British government in India.

It was because of the bungling episode of apology that the Ali brothers, in particular, Mohamed Ali, adopted a more aggressive posture in their subsequent speeches. Addressing a Gujarat Provincial Khilafat meeting in Broach, on June 2, 1921, Mohamed Ali reaffirmed his and his brother Shaukat's faith in Gandhiji's philosophy of non-violence. Yet, he added that though they followed Gandhi's line of non-violence, their religion did not prohibit use of violence and in some situations, for instance, self-defence, it would be the religious duty of a Muslim to use violence. He added that the Khilafatists reserved their right to armed struggle against the enemies of Islam if the Non-coperation strategy failed. Then at a meeting of the CKC in Bombay held on June 15, it was declared that the Muslim soldiers of the British Indian army should refuse to fight if Britain declared a war against Turkey. Again, at a district Khilafat meeting it was announced that India should declare its independence if Britain attacked the forces of Mustafa Kemal Pasha.[38]

The ulama also reinforced a hawkish line by circulating a fatwa issued the preceding year which said that service in the British army and police was a great sin because a Muslim soldier or policeman might be required to fight or fire at his co-religionists. It cited the Quran: "One who kills a Muslim deliberately will be subjected to eternal hellfire." Ahadis were also quoted: "Whoever takes up arms against Muslims, he ceases to be a Muslim..."[39] This fatwa was widely circulated, which discomfited most non-Muslim supporters of the Khilafat stir. At the CKC meeting in Karachi held between July 8 and 10, 1921 the fatwa was endorsed. Mohamed Ali speaking on the occasion laid the blame on Britain that it was systematically destroying Islam and exhorted the people to throw the foreign rulers out of India. A number of resolutions were passed reiterating Muslims' commitment to the cause of Khilafat. One of the resolutions also acclaimed Mustafa Kamal's heroic victories against the enemies of Islam. Nonetheless, one resolution particularly alarmed the governement because it said: "...in the present circumstances the holy Shariat forbids every Muslim to serve or enlist himself in the British Army or to raise recruits for it... it is incumbent on all Muslims in general and all ulama in particular to carry this religious commandment to every Muslim soldier in the British Indian Army."[40] This, in the opinion of the authorities, was an open declaration of revolt and they decided to take action. Though the government did not initiate the action immediately, it had decided to charge the seven prominent leaders present in the Karachi meeting of conspiracy.

One of the consequences of the unfortunate apology episodes was the rupture in the Hindu-Muslim alliance. Above and beyond, the foreign rulers and their local stooges did not leave any stone unturned to break the Hindu-Muslim unity. They succeeded in fanning the flames of communalism as a result of which communal violence broke out at many places. The worst communal flare up was witnessed in August 1921 in the district of Malabar in Kerala. It began as a revolt against the British government that was guilty of using coercive measures to suppress the Khilafat movement. Initially the Khilafat volunteers in the Eranad and Valluvanad talukas of Malabar clashed with the police that would not allow even the peaceful agitation. The police's overbearing methods of suppressing the Khilafat agitation infuriated the Muslim peasants known as Mappilas (also Moplahs)[41] and they went berserk. The violence soon spread out to many other places in the district. The prominent leaders who were spearheading the Mappila rebellion were Variankunnath Kunjahammad Haji, Siti Koya Thangal and Ali Masliyar.[42]

We cannot get the full picture if we treat the incidents of violence in Kerala merely as riots between the Mappilas on one side and the Hindus and the British police and later military on the other. The genesis of the violence lay in the pattern of land distribution and the nature of the relationship between the tillers and the land owners. Under the British the entire agricultural land was owned by the high caste Nambudri Brahmins known as the Janmi. Below them in the agrarian hierarchy were the Hindus of the Nair caste known as Kanakkaran. They were also not the actual tillers but the agents appointed by the Janmis to collect the agricultual produce. At the bottom were the Verumpattakkar, the actual tillers. In the Malabar region almost all Verumpattakkars were Muslims. The rents were as high as 80% of the net produce that left almost nothing except "only straw" to the Muslim tillers.[43] Such an exploitative patron-client relationship had reduced the Muslim tillers of the land to the level of beggars who were "labouring late and early to provide a sufficiency of food for their wives and children."[44] There were violent clashes between the Hindu land owning classes and the Muslim tillers even in 1836. In 1921, however, the Mappilas also had a religious reason, the Khilafat to clash with the police who, in their perception, would always protect the interests of the Janmis. Though the declared objective of the Khilafat volunteers was religious but there was also an undercurrent of resentment against the Hindu land owners. The number of peasants and ordinary people who died in the British retaliation as casualties is estimated at between 500 and 600.[45] The Government of Kerala ultimately officially recognized in 1971, that those participated and those who laid down their lives against the British were freedom fighters.[46]

Despite the upsurge in communal violence, in late 1921, the Khilafatists and the Congressmen had reasons to be satisfied with the successful execution of Non-cooperation during the preceding months. The government, despite its apparent nonchalance was actually scared because the Khilafat and Non-cooperation agitations had brought in crores of people in the fold of political agitation against the British Raj. The growing aggressive posture of the Ali brothers and the circulation of the fatwa all across the country forced the government to arrest the seven prominent leaders, Shaukat Ali, Mohamed Ali, Dr. Kitchlew of Amritsar, Maulana Husain Ahmad Madni of Deoband, Maulana Nisar Ahmad, Pir Ghulam Mujaddid of Matiari in Sindh and Shri Shankaracharya who were present at the Karachi meeting. They were charged with hatching a conspiracy against the government. The trumped up charge against the foremost leaders of the Khilafat and Non-cooperation led to widespread dmonstrations and condemnation of government action throughout India. In the nationwide protests the issue of religious freedom was raised vociferously and the Ali brothers were justified in expressing their point of view in accordance with the precepts of their faith. The prosecution could not substantiate, with concrete evidence, to prove the conspiracy charge. The six Muslim leaders therefore, were found guilty of minor offences and were sentenced to two years imprisonment. Shri Shankaracharya was acquitted of all charges. The government, in view of the upcoming visit of the Prince of Wales put a ban on the volunteer corps that was the youth wing of the Khilafat agitation. The public reacted by enlisting in large numbers in the volunteer corps.

The anti-government demonstration increased manifold because its authoritarian measures infuriarated the masses to no end. At this time Gandhi decided to accede to the popular demand of civil disobedience which was long pending before the Congress. On October 14, 1921, he also issued a statement stating that for an Indian it would not be proper to work under a government either in civil departments or military that created an economic, political and moral crisis in the country. The statement that was issued in the form of a policy document was signed by many Congress leaders. Mohamed Ali's faith in Gandhi's leadership remained firm even after the episode of his apology. He was sentenced to two years' imprisonment and while going to Bijapur jail he said: "The people who are free would look after and speak about our agitation. I want to state this much that after my Prophet, I obey the command of Gandhi." Reacting to the Ali brothers' imprisonment, Gandhi further intensified the Non-cooperation Movement. The foreign rulers could not break the grit and determination of the freedom fighters despite resorting to coercive means.

In the absence of the Ali brothers, Maulana Azad emerged as the principal leader of the Khilafat agitation. On September 22, 1921, he was elected to the post of secretary of the CKC, a post held by Shaukat Ali. Thereafter, he undertook an extensive tour of the country addressing dozens of meetings exhorting people, in particular, Muslims to join Non-cooperation as it was a religious responsibility in the prevailing political conditions. In addition to his tours and speeches, Azad, in collaboration with his trusted colleague, Abdur Razzaq Malehabadi, launched a new Urdu weekly, *Paigham,* from Calcutta. It was a different periodical compared with Azad's earlier journalistic ventures, *Al-Hilal* and *Al-Balagh,* in terms of goals and tenor. Through *Paigham,* Azad had to inspire people to support the Khilafat agitation by non-cooperating with the government. He explained to his Muslim readers that there were two kinds of non-Muslims. One, those who attack Islam to finish it off like the British do. The second category of non-Muslims comprised those who live with Muslims in peace like the Hindu brethren of India. Therefore, it was a religious duty of the Muslims to oppose the British who were enemies of Islam and it was equally a religious requirement for the Muslims to join hands with their Hindu countrymen against the British Raj. A Muslim, therefore, should strive for *Swaraj*. The government reacted by raiding Azad's home and the press and arresting the editor of *Paigham*, Abdur Razzaq Malehabadi, in the first week of December. A few days later, Azad too was arrested on the charges that in two of his speeches he spoke about 'revolution' to be brought about in India. He was sentenced to one year imprisonment.

When the date (November 17, 1921) of the visit of the Prince of Wales was nearing the Viceroy decided to file a case against Gandhi for challenging the authority of the imperial government. The leaders of the Congress and the Khilafat Movement had given a call of a strike. Gandhi was personally supervising the planning of the strike in Bombay. Despite his presence in the city, communal violence broke out in Bombay, not between Hindus and Muslims but between the combined front of Hindus and Muslims on one side and the Christians and the Parsis on the other side. It so happened because the Christians and the Parsis of Bombay had decided to give a warm welcome to the Prince. This led to the clashes at many places in the city that continued for five days. Gandhi was distressed because for him Hindu-Muslim unity was the symbol of unity between majority and minority communities. He had never imagined that the other minority communities would show hostility towards Hindu-Muslim unity. However, he also, chided the Muslims for using violent means to make the strike successful. Gandhi's remark was not acceptable to many Khilafatists. Gandhi was aware that his relations with the Muslims were far from strong . He gave expression to this thought in one of the issues of *Young India*. He wrote: "I can wield no influence over the Muslims except through a Muslim. There are many stalwarts and good Muslims I know. But no Muslim knows me through and through as Shaukat Ali does. Now I feel I have to represent him and to speak to the Muslim things I used always to reserve for him. I observe one of my appeals has already been misinterpreted."[47] With the exception of Bombay, however, the strike was peaceful and complete all through India.

The huge success of the strike alarmed the government and it decided to put an end to the twin movements by force. Consequently, the police raided the offices of the Congress and the Khilafat. Meetings were banned and the activism by the volunteers of the two organizations was prohibited. The limit of repression was that people sporting a Gandhi cap and raising slogans like *Gandhi ki Jai* were arrested. In the month of December, prominent Congress leaders such as Motilal Nehru, Jawaharlal Nehru, Lajpat Rai and C.R. Das were arrested. There was pressure on the Viceroy from his colleagues in India and Britain to arrest Gandhi too but he refrained from doing so. He, instead suggested to Gandhi that a round-table conference should be convened to find a solution. In response, Gandhi demanded that before the proposed conference, the government should roll back all the contentious issues and release the Ali brothers. The Viceroy did not accede to Gandhi's demands. Thus, the confrontation between the agitationists and the government continued.

Both the Congress and the Khilafat Committee were plagued with groupism and factional bickering. The hawks among the Khilafatists led by Abdul Bari and Hasrat Mohani had openly expressed their exhaustion with Gandhi's non-violent line of action. They were also planning to part ways with the Congress and deal directly with the British for a revision of the Treaty of Sevres. The moderate group of Khilafatists, notably Dr. M.A. Ansari and Hakim Ajmal Khan insisted on continuation of the alliance with the Congress and Khilafatists' participation in Non-cooperation. Regarding directly dealing with the British their argument was that Khilafat was not merely about revision of the Treaty of Sevres. It was also about resisting the European presence in the Arab peninsula and within India the Khilafatists should also strive for achieving Swaraj in collaboration with the non-Muslim countrymen. They reiterated the significance of Hindu-Muslim unity.

Within Congress, opposition to Gandhi's policy of Non-cooperation and the forthcoming strategy of disobedience were disputed issues and moderates like Madan Mohan Malviya favoured a policy of entering into negotiation with the government. Though Jinnah had dissociated himself from the Congress, at this juncture he too supported Malviya's idea to appeal to the Viceroy to call a round table conference to discuss what measures the government had to adopt to cancel out the wrongs it did in matters of the Khilafat and Amritsar massacre. Gandhi was not keen on the idea though in principle he was not opposed to a round table conference provided the government released all those arrested in connection with Non-cooperation and, in particular the Ali brothers. It was obvious that the government would not accede to Gandhi's demand and therefore the moderates had to toe the Gandhian line.

In December 1921, the annual sessions of the Congress, the Khilafat Committee and the Muslim League were held in Ahmedabad. The observers noted the Congress session was different in many ways than the earlier sessions. All the delegates were wearing khadi clothes, there were no chairs on the podium, all the people were seated on the mattresses or mats (known as Indian style) and all the communication during the session was made in Hindi / Urdu. There was hardly anyone who was speaking English. The session was presided over by Hakim Ajmal Khan. Speeches were short and to the point. There was no clapping. Though, Malviya and his moderate supporters tried to pass a resolution about the round table conference, they could not make it. Another resolution that was hotly debated was moved by Hasrat Mohani that pushed for the abandonment of the policy of non-violent Non-cooperation altogether and immediate declaration of 'complete independence' from Britain and adoption of violent means if necessary to accomplish the goal. Gandhi was obviously shocked by the impudence that was reflected in the text of the resolution. It was perceptibly rejected. Subsequently, Mohani tried to get it passed in the Muslim League session but in vain. He then moved the same resolution in the Khilafat session where its supporters and opponents had almost come to blows and ultimately the resolution was shelved. Historically speaking it must be underscored, however, it was the first resolution ever moved in the sessions of the Congress and the Muslim League proclaiming *complete freedom* from Britain. In a nutshell the entire proceedings of the Congress session were conducted as per Gandhi's plan. In a significant resolution, Gandhi commended the people of India for the firmness, self-sacrifice and dignity with which they were carrying out the ongoing Non-cooperation and Khilafat agitations and with determination he declared that the agitation against the British rulers would continue till the government took the necessary action against the butchers of the Jallianwala Bagh tragedy and addressed the grievances of the Muslims on the Khilafat issue.

On February 4, 1922, Gandhi wrote to the Viceroy that he had selected a small village of Gujarat, Bardoli as a unit of launching the civil disobedience stir and defiance of the anti-Indian laws of the British. He made it clear to the Viceroy that in Bardoli it was going to be the people's revolt in the interest of the nationalist cause. He further explained that in view of the oppressive and barbaric manner with which the authorities were trying to smother the people's agitation, there was no other alternatve left for the nationalists except to launch a civil-disobedience movement against the government and as a first act of defiance the people in Bardoli would stop paying taxes. Thereafter, when Gandhi was still busy giving final touches to the Bardoli satyagraha, an unfortunate incident took place in a town of UP that ultimately put an end to the Non-cooperation movement.

Chauri Chaura, a town in the Gorakhpur district of UP witnessed a large protest on February 5, 1922, as part of the Non-cooperation movement. The demonstration was actually started a day before when about 2,500 people picketed before a liquor shop. The police arrested one of the leaders. The people got infuriarated and gathered before the police chowki demanding the release of their leader. Armed police arrived and fired at the slogan-shouting protesters. Three people were killed on the spot and many more were injured. This exacerbated the situation further as infuriated protesters irately advanced towards the policemen without bothering about their guns. This astonishing display of courage by the protesters intimidated the policemen and they sought protection in the chowki. The incensed crowd put the chowki on fire which burnt alive the 23 Indian policemen.[48]

The Chauri Chaura incident horrified Gandhi so much that he thought of it as his personal complicity in the bloodshed.[49] As penance for the guilt he suffered from, he went on a five day-fast. He mulled over the point that he failed in training his satyagrahis properly in the method of non-violent agitation. He also felt that Indians were not fully prepared to carry out a peacefuul agitation against the British Raj. He, therefore, declared on February 12, even against the opinion of many of his Congress colleagues, the end of the Non-cooperation movement. That did not deter the authorities to arrest him. He was sentenced to six years imprisonment but he was released on health grounds in February 1924.[50]

The end of the Non-coperation movement had weakened the Khilafat movement to a great extent. The leaders of both the Congress and Khilafat were dismayed by Gandhi's decision. For them it was admission of defeat and betrayal to lakhs of Indians who had sacrificed almost everything to support the twin movements of Khilafat and Non-cooperation. C.R. Gopalachari who was considered to be very close to Gandhi wrote in his diary: "...despite my close relationship with my mentor Gandhi, I fail to understand the reason because of which he called off the movement." Mohamed Ali was in jail. He was completely distraught on learning about it. The Kanpur Khilafat Committee on the prompting of Hasrat Mohani and Maulana Azad Subhani declared to oppose Gandhi's decision. Jamiat-ul-Ulama too expressed its reservation about the principle of absolute non-violence in its Ajmer session held in early March 1922. Khaliquzzaman Chaudhary who was an important leader of the Khilafat movement informed that when the Nehrus, Motilal and Jawaharlal learned about the calling off of the movement in Lucknow jail, they were extremely offended. In his words: "Pandit Motilal was furious... and expressed his deep resentment and anger at what had happened...He... shouted, 'Look here what has happened...This ends the movement because some people in a big country like India have lost their mind and committed violence.' Jawaharlal...did not say anything at that time. However, I could see by his face that he did not like it and shared his father's views."[51] Maulana Abdul Bari was beside himself and in that heat of the moment said: "To me Gandhiji is like a paralytic whose limbs are not in his control, but whose mind is still active. I am doubtful of his [future] success, because he has not yet acquired much success from his [non-violent] movement...There is general depression all over."[52] When Gandhi found out about Maulana Bari's annoyance, he rushed to Ajmer, where Bari had made the statement and did his best to mollify Maulana Bari who in turn issued a conciliatory statement: "I had agreed with Gandhiji that until I had become hopeless of the success of the non-violent Non-cooperation movement, I would not do anything against it openly or secretly."[53]

Gandhi's decision to call off the movement had a huge adverse impact on the Khilafat volunteers. The widespread reaction among them was that they were cheated. On the other hand the authorities were very happy. Harcourt Butler, the Governor of UP had remarked that Hindu-Muslim unity was on the verge of death. With the intention of intensification of hatred between Hindus and Muslims further, the Viceroy sent a telegram to London pleading with the British Government to reconsider the term of the Treaty of Sevres. It was a clever ploy to wean the Muslims away from the mainstream nationalist movement. Sadly, many leaders of the Khilafat movement were caught in the trap. Then, on the prompting of the British Raj, the *Statesman* of Calcutta published the news that there was misappropriation of the Khilafat Fund. This greatly damaged the reputation of the Khilafat leaders. Then came the news from Turkey that Kemal Pasha had brought in radical reforms which had made the future of the institution of Khilafat uncertain. The first swipe at Khilafat was taken by Turkey's Grand National Assembly in November 1922 when the Sultan, Wahiduddin Muhammad VI was deposed and Abdul Majid Effendi was nominated the new Caliph. The separation of the temporal powers from the spiritual office of the Caliph rendered the Khilafat movement of the Indian Muslims inconsequential. Many ulama in India were dismayed on receiving the news because in their view separation of temporal powers from those of spiritual was against Islam. Nonetheless, for some other ulama it was an agreeable development as, they thought, the institution of Khilafat got back its sanctity after its separation from the hereditary position of the Sultan.[54]

The arrest of almost all the prominent leaders left the Khilafat rudderless. Besides Maulana Azad five secretaries of the Khilafat Committee were also arrested. Common Muslims were left high and dry. Many were of the opinion that they should forsake Gandhi and his guidance and should continue opposing the British policies on their own. Muhammad Marmaduke Pickthall, the famous translator of the Quran into English, while presiding over the CKC in Sindh advised the Muslims to desist from turning away from Gandhi. He told the Khilafat Committee volunteers that he was aware that some Muslims did not favour making a Hindu as their leader. Nonetheless, he emphasized that a saintly Hindu who cherished the ethical and sublime principles of life would prove a far better leader for the Muslims than a Muslim sinner who lived an ignoble life. The Khilafat Movement faced the worst crisis particularly after the allegation of misappropriation of the Khilafat Fund by the Ali brothers. Their reputation was at stake. Since they were in jail they could not respond to these allegations propagated widely by the British controlled press.

The allegations of misappropriation of funds became frequent and sharper because by July 1922, there was no money left to run the CKC. It was also reported that the Smyrna and Angora Funds had a combined balance of Rs. sixteen lakhs. In order to meet the expenses of the CKC it was decided that Rs. one lakh should be lent to the CKC from the Angora Fund and Chhotani would transfer Rs. ten lakhs to Turkey. At the October meeting of the CKC it was revealed that the decisions about the funds were not complied with. While Seth Chhotani was the president, his son Ahmad Mian Chhotani was the treasurer of the CKC. What was worse that the father-son duo could not properly explain why they failed to act in accordance with the decision of the CKC. This provided grist to the rumour mill and the allegation of embezzlement hit the CKC hard. Later, the facts were out that revealed massive mis-management of funds. A massive amount of money was spent on questionable heads of expenditure. An unjustifiable huge amount was also spent on the visit of the Khilafat delegation to Europe. Then there were financial difficulties of the Chhotanis. Prior to the Khilafat movement he was one of the preferred contractors of the government. However, the government blacklisted him because of his association with the movement and his business suffered heavy losses. He, therefore, had invested the entire amount of Smyrna and Angora Funds in his business. This exposure created a serious crisis as most leaders of the Working Committee hailing from North India wanted not only to kick out the Chhotanis but file criminal cases against them. Neverthless, Abdul Bari ultimately supported the Chhotanis and asked him to pay back the amount. He signed the papers transferring the ownership of two of his saw mills to the CKC. The father-son duo also resigned from the post of president and treasurer respectively. Despite their misdemeanour, most members felt sorry for the Chhotanis as they had contributed substantially to build the movement in its formative years.[55]

The issue of reforms brought about in Turkey was another subject that put the Khilafat movement in a quandary. The Khilafat leaders could do anything to prevent the revolutionary changes that were being brought about in Turkey. Kemal Pasha was a modernist. He did not approve of those who favoured continuation of the Shariat. He had made up his mind to abolish the institution of monarchy and establish a people's government in Turkey. In the General National Assembly, the ulama strongly opposed the proposed anti-Islam reforms. Kemal Pasha got up and stated that a people's government was not established with the help of the ulama. We had to fight for it. Turkey could regain its lost sovereign government by defeating the imperial powers. If all of you could appreciate this fact then it would be good for the nation. The people's government would prevail in any case. It would however be necessary to kill some people for its survival. The impact of his menacing words left the ulama speechless and his resolution for the reforms was passed unanimously. In a nutshell his reforms can be explained thus: "Mustafa Kemal initiated a series of reforms affecting almost every aspect of Turkish society. The set of these reforms known as Kemalism comprises six ideological traits, viz. republicanism, nationalism, statism, populism, secularism and revolutionary zeal."[56]

Though Khilafat was not abolished at that time but the Sultan was deported from Turkey. The question that troubled the Muslims across the world and, in particular, the Khilafat agitators in India was how could the institution of Khilafat exist without a Khalifa? Kemal Pasha, however, was very clear about his position He did not want any Sultan or Khalifa to rule over Turkey. He had also rejected the concept of a Khalifa controlling the entire Muslim world. For him it was a preposterous idea.

The suspension of the Non-cooperation movement created a void which was soon filled up by Hindu-Muslim acrimony and consequent communal violence. Gandhi and the Ali brothers had mobilized the sleeping masses to fight for their motherland and for the dignty and honour of their co-religionists. The stirring was mammoth. Lakhs of common people who were hitherto hardly acquainted with anything political made great sacrifices just because their leaders had given them a purpose and asked them to live and die for a dream. Then the leaders themselves obliterated the purpose and snatched away the dream from them. Most people felt cheated. The feeling of frustration and hurt was more acute among the Muslim masses. Since Gandhi had called off the popular movement, most Muslims inferred that the Hindus had betrayed them. The activities of Hindu communal organizations exacerbated the already volatile situation further. The Arya Samajists got active in their pet projects of *Shuddhi* and *Sanghathan* which were squarely anti-Muslim missions. Shuddhi was a socio-political movement started by the Arya Samaj, and its founder Swami Dayanand Saraswati and his followers such as Swami Shradhanand, who also worked for the *Sangathan* (consolidation) of Hinduism. Lala Lajpat Rai, at one time also headed the *Sanghathan*. The movement aimed to reduce the conversions of Hindus to Islam and Christianity. In 1923, Swami Shraddhanand established the *'Bhartiya Hindu Shuddhi Mahasabha'* (Indian Hindu Purification Council) that got active in accomplishing the agenda of reconversion. Such a provocative move in an already explosive atmosphere naturally created a flashpoint between Hindus and Muslims. The communal clashes began when the *Shuddhi Mahasabha* attempted the reconversion of Malkana Rajputs in western UP.[57] Later, the movement became controversial and got an image of an anti-Muslim mission which in turn made the Muslims active against it.[58] The Muslim antagonism ultimately led to the death of the leader of the movement, Swami Shraddhanand in 1926. After Shraddhanand's death the Shuddhi movement continued with the usual missionary zeal.[59]

On their part, the Muslims of North India, in addition to countering the Arya Samaji missions like *Shuddhi* and *Sanghathan* also got engaged in establishing their own institutions to keep their co-religionists united and ward off the Hindu proselytization projects. The emergence of Tablighi Jamaat also coincided closely with the Hindu aggressive programmes of *Shuddhi* (purification) and *Sanghathan* (consolidation). To begin with the main purpose of the Tablighi Jamat, though it was not named so immediately, was to educate borderline Muslims to reaffirm their religious and cultural identity who were still practising certain customs and rites that were a throwback to their Hindu past. Thus in the initial years the movement concentrated more on making the Muslims better and purer members of the faith rather than proselytization. The founder of Tablighi Jamat, Maulana Ilyas first started working among the Meos of Mewat (Haryana). The Meos belong to the Rajput ethnic group and even after embracing Islam had retained many Hindu customs and traditions. While working among the Meos, Maulana Ilyas called his movement *Tahrik-e-Imaan*. His initial strategy was to establish a network of *madarsas* located in mosques through which he intended to educate the Mewati Muslims about the basic tenets of Islam and Muslim customs and traditions. Having worked for quite some time in Mewat, Maulana Ilyas realized that his efforts only produced religious functionaries and not preachers. So, he relocated himself in a mosque near the mausoleum of the famous Sufi Saint, Khwaja Nizamuddin Auliya in Delhi and formally launched the Tablighi Jamaat in 1926. Tabligh literally means proselytization and thus the members of Tablighi Jamaat are expected to preach as well. However, they do not proselytize aggressively because every member of the Jamaat first attempts to become a purer and better Muslim before inviting the members of the other faiths to embrace Islam.[60] The Jamiat-ul-Ulama joined in promoting the aims and objectives of the Tablighi Jamaat and surprisingly the Ahmadiya Muslims[61] too becme active in carrying out the mission of proselytization.

Other than these Muslim proselytizing outfits, Dr. Saifuddin Kitchlew had also started his *Jamiat-e-Tanzim* immediately after his release from jail in 1923. Though the declared objectives of Tanzim (Organisation) were to establish schools, charitable institutions, banks and financial institutions for the welfare of the Muslims, it got engaged more in countering the Arya Samaji missions of *Shuddhi* and *Sanghathan*. Kitchlew also launched an Urdu Daily,

Tanzim, to disseminate the ideas and programmes of his organization. It must however, be acknowledged that Kitchlew through his daily newspaper exhorted the Muslims to continue their struggle for achieving Swaraj and should not allow depression to subdue them because of the fiasco of Non-cooperation and Khilafat.

The presence of these organizations with overtly communal agendas intensified the Hindu-Muslim tension particularly in North India that led to frequent communal clashes. For instance, in August 1923, there were Hindu-Muslim riots in Agra and Saharanpur on the occasion of Muharram. It must be remembered that in these towns of Western UP, the Shuddhi activists and the members of Tablighi Jamaat had considerable presence. The irony was that quite a few leaders, both Hindus and Muslims, who were leading the marauding mobs had been active against the British Raj alongside each other a year and half ago during the Non-cooperation and Khilafat agitations. In the following year the incidents of communal violence increased perceptibly. There were communal clashes in Delhi in July 1924 during Eid-ul-Azha, the second most popular festival of the Muslims. Thereafter, a major communal riot broke out in Kohat, NWFP, on September 9 and 10. It is pointless to blame one particular community for starting the communal conflagration because a lot of planning and propaganda take place before the outbreak of a communal riot. In this respect the communal organizations (and in independent India communal political parties too) play a diabolic role.

Mohamed Ali, rotting in a dingy cell of the jail, was not aware of the radical changes that were brought about in Turkey. He would still consider all Muslims the citizens of Turkey. He asserted that despite the fiasco of the Non-cooperation movement, the Muslims of India would continue their struggle for perpetuation of the Khilafat because they were the best Muslims. After coming out of jail in September 1923, he like most nationalists, was naturally distressed because of the worsening communal situation. Therefore, worried nationalist leaders got active to take certain measures to end the rising communal hatred. As part of these measures a special session of the Congress was convened in Delhi in September 1923. It was presided over by Maulana Azad who was released from jail a few months ago, while Dr. Ansari was the host. Mohamed Ali was present. It was Mohamed Ali's first major political act after coming out of jail. The meeting reiterated the Congress commitment to Hindu-Muslim unity. Aẓad, in his presidential address admitted that there was disillusionment and discord among the Congress cadres. He asked every Congressman to help discard the dismal mood. For which he suggested that first of all factionalism within the Congress should be eliminated.

Though Azad, Ansari and Mohamed Ali were present at the special session and committed themselves to work for the Hindu-Muslim cooperation in the national interest, other prominent Muslim leaders mainly belonging to the Khilafat did not take the trouble to attend the session. Abdul Bari, for instance, did not attend pleading ill-health. What was worse, however, was the belligerent statement he issued on the occasion which said: "We can sacrifice our all to obtain self-rule except our beloved faith. A Muslim is a Muslim first and last and if any community wants our support in India it must learn to respect Islam...If the commandments of the *shari'a* are to be trampled underfoot, then it will be the same to us whether the decision is arrived at on the plains of Delhi or the hilltops of Simla. We are determined to non-cooperate from every enemy of Islam whether he be in Anatolia or Arabia or at Agra or Benares."[62] Such an attitude on the part of most Muslim leaders could hardly be conducive to recreate the atmosphere of Hindu-Muslim amity that was witnessed in the initial phase of Non-cooperation and Khilafat agitations.

Mohamed Ali did not have a place of his own. in the capital. His daughter who lived in Bhowali, a small hill-station in UP (now in Uttarakhand) was ill at the time. So he went there to meet her. There he met Dr. Saifuddin Kitchlew. He expressed to him that he was terribly shaken because of the anti-Muslim feelings of some of the prominent Congressmen. He admitted that Gandhi had shown a ray of hope to the Muslims because his objectives were to achieve Hindu-Muslim unity and Swaraj. Next to Gandhi, Mohamed Ali had a high opinion of Nehru whom he was, in the capacity of the president, forced to accept the post of general secretary of the Congress.

In the presidential address of the 1923 session of the Congress held at Cocanada (now Kakinada), Mohamed Ali appealed to the Muslims of the world to support the cause of Indian independence. Speaking about Indian Muslims he pointed out that they had two responsibilities. Their first responsibility was, he emphasized, to struggle for the independence of their country. India was as much their country as it was that of the Hindus...the Muslims should keep struggling for independence even if they were left alone. Mohamed Ali also made a mention about the institution of Khilafat that had lost its standing. He averred that the holy land of Islam was under the control of non-Muslims. Finally, he called attention to Hindu-Muslim unity that was very dear to Gandhi. He, however, pointed out that the members of both the communities should recognize the fact that neither could Hindus throw out the Muslims nor could the Muslims get rid of the Hindus. The only option for both of them was to forget their differences and live together in harmony. He asked the Muslims to make the Hindus familiar with their commitment to India's independence. They should also convince the Hindus that they would always be prepared to lay down their lives in case of any foreign aggression on the country. On the other hand, the Hindus should make the Muslims understand that in independent India the minority community would not be reduced to the level of slavery.

The Khilafat Conference was also held at Kakinada at the same time. In his presidntial address, Shaukat Ali spoke exclusively for the Muslims and on the issues that were dear to the community. He did not refer to the need of Hindu-Muslim cooperation even once. He advised the Muslims not to get disillusioned or dispirited because of the unfortunate political developments. He insisted that Muslims should remain united behind the Khilafat movement, the Turkish reforms notwithstanding. He declared that all the Muslim demands would be ultimately acceded by the "greatest enemy of Islam, the British government" provided the Muslims kept up a united front and work for the achievement of their goals with utmost enthusiasm and devotion. Despite the portentous words, Shaukat Ali's exhortation about Khilafat was a futile act of no consequence. In the aftermath of the Treaty of Sevres, the issue of Khilafat helped mobilize the Muslim masses because at that time the powerful non-Islamic Allied Powers seemed to subjugate a weak and vanquished Ottoman Empire. In the winter of 1923, Turkey was no more an oppressed and tyrannized country. Mustafa Kemal had fought back to restore the honour, dignity and territorial integrity of Turkey. He had also forced the Allied Powers to replace the unfair Treaty of Sevres with a more judicious Treaty of Lausanne. Therefore, it was not the 'greatest enemy of Islam, Britain' that had battered the institution of Khilafat but a proud and valiant Muslim warrior, Mustafa Kemal, who had questioned the relevance of the institution in the changed times. The problem of the Ali brothers was that they could not issue an outrightly communal appeal to unite the Muslim masses and this quandary forced them to keep going back on about Khilafat.

After his release in February 1924, Gandhi was extremely offended because of the atmosphere of mistrust between Hindus and Muslims. He had almost given up hope to unite the two communities. In September he went to Delhi and with the intention of making another attempt to unify the two largest communities of the country he stayed at the residence of Mohamed Ali. Around this time the news of the Kohat riot reached Delhi. Mohamed Ali was on a visit to the home of Dr. M.A. Ansari when he got the news that as an atonement for the riot, Gandhi undertook a 21-day fast. Mohamed Ali implored him to give up the fast but Gandhi refused as he was looking for an antidote to cure the malady of violence. Most people, including Mohamed Ali, were apprehensive that in case something untoward happened to Gandhi at Mohamed Ali's place, it would prove ominous to the cause of Hindu-Muslim unity. Nonetheless, it was Gandhi's premeditated decision to sit for the fast in a Muslim's house. He argued that Mohamed Ali was a brother to him and his choice of the venue for the fast would send the appropriate message to the Hindus and Muslims to shun violence and live in pece.

Fortunately nothing untoward happened and Gandhi ended his fast on October 8. As a token of salutation, Mohamed Ali gifted a cow to Gandhi who was delighted to receive such a present. In response he wrote to Mohamed Ali addressing him as brother and adding that he was more than a brother to him. Gandhi also observed that he prayed to God that the relationship between him and Mohamed Ali and his brother should lead to establish a fruitful relationship between Hindus and Muslims. Mohamed Ali was succeeded by Gandhi in the thirty-ninth session of the Congress held at Belgaum. There appeared a shift at this point of time in the freedom struggle. The focus was now on constructive programmes rather than agitation. Gandhi too was focusing more on issues like entry into the councils which actually meant participating in elections. Another concern was to put an end to the differences between the members of the Congress and Swaraj Party.[63] It was, in fact, a conflict between the votaries of revolution and anti-revolution. The anti-revolution lobby wanted to contest the election and enter the councils. The highlight of the Belgaum session was a compromise between the two factions that came to be known as the Gandhi-Nehru-Das Pact. It paved the way for taking part in the elections.

The Central Khilafat Committee's Annual Conference was held at Cawnpore (now Kanpur) in December 1924 which was presided over by Maulana Azad. Gandhi, the Ali brothers, Mrs. Sarojini Naidu and other Congressmen attended the session. Maulana Hasrat Mohani, who was the chairman of the reception committee vehemently criticized the government of Turkey for abolition of the institution of Khilafat. Maulana Azad too condemned Turkey's decision to do away with the Khilafat. He suggested that the Muslims should have an informal right to choose a Caliph. He was optimistic about the restitution of Khilafat and advised the Muslims to join the freedom movement led by the Congress to free India from the British. Once the British imperialism was weakened, he reasoned, the holy places of Islam would be once again under the control of the Muslims. Mohamed Ali commended Ibn Sand for capturing of Arab peninsula. A resolution to that effect was also passed in the Conference which stated that through this resolution, the Conference wished to express its warm congratulations to Ibn Sand for the peaceful entry of his army into Jeddah. It further stated that the Conference ratified various declarations that the Sultan had made about Hejaz and hoped that the entire Muslim world too would greet them. The Conference also looked forward to an International Islamic Conference to take into account the future of Hejaz. The resolution further waited for the opening of new offices at Jeddah and other places in Hejaz by the Islamic Conference to make available all the necessary facilities to the pilgrims of Hajj.

After the Conference, V.S. Srinivas Sastri wrote an article in *The Hitavad,* the organ of the Servants of India Society censuring Mohamed Ali's departure from the nationalist mainstream and taking back the position of a Muslim separatist. He wondered whether Mohamed Ali lost his love for the Mahatma. In response, Mohamed Ali wrote in his paper *Comrade* that he was still loyal to Gandhi. He praised Gandhi for converting the Congress into a truly nationalist party because despite being a true Hindu, he did not turn his back on Muslims, nor did he ignore their problems. His genuine brand of nationalism had completely changed the political situation in India. Regrettably, he added many of his Hindu colleagues in the Congress could not approve of his viewpoint because like Gandhi they were neither open-minded nor sagacious. Consequently, the Muslims lost their faith in the majority community and, therefore, they demanded separate electorates. Mohamed Ali blamed people like Srinivas Sastri and Lala Lajpat Rai who construed Gandiji's friendly relations with the Muslims as "walking out on the rights of the Hindus". Mohamed Ali averred that in the eyes of the Hindus a Muslim was always a Muslim whether he opposed or supported the orthodox section of his own community. For a Hindu, a Muslim would always be evil.

In 1926, a special session of the CKC was held on May 8 and 9. It was chaired by Syed Sulaiman Nadvi. Besides the Ali brothers, Hakim Ajmal Khan, Maulana Azad and Khwaja Hasan Nizami were other notable delegates. Nadvi forcefully condemned the continuing campaign of shuddhi through which the communal Hindus were spreading hatred against the Muslims. He particularly lamented the stance of some of the playwrights of Maharashtra and Bengal who, through their plays and articles, were encouraging anti-Muslim feelings. A significant issue taken up in the Conference was to amend the Constitution of the CKC in the light of abolition of the institution of Khilafat by Turkey. The amended Constitution emphasized the uplift of the conditions of the Indian Muslims through missionary works and education. The Committee should protect the lives and properties of the Muslims at the times of communal riots and should also rehabilitate the affected families of communal violence.

Then the annual session of the CKC was held in Lucknow on February 26, 1927. Though quite a few prominent members were present, many were conspicuous by their absence. Abdul Majid Daryabadi was the chairman of the Reception Committee. The session was to be presided over by Haji Ibrahim Haroon but he could not attend because of ill-health. Accordingly, Maulana Shafi Dawoodi chaired the session. The next day the International Muslim Conference was held that was presided over by Dr. M.A. Ansari. He clarified that there was no clash of agenda between the International Muslim Conference and the CKC. The former would be engaged in taking into account the issues of the Islamic world while the latter would concentrate on the problems of Indian Muslims. He insisted that Indian Muslims should consider themselves as Indians first and should spurn the communal outlook. He also made it plain that among the Hindus, Lala Lajpat Rai and Madan Mohan Malviya and among the Muslims Mohammad Ali Jinnah and Sir Muhammad Abdur Rahim were not the friends of Muslims. Mohamed Ali in his speech lamented the deterioration of Hindu-Muslim relations. He also expressed his displeasure of Gandhi's dissociation from the task of restoration of Hindu-Muslim unity. He stated that Hindu Mahasabha leaders such as Madan Mohan Malviya and M.S. Anney had become very popular among the Hindus and because of which they had completely ruined the plan of an amicable relationship between Hindus and Muslims.

It must also be recalled that a few days before the CKC session of Lucknow, a meeting of the prominent Muslim leaders was summoned in Delhi's Western Hotel. Thirty leaders belonging to different parties and institutions attended. Most leaders, however, represented the Muslim League and the CKC. The main issue on the agenda was how to restore cordial relations between Hindu and Muslims. Jinnah suggested that a charter of demands of the Muslims should be presented to the Congress for its consideration. Jinnah's charter of dmands included the following issues:

1. Separation of Bombay province from Sindh. 2. Proportional representation on the basis of Muslim population in Assemblies and other democratic institutions. 3. No future plans of partition of Provinces should adversely affect the Muslim majority in Punjab,

Bengal and North Western Frontier Province. 4. Conferring of equal status on NWFP with the other provinces. 5. Continuation of status quo regarding the representation of other communities. A provision should also be inserted stating that any community could give up a separate electorate to opt for joint electorate. After long and animated deliberations, the Muslim leaders agreed on the point that in case Congress agreed to their demands the Muslims would agree to opt for joint electorates. It was then resolved to submit the proposals through M.A. Jinnah to the Congress for its consideration. The charter of demands thus came to be known as the "Delhi Proposals."

The response of the Congress was pleasantly encouraging. The Congress Working Committee hailed the Delhi Proposals and made the decision "that the committee cordially appreciates the decision arrived at by the Muslim Conference to accept the institution of joint electorates all over the country with reciprocal concessions in favour of minorities and appoints the following Sub-Committee to discuss details with representatives of the Muslim Conference and of the Hindu community."[64] The sub-committee included Mrs. Sarojini Naidu, Pandit Motilal Nehru, Srinivasa Iyengar and Maulana Mohamed Ali.

The Congress Working Committee ultimately reflected upon the report of the sub-committee on March 20, and passed a resolution. The salient points of the resolution were as under:

> (1) That in any future scheme of the Constitution, so far as representation in the various legislatures is concerned, joint electorates in all the provinces and in the Central Legislature be constituted.
>
> (2) That, with a view to giving full assurances to the two great communities that their legitimate interests would be safeguarded in the Legislatures, for the present, and if desired, such representation of the communities should be secured by the reservation of seats in joint electorates on the basis of population in every province and in the Central Legislature;
>
> Provided that reciprocal concessions in favour of minorities including the Sikhs in the Punjab may be made by mutual agreement so as to give them representations in excess of the proportion of the number of seats to which they would be entitled on the population basis in any province or provinces; and the proportions so agreed upon for the provinces shall be maintained in the representation of the two

communities in the Central Legislature from the provinces.

(3) a.—The proposal made by the Muslim leaders that reforms should be introduced in the NWF. Province and British Baluchistan on the same footing as in other provinces is, in the opinion of the Committee, a fair and reasonable one.

(3) b.—The proposal that Sind should be separated from the Bombay Presidency and constituted into a separate province is one which has already been adopted in the Constitution of the Congress on the principle of the redistribution of provinces on a linguistic basis and the Committee is of the opinion that the proposal may be given effect to.

(4) That in the future Constitution, liberty of conscience shall be guaranteed and no legislature, central or provincial, shall have power to make any laws interfering with liberty of conscience.

"Liberty of conscience" means liberty of belief and worship, freedom of religious observances and associations and freedom to carry on religious education and propaganda with due regard to the feelings of others and without interfering with similar rights of others.

(5) No Bill, Resolution, Motion or Amendment regarding inter-communal matters shall be moved, discussed or passed in any Legislature, Central or Provincial, if a three-fourths majority of the members of either community affected thereby in that legislature oppose the introduction, discussion or passing of such Bill, Resolution. Motion or Amendment. "Inter-Communal Matters" means matters agreed upon as such by a joint Standing Committee of both communities, of the Hindu and Moslem members of the legislatures concerned, appointed at the commencement of every session of the legislature.[65]

The AICC approved the resolution and asked the entire Congress organization to adopt appropriate measures to implement the recommendations. Nonetheless, the Hindu communal leaders within the Congress were bitterly opposed to give even a minor concession to the Muslims. Their stand was that the recommendation in respect of the joint electorates should be accepted but no other recommendation that found ways to help the Muslims should be agreed to. Thus, the AICC's recommendations were trampled under by the so-called Congress leaders who made the minorities, in particular, the Muslims feel that theirs was a Hindu organization. An advantageous opportunity that could have united all Indians against the British

Raj was lost because of the Hindu fanatics. Sir Tej Bahadur Sapru was extremely upset and he vehemently denounced the Hindu communal leaders who had almost hijacked the Congress and forced the Congress to lose an opportunity to achieve Hindu-Muslim unity.

Mohamed Ali was obviously depressed because of the contempt with which the Hindu fanatics, paricularly members of the Congress from Bombay and Bengal provinces, treated the recommendations of the AICC. His image as a nationalist leader having faith in Gandhi's leadership was also tarnished around this time because of his incensed reaction to the verdict of the Punjab High Court's Division Bench recommending the harshest punishment to the Muslim killer of the author of an anti-Prophet book, *Rangeela Rasool*. Most Muslims condemned the verdict. Mohamed Ali resorted to legal action. In his Urdu paper, *Hamdard*, he blamed the law under which the verdict was pronounced and also criticized the judges for their biased view. He proposed alteration in the law in question and endeavoured with complete commitment to get the law changed by the Central Legislative Assembly. His efforts bore fruits as the altered law is now part of the Indian Penal Code. It reads that if anyone with wilful intention or infamy hurts the religious sentiments of the subjects of His Majesty or a religious community by oration or writing shall be imprisoned for two years or fined.

Since there was no let up in enmity between the Hindus and the Muslims, a special session of the Central Legislative Assembly discussed the deteriorating inter-communal relations. It failed to find a solution. In September 1927, on cue from the CKC, Mohamed Ali convened a 'Unity Conference' in Simla. It also failed to achieve anything concrete. The incessant failures in attaining the objective of Hindu-Muslim unity made Mohamed Ali extremely despondent. Around this time the British announced the arrival of the Simon Commission comprising only the white members of British origin to explore the prospect of making a constitution for India. Like the reaction of all nationalists, Mohamed Ali's response to the announcement was entirely intimidating. For him it was highly insulting to the honour and dignity of the nation. These were trying times for Mohamed Ali. His health was worsening and the financial condition of the CKC was also very poor. The Khilafat Movement, by now, had lost it attraction and the very purpose. In Hejaz, though Ibn-e-Saud had successfully driven out the puppet of the British, Hussain (Sharif of Mecca), and he himself had established an absolute, hereditary monarchy in the region. He had also introduced a rigid and extremely puritanical mode of Islam, Wahabism (Salafism) as the official religion of the kingdom. Acting as per the precepts of the fundamentalist and inflexible version of his faith, Ibn-e-Saud bulldozed the graves of the companions of the Prophet. These developments gave a rude shock to the Ali brothers because with the establishment of the Saudi kingdom based on the principle of heredity, the hope of establishing a new seat of the Caliphate in the Arab peninsula was also shattered.

Mohamed Ali's health kept deteriorating. The Maharaja of Alwar advised him that he should go to England for medical treatment and offered financial assistance for the purpose. He was hesitant initially but because of Shaukat Ali's persuasion and some close friends he agreed to go to London. Having spent a few months in London, he came back as his health had improved. During his absence from India, the Nehru Committee Report was accepted by the INC.[66] Mohamed Ali was taken aback because among the supporters of the Report were people like Dr. M.A. Ansari and Maulana Azad, who were once his closest allies. Mohamed Ali's main objections to the Report were two: a) it had rejected the principle of separate electorates based on faith by opting for the joint electorates throughout the country; and b) it agreed to accept the dominion status for India instead of complete independence.

On December 24-25, 1928, the CKC held its session in Calcutta under the presidentship of Mohamed Ali. In its second session he launched a scathing attack on the Nehru Report mainly because of joint electorates, which in his opinion, was brazen betrayal of the Muslims of the subcontinent. Another delegate Azad Sobhani remarked that the Report was not in the interest of Indians as it acquiesced to dominion status for the country under British imperialism. Sobhani asserted that the prime duty of the Muslims was to get rid of the British rule and the Muslims under the CKC were committed to struggle for the attainment of freedom. Maulana Zafar Ali Khan underscored that the Nehru Report was a document that perpetuated the slavery of Indians. Maulana Hasrat Mohani moved a resolution, the salient points of which were as follows:

1) The future Constitution of India should establish a federation comprising autonomous provinces of the country.
2) All the federating units (provinces) should have genuine autonomy within their territories having its own legislature and popularly elected governor.
3) The federal legislature (parliament) should also be composed of the popularly elected members and the federal government should be vested with the powers necessary to look after the subjects of national importance.

Mohani declared that any future constitution of India bereft of these principles would not be acceptable to the Muslims. He expressed that it was a matter of satisfaction that most prominent Muslim leaders had rejected the Nehru Report.

Maulana Shafi Dawoodi spoke in support of the resolution by insisting that the dominion status for India would never be acceptable to the Muslims who were entirely dedicated to the independence of the nation. In short, the mood of the majority of the office bearers seemed to be in favour of the resolution moved by Mohani and consequently it was passed. The prominent leaders who opposed the resolution included Dr. M.A. Ansari, Maulana Azad and Dr. Saifuddin Kitchlew. A short while later these leaders dissociated themselves from the opponents of the Nehru Report and made a declaration that the majority of the members of the CKC were with them. They elected Dr. M.A. Ansari as their president and in a separate session passed the following resolution:

> We, the signatory members of the CKC feel dutybound to make public the reasons for differences between us and the office bearers of the CKC with whom we have worked for decades to build up and fortify the Khilafat Committee. In order to clarify our position we would like to put on record the following facts:
>
> 1) First of all we want to state that we have had a majority of 70 delegates in the session held on December 24. Despite this the President adopted an antagonistic attitude towards us and arbitrarily passed the contentious issues by ignoring to put them to vote;
>
> 2) We have been striving for arriving at some amicable decision on

the Nehru Report agreeable to all the members of the CKC. However, because of the impediments created by the office bearers our efforts have failed;

3) The Bengal Khilafat Committee that favours the Nehru Report has been engaged in taking a vote on the issue. When the President of the CKC got the news he personally went to the venue along with the Secretary of the CKC and about a hundred goons and tried to stop the voting. When he realized that his unruly tactics would fail to stop the voting, he engineered a mayhem there. The Bengal Khilafat Committee had elected 30 delegates for the CKC. The President of the CKC had unlawfully confiscated the muster of the members of the Bengal Khilafat Committee. Next day, without any notice he ordered fresh elections of the delegates from the Bengal Khilafat Committee to the CKC. This election was totally illegal as the electorates were only from the city of Calcutta. The members of the district committees were neither present nor were their names invited for the purpose of voting. Besides Bengal there were Khilafat Committees of Bihar and the NWFP that were not in favour of the stance of the President and other office bearers on the Nehru Report. All these members were disallowed to participate when the vote was taken for rejecting the Nehru Report.

4) At the meeting of the Working Committee, the unlawful actions and decisions taken by the President were fully exposed. The elections that were held under the instruction of the President for electing the delegates to the CKC from the Bengal Khilafat Committee were declared void by the majority vote in the Working Committee.

5) Thereafter at a meeting of the CKC held late in the evening, the behaviour of the President naturally came under attack. In response his supporters became violent and started swearing and verbally abusing their opponents. A member of the CKC suddenly whistled after which a few hoodlums armed with knives and batons entered the *pandal*. A goon was wrathfully gesticulating with a big hunter knife. It took a lot of patience and persuasion of many members to talk into the hoodlums to go out of the *pandal*. It was plain for everyone to see that these goons were asked to wait outside the *pandal* and on getting the cue should enter and create a pandemonium. In such conditions we were left with no choice but to walk out of the meeting. However, even after the walkout of the majority of the members, the President not only continued the proceedings of electing the members of the Subject Committee but also helped reinstate the thirty members from the Bengal Khilafat Committee to the CKC who

were disqualified by the Working Committee. He also elected the Secretary and the Executive Members of the CKC in the absence of the majority of the delegates. We say publicly that the elections of office bearers and the members of the executive committee have been null and void.

In the light of the policy adopted at the Lucknow session, the dissident members passed the following resolutions:

1) The members of the CKC should keep attending the all-parties' conventions as they have been doing till now.
2) While keeping hold of the objective of complete independence of the country, the Nehru Committee Report should, by and large, be accepted. The issue of communal electorates should also be retained with minor alterations. The pact that was signed at Lucknow with the representatives of Punjab and which was submitted to the All Parties Convention by the CKC should be adopted forthwith and as per its provisions a demand of reservation of seats for ten years should be made. The demands of the province of Bengal should be tuned with the Punjab Pact.
3) In accordance with the principles endorsed by the All Parties' Convention separate electorates for Muslims in all legislatures should be retained until the minority community decides otherwise.
4) The representatives of the CKC to be nominated for participation in All Parties Convention should have complete authority.

Ali brothers did not take the opposition to their stance on the Nehru Report lying down. They pulled together their supporters and goaded them to hijack the meetings of their opponents and also thrash them. Some leaders were indeed beaten black and blue. This was the worst episode in the history of the Khilafat Movement. It was followed by a series of communal riots in different parts of the country.

Despite a virtual break away from the Congress, the Ali brothers kept on opposing the British Raj in India. Though they were quite rattled because of Congress's stand on the communal question, they were equally hostile to the Raj that, they believed, was mainly responsible of creating a rift between Hindus and Muslims. Mohamed Ali would often say: "We get divided and they rule over us." The Ali brothers along with all the members of the CKC decided to oppose the Simon Commission that had arrived in India to get the feedback for framing a new constitution for India.[67] The Congress was also opposed to the all-white commission. Quite a few Muslim leaders including Dr. Muhammad Iqbal welcomed the Simon Commission. For Mohamed Ali these leaders were suffering from the slave mentality. Iqbal's position, in particular, agitated him immensely.

He showed his disapproval of Iqbal's stance in his weekly, *Hamdard*: "During the First World War, Allama Iqbal was free and we were rotting in jail. After the conclusion of the war, the British Raj imposed martial law under which hundreds of people were arrested including the prominent leaders of Punjab. Yet, this time too Iqbal was not touched." Mohamed Ali also wrote that Iqbal had always kept away from joining the Khilafat Movement on one pretext or the other. Once Iqbal was instrumental in procuring an edict (*fatwa*) in favour of Khilafat which was signed by five hundred *maulavis*. Notwithstanding it, he kept away from the Khilafat Movement stating that he would like to be engaged in constructive works. Iqbal had also advised the Muslims to concentrate more on seeking technical education. Mohamed Ali commented acerbically that Iqbal was sermonizing about technical education and writing his poems sitting comfortably in Anarkali of Lahore, whereas we read his poems and rotted in jails.

Though Mohamed Ali considered Iqbal as his teacher, he refused to accept his politics. Iqbal never thought highly of Mohamed Ali's Khilafat Movement. He had, in fact, said the "Khilafat Movement was a foolish action", a lifeless lobby that had no correlation with Indian Muslims. When Kemal Pasha ended the institution of Khilafat, Iqbal was not overtly agitated though he described Pasha's action as heresy. Iqbal maintained that a phony reverence of history and its false revival was a waste of time for those who were striving to improve their conditions. Though some Muslims of the time were in agreement with Dr. Iqbal, those associated with the Khilafat Movement were totally opposed to his ideas. In order to make Iqbal realize that the overwhelming majority of the Muslims was behind the Khilafat agitation, Mohamed Ali once invited Iqbal to share a platform with him to address the Muslims either at Lahore or any other place of his choice. Iqbal scornfully rejected the offer with the comment, "I do not like such craftiness."

Regardless of Khilafatists' earnest efforts the relations between the Hindus and Muslims did not improve. Communal riots kept recurring frequently. The Muslims were not in the right frame of mind to trust Hindus because they believed that the majority community did not favour sharing power with the Muslim minority. Hindus, on their part, supposed that Muslims were not interested in joining hands with them to free the country from the British and to camouflage their real intention they kept creating problems for the nationalist movement. The rift between Gandhi and Mohamed Ali kept widening. Mohamed Ali seriously believed that the Nehru Report was a document that was designed to legalize the majority community's domination over the Muslim minority. It was a device to act towards the majority community's communalism as nationalism. The Muslims' efforts to protect their interests from the offensive of the majority community was construed to be as communalism.

A conference of all the Muslim parties and organizations was held on January 11, 1929. It was chaired by Aga Khan. The Ali brothers attended the conference as the representatives of the CKC. The Conference rejected the Nehru Report. A Muslim manifesto enlisting Muslim demands to be incorporated in the future constitution of India was released. The inflexible stance of the Muslim Conference on the Nehru Report alienated a few Muslim leaders like Dr. M.A. Ansari, Maulana Azad, Dr. Saifuddin Kitchlew, Khaliquzzaman Chaudhary et al. These leaders preferred to be associated with the Congress.

It was the time when the Ali brothers were passing through the worst financial crisis. Both the weeklies, *Comrade* (English) and *Hamdard* (Urdu) of Mohamed Ali went out of business. The more serious problem, however, was his constantly failing health. He was diabetic and was also suffering from high blood pressure. He had lost one eye and the sight of the other one was also weak. In his famous speech at the Round Table Conference, Mohamed Ali talked about his ailments thus: "A man with my dilated heart; with my approaching and recurrent blindness through retinitis; with my once-gangrened foot, with neuritis—this huge bulking foot through oedema; with albuminaria; with diabetes, and the whole long list..."[68] Many of his colleagues believed that he had lost his worth. Regardless of these disadvantages, Mohamed Ali kept corresponding with the Viceroy on the Muslim issue. The Nawab of Bhopal invited Mohamed Ali to his city and made a genuine effort to provide the best possible medical treatment. However, it was too late. His health barely improved. Around this time the Viceroy invited him to participate in the Round Table Conference that was convened by the British Prime Minister and was to be held at London in November, 1930. Disregarding his doctors's advice, Mohamed Ali went to London. His friends and well-wishers in London advised complete rest but he ignored their advice and got engaged in preparing for the conference. He knew that he would not survive for long.

In his speech at the Round Table Conference, Mohamed Ali forcefully argued for complete independence of India and insisted "I want to go back to my country if I can return with the substance of freedom in my hand. Otherwise I will not go back to a slave country. I would even prefer to die in a foreign country, so long as it is a free country; and if you do not give us freedom in India you will have to give me a grave here."[69] He emphasized the need for Hindu-Muslim unity and explained the root cause of the rift between the two main communities of India. In his words: "The real problem which is upsetting us all the time has been...this Hindu-Muslim problem; but that is no problem at all. The fact is that the Hindu-Muslim difficulty, like the Army difficulty, is of your own creation. But not altogether. It is the old maxim of "divide and rule." But there is a division of labour here. We divide and you rule. The moment we decide not to divide you will not be able to rule as you are doing today. With this determination not to be divided, we have come here."[70] Thus, he hit the nail on the head by blaming the British for dividing Indians on communal lines to perpetuate their unjust rule over India.

Reflecting on religion, its linkages with politics and his position as a Muslim leader Mohamed Ali said: "It is a wrong conception of religion that you have, if you exclude politics from it. It is not dogma; it is not ritual! Religion, to my mind means the interpretation of life. I have a culture, a polity, an outlook on life—a complete synthesis which is Islam. Where God commands I am a Muslim first, a Muslim second, and a Muslim last, and nothing but a Muslim. If you ask me to enter your Empire or your Nation by leaving that synthesis, that polity, that culture, that ethics, I will not do it. My first duty is to my Maker, not to H.M. the King..."[71] He was extremely forthright while commenting on a Muslim's position towards his country and the love of his country that goes by the popular idea of nationalism. His words put across the point very apparent that though he was striving sincerely for the independence of India, he did not believe in nationalism. It makes him a complex man whose ideas were enmeshed with each other and as a result of it, his critics rightfully blamed him for inconsistency. Consider this segment of the speech: "I belong to two circles of equal size, but which are not concentric. One is India, and the other is the Muslim world. When I came to England in 1920 at the head of the Khilafat delegation, my friends said: 'You must have some sort of a crest for your stationery.' I decided to have it with two circles on it. In one circle was the word 'India'; in the other circle was Islam, with the word 'Khilafat.' We as Indian Muslims came into both circles. We belong to these two circles, each of more than 300 millions, and we can leave neither. We are not nationalists but supernationalists, and I as a Muslim say that 'God made man and the Devil made the nation.' Nationalism divides; our religion binds. No religious wars, no crusades, have seen such holocausts and have been so cruel as your last war, and that was a war of your nationalism, and not my Jehad."[72]

III

Mohamed Ali's speech delivered at the First Round Table Conference was his swan song. The Khilafat Movement had died much earlier than the death of its charasmatic, though controversial, leader. He was a true representative of Indian Muslims in the sense that like an overwhelming majority of them, he too had an emotional rather than an objective or pragmatic approach to deal with the community's problems. It was the dominance of Mohamed Ali over the Khilafat Movement that had never allowed it to rise above the level of an emotional outburst against the wrongs done to the Muslim interests by British imperialism. His ideas were mostly the product of his emotions and he expressed them in his inimitable vociferous and sensational style. In the typical tradition of Muslim politics in India, Mohamed Ali's political strategy was to give a fearless expression to what he construed to be the truth. A sagacious and malleable political strategy was not his forte. Political guidance is an accommodating and hardnosed task. It requires persistence, prudence, adaptability, vision, sobriety and pliability, the qualities woefully absent in the persona of Mohamed Ali. He relied mostly on courageous confrontation and emotional appeal that hardly impressed his British adversaries. It has been reported that the "Government officials associated him (Mohamed Ali) with the extreme faction of the 'Muslim community', the 'Advanced Party' and the 'hot-headed Nationalist Party'. He led a clique of noisy and aggressive Muslims of the 'young party', who made the raja's house [Raja of Mahmudabad] their headquarters and lived and agitated at his expense. He left trouble whereever he went, reported the viceroy."[73]

The Khilafat Movement was the the first biggest mass movement of the Indian Muslims that had proverbially started with a bang but ended with a whimper. Nevertheless, during its heyday it accomplished the objective of Hindu-Muslim unity that was considered to be almost impossible. The regrettable point is that it could not sustain the ambience of inter-communal amity for long mainly because of the incongruity of its leading lights, viz. Gandhi and Mohamed Ali. While the former was a soft-spoken visionary, the latter was a fiery confrontationist. For most Muslims, the Khilafat Movement was a religious issue while for Gandhi and most Congressmen it was a political strategy to create a formidable united front comprising the two major communities of the country against the British. It was mainly because of the Ali brothers and the ulama who backed them, that Khilafat could not be transformed from a Muslim issue into a nationalist movement. Though Jamiat al-Ulama was born at the same time that the Khilafat Movement was launched, most members of the former preferred to go along with Gandhi for the sake of nationalist goals. The leading members of the CKC, however, were unable to latch on their objectives to the mainstream nationalist struggle.

Mohamed Ali and his colleagues failed miserably to chalk out a constructive political plan through their movement that could help create an enlightened Muslim leadership. No doubt that the involvement of the Muslim masses, particularly in Northern India, in political agitation was largely because of Khilafat. It was politically a healthy development. When the international scenario, over which neither the Ali brothers nor any other Indian leader had any control, rendered the very issue of Khilafat superfluous, Mohamed Ali could have turned the force of the Muslim masses to back the nationalist cause as was the expectation of Gandhi, about whom he once said, "I cannot find in any community—Jewish, Christian or any other—a man who has as noble a character as Mahatma Gandhi." And, on parting ways with Gandhi and the Congress, he estimated Gandhi thus: "Even the most degraded Muslim was better than Mahatma Gandhi."[74] However, it seems his understanding of nationalism was flawed. For him nationalism merely meant anti-British rhetoric. His pan-Islamist bent of mind probably did not allow him to recognize the conceptual advantages of nationalism. It was for this reason that he could not figure out the political stance of the Arabs during and after the First World War.

5

Beyond the Movement

What an excellent idea to renovate and reactivate the old 'Khulafat House'. It is hallowed with remembrance of stalwarts of our freedom struggle and has been an active centre of Hindu-Muslim Unity.

– Indira Gandhi

It was at this place (Khilafat House) her grandfather Motilal Nehru, her father Jawaharlal Nehru, Mahatma Gandhi, Mrs. Sarojini Naidu, Madan Mohan Malviya, Hakim Ajmal Khan, Dr. M.A. Ansari, Maulana Abul Kalam Azad and the Ali brothers would discuss the national issues.

– Rafiq Zakaria

If one takes a turn towards the east at the crossroad of Byculla Police Station that is located just by the flyover in the street that earlier had a very romantic name—*Love Lane*—that was later changed because of the bigotry of politicians who seek a vicarious pleasure in changing the old names of streets, cities public places and institutions and never lose any opportunity to mention such acts to their followers as some of their "great accomplishments". The present name, Motishah Lane is not only banal but also has a mercantilist ring to it. So, in independent India love got transformed into merchandise. The current name of the street, all the same, suits the surroundings that can best be described as the lower middle class market. About a furlong from the police station one will be surprised to see a big Mughal style archway on the right. The element of surprise could be because the archway and its name engraved boldly in *Nastaliq* script—Baab-e-Omar—at the top of the archway look incongruous in the dowdy surroundings with decrepit shops dotted all around owned mostly by Jain-Hindu traders. There is also a Jain temple located just opposite the imposing gateway. More information is engraved on the two marble plaques fastened to the two pillars of the archway. The English text on the left one reads: "Bab-e-Omar (Omar Gate)/In Loving Memory of Omar Sobani Marhoom/Born Bombay, April 11, 1888 AD/Died Bombay July 6, 1926 AD. Devoted worker in the cause of Khilafat, a true patriot and generous loving friend./ Erected by his admirers and co-workers." The right side plaque provides the same information in Urdu but a (*sher*) couplet of the renowned Persian poet Hafiz is also engraved at the end:

> *Hargiz nameerad aan ke dilash zinda shud ba-ishq*
> *Sabt ast bar jareeda-e-aalam dawam-e-ma*
>
> (One whose heart got engrossed in true love, cannot die/His (name) is eternally affixed in the chronicle of the earth)

This is the archway of the precinct wherein is located the headquarters of the Central Khilafat Committee. Though the building and the objectives of the organization it houses have undergone changes, it still transports the visitor to the glorious days it has seen and makes him picture the prominent freedom fighters it has hosted. Currently, it houses the Khilafat College of Education and the prospectus of the College provides very briefly the basic information about the CKC. It says: "All India Khilafat Committee, with its headquarters in 'Khilafat House', Bombay, has a hoary historical past. Started as an organization of Indian Muslims to voice their resentment against the British rule at the end of the First World War in 1919 by the famous Ali brothers—Maulana Mohamed Ali and Maulana Shaukat Ali—with the active support of Mahatma Gandhi, it soon became the chief instrument of opposition. It mobilized under its banner Muslims from everywhere in the subcontinent and under the guidance and leadership of the Mahatma launched the first Non-cooperation movement in 1920; the Indian National Congress joined this movement six months later. As a result, not only Gandhiji and the Ali Brothers but lakhs of Khilafatists were imprisoned and tortured and their properties were confiscated.

"Hence in India's struggle for freedom, 'Khilafat House' played a most important role: it was the beehive of Gandhiji's activities in the early 1920s. Initially, the meetings of the All India Khilafat Committee were held at 'Chotani House' situated at Khadak, Bombay, but later, the Sobani family under the leadership of the well-known patriot and freedom fighter, Mr. Umar Sobani, handed over their ancestral property at Love Lane, Byculla to the All India Khilafat Committee and named it 'Khilafat House'."[1]

Though the Khilafat Movement had died much before the demise of its star campaigner, Mohamed Ali, on January 4, 1931, the CKC headquartered at Bombay did remain a focal point of Muslim politico-religious activities. Maulana Shaukat Ali who was once a close ally of Gandhi during the heyday of the Non-cooperation-Khilafat agitation had, by now, parted company with the Congress and its political positions. In the post-Khilafat days he made Khilafat House the headquarters of his activities that were ideologically in contrast with the mission of the Congress. His popularity among the people, in particular, the Muslim masses, was primarily because of the Khilafat Movement. With the withering away of the Movement, most Muslim masses turned away from the Ali Brothers as well as the Congress. In the changed political scenario, Maulana Shaukat Ali too began to identify himself exclusively with the Muslim causes that, more often than not, were rooted in Muslim separatism. For instance, the Congress had given the boycott call of the Round Table Conference and its representatives did not attend the first two of the three conferences. However, the Ali Brothers attended these conferences as the Muslim representatives. After the death of his younger brother, Maulana Shaukat Ali took upon himself the responsibility of advocating the *Muslim cause* not only in India and Britain but all across the world. He visited almost all the Muslim-dominated countries of the Middle East and Africa. He was also a proactive organizer of the World Muslim Conference held in Jerusalem in 1931. He went on a lecture-tour of the US and delivered lectures in many American cities highlighting the plight of the Muslims in general and the myriad problems of the Indian Muslims in particular.

The Khilafat House was made the headquarters of the CKC in

1924 and even after the collapse of the Movement it retained its identification as a meeting place for those who were involved in the Khilafat agitation. Nonetheless, an ideological shift came about in Muslim politics in India with the abolition of the institution of the Khilafat. The Muslim masses who were mobilized by the ulama and the Khilafat leaders on the slogan of *'Islam in danger'* during the halcyon days of the Khilafat agitation had also made a common cause with their Hindu brethren as Gandhi had launched the Non-cooperation Movement simultaneously to support the Muslim cause. As a result, the twin agitation was truly an Indian agitation because India, for the first time, had witnessed the unprecedented Hindu-Muslim unity against the British imperialists across the subcontinent. It was too good to believe and sadly it did not last long. Gandhi's decision to suspend the Non-cooperation Movement in the aftermath of the Chauri Chaura incident disappointed most of the political activists, both Hindus and Muslims, but the wily orthodox Mullahs interpreted it as treachery by the 'Hindu' Congress and its supreme leader. This engendered a sea change in the Muslim political attitude towards the INC and the concept of composite nationalism.

First of all, the Muslim masses who had joined the agitation on the catchphrase of *'Islam in danger'* and who did not have any inkling about the imperialist designs of the British against the Ottoman Empire, had lost all interest in the agitation once the Muslim political elite became dormant on the issue after 1924. Secondly, most Muslim leaders, including the Ali Brothers, had blamed Gandhi and the INC for weakening the Khilafat agitation when it was at its peak. Though the Ali Brothers did not snap their affiliation with the INC in 1922, the drift away from a united front against the foreign rule had set in. Thirdly, the abolition of the institution of Khilafat by Mustafa Kemal had left the Movement without its raison d'être and the Ali Brothers without a cause. It was, therefore, expected from the two towering leaders of the Khilafat to continue within the Congress fold and also advise their followers to rally behind the nationalist platform. The point of departure, nonetheless, came when the Nehru Report was prepared in 1928, as an alternative to the British government's plan to frame yet another constitution for India. The Ali Brothers and under their instructions the Central Khilafat Committee strongly disapproved of the Nehru Report mainly because it did not provide for separate electorates for any religious community including the Muslims. Thereafter, defying the INC diktat, Maulana Shaukat Ali attended the first two Round Table Conferences in London.

Maulana Shaukat Ali had no reason to support the Muslim League because that organization had openly opposed the Khilafat Movement. Nevertheless, he was not politically as sagacious as he was dexterous in campaigning for a religious issue that could immediately connect with the Muslim masses. He, therefore, joined the All India Muslim League in 1936, and thereafter became a campaigner to disseminate the separatist ideology of his new camp. This, unfortunately is the case of quite a few Indian Muslim political leaders that their popularity and fame among the members of their community owes a lot to their craftiness in concealing political ambitions in religious idioms. Mohammad Ali Jinnah's is a case in point. At the beginning of the twentieth century he emerged as one of the most secular Congress leaders. He was one among the leading lights of the moderate Congressmen. His politics then was deeply immersed in the categorical commitment to liberal-constitutional, democratic and secular principles. He was totally opposed to intermixing of religious issues with political ones. In fact, his conflict with Gandhi was mainly on this issue. His opposition to the Khilafat Movement was also on the ground that, in his view, Khilafat was absolutely a religious issue and making it a part of the nationalist struggle was erroneous. In those days, though Jinnah was the darling of the young Congressmen, the Muslim masses hardly knew him and the Muslim political elite despised him. The same Jinnah became a rage among the Muslim masses as well as political elite when he got transformed into a communal leader with his two-nation theory and the demand for Pakistan.

In the post-Communal Award scenario, therefore, Maulana Shaukat Ali's political expediency made him jump on to the bandwagon of the Muslim League that was being driven by *Qaid-e-Azam* of the Muslims of the Indian subcontinent. The Communal Award that was announced after the conclusion of the three Round Table Conferences in 1932 by the British Prime Minister, Ramsay

MacDonald, had, besides continuing the separate electorates for the Muslims, also extended it to other religious minorities including the Dalits. The one clause that gave a fresh lease of life to the Muslim League that had, till then, remained a political organization of the Muslim *zamindars* and *ashraf*, provided that the British Government henceforth would not take any important political decision regarding India unless the two major political parties, viz. the INC and the Muslim League did not concur on it. In a way, it empowered the Muslim League with a veto power to scuttle any proposal the INC would put forth in future. In this, Jinnah's brilliant legal mind saw an opportunity to settle scores with his arch political adversary, Gandhi, and thus he revived the listless Muslim League by transforming himself as the chief spokesman of the Muslims of India. Thereafter, not only Maulana Shaukat Ali but most Khilafatists who were still politically active dissociated from the INC and joined the Muslim League.

On joining the Muslim League, Maulana Shaukat Ali was appointed the member of the Working Committee of the organization, the position that he held till his death. Gandhi was quite hurt on hearing the news that Maulana Shaukat Ali got dissociated with the INC and not only became a proactive leader of the Muslim League but also a fervent advocate of Jinnah's 'two-nation theory'. Since Jinnah's emergence as the undisputed leader of the Muslim League, the other Muslim leaders hardly had any power to make any noteworthy contribution to the policies and political strategies of the organization. Everyone was expected to toe the line adopted by the *Qaid-e-Azam*. Soon enough, Maulana Shaukat Ali realized that despite his membership of the Working Committee and the camaraderie with Jinnah, his position in the Muslim League only had a cosmetic value. Consequently, he dedicated himself more to the purely religious activities. He set up an institution, *Khudam-e-Kaaba* (Servants of Kaaba), that looked after various needs of the pilgrims going to Mecca for Hajj. In those days most pilgrims would travel to Mecca by sea and, therefore, they had to come from distant places of the Indian subcontinent to Bombay to take a ship to Saudi Arabia. During their stay in Bombay, the *Khuddam-e-Kaaba* would make arrangements for their lodging and boarding, would help them buy the most economical passage fare, take care of the necessary documents and, as a rule, make available for them the services of a doctor. In short, Maulana Shaukat Ali's organization performed a similar kind of role for the pilgrims that is currently carried out by the Hajj Committee.

Another activity of the Khilafat House that continued under the supervision of Maulana Shaukat Ali was to take out the annual procession on the birthday of Prophet Muhammad (*Yum-e-Milad-un-Nabi*), a tradition that continues till now. As a matter of fact, the practice of taking out a procession on the birthday of the Prophet was started with Gandhi's blessing during the heyday of the Khilafat Movement in 1920. For the devout Muslims, his birthday is not an occasion to express unbound happiness and exuberance because as per the Islamic calendar the day of his death is also the same as the 12th Rabi-al-Awwal. The Muslims across the world, therefore, do not go overboard in observing the day as the Christians do on December 25th. It was precisely for that reason there was no tradition of taking out a procession on *Yum-e-Milad-un-Nabi* anywhere in the Indian subcontinent. Gandhi, in alliance with the Ali Brothers, started it emulating the strategy perfected by Bal Gangadhar Tilak two decades earlier when he pioneered the public celebrations of *Ganesh Utsav*. Public Ganesh Utsav provided Tilak and his supporters a conduit to give expression to his political agenda and furtively cultivate mass-opinion against the British. It was obviously an intermixing of religion and politics but Tilak never bothered about sticking to the value of secularism. So taking a cue from Tilak, the Ali Brothers and Gandhi laid down the tradition of a procession to commemorate the Prophet of Islam on his day of his birth and also use the occasion to endorse the Non-cooperation-Khilafat agitation. The major difference between Tilak's public celebration of *Ganesh Utsav* and the *Yum-e-Milad-un-Nabi* procession is that while the former is an affair exclusively of the Hindus, whereas the latter lays emphasis on the requirement of *Hindu-Muslim unity*. In the early 1920s, as has been noted in the previous chapter, the Indian freedom struggle witnessed the unprecedented scenes of Hindu-Muslim camaraderie because of the alliance between Gandhi and the Ali Brothers and for them the Prophet's birthday procession provided an opportunity to appeal for amity between Hindus and Muslims. Nonetheless, when the Khilafatists got dissociated with the Congress, the annual procession on the day of the Prophet's birth was usurped by the Muslim League to enlist the supporters for its separatist political agenda.

Rafiq Zakaria on taking charge of the affairs of the Khilafat House in 1970, earnestly tried to restore the all-inclusive character of the annual procession on the Prophet's birthday by forcefully asserting that it epitomized Hindu-Muslim unity as was witnessed between 1919 and 1922. On many occasions he had appealed to the Hindus, Christians, Sikhs, Jains, Buddhists and Parsis of the city of Bombay to join the procession to support the cause of communal harmony. Another tradition that he had revived was to invite mostly non-Muslim prominent personalities to lead the procession. The first procession of *Milad-e-Nabi* was led by Gandhi in 1920 and other well-known leaders such as Pandit Motilal Nehru, Pandit Jawaharlal Nehru, Madan Mohan Malviya and others also participated. Under Zakaria's leadership, besides quite a few Chief Ministers and Union Ministers, the President of India, Giani Zail Singh and the Prime Ministers, Rajiv Gandhi and P.V. Narasimha Rao also led the procession. Addressing a large crowd prior to leading the procession, Narasimha Rao said that the Khilafat Movement had consolidated the secular and nationalist feelings in the country and unified the Hindus and Muslims that had shaken the foundation of British colonial rule. It was because of Hindu-Muslim unity achieved during the peak of the Khilafat and Non-cooperation movements that Gandhiji got transformed into the greatest leader of our freedom struggle. The All India Khilafat Committee had always celebrated its annual day on the birthday of the Prophet and in this manner it had been making attempts to fortify the ideal of Hindu-Muslim unity. Narasimha Rao congratulated the members of the Khilafat Committe for keeping alive the practice of taking out the procession on the birthday of the Prophet.

It must, however, be noted with a sense of despondency that of late and in particular since the death of Rafiq Zakaria in 2005, the all-inclusive character of the procession seems to have been eroded. It is not entirely the fault of the members of the Khilafat Committee because the current Chairperson, Mrs. Fatma R. Zakaria, is as much committed to secularism and the cause of Hindu-Muslim unity as her late husband was. The Vice-Chairperson, Sarfaraz Arzoo is a veteran journalist and a social activist. He too is a man who believes in the secular and all-inclusive character of Indian society. Despite the sincere efforts of the Chairperson and Vice-Chairperson, the annual procession on the birthday of the Prophet seems to have acquired the image of an exclusive Muslim event. The obvious reason is the ever increasing gulf between the Hindus and Muslims because of the rise of Hindu and Muslim fundamentalism. The politics of *Hindutva* brought its proponents to power and had almost marginalized the secular forces. Nevertheless, we must also censure the attitude of the secular-minded Hindus and Sikhs. They would be participating in the procession in large numbers till the end of the last century. Their lack of interest not only in this event but in quite a few other issues of an all-encompassing nature is a major setback to the cause of Hindu-Muslim unity. The dream of a peaceful secular and harmonious India cannot be translated into reality merely by sermonizing about it but it could become a certainty only when the secular-minded members of all the communities take concrete steps for it. The Hindus being the majority community have a greater obligation to take the lead to strengthen traditions and practices that are designed to achieve Hindu-Muslim unity.

Maulana Shaukat Ali died in the morning of November 27, 1938 at Delhi. The next day he was buried in front of Jama Masjid on the eastern side.[3] Though for about a decade Shaukat Ali was not close to the Congress leaders and had got himself involved more in the politics of the Muslim League, the leading leaders of the INC paid rich homages to him on his death. In a message Gandhi said: "Please convey to the proper quarters my grief at big brother's death. In spite of later differences, I could never forget our past warm friendship. Maulana always held me in his pocket for Hindu-Muslim unity which, though it could not be ahieved during his lifetime, let us hope his death will make both communities achieve it."[4] The point to be noted here is that Gandhi remembered Maulana Shaukat Ali in the condolence message for the cause which was at one time closest to their hearts, viz. Hindu-Muslim unity. Despite the failure of both the leaders to make the unity of the two leading religious communities of India a reality during the lifetime of

Shaukat Ali, the optimist Gandhi hoped that the members of the two communities would strive to achieve it.

Likewise, Pandit Jawaharlal Nehru expressed his feelings in a message: "I am deeply grieved to learn of the death of Maulana Shaukat Ali. One by one the brave old comrades in our fight for freedom pass away and Maulana Shaukat Ali was the bravest of these. Together with Maulana Mohammad Ali he became an emblem of the new spirit for freedom among the Muslims of India, and in the great days of non-cooperation. Eighteen years ago, his towering figure became familiar in every nook and corner of India. For these many years I had the privilege of close comradeship with him and subsequent differences of opinion on political and other matters cannot take away that memory or lessen the grief at the passing away of one who has played a great part in India's struggle. Essentially a fighter, he has died in harness and India must pay homage to his memory."[5] For Nehru, the role of the Ali Brothers in the Non-cooperation was of immense significance and, therefore, he remembered the deceased leader for his role in the agitation that was in tandem with the Khilafat Movement.

Maulana Abul Kalam Azad expressed his deep shock at the death of Maulana Shaukat Ali. He also added: "His death will be mourned not only throughout India but abroad as well. His name has been so closely associated with the most important event of the political movements in India that we cannot recollect those without recalling his memory. His services and sacrifices which he rendered during the 1919-20 movement shall remain as his everlasting memorial."[6] The significant point is that no Congress leader, including Azad, remembered Maulana Shaukat Ali in the context of the Khilafat agitation which was supported by the INC. Nonetheless, by the late 1930s, it seemed that the INC leaders preferred to forget that phase of their struggle. Subhas Chandra Bose was the President of the INC at that time. He too did not make a mention of the Khilafat Movement while remembering the departed leaders in these words: "I am sorry to hear of the sad demise of Maulana Shaukat Ali. He was a great leader and one of the fighters in the nation's cause."[7]

Maulana Shaukat Ali's last phase of political activism was with the Muslim League during which time he was quite close to

Mohammad Ali Jinnah. It was, therefore, obvious for Jinnah to be extremely grief-stricken. In an interview to the *Associated Press*, he said: "I am deeply grieved to hear the most distressing news of the sudden death of Maulana Shaukat Ali who was my personal friend and colleague. In him the Muslims in India have lost a great leader who was true and loyal to his people and no sacrifice, however great could stand in his way or deter him from serving and standing by his people at all critical moments. He was ready to sacrifice his life and all for the Muslims. The Muslims have lost in him one of the greatest leaders, a fearless worker and a champion of Islam".[8] One can easily discern overemphasis on 'Muslim' and Islam in this statement which was the prime concern of Jinnah and the Muslim League. Maulana Shaukat Ali's earlier efforts to make Hindu-Muslim unity happen were completely disregarded and he was remembered simply for his concerns about his community.

After the death of Maulana Shaukat Ali, his son Zahid Ali took on the affairs of Khilafat House. He, however, was not inclined to get involved in socio-political activism. He, therefore, restricted himself to oversee the religious affairs of the Muslim community that were mostly about looking after lodging and boarding facilities of the pilgrims on the way to Mecca and organizing the annual procession on the birthday of the Prophet. The Muslim politics in those days was completely dominated by the Muslim League and the movement for Pakistan. Zahid Ali could not play a significant role in that area too because by nature he was not cut out to be a man of politics. The partition of the country and creation of Pakistan put the Muslims who decided to stay put in India in great trouble all over India. The Khilafat House that had been a witness to the vicissitude of Muslim politics was also a target of anti-Muslim policies of the state government. In 1954, Morarji Desai, who was the Chief Minister of the then Bombay State issued a notice to Zahid Ali to check out of the Khilafat House as the government was planning to establish a charitable trust in the building. This notice stunned Zahid Ali and he was in a fix as how to deal with the adverse situation. At this time he decided to get in touch with Dr. Rafiq Zakaria, a young barrister and a committed Congressman.

At this point it is appropriate to say a few words about Dr. Rafiq Zakaria and his contribution to national and Muslim politics.

Dr. Rafiq Zakaria had a vision to build a progressive, self-reliant, prosperous, democratic and secular India and fought for accomplishing it. Dr. Zakaria was a multi-faceted person. He was an Islamic scholar, a staunch nationalist, a social scientist, an educationist, a prolific writer and a public figure committed to secularism and liberal democracy. Dr. Zakaria was a Muslim political thinker in the tradition of Syed Husain Ahmed Madani who loved his motherland intensely without being apologetic about his Muslim identity because he did not find any mismatch between nationalism and the precepts of Islam. Prior to Dr. Zakaria's writings, Madani's intellectual legacy could also be located in the political thought of Badruddin Tyabji, Hakim Ajmal Khan, Mukhtar Ahmed Ansari and Maulana Abul Kalam Azad. Among these stalwarts, Dr. Zakaria could be compared more closely with Maulana Azad because both were resolute nationalists, Islamic scholars, political activists, journalists and prolific writers. In fact, besides Azad, no other Muslim political thinker, with the exception of Dr. Zakaria, has produced so many scholarly tomes about Islam, Indian politics, Muslim politics, nationalism, democracy and secularism.

The present-day generation can barely conceive the significance of being a proud Muslim and a steadfast nationalist in the pre-independence period in India. Though the overwhelming majority of the Muslim masses loved their motherland as much as any other countryman, a considerable majority of the Muslim elite were wedded to the separatist political ideas that were being disseminated by the Muslim League. The nefarious 'two-nation' theory was the logical conclusion of the separatist politics that ultimately divided the country. A young Zakaria had shown remarkable political sagacity even during his college days not only to shun but passionately oppose Muslim separatism. He was unreservedly committed to the political ideals of the Indian National Congress. In the city of Bombay, where Zakaria was brought up, studied and took part in the freedom struggle, it was extremely difficult for an educated young Muslim to oppose the politics of the Muslim League because it was also the city where M.A. Jinnah lived and participated in politics. The task of a nationalist Muslim was also arduous because a majority of the

Muslim elite, in particular, the rich business community, had completely thrown its weight behind Jinnah and his brand of politics. Zakaria was one of those rare Muslim youths who had firmly opposed Jinnah and the *'two-nation'* theory without undermining his Muslim identity. His heroes among the Indian National Congress were Pandit Jawaharlal Nehru and Maulana Azad. He had paid his tribute to both of them by writing a scholarly book on the former while christening a reputed college after the name of the latter.

In the post-independence period, Dr. Zakaria completely devoted himself to the task of nation building. This he did both by his scholastic writings and active politics. He was not one of those intellectuals who live in their ivory towers and lament the 'deteriorating conditions' of the nation. Zakaria was a Congressman right from his student days. He successfully contested quite a few elections and served as a cabinet minister in the state of Maharashtra. He was aware that the creation of Pakistan in the name of Islam had positioned the Indian Muslims in a precarious situation. He knew that they had to suffer from innumerable woes including social and political exclusion. Dr. Zakaria was one of those leaders who helped the hapless Muslim community gain confidence and respect as the proud citizens of a secular democratic state. He had also realized that despite concerted efforts since the Aligarh Movement, the Muslims, in the field of modern, technical education, lagged far behind their Hindu counterparts. In order to address this anomaly he established quite a few educational institutions in Aurangabad and Bombay. These institutions epitomize his socio-political thought. They cater to the educational needs of all but take extra care of the Muslims who happen to be educationally backward. This is an exceptional illustration being committed to secularism without disowning your faith.

Since he was a prolific writer he had written as many as seventeen scholarly books in which his depth of knowledge about Islam, his insight regarding politics particularly Muslim politics, his commitment to nationalism, his profundity concerning secularism and his vision as to an all-inclusive democratic India are on display. These books constitute an indispensable source of value-based politics, which contemporary India is lamentably deprived of. Dr. Zakaria is perhaps the most neglected among the Indian political thinkers. It is futile to go into finding the reasons for this criminal neglect and start the blame game. The need, in fact, is to revisit Dr. Zakaria's intellectual contribution and offer a critique of his thought in the light of contemporary political realities. Such an exercise will definitely help the contemporary political elite, academicians, activists and, more importantly the youths, reinstate their conviction in value-based political processes. They may also seek inspiration from the life and works of Dr. Zakaria and get engaged in protecting and promoting progressive political ideas such as nationalism, democracy and secularism without turning away from their faiths.

Thus, when Zahid Ali met Dr. Zakaria and explained to him the hostile approach of the Morarji Desai government towards Khilafat House, the young barrister who had recently arrived from London advised him to make a selection from the two options available in the circumstances. The first option was to challenge the state government's notice in the appropriate court and the second one was to appeal to the then Prime Minister of India, Jawaharlal Nehru. Accordingly, Zahid Ali challenged the government's notice in the Bombay civil court. As is the practice with the Indian judicial system, particularly in matters of civil litigation, it takes years to reach the settlement stage. It is time-consuming as well as expensive. The Morarji Desai government was adamant on getting hold of Khilafat House and convert it into a government institution by completely erasing the memory of the Khilafat Movement.

Finding himself in a jam, Zahid Ali finally decided to write a letter to Nehru explaining the background of the Khilafat House and the intimidating attitude adopted by the state government headed by Morarji Desai. Nehru's response was sympathetic. He advised Morarji Desai to be lenient towards Zahid Ali, the son of Maulana Shaukat Ali, and by taking into consideration the significance of the Ali Brothers and the Khilafat House in the history of India's freedom struggle find an amicable settlement of the dispute. Nehru's intervention forced Morarji Desai to change his stance on Khilafat House from rigidity to flexibility. He instructed the government pleader in the case to work on an agreement with

Zahid Ali that might help his continuity of residence in the Khilafat House. As a result of the changed stance of the state government in the dispute, the Bombay civil court adjudicated on May 26, 1964 that Zahid Ali would continue to reside in the Khilafat House and he was also allowed to look after the affairs of the Khilafat Committee.[9]

The verdict engendered a major change in the basic character of the institution. Though the word Khilafat was retained in the name of the new organization, it was converted into a trust that would carry out socio-cultural activities instead of political agitation. As per the draft of the schedule for the management and administration of a public trust registered under No. B-703, Bombay, the Charitable Public Trust "shall be designated by the name of the All India Khilafat Committee." The draft further says that the "registered office of the Trust shall be Khilafat House, Love Lane, Bombay-27". The objects of the Trust *inter alia* include the following:

a) Religious, educational, social and economic upliftment (sic) of Indians and particularly of Muslims.
b) To establish a fraternal relationship and unity with the other countries.
c) To achieve the said objects, to run and conduct the paper *Khilafat*.

The draft of the trust also specified that the number of the Trustees "shall not be less than five and more than eleven".[10] The list of the first Trustees include eleven names which are:

1. Shri Mohammad Ali Zainal Aliraza
2. Dr. Rafiq Zakaria
3. Shri Mustafa Faki
4. Shri Zahid Shaukat Ali
5. Shri M.Y. Nurie
6. Shri Ismail M. Kanga
7. Dr. K.A. Hamied
8. Shri Mustafa M. Shaikh
9. Shri H.H. Ismail (Managing Trustee)
10. Dr. Syed Mahmud
11. Shri Mulla Jan Mohammad[11]

It was also provided that the trustees would elect someone from amongst them as a chairman at the beginning of each year. Accordingly, Zahid Shaukat Ali was elected the first Chairman of the Khilafat Committee and he was also allowed to reside at the Khilafat House. This privilege was consented to him because of the pivotal role played by his father and uncle in the Khilafat Movement. In keeping with one of the objects of the Khilafat Committee, an Urdu daily *Khilafat* was also launched under the editorship of Zahid Ali. Making a departure from political preferences of Maulana Shaukat Ali during the last phase of his political career, *Khilafat* adopted a pro-Congress policy. It was in tune with the objects of the Khilafat Committee. Furthermore, as the famous script writer Javed Siddiqui, a nephew of the Ali Brothers who also worked for sometime as a journalist with the *Khilafat*, pointed out that in those days a newspaper brought about by a Muslim institution could not even think of espousing any other line of thought except toeing the Congress line.[12] Though *Khilafat* was not among the leading Urdu newspapers of India, nor did it have a wide circulation. Its reputation solely rested on the memories of the Ali Brothers and their brand of politics. The paper continued to be published till 1960. Sadly, we cannot assess the worth and depth of the daily now because no record of the newspaper is available with anyone. As per the stipulation, the publisher of every newspaper and magazine has to preserve a copy of each issue. In the case of *Khilafat,* however, not a single issue of the newspaper is to be found because as per the statements of the registrar and librarian of the Khilafat College of Education the copies of the newspaper were devoured by white ants.

Zahid Ali was also a passionate aficionado of Urdu poetry. Those were the days when many famous Urdu poets and writers, in particular, belonging to the Progressive Writers' Movement were present in Bombay. So, besides editing the daily newspaper, Zahid Ali would frequently "also hold *mushairas* and *mehfils* at Khilafat House." Zahid Ali was quite popular among the Urdu poets and writers for "his famed hospitality—food would come free from the nearby Haji Hotel, which Zahid would share with his friends."[13]

After Zahid Ali's death in 1970, Dr. Rafiq Zakaria was unanimously elected the Chairman of the Khilafat Committee, the position that he held till his death in 2005. At that time Zakaria was a cabinet minister in the Government of Maharashtra. Additionally, he was an influential member of the All India Congress Committee. Since the closure of the newspaper *Khilafat* a decade ago the only activity, discounting the frequent *mushairas* and *mehfils*, that was being performed by the Khilafat Committee was the organization of the annual procession to commemorate the birthday of the Prophet. Zakaria, a man with a modern vision with a commitment to uplift the socio-economic condition of Indians, particularly the Muslims, made up his mind that instead of holding literary meets, the Khilafat Committee should carry out some constructive activity in the interest of the community.

The Muslims and Muslim institutions have always been the target of the Hindu communal organisations. An unfortunate development since independence has been penetration of the Hindu communal elements in bureaucracy and other public institutions. These elements never miss an opportunity to destroy Muslim interests wherever possible. The location of Khilafat House in a business area of Bombay and its fairly large premises made it an obvious target of Hindu harassment. Though in the changed circumstances and since the formation of the All India Khilafat Committee Trust, the historic building of the Khilafat House had become a centre for Hindu-Muslim unity and communal harmony. For the Hindu communal elements it was still an abode of Maulana Shaukat Ali who at the last leg of his life had supported the Muslim League. Therefore, a communally motivated officer attached to the Archaeological Survey of India made up his mind to play a fraudulent caper to harass the trustees of the Khilafat Committee.

His plan was absolutely imprudent but malicious that can be gauged by the letter of the manager of the Khilafat House written to Dr. Rafiq Zakaria on July 16, 1978. It reads: "I have to bring to your kind notice that two monument attendants (peons) called at Khilafat House on July 9, 1978, at about 2 pm and informed the Khilafat peon (Lala) that they had been sent by G.V. Vidwans, the Conservation Assistant, Archaeological Survey of India, Bombay Range Sion Fort, Bombay-22 (Tel. No. 471102), to take charge of the Khilafat House.

"We are informed by the two attendants that they were acting under the orders of the Central Government to whom one organization named 'Muslim Youth Circle, Bombay' had applied... stating that Khilafat House was a historical monument and should be taken over by the Archaeological Department, Government of India."[14] It is needless to add that the complainant organization was a fictitious one, a creation of the communally fertile imagination of the scheming officer. The letter further says:

> "Acting on this sudden move by the Archaeological Department without any notice whatsoever to the Khilafat Trust, our Trustee Mr. Habib A. Shaikh rushed to the Archaeological Office at Sion Fort, on July 12, 1978, and contacted one Mr. G.V. Vidwans and investigated (sic) the reason for the sudden step taken by the said Department. G.V. Vidwans, though did not part with any written order, informed Mr. Shaikh that he was acting under the orders of the Central Government, as a result of an application of the Muslim Youth Circle as stated above. Repeated requests by Mr. Shaikh to show the orders of the Central Government, the officer concerned declined to show the orders or give the copy thereof, failing which Mr. Shaikh informed the said officer that he would have to lodge a complaint of criminal trespass against the said Department."[15] Since the whole plan was fabricated by the officer himself, how could he show the imaginary 'orders of the Central Government'? Anyhow, on getting to know the possibility of a criminal case against his department, "the said officer softened and told Mr. Shaikh that he would withdraw his men forthwith from the Khilafat House, which he did in the afternoon of July 12, 1978."[16]

The entire episode was planned by anti-Muslim Conservation Assistant of the Archaeological Survey of India, Bombay was later confirmed when Mr. Habib A. Shaikh met Mr. B.K. Thapar, the Additional Director, Archaeological Department who was on a visit to Bombay. Informing the Chairman of the Khilafat Trust about this meeting, Mr. Habib wrote: "I met Mr. Thapar on the July 16, 1978, at 6 pm at Sion Killa, Government Guest House, Bombay. He informed me that it was 'a fault' on the part of the Bombay Office of his department to have sent two monument attendants (as they are called) to take 'charge' of the Khilafat House and that my action in warning them of this illegal step was correct."[17]

A Hindu communal officer's plan to the newly constituted Khilafat Trust of its headquarters was thus frustrated by the prompt and correct action of a trustee. However, this was an alarming signal that made Dr. Zakaria think that some concrete activity should be undertaken by the Khilafat Committee. His first intent was to renovate and remodel the ramshackle building of the Khilafat House. It was an expensive project for which Zakaria appealed to the generous donors to contribute openhandedly for the renovation of the old building. His appeal met with superb success as in addition to the contributions made by the individual patrons, the Government of Maharashtra and the Bombay Municipal Corporation too donated Rs. 1,00,000 each for the cause. The other notable donors were:

1. Embassy of Libya in India	Rs. 75,000
2. Taj Group of Hotels	Rs. 50,000
3. Zenith Tin Works	Rs. 25,000
4. Wadia Foundation	Rs. 25, 000
5. Kapadia Group of Companies	Rs. 25,000
6. Maharashtra Marketing Federation	Rs. 5,000[18]

It was not an easy project considering the fact that the building was a hundred years old and for that reason it was imperative to carry out the renovation work without damaging the old facade of the structure. This kind of task could only be accomplished by an expert architect. Zakaria, therefore, hired the services of Roshan Nanavati, who was the most sought after architect at that time. Nanavati accepted the assignment as a challenge and ultimately did a commendable job by transforming the old structure into a modern and more spacious building while retaining the beauty of the old edifice. It could only be accomplished because of Nanavati's architectural expertise.

On completion of the new building, Zakaria invited Indira Gandhi, the then Prime Minister of India to inaugurate the renovated and remodelled Khilafat House. The inaugural function presided over by A.R. Antulay, the then Chief Minister of Maharashtra, was held on April 19, 1981. In his welcome address Dr. Zakaria drew Mrs. Gandhi's attention to the historical background of the Khilafat House mentioning that it was at this place her grandfather Motilal Nehru, her father Jawaharlal Nehru, Mahatma Gandhi, Sarojini Naidu, Madan Mohan Malviya, Hakim

Ajmal Khan, Dr. M.A. Ansari, Maulana Abul Kalam Azad and the Ali Brothers would discuss the national issues. Congratulating Dr. Zakaria "for his untiring efforts for keeping this national monument alive and active", Mrs. Gandhi observed in her inaugural address: "What an excellent idea to renovate and reactivate the old 'Khulafat House'. It is hallowed with remembrance of stalwarts of our freedom struggle and has been an active centre of Hindu-Muslim unity... The strength of our nation lies in its secularism, giving equal regard to all religions and equal rights and opportunities to all our citizens. Those who are fewer and weak because of economic or social reasons must get special protection...We are proud of the sacrifices made by our Muslim leaders and of the contribution to our culture and development. Muslim scholars, Muslim weavers and artisans have given a rich heritage and (they) now work for a better future along with Hindu, Christian, Sikh, Buddhist, Jain and Parsi brothers. My good wishes to the Khilafat House."[19]

In his presidential address Antulay stressed the point that Khilafat House was the symbol of Hindu-Muslim unity. He added that the edifice was the interpretation of the dream of the renowned poet Allama Iqbal. He had dreamt of a *Naya Shiwala* (New Shrine) that would be higher than the skies and a focal point of love and harmony. In its precinct the Hindus and Muslims would together supplicate for communal amity and peace and order in the country. The particular poem, *Naya Shiwala,* belongs to the first phase of Iqbal's poetry during which the patriotic feelings dominate most of his poetry. To estimate the significance of the analogy suggested by Antulay, we must take into consideration a few couplets of the poem:

Patthar ki Mooraton mein samjha hai tu khuda hai
Khak-e-watan ka mujh ko har zarra devta hai

(You believe that God resides in the statues of stone/For me each particle of motherland's soil is God.)

Aa ghairiyat ke pardey ek bar phir utha dein
Bichhdon ko phir mia dein, naqsh-e-dooi mita dein

(Draw closer! Let us remove the veils of the rift again/Let us unify the parted ones, (and) erase the mark of duality.)

Sooni padi hui hai muddat se dil ki basti
Aa ik naya shiwala is des mein bana dein

(The habitat of the heart is deserted for long/Draw closer to build a new shrine in this country.)

Duniya ke teerathon se ooncha ho apna teerath
Damaan-e-aasman se iska kalas mila dein

(Let our shrine be taller than other shrines of the world/Let us link its pinnacle with the declivity of the sky.)

Shakti bhi shanti bhi bhagaton ke geet mein hai
Dharti ke baasiyon ki mukti preet mein hai

(The power and peace both dwell in the songs of the devotees/The emancipation of the people of the earth inhabit in love.)

Though all the five couplets cited above from the poem orate love and amity among people belonging to different faiths, the second one is particularly more germane considering the background of the Khilafat Movement. It has been argued consistently that for almost three years between 1919 and 1922, of our freedom struggle when the twin movements Khilafat and Non-cooperation were on in tandem, the Hindus and Muslims could forge together an invincible nation. The scenes of Hindu-Muslim unity during those days were so inspiring that ordinary people had forgotten their communal differences and were coagulated into a national rock against the foreign rulers. In Iqbal's couplet the word *again* is very significant. If read in the context of the Khilafat House, the message becomes loud and clear that through this *new shrine,* the trustees hope to recreate the similar atmosphere of communal unity *again* as it existed during the days of the Khilafat-Non-cooperation Movement.

Having renovated the building, Dr. Zakaria had to address the financial aspect of the All India Khilafat Committee's Trust. There was practically no financial source of the institution except occasional donations by the member trustees and their friends for routine expenditure. He, therefore, decided to generate funds by letting out the newly constructed hall, named after the Ali Brothers, of the building for meetings and socio-cultural functions. In order to execute the plan he circulated a letter among his friends and acquaintances. The letter dated April I, 1985, reads:

> Dear Friend (s), The Khilafat House...is under the Charitable Trust, managed by the All India Khilafat Committee...Under the Scheme of the Trust approved by the Government of Maharashtra, the Khilafat

> House (Ali Brothers Memorial Hall) is open to all citizens of India, without distinction of caste and creed...The House consists of a spacious hall on the ground floor with a space of 300 chairs. It has a permanent stage for VIPs. In order to run the institution, the Board of Trustees have fixed the following lowest remuneration without any idea of gain, for the use of the House to all citizens:
>
> 1. Rs. 500...for the use of the Hall per day and Rs. 125...for service charged per day for the occasion.
>
> The engager would be charged extra remuneration for the use of the compound abutting the Hall.
>
> ...We are proud to say that the Freedom Movement started from this institution by Mahatma Gandhi, Lok Manya Tilak, Motilal Nehru, the Ali Brothers and other leaders of international repute.
>
> You are cordially invited to take advantage of this non-commercial institution for your educational, cultural and social needs.[20]

It was a commendable move that yielded good results as many organizations and even individuals started booking the Ali Brothers Memorial Hall of the Khilafat House for holding their functions. This activity continues even today. Nonetheless, Dr. Zakaria intended to use the Khilafat House for some truly constructive purposes that would help socio-educational uplift of the community. In consultation with other trustees he settled on opening a teachers' training college for Urdu medium schools at the premises of the Khilafat House. Having obtained the unanimous consent of all the trustees, Dr. Zakaria wrote a letter on May 8, 1989, to Prof. Javed Khan, the then Minister of Education, Government of Maharashtra. The letter *inter alia* underscores the need for an Urdu medium teachers' training college. It reads:

> ...As there is no college of education for B. Ed. (Bachelor of Education) degree course in the city of Bombay for Urdu medium teachers, we have been approached by several of them to start one. On taking the survey of the facilities available in Maharashtra, we find that except for one college in Aurangabad, there is no other such college in the whole of Maharashtra. The Urdu speaking population in the state is more than 12 per cent and hence it is most unfair that they should not be provided the much needed facilities for their training...
>
> The All India Khilafat Committee which is a registered Public Trust, is prepared to start or arrange to get such a college at its premises at

> Bycuulla, which is most central for Urdu teachers in Bombay. The credentials of the Committee are well known. It has a hoary historical past and one of its aims and objects is the promotion of education among Muslims, who are mostly Urdu speaking.
>
> ...As we propose to start the college in June, there is not much time, hence an immediate reply will help us to organize facilities required on an emergency scale.[21]

Dr. Zakaria's efforts had in the desired effect as the Government of Maharashtra granted the permission to the All India Khilafat Committee to start a College of Education at its premises from the academic year 1989-90. The College got affiliated to the University of Mumbai. In order to keep the record straight an Indenture was also signed among the Trustees of the All India Khilafat Committee on November 15, 1989. It *inter alia* mentions:

> "This Indenture made at Bombay...between the All India Khilafat Committee Trust...hereinafter called the SETTLOR...and
>
> 1. Dr. Rafiq Zakaria, Chairman
> 2. Dr. M.A. Aziz, Hon. Secretary
> 3. Shri Akbar Premji, Managing Trustee
>
> All of Bombay inhabitants, hereinafter called 'The Trustees'...
>
> Whereas the All India Khilafat Committee Trust the Settlor has started and is carrying on and running and conducting since the past about this year various educational institutions in Bombay and in rendering cooperation in the field of education...
>
> And whereas the said All India Khilafat Committee Trust has also started with the necessary sanction of the Bombay University and Government from the Academic Year 1989-90 of the University of Bombay that is from the seventeenth day of July 1989-90, a college of Education at Byculla at present known as the All India Khilafat Committee, College of Education.[22]

Though, the alacrity of the Government of Maharashtra in granting permission to an Urdu medium college of education must be appreciated, the proviso that has placed the responsibility on the All India Khilafat Committee Trust to raise the funds itself for running the college is somewhat dicey. The poor socio-economic condition of the Urdu-speaking people, an overwhelming majority of whom happen to be Muslims, is well known. The findings of the Sachar Committee may be referred to in this context. Moreover, the persons who opt for a teaching career among Muslims invariably belong to the lower-middle or lower strata. Obviously, the All India Khilafat Committee cannot propose exorbitant fees for the bachelor course in education because most of the students enrolling for the course belong to the poor financial background. Despite this the All India Khilafat Committee, College of Education has done reasonably well during its existence of more than a quarter of a century.

The yardstick for assessing the success of such an institution has to be different from the one that is applied to the elite educational institutions of India. This institution has a social commitment to generate a climate congenial for Hindu-Muslim unity. It was the prime objective of Gandhi and the Ali Brothers when they first launched the Khilafat Movement. Dr. Rafiq Zakaria, was equally committed to the ideal of communal harmony and for that reason he, through the All India Khilafat Committee Trust, made constructive efforts for the cause of Hindu-Muslim unity. The establishment of the Khilafat Committee College of Education with 'Hindu-Muslim Unity' as its motto is one of those efforts. As the *Self Appraisal Report* of the College suggests: "...this institution was established to carry forward the ideology to develop a dynamic society by empowering the community. The strength of our institution lies in its unique status as a link from the glorious past to a vibrant present and a promising future. The institution has a great historical background which provides direction to the institution to frame its mission, vision and goals. These values permeate into all the programmes organized by the institution. In order to develop values among student-teachers, the institution organizes visits, community work, extension work and assemblies based on core values and life skills. Our co-curricular activities reflect the national and global values.[23] These are indeed the characteristic features of an educational institution that is devoted to defend and promote values of peace, communal harmony and socio-economic development of a plural society.

The choice of Urdu medium for the College was also a thoughtful one. The first objective was obviously to help the Muslim community to raise its socio-economic standard. It is also a fact that the overwhelming majority of Muslims in Mumbai comprises Urdu speakers. Secondly Urdu has been, and despite various setbacks, continues to be the most potent symbol of Hindu-Muslim unity and the composite culture of India. It has undeniably played a pivotal role in India's freedom struggle. During the golden phase of Hindu-Muslim unity, when the Non-cooperation and the Khilafat Movements were simultaneously on, Urdu was the most preferred vehicle of campaigning. Besides, the Ali Brothers were the true lovers of the language. Maulana Mohamed Ali, besides being a valiant freedom fighter was also a reasonably good poet of Urdu. His nom de plume was Jauhar and quite a few of his Urdu couplets are still popular among the Urdu speakers. His reputation as a competent journalist though was settled on because of his English weekly *Comrade,* he was equally proficient in Urdu journalism that was reflected in the issues of the Urdu weekly *Hamdard,* that he edited. Maulana Shauukat Ali too was an enthusiastic patron of Urdu language and literature. When he was solely running the affairs of the Khilafat House after the death of his younger brother, he started publishing the Urdu daily *Khilafat* and continued editing it till his death in 1938. Thereafter his son, Zahid Ali took over the editorship of the newspaper. Though Dr. Zakaria's major works (he has written as many as 17 books) are in English, he too was a lover of Urdu language and literature. In particular he was an aficionado of Urdu poetry and would often quote many Urdu couplets in his speeches to emphasize on a particular point. Most importantly, he was Chancellor of Jamia Urdu, Aligarh (A deemed university) for many years. It was, therefore, natural for the All India Khilafat Committee Trust to establish an Urdu medium College of Education.

Dr. Rafiq Zakaria had also planned to establish a Hindu-Muslim Relations Research Centre in the premises of Khilafat House. He had envisaged to create an excellent research institution having all the pertinent source materials to study more than a thousand years of religious, political, economic, social and cultural interactions between the Hindus and the Muslims of the Indian subcontinent. In order to concretize his plan he had got in touch with the then Prime Minister of India, Inder Kumar Gujral. Zakaria put forth his point of view before the Prime Minister that one of the best ways of celebrating the Golden Jubilee of India's independence was to establish a research centre that would provide the necessary facilities to the scholars to carry out research on the causes and impact of Hindu-Muslim conflict. The proposed research centre was also expected to work for establishing affable relations between the two major communities of the country. Gujral appreciated Zakaria's plan to establish a research centre exclusively dedicated to the research on Hindu-Muslim relations. He was also convinced that there could not be a more suitable organization to start such a centre than the All India Khilafat Committee for Hindu-Muslim unity was one of its objectives. I.K. Gujral had also promised that the Government of India would extend all necessary support to the All India Khilafat Committee to establish the research centre. Subsequently, on the instructions of the Prime Minister, the Ministry of Cultural Affairs, Government of India, sent its Joint Secretary, S. Satyamurthy, to Mumbai for consultation with the trustees and office bearers of the Khilafat Committee. Satyamurthy paid a visit to Khilafat House as well and got acquainted with various activities of the organization. His interaction with the trustees and office bearers of the AIKC proved rewarding as he submitted a flattering report to the Government of India recommending financial assistance to the Khilafat Trust to establish the Hindu-Muslim Relations Research Centre at Khilafat House.

The change of government at the Centre, nevertheless, impeded the realization of the project because I.K. Gujral was succeeded by A.B. Vajpayee as Prime Minister and the coalition government led by the Bharatiya Janata Party (BJP) was less than disposed to the idea of a research centre to study Hindu-Muslim relations. The research centre that was to include a large research library relevant books, private papers, manuscripts, official and non-official reports, research journals and magazines as well as audio-visual facilities and an attached reading room for the scholars originally required Rs. 5,00,0000 to get going. The Vajpayee government, however, sanctioned a paltry sum of Rs. 5,00,000.[24] The paucity of funds, therefore, is the main factor that has delayed the establishment of the proposed research centre.

The current Chairperson, Fatma R. Zakaria is, nevertheless, ceaselessly striving to convince the Union as well as the state governments about the need and significance of the proposed research centre to encourage inter-community dialogue that is an essential requirement of a plural society such as India. Moreover, she has also approached a few philanthropists who may feel inclined to extend a helping hand for the establishment of the research centre. Hopefully, the efforts of the AIKC and its Chairperson will bring in the desired result and a Hindu-Muslim Relations Research Centre will ultimately be established in future. If it comes about then it will certainly facilitate the research scholars in myriad ways to inquire into areas of conflict between the two major communities of India and then suggest the appropriate policies to create conditions for communal harmony.

6

Conclusion

The institution of Khilafat has been mired in controversies and internal strife right from the beginning. An objective critique of the history of the institution may reveal the fact that factionalism in Islam was an end-result of the political bickering that had gone together with the appointment of the Caliph from the word go. Three major factions emerged led by three leaders to stake their respective claim over the post of the Caliph. The three groups that had laid claim to the Caliphate included Banu Hashim led by Ali, Muhajirun or the Quraish of Mecca led by Abu Bakr and Umar and the Ansar whose chief was Saad bin Abada. Most Sunni ulama assert that the first Caliph and the subsequent three Khulfa-e-Rashidun were democratically elected. If it was so, then bin-Abada should have been the first Caliph as Ansar constituted the majority and they had unanimously expressed their desire to elect bin-Abada. They were, however, restrained to exercise their democratic right on the dubious claim that the Caliph had to be from the tribe of the Quraish. Paradoxically, two years before the leaders of the Quraish group, Abu Bakr and Umar, denied the Ansar the post of the Caliph on account of their purported inadequacy compared with their own pre-eminence, the Prophet had declared in his sermon after the conquest of Mecca: "Bear in mind that every claim of privilege, whether that of blood or property is abolished except that of the custody of the Ka'aba and supplying water to the pilgrims." Then addressing the Quraish of Mecca directly he continued: "People of Quraish, surely God has abolished from you all pride of the time of ignorance and all pride in your ancestry, because all men are descended from Adam, and Adam was made of clay."[1] Despite the clear stipulation of human equality that is one of the most sublime principles of Islam, the dominant albeit numerically smaller group of the Quraish practised the custom of tribal superiority and ignored the path shown by the Prophet of Islam. The ignoring of the public declaration of the Prophet at Ghadir Khumm nominating Ali as his successor was a shocking defiance by the leaders of the Quraish and most of the *sahaba* (companions). This was solely responsible for splitting the nascent *ummat* into two, the *Shiyan-e-Ali* (the party that supported Ali) and those who opposed his nomination as the first Caliph. This proved to be the genesis of sectarianism in Islam. The Shia-Sunni divide that has played havoc in Islamic history was a harmful corollary of denying Ali the position that the Prophet had willed for him. The Khilafat should remain among the members of *Ahl-e-Bait* from the lineage of Fatima is also an unreasonable position that most Shia sects had later taken on. This stipulation is as much unwarranted as the Sunni stance that only a member of the Quraish tribe can become a Caliph. Nevertheless, all this squabbling possibly would not have happened had the companions acted according to the wish of the Prophet. In that case there might not be a schism in Islam. The sect of the Khawarij, that intensely opposes both the Shia and the Sunni sects and whose members had been creating devastation across the Islamic world until recently, was also born as an end result of rivalry on the issue of Khilafat.

Despite the democratic pretention of the institution of Khilafat, the governance that ultimately emerged under it was awfully totalitarian that demanded complete surrender of an individual at the altar of the temporal-religious authority, which purportedly represented the will of the *ummat*. It was a kind of despotism that controlled an individual's entire life including food and drink choices, the issues that usually fell in the private realm. In order to ensure the complete obedience of the subjects a few ahadis were frequently invoked. For instance, a hadis such as, "The Apostle of God said: Whoso obeys me, obeys God, and whoso rebels against me, rebels against God; whoso obeys the ruler, obeys me; and whoso rebels against the ruler, rebels against me" would often be quoted.[2] A hadis guaranteeing the people that Allah would not hold them responsible for doing wrong things on the commands of the ruler was also in circulation. The particular hadis is: "Obey your rulers whatever may happen, for if they bid you do anything different to what I have taught you, they shall be punished for it and you will be rewarded for your obedience; and if they bid you do anything different to what I have taught you, the responsibility is theirs and you are acquitted of it."[3]

Taking advantage of such ahadis, the Caliphs made quite a few innovations that were later legitimized by integrating them with Shariat. The political doctrine that ultimately emerged out of such a governing system had, in fact, neutralized people's concerns as well as their participation in the affairs of the state. To control the behaviour of the subjects, ahadis and in the later phase the Shariat were usually invoked. The people were made to believe that the ruler would be punished for his unjust actions by Allah and they, as the believers of Islam, had no role to play, rather no right to question, the commands and deeds of the ruler even if they were openly sacrilegious. The people's minds were dulled by making them believe that their religious duty was to obey their ruler for which they would certainly be rewarded by the Almighty. The burden of suffering under an unjust and oppressive ruler was also indirectly situated on the fate of the people in a hadis that goes like this: "When God wishes good for a people, He sets over them forbearing and wise, and places their goods in the hands of generous rulers; but when God wishes evil for a people, He sets over them the witless and base and entrusts their goods to avaricious rulers."[4]

Considering the times of the inception of the Caliphate it was not out of the ordinary because absolute monarchy was the legitimate form of governance then. The element of surprise on the part of the inquirer though is because of the intensity and the persistent claim by the apologists of Khilafat with which the institution is described as a democratic polity. It was never so. The first phase of the Caliphate known as the age of the rightly guided Caliphs lasted less than thirty years in which the four Caliphs, all of whom were the prominent companions of the Prophet ruled over the nascent community of Islam. There was no division of powers because the executive and the judicial powers were combined in the position of the Caliph and there was no question of the legislative wing of the government because the Quran and

Sunna were acknowledged as the ultimate laws for the welfare of the people in this life as well as in the hereafter. The rightly guided Caliphs were, nonetheless, committed to the Quranic concept of equality of all the *Muslims*. This should not be confused with the modern principle of equality of all people. Despite the condemnation by the Shias of the rule of the first three Caliphs, the first two Caliphs, nevertheless managed the affairs of the Islamic state competently. The fourth Caliph, Ali, was best suited for the job in every respect. However, his opponents intermittently forced him to get engaged in suppressing a series of intentionally generated rebellions.

The end of the era of the rightly guided Caliphs also heralded the end of the pretension of democratic foundation of the Islamic state. Muawiyah, who usurped the absolute suzerainty of the territories under the control of the Muslims after the assassination of Ali in 661 had completely abandoned the ostensible electoral or consensus element from the institution of the Caliphate. Six years later after assuming complete power and about four years before his death, Muawiya firmly laid the foundation of the hereditary monarchy by nominating his son Yazid as his successor. Once established at the beginning of the Umayyad Caliphate, the practice of nominating a son or some other close male relative as successor was never officially cast off all through the history of the Khilafat. In a way, Muwaiyah also toned down the religious zeal from the institution of Khilafat to a large extent by establishing a grand monarchical order in the tradition of the Persian and Roman royalty. The extension of Islam that followed beginning from the second half of the seventh century was, therefore, not out of the proselytizing mission of the Muslim warriors but in actuality it was an expansionist project of the Arab militant tribes to capture the fertile lands and huge treasures that were under the control of the Persians and the Romans. The Arab expansion also brought in a large number of non-Arab people under the fold of Islam. This development put an end to the notional egalitarianism of the Muslim brotherhood because the conquering Arab tribes would not treat the non-Arab Muslims as their equals but would show signs of self-importance because of their race and would seek pride in their ancestry. It was actually the revival of the prejudices and the false notions of racial superiority that the Arabs were accustomed to in the pre-Islamic Arab peninsula.

The Umayyad Khilafat was very successful so far as expansion was concerned. Close to its extremity, the Caliph was the master of the huge territories that bordered China in the east and the shores of the Atlantic in the west. In short, the entire area under the erstwhile Persian empire and most of the eastern provinces of the Roman empires were conquered and brought under the Muslim dominance. A branch of the Umayyad had also established its rule over Spain. It was the staggering size of the territory and the grandeur, the result of the immense riches, that bestowed immense dignity to the title of Khalifa at that point of time throughout the known world.

The Abbasid Caliphate was marked by the constantly escalating Iranian influence. The Abbasids on the suggestion of their Iranian officials had decided to change the *Dar-ul-Khilafa* (the capital) from Damascus to Baghdad in Iraq. The Abbasid Caliph Mansur, therefore, assigned the responsibility to Barmakids to construct a new capital city. Thus, Baghdad was founded in 762, and made the new seat of the Khalifa. Thereafter, the important positions in the court of the Abbasid Caliphs were gradually held by persons of Iranian origin. The induction of Iranians to significant positions transformed the essentially clannish Arab administration into a more cosmopolitan and broad-based governing system representing the true demographic characteristic of the expanding Caliphate. The encounter of the simple tribal lifestyle of the Arabs with hugely advanced Iranian civilization resulted in a marvellous synthesis of a refined set of customs and norms which, is usually, referred to as the Islamic civilization the world over. It must be acknowledged that an overwhelming segment of the professed Islamic culture, cuisine, painting, literature, music, dance, dress and mannerisms has its roots in Iranian culture.

The most significant change that this inter-mingling of Arab and Iranian civilizations brought about was the intellectual and scientific advancement that is popularly known as the *Golden Age of Islam*. Most Abbasid Caliphs, taking their cue from the Iranian officials got engaged in intellectual and academic discussions and debates and promoted inquiry and research in myriad disciplines such as theology, philosophy, mathematics, history, governance, astronomy, architecture, scientific discoveries, poetry, music, dance, painting, etc. The historians usually identify six centuries of Abbasid rule, i.e. from the eighth century to the thirteenth century as the Golden Age of Islam that was marked by scientific, cultural, philosophical and economic advancement forcefully supported by the Caliphs.[5] The commencement of the Islamic Golden Age coincided with the coming to power of Harun Rashid (786-809) who established a House of Wisdom in Baghdad, which was a unique institution of Advanced Study open to scholars of the world irrespective of their race or religion.

An extraordinary development that mainly affected Islamic theology was adoption of Mutazilism as the official doctrine by Khalifa Mamun. In fact, Mutazilism originated before the establishment of the Abbasid Khilafat but the general climate that was conducive to the intellectual and scientific thought during the beginning of the ninth century in Baghdad helped this rationalistic Islamic movement prosper. It was the peak of the golden age as Muslim philosophers, scientists and intellectuals in the company of their Iranian, Jewish and Greek counterparts strived to unravel, comprehend and adopt the philosophical, social and scientific theories produced by the Hellenistic and Greek civilization that was either wiped out or discarded as the 'false body of knowledge' by the Holy Roman Empire. It was commendable that the Abbasid Caliphs not only encouraged the revival of the philosophical and scientific ideas of the Ancient Greece but allocated huge amounts for their translations into Arabic, Persian and Latin. The Golden Age of Islam did not, therefore, merely enrich the Muslim intellectual traditions but it also directly helped the European civilization to reclaim their intellectual legacy that was condemned to annihilate by the orthodox Romans. Mutazilism was adopted in such an enlightened climate as the official creed of the Abbasid Khilafat. It was a creditable attempt to free Islam from the vice-like grip of the orthodox mullahs for whom natural laws and reason were anathema. It was unfortunate that the later Abbasid Caliphs not only abandoned Mutazilism but hounded and banished its adherents. Though, the major cause of the end of the Golden Age of Islam was Halaku's invasion and sacking of Baghdad in 1258, the real reasons included the relapse of the Abbasids to orthodoxy and banishing science and reason from the Muslim world.

An important landmark in the Khilafat narrative is the emergence of a Shia Caliphate in north-west Africa in the first quarter of the tenth century. Known in history as the Fatimid Caliphate because its pioneers claimed descent from the fourth daughter of the Prophet, Fatima, the wife of the fourth Caliph, Ali. In the contemporary discourse of Shiaism, Khilafat is usually debunked as a debatable institution mainly for historical reasons. Considering the fact, the emergence of the Fatimid Caliphate was an astonishing development of Islamic history. At its zenith, the Fatimid Caliphate had under its control a huge territory that included Egypt, Maghreb in North Africa. Sudan, Sicily, Hejaz and the entire Levant, an area that included the present-day nations of Syria, Lebanon, Jordan, Palestine and Israel.

Factionalism, that plagued the Fatimid armed forces innately existed in it and this was one of the major factors that led to the gradual decay and decline of the Caliphate. Fatimid armed forces did not comprise a single ethnic group. In the initial phase, Berbers dominated it but in later years the Turkish and Black African soldiers were also recruited. Despite the fact that all of them professed Islam as their faith they could hardly maintain a common front. Initially the Berbers resented the entry of the Turks and later both the Berbers and Turks made a common front against the black Africans. Thus, the Fatimid army was a divided house which engendered disunity and internal rivalries. It is quite obvious that if the armed forces lack unity, they cannot be truly fighting forces against the enemy forces. This exactly happened because shortly after the mid-eleventh century, the three factions of the army were fighting among themselves.

In addition to the internal discord of the armed forces there were external forces too that posed threats to the Fatimid Caliphate. The Turks and the Crusaders had captured many provinces in the Levant. This led to the beginning of the decline and gradually the Fatimid control got confined only to Egypt. Then a dispute about succession also appeared that further weakened the Fatimids. First dissent about succession made its appearance after the death of the eighteenth Caliph Mustansir and ascension of Mustaaili as the new Caliph. A group supported the claim of the eldest son Nizar as the rightful heir but Nizar was ultimately killed. A similar dispute also surfaced after the death of the twentieth Caliph Aemir who did not leave behind a male heir. The weakening of the central authority emboldened the governors of various provinces to become autonomous. Thus by 1160, the Zengis of Syria captured Egypt through their Ayyubi commanders. By 1169, the Ayyubi Sultanat was established in Egypt.

The Ottoman Caliphate (*Khilafat-e-Osmania*) was unique in the sense that its rulers were non-Arabs and none of them pretended to be a scion of the family of the Prophet, his son-in-law Ali or his daughter Fatima. What is more many of the Ottoman rulers did not care much about calling themselves 'the Khalifa.' The Ottomans were Turkish by origin who became the masters of the Muslim world after the sacking of Baghdad by the Tartars in 1258. Earlier, they started as the fortune hunters from Central Asia and then became part of the Seljuqui forces. It was principally because of the Turkish warriors that the Seljuqs could occupy Baghdad in 1055. By 1071, they were de facto rulers of many areas of the present-day Syria though the nominal rule was that of the Seljuqs. The title of Khalifa was officially assumed by Murad I in the second half of the fourteenth century and thereafter they were recognized as the supreme authority all across the Muslim lands where Sunni Islam was the dominant force. At their peak the Ottomans controlled Asia minor, the entire Middle East, North Africa, the Caucuses and most of Eastern Europe. The Caliphate survived for almost six centuries and at one time it was the largest, second only to the British Empire.

The 37 Sultans who ruled over six hundred years of the Ottomans did not take any special care to strengthen the institution of Khilafat from the point of view of orthodox Islam. First nine of them did not even care to use the title Khalifa for themselves. The long rule spread over six centuries is usually divided into two categories. The first phase commencing from the establishment of the dynastic rule in 1261 by Osman I came to an end in 1603 with the extremity of the reign of Muhammad III. This phase was characterized by expansion, prosperity, overall progress and grandeur. The Achilles Heel of the Ottomans throughout had been the interference of the orthodox mullahs in the affairs of the state. This was true about most Muslim rules that emerged and perished in different parts of the world. Nevertheless, one particular incident that had relegated the entire Muslim world to backwardness compared to the future emergence of Christian Europe as a technologically advanced and powerful region, was the banning of the use of the printing press within the territories of the Caliphate.

As it is well known that Johannes Gutenberg of Germany invented the printing press with movable type in 1439. Fifty years later the technology was brought to Istanbul by the Jews who were thrown out by the Christians of Spain and Portugal during the Inquisition in 1492. They found the safe haven in the Caliphate and established units of the printing press in the capital of the Ottomans. Though they were allowed to establish their presses, the *Shikh-al-Islam* of the time issued a fatwa against the use of printing technology. Under the pressure of the orthodox mullahs, the Caliph had to ban the most efficient technology to disseminate knowledge and ideas which was soon to revolutionize the world, as un-Islamic. The mullahs banned the printing press because in their biased opinion it would be a great dishonour to the Quran if it was printed by a machine. The irony is that the Muslim fundamentalists and orthodox mullahs of the contemporary world seek immense pride by citing the fact that the Quran is among the largest printed books of the world.

The orthodox mullahs of the fifteenth century, however, were hell-bent upon banishing the printing technology from the world of Islam. On the advice of the Sheikh-al-Islam, Bayazid II issued a firman in 1483 prohibiting the use of the printing press and the printed books by the Muslims. The violators of the official edict were to face the penalty of death. The succeeding Sultan Salim I confirmed the firman in 1515 and thus, the ban on the press remained in place. On the other hand, the fields of scientific education, mathematics, philosophy and culture in Western Europe progressed by leaps and bounds while the Muslims under the Caliphate stagnated. Then in 1720, Ahmed III visited the Court of Louis XV along with his father who was the ambassador to France, and was completely taken by the printed books and the printing technology. He was determined to introduce the press in the

Caliphate. In order to execute his idea he got in touch with the Grand Vizier, Ibrahim Pasha, an enlightened person. Pasha promised to procure the positive firman from the Sultan. Though Ahmed III, the Sultan, issued the official edict permitting the use of printing technology within the territories of the Caliphate, he prohibited the printing of the Quran and other religious books of Islam under the pressure of the orthodox mullahs and thousands of copyists for whom making copies of the Quran was a lucrative business. Thus, printing technology, albeit on a very limited scale was introduced to the world of Islam in the eighteenth century, about three hundred years after it was used widely in Western Europe. The pace of printing non-religious books after the official sanction was so slow that in about twenty years, i.e. till 1746, merely 16 books were printed that included two volumes of the Turkish-Arabic dictionary.[6]

In practical terms, printing technology made its wider appearance in the Muslim world only in the nineteenth century. By that time, Western Europe that was rotting under the yoke of the Holy Roman Empire and the consequent Dark Ages, made the optimum use of printing technology, all kinds of books got published, ideas, especially scientific ideas could be easily disseminated by printed books, which ultimately led to the Renaissance, the Age of Reason and the Industrial Revolution. Though the orthodox mullahs had always hindered the progress of science and technology, their opposition to the printing press in the fifteenth century was the most damaging one that relegated the Islamic world compared to Europe. In the opinion of a scholar: "The late arrival of the printing house in the empire has often been cited as one of the major causes of the relative decline of Ottoman science and culture compared with Europe. It should be noted, however, that the major Ottoman printing houses published a combined total of only 142 books in more than a century of printing between 1727 and 1838. When taken in conjunction with the fact that only a minuscule number of copies of each book was printed, this statistic demonstrates that the introduction of the printing press did not transform Ottoman cultural life until the emergence of vibrant print media in the middle of the nineteenth century"[7]

The second phase of the Ottomans commenced with the

inauguration of the reign of Ahmed I in December 1603. Nevertheless, the putrefaction that got set in the first phase led to overall stagnation and subsequently to defeats, losses, humiliation, decline and finally the annihilation of the Sultanate as well as the Caliphate with the dismissal and expulsion of Abdul Majeed II in 1924. On the issue of Khilafat, most of the Ottoman rulers did not give much consideration to its temporal aspect, except invoking the title in times of difficulties to take advantage of the religious sentiments of the people of the Muslim world. Another shortcoming of the Ottomans was an offshoot of their belief. Since they were the followers of the Hanafi school of Sunni jurisprudence, their Caliphate remained confined to the areas where Muslims subscribed to the Hanafi school. For the Shias and even for the non-Hanafi followers of the Sunnis, for instance, Malikis, the Ottoman Caliphate did not have any appeal. Most Ottoman Sultans on their part did not pay much heed to the issues, grievances or needs of people belonging to other sects of Islam.

By the time of the outbreak of the First World War, the Ottoman Empire had major problems such as political instability, collapse of administrative machinery and financial crisis that were the end results of a long period of corrosion of effective rule. The Ottomans had lately faced quite a few humiliating defeats and the consequent loss of territories and honour had frustrated the people and demoralized the armed forces. The general discontent with the ruling clique provoked the disgruntled army officers to cause the second coup d'état in 1913. Though the nominal rule of Sultan-cum-Caliph was retained the real powers were exercised by the military commanders. It was under such circumstances that the Young Turks acquired tremendous power and it was because of their diktat that the Ottoman Empire entered into an alliance with Germany and joined the war as an ally of the Central Powers. In retaliation Britain, France and Russia immediately declared war on the Ottomans. At the end of the war, the Ottomans found themselves to be on the losing side and one of the most sadistic and vindictive peace treaties, the Treaty of Sevres, put an end to the Ottoman Caliphate.

For many international scholars, the movement that was launched for the restoration and continuation of the Ottoman

Khilafat by the Indian Muslim elites and soon after endorsed by the nationalist leaders, the most prominent of them being Gandhi, is somewhat bizarre for in no Muslim-dominated country was such a movement even thought of. What is more, a political front that claimed to be promoting and protecting the religious, social, political and economic interests of the Muslims of the Indian subcontinent, the Muslim League, did not even bother to make a common cause with the leaders of the Khilafat movement. The most paradoxical dimension of the issue was that in the Arab lands, in particular the Arab peninsula, the epicentre of Islam, the people were struggling to shed the yoke of the Ottoman Khilafat. Why then, were only the Indian Muslims, despite the indifference of the Muslim League, emotionally involved in a movement to restore an institution that was vehemently condemned and assailed by a huge majority of Muslims outside the Indian subcontinent?

The answer to this reasonable question may be sought in the unreasonable political agenda of the Muslim leaders of India. Most Muslim political elites in modern Indian history showed an appalling apathy towards the overall backwardness of the common Muslims. For them social, economic and educational retardation of the overwhelming majority of the community was hardly an issue to be addressed. Except for Sir Syed, no other significant Muslim leader sincerely attempted to bring about progressive socio-religious reforms in the community. Most Muslim leaders approached the socio-political problems of the community with a mindset stuck in the intellectual milieu of a tribal desert society that existed fourteen centuries ago in the Arab peninsula. This partly explains the obsession of the Muslim masses with religion. Added to this, has been the peculiar position of the Indian Muslims. The Muslim percentage in the population in undivided India was slightly less than one-third but they constituted one of the poorest and the least educated segments of the society. The mullahs and the self-proclaimed Muslim leaders had developed a vested interest in keeping the community perpetually occupied in religious issues by relentlessly raising the bogey of *'Islam in danger'*. Most importantly, the British became the political masters of India by displacing the so-called Muslim rule. In the immediate aftermath of the uprising of 1857, the British had also markedly persecuted the Muslims particularly in northern India. The Muslims, therefore, hated the British Raj more than any other Indian community. Consequently, when the Ottomans joined Germany against the Allied Forces in the First World War, the Muslims in India emotionally sided with the Axis Powers. The defeat of the Turks and the imposition of an unjust Treaty of Sevres on the Ottomans had obviously threatened the continuation of the institution of Khilafat, which according to the emotionally charged leaders of the Khilafat movement was a matter of survival of Islam. A sizable minority community surrounded by an inconsiderate, if not hostile, Hindu majority and ruled over by a foreign power that was out to destroy the sacrosanct institution of Khilafat, had a strong reason to retreat into the religious cocoon for safety. This vulnerability of the Muslim masses was exploited to the hilt by the Khilafat leaders.

In this backdrop we must assess the Khilafat movement, which happened to be the first mass movement of the Indian Muslims that met with tremendous success all across the country. Nevertheless, the popularity of the movement fizzled out very soon. It must, however, be acknowledged that during its peak it had managed to achieve one of the most difficult objectives of Hindu-Muslim unity. Sadly, it could not sustain the nationalist cause of inter-communal amity for long mainly because of the ineptness of its prominent leaders, viz. Gandhi and Mohamed Ali. While the former was a soft-spoken visionary, the latter was an emotional and fiery confrontationist. The Ali Brothers presented the issue of Khilafat to the gullible Muslim masses as a religious question for which a true Muslim should not hesitate even to lay down his life, while for Gandhi and most Congressmen it was a political strategy to create a formidable united front comprising the two major communities of the country against the British. In retrospect, one can only lament that the Ali Brothers and the short-sighted ulama who backed them, did not allow the Khilafat to be transformed from a Muslim issue into a nationalist movement. The leaders of the Khilafat failed miserably to latch on their objectives to the mainstream nationalist struggle. The movement also failed to produce a truly progressive political leadership that could put the Muslim masses who got involved in large numbers to save Khilafat, on the path of social reform, education and development. The ironical aspect about the movement was that its leaders proclaimed to protect the interest of Islam, whereas no Muslim-dominated country shared their point of view. At one point even the Turks themselves opposed the continuation of Khilafat. Such incongruity was the result of the myopic approach of the Khilafat leaders many of whom, despite their modern English education, were ill-equipped to negotiate with serious socio-political issues.

Though the Khilafat movement was practically over in 1922, the Central Khilafat Committee based in Mumbai has survived albeit with altered objectives and still playing its bit role for the uplift of the Muslim community. After the death of Mohamed Ali in 1930, his elder brother Shaukat Ali did not pull the plug on the CKC; he used it to promote his own political agenda. The natural course left for those associated with the Khilafat movement was to join together with the Indian National Congress and carry forward the struggle against the British. Regrettably, Shaukat Ali and quite a few Khilafatists along with him made a common cause with the Muslim League, an organization that had spurned the very idea of the Khilafat movement. Shaukat Ali could become a Muslim leader of national importance only because of the Khilafat movement and the support Gandhi lent to it. Nevertheless, when the movement had outlived its utility, he joined hands with Muhammad Ali Jinnah, the sworn enemy of Gandhi.

In the changed circumstances, Shaukat Ali converted the Urdu daily, *Khilafat,* published from the Khilafat House, an organ of the Muslim League that was an act of betrayal and because of which Gandhi was justifiably offended. The situation changed radically after the independence of India and creation of Pakistan, when Shaukat Ali's son, Zahid Ali as the editor of the daily started supporting the policies of the Congress. However, he neither had the vision nor the inclination to make use of the premises of the Khilafat House for some constructive activity for the benefit of the Muslim community. It was Dr. Rafiq Zakaria who transformed the Khilafat House from a place of no consequence to one of the major premises that count as one of the important centres of social, educational and political activities of the Muslims in India. The annual procession that is taken out on the birthday of the Prophet eptomizes Hindu-Muslim unity and Zakaria fortified this dimension of the annual event with utmost conviction. He reinvented the Khilafat trust by appointing active and resourceful people as its members. His decision to start a Khilafat College of Education on the premises satisfied an indispensable need of the community in the city of Mumbai. He also had a vision to start a Hindu-Muslim Relations Research Centre for the optimum usage of the premises. After his death, however, the plan remained unfinished.

The current members of the Khilafat Trust under the Chairmanship of Fatma R. Zakaria are committed to carry forward the ideal of Hindu-Muslim unity, which was the major positive outcome of the Khilafat movement. They are also managing the affairs of the Khilafat College of Education in the light of the aims and objectives for which it was established. The annual procession on the birthday of the Prophet continues to be organized. Yet, of late its prime justification, i.e. to spread the message of Hindu-Muslim unity seems to be toned down slightly. It may be because of the less than enthusiastic participation of the Hindu brethren in the procession. One must not forget that it was Gandhi who had started this annual event. In order to keep the spirit of communal amity alive, it is absolutely necessary that each year a prominent Hindu person should be invited to lead the procession. Another project that needs the serious consideration of the members of the Khilafat Committee is to revisit Rafiq Zakaria's plan of establishing a Hindu-Muslim Relations Research Centre. The paucity of funds may be a major hindrance but it is not such an impediment that cannot be overcome by dedicated members of the Khilafat Committee.

Notes and References

Chapter 1 – Theoretical Framework

1. Holy Quran 24:55, English Translation of the Meanings... by Abdullah Yusuf Ali, King Fahd Holy Quran Printing Complex, Medina, 1987, p. 173.
2. 6: 165, Ibid., p. 66.
3. 7: 69, Ibid., p. 71.
4. 7: 74, Ibid., pp. 71-72.
5. 2: 30, Ibid., p. 2.
6. 38: 26, Ibid., p. 228.
7. The hadîs is recorded by al-Hâkim in his *Mustadrak*. It is supported by narrations in *Musnad Ahmad, Sunan al-Nasâ'î al-Kubrâ,* and *Musannaf Ibn Abî Shaybah*. http://en.islamtoday.net
8. Ibid.
9. Ibid.
10. *Masnad--Ahmad, Mishkat,* Chapter Al-Anzar Wal Tahzir, https://ahmadiyyatzindabad.wordpress.com/khalifatul-masih/
11. Source: Sahih Muslim, 1847, www.oxfordislamicstudies.com/article/opr/t125/e2057
12. Abu Dawood, *Sunan, Kitaab al-Sunnah, Baab Sharh al-Sunnah.*
13. See Musawi ash-Shirazi, Sayyid Muhammad, *Peshawar Nights*. Hamid Quinlan, Charles Ali Campbell. New York: Pak Books, 1996.
14. 5: 70, The Holy Quran, op. cit., p. 52.
15. Veccia Vaglieri, Laura, "Ghadîr Khumm", *Encyclopedia of Islam*, Brill Online, 2012.
16. Ibid.
17. See Ali, Zaheer (ed.), *Reading History: A Bunch of Papers*, Introduction, Centre for Promotion of Democracy and Secularism, Aurangabad, 2013, p. 32.
18. Higgins, Annie C, "Kharijites, Khawarij", in Martin, Richard C., *Encyclopedia of Islam and the Muslim World*, Vol. 1, Macmillan, 2004, p. 390.

19. "Schisms and Heterodoxy among the Muslims" by Javeed Akhtar, http://www.irfi.org/articles/.
20. Glasse, Cyril, *The New Encyclopedia of Islam.* Altamira Press, California, 2001 pp. 255–56.
21. See Dr. Ghulam Nabi, *Khilafat in Theory and Practice,* Adam Publishers and Distributors, New Delhi, 2008, pp. 131-136.
22. https://en.wikipedia.org/wiki/Al-Mawardi.
23. Hunt, Janin, *The Pursuit of Learning in the Islamic World,* McFarland, 2004, p. 83.
24. Nicholson, Reynold Alleyne, *A Literary History of the Arabs,* Cambridge University Press, London, 1966, p. 382.
25. Hunt, Janin, op. cit.
26. Ibid.

Chapter 2 – The Rightly Guided Caliphs

1. The Shias claim that the Prophet did name Ali as his successor while the Sunnis contest the claim. The issue is controversial and was one of the prime reasons for the schism of the ummah into Sunni and Shia sects
2. See Fred Donner, *The Early Islamic Conquests,* Princeton University Press, New Jersey, 1981.
3. Syed Amir Ali, *Spirit of Islam,* Islamic Book Trust, Delhi, 1981, p. 123.
4. Ibn Hisham, *Sirat-un-Nabi,* Vol. I (Urdu Translation by Abdul Jalil Siddiqui), Aetiqad Publishing House, New Delhi, 1982, pp. 273-74.
5. Ukaz was a market town located on a plain in the hills halfway from Taif to Mecca. An annual fair was held at this market town in which the merchants from all across the Arab peninsula would reach to sell their merchandise and to witness and participate in various activities such as group conversations, horse and camel races and poetry recitation sessions. During the four months' duration of the fair there would be no violence as a "holy truce" would be observed and all men would avoid carrying weapons, treat prisoners judiciously and, most importantly, participate in poetry competitions. The best poems of the poets would be written in molten gold on the finest silk and suspended on the holy temple of Mecca. For these reasons the finest poems were known as *mualaqat* (suspended) in Arabic.
6. Shibli Nomani, *Al-Farooq,* Vol. I (Urdu), Farid Book Depot, New Delhi, n.d., p. 19.
7. Ibn Hisham, op. cit., p. 274.
8. Ibid., pp. 274-77.
9. Quran, 92: 5-7.
10. Ibid., 92: 18-21.
11. Ibn Hisham, op. cit., p. 534.

12. Ibid., pp. 534-36.
13. Quran, op. cit., 9: 40.
14. Ibn Hisham, op. cit., p. 542-44.
15. Abdur Rahman later converted to Islam and achieved prominence as a valiant warrior during the Muslim conquest of Syria.
16. Sahih Bukhari, Vol. I, Book 8, No. 456, www.sahih-bukhari.com/ Pages/results.php5
17. Ibn Jafar al-Tabari, *History of the Prophets and the Kings,* Vol. 9, State University of New York Press, 2007, p. 184.
18. Quran, op. cit., 3: 144.
19. Quoted in Syed Amir Ali, *A Short History of the Saracens,* Kitab Bhavan, New Delhi, 1981, p. 23.
20. Musaylimah had joined hands with another 'prophetess' Sajah of the Banu Tamim by marrying her. Together they succeeded in raising an army of forty thousand warriors and had defeated two Muslim armies before Khalid bin Walid vanquished them after a tough battle fought at Yamama, the present Riyadh. Interestingly the present rulers of the Kingdom of Saudi Arabia, who pompously call themselves the 'guardians of the holiest places' of Islam and large sections of credulous Muslims across the world believe they trace their ancestry to the same Musaylimah, the Kidhab (Liar). No wonder Riyadh is the capital of Saudi Arabia.
21. Philp K. Hitti, *History of the Arabs,* Macmillan, New Delhi, 2001, pp. 141-2.
22. Quoted in Amir Ali, op. cit., pp. 21-22.
23. Hitti, op. cit., p. 150.
24. For a perceptive history of the Quran see Muhammad Hamidullah, *The Emergence of Islam,* Khan Publishers, Delhi, 2004, pp. 3-38.
25. Making use of personal reasoning in case clear guidance is not available in the Quran and reliable ahadis to select the appropriate course of action. However, the practice of *Ijtihad* was, in reality, approved by the Prophet himself. It is reported that the Prophet permitted Muaz bin Jabal at the time of his appointment as governor of Yemen to use his reasoning to deal with an issue about which he could not find a clear ruling in the Quran or *sunnah.* (See Ibid., pp.77-8).
26. Ibn Hisham, op. cit., p. 794.
27. Ibid., p. 29.
28. Ibid., p. 30.
29. Ibid., p. 377.
30. Ibid., p. 378.
31. Jalaluddin as-Suyuti, *The History of the Khalifahs,* digitized version on Book & Web Design...
32. Ibid.

33. Ibn Hisham, op, cit., p. 794.
34. Shibli, op. cit., p. 58.
35. Ibid., pp. 132-4.
36. For a detailed account see Ibn Hisham, Vol. II, op. cit., pp. 806-813.
37. Syed Amir Ali, op. cit., p. 234.
38. Shibli, op. cit., p. 161.
39. Hitti, op. cit., p. 152.
40. Amr bin al-Aas, in Islamic History, occupies a very high position as a ferocious military general, next only to Khalid bin Walid. Prior to the conquest of Egypt he had conquered Palestine carrying the banner of Islam. Later, he was the one who shrewdly helped his childhood friend Muawiya to seize the headship of the Muslim state for which he earned for himself the soubriquet 'one of the four Arabian political geniuses.'
41. Quoted from Hitti, op. cit., p. 160.
42. Ibid., p. 163.
43. For a detailed account of Umar's administrative reforms see Shibli, op. cit., Part II, pp. 12-119.
44. Quoted from Shibli Nomani, *Al-Mamun,* Maktba-e-Muarif, Azamgarh, 1957, p. 199.
45. Thomas Carlyle, *On Heroes and Hero Worship and the Heroic in History,* AMS Press, New York, 1974, p. 77.
46. Bernard Lewis, *The Arabs in History,* Oxford University Press, 2002, p. 59.
47. R.V.C. Bodley, *The Messenger,* Doubleday & Co., London, 1946, p. 271.
48. *The Meaning of the Glorious Quran,* translated by Marmaduke Pickthall, Idara Isha'at-e-Dinyat, New Delhi, 2006, p. 51.
49. Quoted from Dakake, Maria Massi, *The Charismatic Community: Shi'ite Identity in Early Islam*. SUNY Press, 2008, pp. 39-40.
50. Ibid., p. 35.
51. Umme Ayman was a maid of Amina bint Wahab, the Prophet's mother. At the time of his mother's death, the Prophet was barely six years old. Thereafter, it was Umme Ayman who, like a real mother, rendered selfless service to the Prophet. The Prophet, all through his life, called her 'mother after mother.'
52. Shibli has quoted this hadis from Sahih Bukhari. Shibli Nomani, op. cit., p. 54.
53. Ibid., p. 56.
54. For instance, Syed Abul Aala Maududi insists that Khilafat is a democratic institution in his *Khilafat-o-Mulukiyat* (Urdu) Idara-e-Tajuman-ul-Quran Pvt. Ltd., Urdu Bazar, Lahore, n.d.
55. Shibli, op. cit., pp. 57-58.

Chapter 3 – Transformation of Khilafat

1. Bin-e-Hisham/Bin-e-Ishaq, 1955 edn. pp. 380-88.
2. Wilfred Madelung, *The Succession to Muhammad: A Study of the Early Caliphate*, 1997, p. 232. Also see H.U. Rahman, *A Chronology of Islamic History 570-1000 CE*, 1999, p. 59.
3. Holt, P.M., *The Cambridge History of Islam*, Vol. I, Cambridge University Press, 1977, pp. 67-72.
4. See for instance, Aslam Jairajpuri, *Tareekh-ul-Ummat*, Vol. IV (Urdu), Maktaba-e-Jamia, Delhi, 1958, p. 109.
5. Encyclopedia of Islam, 2 ed., Vol. 1, pp. 1033 ff. Online as: "al-Barâmika." *Encyclopaedia of Islam*, Second Edition. Brill Online, 2012.
6. Ibid.
7. See J.A. Rogers, *World's Great Men of Color*, Vol. II, Simon & Schuster, New York, 2009.
8. Marshall Broomhall, *Islam in China: A Neglected Problem*. London 12 Paternoster Buildings, E.C.: Morgan & Scott Ltd., pp. 25, 26. Retrieved December 14, 2011.
9. The term *Zindiq* has its origin in old Persian, rooted in Zoroastrian literature. In medieval Islam it was usually applied to a person who, in the eyes of the mainstream Muslims, was guilty of heresy. During the Abbasid Caliphate a Muslim who was accused of secretly following Manichaeism. (It was a major religion of Persia that spread widely during the Sasanian Empire. Its founder Mani c. 216-276 AD believed in the concept of dualistic cosmology, i.e. a constant struggle between good and evil. The good was represented by the spiritual realm of light and the evil was epitomized by the material world of darkness.) In medieval Islam the charge of *zandaqa* was a serious offence punishable by death. Later, the Muslim ulama started applying the term *zindiq* to a person who had differed with the basic dogmas of Islam. The term could be used interchangeably for apostate or infidel. Sometimes, under political pressure, the ulama also charged the political dissenters of *zandaqa*.
10. Jairajpuri, op. cit., p. 99.
11. When the Abbasids ultimately crushed the Umayyads in the struggle for the position of the Caliphate in 750 and later launched an atrocious mission of hunting for and executing every member of the erstwhile ruling tribe. A scion of the Umayyad, Abdur Rahman I had somehow survived. Having spent about six years in exile, he first conquered the Muslim principalities in North Africa and ultimately succeeded in establishing himself as the emir of Cordoba in 756. Thus, the Muslim sovereign power was implanted in Spain. Abdur Rahman I and his successors used the title of Emir or Sultan for almost a century and half. Thereafter, to fight off the Fatimids

who had begun the military expeditions against the Emirate of Cordoba, they adopted for themselves the title of Caliph to rival their adversaries who had styled their reign as the Fatimid Caliphate in defiance of the widely known and accepted Caliphate of the Abbasids. Though the Fatimids failed to overpower the Muslim state of Spain, Abdur Rahman III, the Cordoba Emir of the time retained the exalted title of the Caliph for himself. His successors too continued to use the honorific, Consequently, after 929 there emerged three Caliphates, each claiming its own legitimacy to rule over the Muslim world. The Cordoba Caliphate survived till 1031. Thereafter, a civil war broke out over the issue of succession between the inheritors of the last Caliph Hisham II and the supporters of his rival, Mansur. After months of intense and violent battles the Caliphate disintegrated into many independent Muslim Kingdoms (*Taifa*).

The Cordoba Caliphate attained an enviable level of prosperity and overall advancement in the tenth century. It was Abdur Rahman III who had expanded and unified the areas of Muslim dominance by subjugating the Christian kingdoms of Northern Spain. During this period, the Caliphs also established amicable relations with the nearby Christian kingdoms of Europe and the Berber-ruled states of North Africa. Hakam II, the successor of Abdur Rahman III, continued with the diplomatic policies of his father as a result of which, the Cordoba Caliphate had fruitful relations with countries like Germany and France. The death of Hakam II in 976 led to the bloody civil wars for succession that ultimately led to the fall of the Caliphate and emergence of various smaller kingdoms. Thus the civil war permanently broke the back of the Muslim power in Spain.

(For more details see: Azizur Rahman, Syed, *The Story of Islamic Spain*, Goodword Books, New Delhi, 2001; Barton, Simon, *A History of Spain*, Palgrave MacMillan, New York, 2004; Chejne, Anwar G., *Muslim Spain: Its History and Culture*. The University of Minnesota Press, Minneapolis, 1974; Reilly, Bernard F., *The Medieval Spains*, Cambridge University Press, Cambridge, 1993)

12. The defeat of the supporters of the house of the Prophet (*Ahl-e-Bait*, also known as the Alids) led by Husain bin Ali, a grandson of Hasan bin Ali in the Battle of Fakhkh, near Mecca, fought on June 11, 786 at the hands of Sulaiman bin Jafar, a son of the Abbasid Caliph Mansur dealt a crushing blow to the Shias in their struggle for the Caliphate. Husain bin Ali along with most of his supporters was executed by the victorious Abbasids. However, one member of the Alids, Idris bin Abdullah, somehow managed to get away from execution and later ran off to the Maghrab (present-day Morocco). He was the founder of the Idrisid dynasty in North Africa.

The Idrisid dynasty existed between 788 and 974. The Idrisids belonged to the Zaidi branch of Shiaism. Idris bin Abdullah first reached Tangier and later settled in the ancient Roman city of Volubilis (Walili). The area was dominated by the Berbers who on their own accord conferred upon Idris the title of the Imam because of his lineage that could be traced to the Prophet of Islam. Though the Berbers were Muslims, the population of Jews and Christians was also significant in the area. Idris being the Imam was also recognized as the temporal head and thus was the pioneer of the Idrisid dynasty. He built a new city near Volubilis and named it Madinat ul-Fez, which subsequently came to be known only as Fez. The Abbasids were disconcerted because of the emergence of the Idrisid dynasty and, therefore, an agent of the Abbasid Caliph poisoned Idris in 791. He was succeeded by his son Idris II as the new Imam. The effective control of administration during the reign of Idris I was entirely in the hands of the local Berbers. Idris II, nonetheless, adopted the policy of appointing Arabs as viziers and the judges (Qazi). Consequently, the leader of the Berbers, Ishaq hatched a conspiracy in collaboration with the Aghlabids of Tunisia to eliminate Idris II. However, the Imam got wind of the plot and executed Ishaq. Thereafter, in 809 he shifted the capital of the dynasty from the Berber-dominated Volubilis to Fez. He also encouraged the people of Arabic origin from Cordoba and Tunisia to emigrate and settle in and around the new capital city. Idris II also expanded the territory of his dynasty by subduing the adjacent principalities as a result of which, when he died in 828, the area of the Idrisid dynasty bordered Algeria in the West and Sous in Southern Morocco.

The son of Idris II Muhammad became the new Idrisid Imam on the death of his father. He, however, was not a competent ruler. Though he ruled between 828 and 836, he did not have solitary control over the kingdom. It was divided among seven of his brothers. However, during this period the Moroccan urban society was significantly Arabised. The Berber culture prevailed in the rural areas that influenced the immigrant Arabs to adopt many of local traditions and customs. The cultural transition was thus a two-way process. In the eleventh century the deeply Berberised Idrisids, the Hammudids rose as new political masters by bringing many cities in Northern Morocco and Southern Spain under their control. In 868, the Berbers belonging to the Khariji sect defeated the Idrisid forces and killed the reigning Imam Ali bin Umar. Twelve years later, Ali's brother Yahya routed the Kharijis and took control of Fez. In 917, the forces of the allies of the Fatimids attacked the Idrisid kingdom and forced the Imam to acknowledge the authority of the Fatimid Caliphate. The Fatimids also deposed Yahya in 921. Four

years later a member of the Idrisids, Hasan I, managed to conquer Fez and many parts of the kingdom. He, nonetheless, proved to be the last ruler of the Idrisid dynasty. He could rule only for two years as in 927, the local Berbers in collaboration with the Sunni rulers of Cordoba launched a systematic campaign to track down and kill the Idrisids.
(For more details see: Hodgson, Marshall, *Venture of Islam,* University of Chicago Press, Chicago, 1961)

13. The Aghlabid dynasty existed between 800 and 909 in Ifriqiyah (present-day Tunisia and Eastern Algeria). The dynasty's name was derived from its founding ruler Ibrahim bin Aghlab who was appointed by the Abbasid Caliph Haroon Rashid as Emir of Ifriqiya in 800. At that time the law and order had been completely broken in the province and Ibrahim bin Aghlab who was the son of an Arab commander from Khurasan was expected to end anarchy and restore peace. Aghlab, in the capacity of Emir enjoyed considerable autonomy and with the passage of time his successors became de facto rulers of the province. The capital city of the Ifriqiyah was Kairouan (al-Qayrawan in Arabic), which is located in present-day Tunisia. Having restored order in the region, Ibrahim built a new city Abbasiyya near Kairouan and made it the capital of his dynasty. Additionally he also built quite a few magnificent buildings and mosques as well as improved the irrigation and water supply system in the entire province.

    The Aghlabids during the reign of Ziyadatullah (817-838) conquered Sicily that remained under the control of the Arabs for the next two centuries. The golden age of the Aghlabid dynasty was under Ahmad bin Muhammad (856-863), when the province of Ifriqiya became prosperous because of improved agriculture and thriving trade. Abbasiyya at the time achieved the status of one of the most significant centres of Islamic theology and jurisprudence. The decline of the dynasty set in motion under the reign of Ibrahim II bin Ahmad (875-902) when the Aghlabid forces had to repulse the attack of Egypt and suppress the internal rebellion of the Berbers with a huge loss of life. Thereafter, the dynasty had to face a series of rebellions mostly of the Shia supporters of the Fatimids. Consequently, in 909, the Aghlabid dynasty was overthrown and the province was made a part of the Fatimid Caliphate.
    (Reference Georges Marçais' entry, "Aghlabids," *Encyclopedia of Islam,* 2nd ed., Vol. I, pp. 699–700.)

14. Paul Lunde, Caroline Stone, *The Meadows of Gold: The Abbasids,* Kegan Paul International, 1989, p. 62.
15. Bernard Lewis, *Race and Color in Islam,* Harper Torchbooks, (Paperback), 1979.

16. P.J. Bearman, Th. Bianquis, C.E. Bosworth, E. van Donzel, W.P. Heinrichs et al. (eds.), *Encyclopædia of Islam*, 2nd Edition, Leiden: E. J. Brill, 1960–2005.
17. Jairajpuri, op. cit., p. 181.
18. The sect referred to is *Kharajite* (seceders), the earliest sect of Islam that emerged in c. 657. The *Kharjites* who were supporters of the fourth Caliph Ali later revolted against him for his acceptance of the principle of arbitration to resolve the conflict with Muawiyah, the then governor of Syria. Their slogan was *la hukma illa li-l-Lah* (arbitration belongs to Allah alone.) In case of the issue under consideration, the Kharjites' position is that a Muslim who commits a grave sin and dies before penitence ceases to be a Muslim and in the hereafter his permanent residence will be hell.
19. It is a reference to the *Murjites.* The sect emerged in the Umayyad period. Its focus was on the suspension *(irja)* of judgment regarding believers who commit sins. See Hitti, Philip K., *History of the Arabs,* Macmillan, Delhi, 2001, p. 247.
20. Nicholson without naming the source, mentions, "according to another tradition, Amr b. 'Ubayd." See Nicholson, R.A., *A Literary History of the Arabs,* Adam Publishers, New Delhi, 2003, p. 223.
21. The battle was fought on the outskirts of Basrah on December 9, 656, between the fourth Caliph Ali and a few prominent opponents to his Caliphate such as Zubayr bin Awwam, Talhah bin Abdullah and Aisha, one of the wives of the Prophet. The battle is known in Islamic history as 'the Battle of Camel' because Aisha joined the battle riding a camel.
22. Nicholson, R.A., op. cit., p. 223.
23. Ibid.
24. The Meaning of the Glorious Quran, xxxix: 10, translated by Muhammad Marmaduke Pickthall, Idara Isha'at Dinyat, New Delhi, 2006, p. 330.
25. Ibid., vi: 1651.
26. Ibid., vi: 164, p. 121.
27. Ibid., xlix: 9, pp. 368-9.
28. Hitti, op. cit., p. 315.
29. Ibid., p. 310.
30. Ibid., p. 431.
31. *Ikwan us Safa* (Brothers of Purity) was one of the few rationalist movements in the history of Islam that flourished in the last years of the tenth century in Basra. Its main objective was to synchronize Islam with reason. The Brothers of Purity also attempted to develop a universal system of religious philosophy. (See Nicholson R.A., op. cit. pp. 370-72)
32. The followers of Jehm Bin Safwan, who was perhaps the first Muslim

theologian who asserted that the Quran was a created word of Allah. He had also declined to accept the ideas such as Abraham's friendship to God and the conversation between Moses and the Almighty. *Shorter Encyclopaedia of Islam*, p. 83, Leiden 1974.

33. Hugh Kennedy, *Early Abbasid Caliphate*, Croom Helm, 1986, p. 157.
34. Ibid., p. 163.
35. Tayeb El-Hibri, *Reinterpreting Islamic Historiography*, Cambridge University Press, 2011, p. 296.
36. See C.E. Bosworth chapter 'Abbasid Caliphs' in *Encyclopedia Iranica*, Columbia University Press, 1985.
37. Tayeb El-Hibri, op. cit., pp. 291–292.
38. Jairajpuri, op. cit., Vol. V, p. 21.
39. Ibid., p. 25.
40. See Hitti, op. cit.
41. The Zanj were the people from East Africa who were bought as black slaves in thousands by the landowners of Basra and surrounding areas in the mid-seventh century to work as agriculture labourers. The marshlands of the region of Basra were allotted to loyal supporters, officials and wealthy businessmen first by the Umayyad and subsequently validated by the Abbasid Caliphs with a rider that the owners would turn them arable and would keep cultivating to help plantation economy grow. This necessitated the demand for farm hands and the land owners of Mesopotamia, in particular, Basra imported Zanj slaves in large numbers from Africa.

    The Zanj were extremely exploited and paid bare minimum subsistence wages as a result of which their living and working conditions were awfully miserable. They were also subjected to frequent beatings. In view of this the Zanj slaves revolted time and again. The two significant revolts by Zanjs against their masters were recorded in 689-90 and 694. However, these were ruthlessly suppressed. The major uprising known as the Zanj Rebellion began in the period of the Abbasid Caliph Muatazz in 869 and ended 14 years later in the reign of Muatamid. According to a moderate estimate around 5,00.000 people were killed in the uprising, The revolt was led by Ali bin Muhammad, who claimed to be a descendant of Ali bin Abi Talib. However, this claim was contested by most historians.
42. Zetterstéen, K.V., "al-Mu¿taid Bi'llâh", in Houtsma, Martijn Theodoor. *E.J. Brill's First Eencyclopedia of Islam, 1913–1936*, Vol. VI: Morocco–Ruzzik. Leiden: Brill. 1987, p. 777.
43. The Carmathians who are known as Qaramita in Arabic were an extremist sect of Ismaili Shiaism. Their headquarter was al-Hisa in Eastern part of Arabian peninsula where they had established their republic in 899. They were strict vegetarians and for that reason

they were also known as al-Baqliyyah in Arabic which can be translated as green-grocers. There is no solitary view about why the sect came to be known as Carmathians. According to the dominant view, the name was derived from the surname of pioneer of the sect Hamdan Qarmat. Another explanation is that the name is drawn from the Arabic verb that means "to make the lines close together in writing" or "to walk with short steps."

Though the Alids played a pivotal role in the overthrow of the Umayyads and the establishment of the Abbasid Caliphate in 750, they felt embittered by the policies of the successive Abbasid Caliphs. Consequently, the Shias would intermittently raise the banner of revolt at different places against the Abbasid rule. Shiaism too got divided into various sects, the most prominent being the Isna-e-Ashari (the Twellers) and the Ismailia. The Ismailia maintain that the sixth Imam, Jafar as-Sadiq (702-765) had designated his second son Ismail bin Jafar as his successor to the Imamate. However, Ismail passed away before his father. This brought a split among the Shias. The group that later came to be known as the Ismailia recognised the deceased Ismail's son Muhammad bin Ismail (746-809) as the legitimate Imam. He resided mostly in Kufa. His death caused further split in the Ismailia. The majority group refused to accept his death by maintaining that he distanced himself from worldly affairs and would ultimately return as Mehdi. The minority group accepted his death, which ultimately ended up as the Ismailia that supported the Fatimid Caliphate.

The members of the majority group settled in Salamiya (in present-day Syria). Their leader Husain Ahwazi adopted Qarmat as part of his name and started preaching a new faith that is known as Carmathian or Qaramita. Qarmat and his brother-in-law Abdan increased the number of their followers and acquired military and financial power in southern Iraq. Their other strongholds were Yemen and Bahrain, which was subsequently to become the most powerful centre of the Carmathians. When the Abbasid power was seriously struggling to hold on because of the Zanj Rebellion, the Carmathians seized the opportunity under the leadership of Abu Saeed Jannabi against the Abbasid Caliphate. The Carmathians swiftly conquered Hajr, capital city of Bahrain and also the city of Hasa that served as the capital of the Carmathian republic.

The Carmathians opposed many precepts of Islam. For them Hajj was a superstitious tradition and for that reason for long they continued to assault Hajj caravans and kill the pilgrims. In 906, they attacked a huge caravan returning after performing Hajj and massacred twenty thousand pilgrims. They acquired so much military power that in 927 they had almost captured Baghdad. In

930, they entered Mecca and then Medina and hugely desecrated the holiest sites of Islam. They filled the Zamzam well with corpses and carried Hajr-e-Aswad (the Black Stone) with them to Hasa. It was returned in 952 after prolonged negotiations and payment of a huge ransom by the Abbasid Caliph. The Caemathians were ultimately defeated by the Abbasid forces in 976 and thereafter the sect disintegrated and finally collapsed.
(Sources: Madelung, Wilferd. "$amdan Qarmat". *Encyclopædia Iranica*. Retrieved April 24, 2016;. Farhad Daftary, *The Isma'ilis: Their History and Doctrines,* Cambridge University Press, 1992; John Joseph Saunders, *A History of Medieval Islam*, Routledge 1978)

44. Jairajpuri, op. cit., pp. 75-76.
45. See Kennedy, Hugh N., *The Prophet and the Age of the Caliphates: The Islamic Near East from the 6th to the 11th Century* (second ed.),. Harlow, Pearson Education Ltd., UK, 2004.
46. See William Muir, www.*answering-islam.org/Books/Muir/Caliphate.*
47. Imam Ahmad bin Hanbal (d. 855) was an Iraqi Islamic scholar whose ideas were institutionalized by his students into one of the four schools of Sunni jurisprudence. It has the least number of adherents. Hanbali jurisprudence is primarily based on the Quran, ahadis and the views of companions (*sahaba*) of the Prophet. Hanbalis do not accept jurist discretions or customs even in matters that cannot be explained in the light of the Quran or ahadis. They would rather prefer to go along with the weaker ahadis or suspect the opinion of an individual companion (*sahabi*). Of the four schools of Sunni Islam, it is the most conservative. It was because of their questionable views, the Hanbalis came into conflict with political power at different stages of Islamic history. (Source: Gregory Mack, Jurisprudence, in Gerhard Böwering et al., *The Princeton Encyclopedia of Islamic Political Thought,* Princeton University Press, 2012, p. 289.
48. Al-Hasan bin Ali al-Barbahari (d. 941) was a Sunni theologian and a follower of Ahmad bin Hanbal from Iraq. He was extremely hostile to Shias, Qadaris, Mutazilis and Asharis and would not even include them in the sphere of Islam. He was responsible for the killings of many Shias, Qadaris and common Muslims who did not subscribe to Hanbali doctrine. In short, he was a bigot who openly advocated use of force to diffuse the tenets of the Hanbali school. In fact he did not contribute much to jurisprudence but acquired infamy as a polemicist. (Source: Michael Cook, *Forbidding Wrong in Islam: An Introduction,* Vol. 3 of *Themes in Islamic History*. Cambridge: Cambridge University Press, 2003, p. 103.
49. Jairajpuri, op. cit., Vol. V, pp. 97-98.
50. Hanne, Eric J., *Putting the Caliph in His Place: Power, Authority, and the Late Abbasid Caliphate*. Fairleigh Dickinson University Press, 2007,

p. 55.

51. Bennison, Emira K., *The Great Caliphs: The Golden Age of the Abbasid Empire*, Princeton: Yale University Press, 2009, p. 47.
52. Sources: Corbin, Henry, *History Of Islamic Philosophy*, Routledge, 2014, p. 119; Gibb, H.A.R. (1960–1985). *The Encyclopedia of Islam*, Vol. 8. Leiden: Brill. 1995, p. 70, and H. Bowen, C.E. Bosworth: *Nizâm al-Mulk.* in *Encyclopaedia of Islam*, Leiden: Brill. 1995.
53. Excerpted from: Komroff, Manuel, Giovanni, Willem van Ruysbroeck, Odorico, and Benjamin. 1928. after the first four Rightly Contemporaries of Marco Polo, consisting of the travel records to the eastern parts of the world of William of Rubruck (1253-1255); the journey of John of Pian de Carpini (1245-1247); the journal of Friar Odoric (1318-1330) and the Oriental travels of Rabbi Benjamin of Tudela (1160-1173). New York: Boni & Liveright. William Muir's public domain, *The Caliphate: Its Rise, Decline, and Fall.*
54. Shajar-e-Dur (lit. tree of pearls) was the widow of Salih, the Ayyubi Sultan who valiantly repulsed and ultimately defeated the Crusaders in their seventh conquest against the Muslims. Most Muslim historians report that she was Turkish of origin whom Salih bought from the slave market when he was still a prince. Later, when she gave birth to a son, Salih married her. Shortly before the commencement of the Seventh Crusade in 1249, Salih died but in view of turbulence engendered by the imminent Crusade, the news of the death of Sultan was not made public. It was at this time, Shajar-e-Dur took charge of the administration and armed forces in her hands and defeated the crusaders in 1250. Thereafter, she was crowned as Sultana (Queen) with regnal name Malika-e-Asmat-ud-Din Umm-e-Khalil, on May 2, 1250.

    The patriarchic tradition of the Abbasid Caliphate required Mustasim to reject Shajar-e-Dur as the monarch of a Muslim province that was a huge setback for the Mamluks who were behind her rise. They devised a strategy to go around the opposition of the Caliph to a lady as monarch by getting her married to a Mamluk nobleman, Aizazuddin Aybak, who was then installed as the new Sultan. In Islamic history, Shajar-e-Dur is remembered for two reasons; One, the crushing defeat she made happened to the Christian forces in the seventh crusade and, two, her crowning as Sultana marked the end of the Ayyubi dynasty and the birth of the Mamluk Sultanate that ruled over the provinces in the southern Mediterranean for many decades.
55. Jairajpuri, op. cit., pp. 193-194.
56. See *The Travels of Marco Polo*, EBook #10636, released on January 8, 2004.
57. Jairajpuri, op. cit., Vol. V, pp. 197-198.

58. Jairajpuri, op. cit., Vol. VI, p. 91 fn.
59. Samy S. Swayd, *Historical Dictionary of the Druzes*. Vol. 3 of *Historical Dictionaries of People and Cultures*, 2006.
60. Jairajpuri, op. cit., pp. 95-96.
61. Delia Cortese and Simonetta Calderini, *Women and the Fatimids in the World of Islam*, Edinburgh University Press, 2006.
62. Jairajpuri, op. cit., p. 96.
63. Wilferd Madelung. *Journal of Near Eastern Studies:* Vol. 37, No. 3, p. 280.
64. See, Willi Frischauer, *The Aga Khans*, Bodley Head, 1970.
65. Ismail K. Poonawala. "Review: The Fatimids and Their Traditions of Learning", *Journal of the American Oriental Society https://en.wikipedia.org/wik.*
66. Jairajpuri, op. cit., p. 97.
67. Dr. Farhad Daftary, "al-Hakim bi-Amr Allah". *Encyclopaedia Iranica,* Vol. 11, pp. 572-573, (ed.) Ehsan Yarshater, Institute of Ismaili Studies, New York, 2003; Makarim, Sami Nasib *The Druze Faith,* Caravan Books, New York, 1974, p. 25.
68. Jairajpuri, op. cit., p. 98.
69. Ibid., p. 100.
70. Ibid.
71. See *A Brief History of Sicily*, Digital edn. web.stanford.edu.
72. Jairajpuri, op. cit., p. 114.
73. Jairajpuri, op. cit., pp. 125-130.
74. S.M. Stern, *The Succession to the Fatimid Imam Emir,* Brill, pp.196-197, http://www.jstor.org/stable/1579511.
75. Jairajpuri has mentioned four of such histories that are supposed to be most reputed among Sunni academicians which speak of the 'heretic', 'innovative' 'cruel' and 'oppressive' characteristics of the Fatimid Caliphate. These accounts are: *Kashf-ul Asrar* by Qazi Abu Bakr Baqlani, *Tabthit-ul Nabuwat* by Abdul Jabbar Basri Muatiziki and the historical accounts by two other scholars, Abu Shama and Haafiz Abul Qasim, Jairajpuri, op. cit., p. 135.
76. Wintle, Justin, *History of Islam*. Rough Guides Ltd., London, 2003 pp. 136–7.
77. See Hasan al-Amin, *Shorter Shi'ite Encyclopaedia*, Ansariyan Pubilcations, first edition, 1997.
78. Jairajpuri, op. cit., Vol. VII, 12.
79. Ibid.
80. Ibid., pp. 12-13.
81. Jairajpuri, op.cit. p. 19.
82. Ibid., p. 20.
83. The geographical region of Balkans is a peninsula that got its name because of the range of Balkan mountains that extends from eastern

Serbia to the Black Sea touching the eastern coast of Bulgaria. The region of Balkans include the present-day countries of Albania, Bosnia and Herzegovina, Bulgaria, Croatia, Greece, Kosovo, Republic of Macedonia, Serbia, Slovenia and the European part of Turkey. See Colin S. Grey and Geoffrey Sloan, *Geopolitics, Geography and Strategy*, 2014; "Balkans" in *Encyclopedia Britannica*, 2015.

84. Fine, John. *The Late Medieval Balkans*, University of Michigan Press, 1994.
85. Jairajpuri, op. cit., pp. 20-21.
86. Ibid., p. 27.
87. See Finkel Caroline, *Osman's Dream: The History of the Ottoman Empire*, Basic Books, 2005, pp. 43.
88. Jairajpuri, op. cit., pp. 32-33.
89. "Dates of Epoch-Making Events", in *The Nuttall Encyclopaedia*, Project Gutenberg. May 1, 2004. Online version retrieved 2007.
90. Lowry, Heath W., *The Nature of the Early Ottoman State*. Albany, NY: SUNY Press, 2003, pp. 115-116.
91. Jairajpuri, op. cit., pp. 47-48.
92. Kupperman, Karen Ordahl, *The Jamestown Project*, Harvard University Press, 2008, p. 40.
93. Ibid., p. 41.
94. Jairajpuri, op. cit., p. 53; Quataert, Donald. *The Ottoman Empire, 1700–1922*, Cambridge University Press, 2000, p. 90.
95. Finkel, Caroline, op. cit., p. 175.
96. Amber, Colin. *The Ottoman Empire: The Structure of Power*, 2nd ed. New York: Palgrave Macmillan, 2009, pp. 98-99.
97. Jairajpuri, op. cit., p. 56-57; Kramers, J.H. "Mustafa I." *Encyclopedia of Islam, New Edition*. Vol. VII. Ed. C.E. Bosworth, E. Van Donzel, W.P. Heinrichs and Ch. Pellat. Leiden: E. J. Brill, 1993. p. 707.
98. Selcuk Aksin Somel, *Historical Dictionary of the Ottoman Empire*, Scarecrow Press, Lenham, 2003, p. 201.
99. Börekçi, Günhan, Ibrahim I., *Encyclopedia of the Ottoman Empire*. Gábor Ágoston and Bruce Masters (ed.), New York: Facts on File, 2009. p. 263.
100. Gökbilgin, M. Tayyib. "Ibrâhîm." *Encyclopaedia of Islam*, Second Edition. Brill Online, 2012. Accessed July 10, 2012 <http://referenceworks.brillonline.com/entries/encyclopaedia-of-islam-2/ibrahim-SIM_3433>
101. Jairajpuri, op. cit., p. 60; Streusand, Donald E., *Islamic Gunpowder Empires: Ottomans, Safavids, and Mughals*, Westview Press, Boulder, Colo., 2011, p. 57.
102. Jairajpuri, op. cit., p. 67.
103. Ibid.
104. Ibid., p. 68.

105. Ibid., p. 69.
106. Hoiberg, Dale H., (ed.), "Abdulhamid I". *Encyclopedia Britannica.* I: A-ak Bayes (15th ed.). Chicago, IL, 2010.
107. https://archive.org/stream/ottomanempireref00lanc#page/n99/mode/2up.
108. Cleveland, William, *A History of the Modern Middle East,* Westview Press, Boulder, Col., 2013, pp. 57–58.
109. Lord Kinross, *The Ottoman Centuries: The Rise and Fall of the Turkish Empire,* Perennial, New York, 1977, p. 437.
110. Jairajpuri, op. cit., p. 78.
111. Shaw, Stanford J. and Shaw, Ezel Kural, *History of the Ottoman Empire and Modern Turkey,* Cambridge University Press, 1977.
112. Jairajpuri, op. cit., pp. 79-80.
113. Hoiberg, Dale H., (ed.), "Abdulmecid I". *Encyclopedia Britannica.* I: A-ak Bayes (15th ed.). Chicago, IL, 2010; Jairajpuri, op. cit., p. 83.
114. Hoiberg, Dale H. (ed.), "Abdulmecid" *Encyclopedia Britannica.* I: A-ak Bayes (15th ed.), .Chicago, IL, 2010; http://www.measuringworth.com/ukcompare/relativevalue.php?amount=10000 & year_source=1847&year_result=2013; http://www.theguardian.com/commentisfree/belief/2011/oct/07/ottoman-empire-secular-history-sharia; http://faith-matters.org/images/stories/fm-publications/the-tanzimat-final-web.pdf
115. The Urabi Revolt (1879-1882) was a nationalist uprising led by an Egyptian Colonol Ahmed Urabi whose primary objective was to depose the then Khedive (Viceroy) Tawfiq Pasha and to restrict the British and French influence over Egypt and Sudan. The revolt could only be quelled by the British bombardment and occupation of Egypt and Sudan that continued until the end of the First World War.
116. Hoiberg, Dale H., op. cit.
117. Jairajpuri, op. cit., p. 86.
118. Palmer, Alan. *The Decline and Fall of the Ottoman Empire,* Faber & Faber Ltd. London, 2011, pp. 141-143.
119. Jairajpuri, op. cit., p. 87.
120. Hoiberg, Dale H., op. cit., p. 22.
121. "Curios Information About Armenia". Armenica.org.
122. See Rodogno, Davide, *Against Massacre: Humanitarian Interventions in the Ottoman Empire, 1815-1914,* Princeton University Press, 2012.
123. Hoiberg, Dale H., op. cit.
124. Jairajpuri, op. cit., p. 91.
125. *The Encyclopedia Britannica,* 15th Edition, 1983, p. 788, Vol. 13.
126. Jairajpuri, op. cit., p. 92.
127. Jairajpuri, op. cit., p. 93.
128. Lawrence Sondhaus, *World War One: The Global Revolution,* Cambridge University Press, 2011, p. 91.

129. *The Times* (London), January 30, 1928, Editorial. http://www.thetimes.co.uk/tto/news/
130. Fromkin, David, *A Peace to End All Peace: The Fall of the Ottoman Empire and the Creation of the Modern Middle East*. Owl, New York, 1989, pp. 286, 288.
131. Jairajpuri, op. cit., pp. 96-97.
132. See Hanioglu, M. Sukru , *A Brief History of the Late Ottoman Empire*. Princeton University Press, 2008.
133. Jairajpuri, op. cit., p. 98.
134. Ibid., p.100.
135. Ibid., pp. 101-102.
136. Ibid., p. 102.

Chapter 4 – Khilafat Movement

1. The Wahabi Movement (1820-1870) was essentially a revivalist movement which intended to purge all the innovations and alterations that, according to its supporters, had crept into Muslim societies. So, its campaigners believed that the return to the pristine and true spirit of Islam of the period of the 'Rightly Guided Caliphs' was the only way for the community to get rid of the socio-political plight and decadence that enfolded the Muslims in the first half of the nineteenth century in India. It was so named as its Indian promoters were greatly influenced by the teachings and the orthodox puritanical movement of Muhammad bin Abd al-Wahhab (1703-1792) of Arabia. The loss of political power at the turn of the nineteenth century had distressed the ulama and the political elite so much that they had considered a few options to put an end to further mortification of the community. The alternatives they thought of included migration of all Muslims to a safer Muslim state, inviting a Muslim sovereign, for instance, the Emir of Afghanistan, to invade India to free it from the British infidels or to launch an armed struggle (jihad) against the East India Company rule. Finally, the ulama rejected the first two options for being unrealistic and impracticable and chose the third one. Thus, Syed Ahmed Barelvi was elected as *Emir-ul Momineen* and entrusted the task of carrying out jihad against the rule of the infidels. Ahmed, instead of challenging the British, decided to overthrow the rule of the Sikhs from Punjab. However, his adventurism ended shortly as the Wahabis were defeated by the Sikh forces at the battle of Balakot in 1831. Ahmed died on the battlefield. Thereafter, the Wahabis also fought against the British in the uprising of 1857. Despite religious and nationalistic pretentions the real intention of the movement was to revive Muslim power in India.
2. Aligarh Movement: The disastrous consequences of the uprising of

1857, had affected the Muslims of North India the most. The British blamed the Muslims for the uprising which they preferred to call the 'sepoy mutiny' and, therefore, deliberately designed the anti-Muslim policies in all the affairs of the government. Having finished the Mughal rule, the British embarked on a policy to erase all the vestiges of Muslim culture from India. They introduced a new educational policy that did not have any place for the learning of Arabic, Persian and Islamic history. English became the medium of instruction in government schools. English had already become the official language in 1835 by replacing Persian. All these changes and the overall anti-Muslim policy of the British demoralized the Muslims.

In order to pull the community out from the atmosphere of despondency, Syed Ahmed Khan started a series of constructive measures that are collectively defined as the Aligarh Movement. In the history of Indian Muslims, the Aligarh Movement has proved to be the most fruitful and beneficial for the community. It helped the Muslims, to some extent, to abandon the medieval outlook and get acquainted with modern scientific education. The main objectives of the Aligarh Movement were:

a. To create an atmosphere of mutual understanding between the British government and the Muslims.
b. To persuade Muslims to learn English education.
c. To persuade Muslims to abstain from politics of agitation.
d. To produce an intellectual class from amongst the Muslim community.
e. To bring social and cultural reform amongst the Muslim community.
f. To maintain, and as far as possible, promote the political and economic importance of Muslims in the affairs of the country to the extent that was possible in a country under foreign rule.

(See Minault, Gail, *The Khilafat Movement*, Columbia University Press, New York, 1982, pp. 14-24)

3. The Deoband or Deobandi movement was started a decade after the failed uprising of 1857 by the leading ulama of the time who were inspired by the soocio-religious ideas of Shah Waliullah (1703–1762). The main thrust of the movement was opposition to British imperialism and revival of the true Islamic teachings of early Islam. The Deobandi ulama were also opposed to modern, scientific, English education that was being promoted by Syed Ahmed Khan's Aligarh Movement. In order to counter the 'evil' influences of English education the ulama such as Muhammad Qasim Nanotvi, Rashid Ahmed Gangohi, Muhammad Yaqub Nanotvi, Shah Rafiuddin, Sayyid Muhammad Abid, Zulfiqar, Fazlur Rahman Usmani et al established an Islamic seminary, Daul Uloom at Deoband, in 1867.

The significant aspect of the ideology behind the movement was its anti-British stance. Most ulama associated with the movement were committed nationalists. Later Deobandi ulama had also established a religio-political organization, Jamiat al-Ulama-e-Hind in 1919. There was a split among Deobandi ulama on the issue of Pakistan. While most of the ulama opposed the movement for Pakistan a minority faction broke away to form the Jamiat al-Ulama-e-Islam and supported the demand for a separate homeland for the Muslims. Source: Brannon Ingram's article: 'Suûs, Scholars and Scapegoats: Rashid Ahmad Gangohi and the Deobandi Critique of Suûsm', in *The Muslim World*, first published online: June 24, 2009. Also see Minault, op. cit., pp. 25-32.

4. Mujumdar, R.C., *History of the Freedom Movement in India*, Vol. I, Calcutta, 1953, p. 492.
5. For more details see Chand, Tara, *History of the Freedom Movement in India*, Vol. III, Publication Divisions, Government of India, New Delhi, 1972.
6. Minault, Gail, op. cit., p. 81.
7. Ibid.
8. Smith, W.C., *Islam in Modern History*, Princeton University Press, Princeton, NJ, p. 285.
9. Chhotani, Mian Mohammad Haji Jan Mohammad was a Bombay-based businessman. He belonged to the Halai Memon community. Like most Memons he too grew up in religious surroundings. He was basically a timber merchant but made a fortune as a government contractor. It was he, who had taken the lead to launch the Khilafat Movement when he presided over a meeting of about 15-20,000 Muslims on March 19, 1919, at Dongri (Khadak) which adopted the resolutions on the Khilafat issue and also authorized the establishment of a Khilafat Committee. He was chosen as the first President of the Khilafat Commiteettee that was later christened as the Central Khilafat Committee (CKC). He was one of the members of the Deputation to the Viceroy (January 1920) on the Khilafat issue. He was also a member of the Sub-Committee that was set up by CKC (May 1920) to work for the starting of Non-Cooperation Movement. He also served as the treasurer of the CKC. He was a member of the Second Khilafat Deputation to Europe (February 1921) and was a signatory to a Manifesto regarding Turkish Peace Terms (1922). He came in for considerable criticism for his administration of the Angora Fund as 17 lakhs out of it had been diverted to his own use. Later, he handed over to CKC two saw mills (valued at Rs. 18 lakhs) as compensation. He was also associated with the Indian National Congress and was a member of the All India Congress Committee, Lucknow (June 1922). His

initiative to start the Khilafat Movement adversely affected his business and the governemt stopped giving him business contracts. He was offered a baronetcy on condition of his severing all contacts with the Khilafat Movement but he refused. He died in Medina (June 1932), while undertaking Hajj.

(Source: *Muslims in India, A Biographical Dictionary,* Edited with an introduction by Naresh Kumar Jain, Published by Manohar, New Delhi, 1979 (India Office, V22587, Vol I, p. 142)

10. For instance, Aziz Ahmed in *Studies in Isamic Culture in the Indian Environment,* Part I, Oxford India, 1999, maintains this position.
11. Maulana Shaukat Ali was one of the two famous Ali Brothers who dominated the Khilafat Movement almost from its inception till his death. He was older than Mohamed Ali. The Ali Brothers were not the product of any madarsa. Both of them got educated in modern, English institutions. The honorific, Maulana, which is prefixed before their names was accorded by their fans when they became the most prominent leaders of the CKC. Shaukat Ali was born in 1873 in Rampur state now a part of Uttar Pradesh. He was educated at the M.A.O. College, Aligarh. He was a very good cricketer and captained his university on more than one occasion. Having completed his education, Shaukat Ali joined the civil service of United Provinces of Oudh and Agra in 1896. He left the civil service in 1913 as he started taking an interest in politics. He was very impressed by Gandhi's leadership and it was under the guidance of the Mahatma that he became an active member of the Congress. He was mainly responsible for nurturing the leadership potential of his younger brother, Mohamed Ali. He made great sacrifices by sending Mohamed Ali to Oxford and later helped him start an English weekly, *Comrade* and the Urdu weekly *Hamdard.* He was jailed in 1919, for publishing an article, which the British government construed as seditious. When the Bombay Khilafat Committeee was converted into a national CKC, Shaukat Ali was elected as its first General Secretary. He was again arrested in 1921 for participating in the Non-Cooperation movement and remained in jail till 1923.

The Ali Brothers had a serious disagreement with the Congress on the Nehru Report and that was the beginning of the end of bonhomie between the Khilafat Movement and the Congress. Shaukat Ali was also not entirely devoted to Gandhi's principle of non-violence. He hated the British so much that to throw them out from India he was ready to resort to armed struggle. It is reported that he supplied guns to the Bengali revolutionary, Sachindranath Sanyal. Shaukat Ali attended the first and the second Round Table Conferences in London. After Mohamed Ali's death in 1931, he continued to be active in Muslim politics in India as well as taking an interest in the political developments in the Middle East. A short while after the death of Mohamed Ali, he organized the World Muslim Conference at Jerusalem. He travelled all over the Middle East, building support for India's Muslims and their struggle for independence. In 1936, Shaukat Ali joined the All India Muslim League and closely worked with Muhammad Ali Jinnah. He served as a member of the Central Assembly from 1934 to 1938. Shaukat Ali died on January 4, 1939. [Sources: Minault, Gail, *The Khilafat Movement*, Columbia University Press, New York, 1982; See also Mohamed Ali, *My Life: A Fragment*, (Edited and annotated by Mushirul Hasan), Manohar, New Delhi, 1999]

12. Mohamed Ali Jouhar was born on December 10, 1878 in the state of Rampur. Besides being the most prominent leader of the Khilafat Movement he was a freedom fighter, scholar, journalist and a poet. Jouhar, the suffix that is often attached to his name was actully his nom de plume and like his elder brother, he was also called a Maulana by his admirers. Despite his Oxford education, his commitment to free India from the clutches of British imperialism was unyielding. He first studied in the M.A.O. College, Aligarh and in 1898, joined Lincoln College, Oxford, majoring in modern history. After his return from Oxford, first he served his native state of Rampur as the director of education and later joined the Baroda civil service. He was a persuasive orator and a fine writer both in English and Urdu. His interest in politics did not allow him to be a civil servant for long. Upon leaving his job, he started in 1911, a weekly in Urdu, *Hamdard* and an English weekly, *The Comrade* from Calcutta. He shifted base to Delhi in 1913. His involvement in the Khilafat Movement and staunch nationalism brought him closer to Gandhi and the Congress. He was the sixth Muslim to be elected as the President of the Congress in 1923, though he remained in that position only for a few months. He was one of the founder members of the All-India Muslim League and was elected as its President in 1918. He was one of the co-founders of the Jamia Millia Islamia, when it was first started at Aligarh.

    As a Khilafat leader he was one of the members of the delegation that visited England in 1919, to appeal to the British authorities not to depose the Sultan of Turkey who was also the Caliph. The British unceremoniously rejected the demands of the delegation. Thereafter, Mohamed Ali devoted himself completely to the cause of the Khilafat and the Muslim question in Indian politics. He, along with his elder brother, Shaukat Ali emerged as a formidable force challenging the British Raj in India. In order to turn the Khilafat Movement into a national agitation he joined hands with Gandhi. It was under Gandhi's leadership that the twin agitations, the Non-cooperation

Movement and the Khilafat Movement were launched simultaneously. Consequently, many Hindu leaders also campaigned for the Khilafat. During this phase, Mohamed Ali attained the status of a true national leader.He was arrested for, in the opinion of the British authorities, a seditious speech, and imprisoned for two years.

When Gandhi called off the Non-Coperation Movement in the aftermath of the Chauri Chaura incident, it also weakened the Khilafat Movement. Mohamed Ali was extremely disappointed by Gandhi's decision. At the time he was in jail and was in no position to influence Gandhi to change his decision. Though upon his release he became the President of the Congress for a short period, he started drifting away from Gandhi and the Congress. The ultimate splitting up with the Congress came on the issue of the Nehru Report in 1928. Though a section of the Khilafat movement comprising the prominent Muslim leaders having affiliation with the Congress was in favour of accepting the Nehru Report, the Ali Brothers and their supporters were absolutely opposed to it. Mohamed Ali's opposition to the Nehru Report was on two counts: a) it advocated dominion status for India; and b) it recommended joint electorates. When the Nehru Report was placed before the All Parties Conference, as many as 30 members of the CKC were present at the Conference including the prominent ones like Shaukat Ali, Begum Mohamed Ali, Abdul Majid Daryabadi, Azad Sobhani, Maghfoor Ahmad Aejazi, Abul Mohasin Mohammad Sajjad and others. They were not entirely convinced with the provisions of the Report.

Mohamed Ali attended the first Round Table Conference. The Khilafat issue by that time had become extraneous. In his famous speech at the Conference he valiantly argued for complete independence of India and declared that he would not go back to an enslaved India. His failing health helped him stick to his words as he died a short while after the Round Table Conference on January 4, 1931, and as per his wish was buried in Jerusalem.

In recognition of his role in India's freedom struggle, the State Government of Uttar Pradesh recently named a university after him. This is incidentally the first significant move acknowledging Mohamed Ali's contribution. Most people believe that the famous Muhammad Ali Road in Mumbai is named after him. It is not. It is named after the renowned philanthropist from Konkan, Muhammad Ali Roghey.

(Soures: Mohamed Ali, *My Life: A Fragment*, (Edited and annotated by Mushirul Hasan), Manohar, New Delhi, 1999. See also Gail Minault, *The Khilafat Movement*, Columbia University Press, New York, 1982)

13. Choudhary, Khaliquzzaman, *Pathway to Pakistan*, Longmans, Lahore, 1961 pp. 47-49.
14. Ibid., p. 48.
15. Minault, op. cit., p. 77.
16. The names of the delegates that were cleared in the Conference included the Raja of Mahmudabad, Fazlul Haq, Raza Ali, Sayyid Husain, Dr. Ansari, Seth Chhotani and Maulana Abdul Bari. However, they never went. Instead Mohamed Ali went with another group of delegates.
17. For more dtails about the rumour of a 'deal' on cow slaughter see: Thursby, G.R., *Hindu-Muslim Relations in British India,* Leiden, E.J. Brill, 1975. on ResearchGate, the professional network for scientists.
18. Husain bin Ali al-Hashmi was the Sharif and Emir of Mecca under the suzerainty of the Ottoman Empire between 1908 1nd 1917 and thereafter, he proclaimed himself the King of Hejaz. In 1916, he revolted against the Ottoman Empire probably because of the machinations of the British. He was the last of the Hashmite Emirs of the Hejaz to be appointed by the Ottoman Sultan. It was because of his noble lineage, i.e. a descendant of the Prophet, he was extremely respected in the Islamic world. It is also argued that because of the rise of Turkish nationalism that was manifested in the Young Turk Revolution of 1908, the Hashmites began drifting away from the Ottomans and opened secret negotiations with the British. The British High Commissioner, Henry McMahon assured Husain that if the Arabs helped the British during the First World War, he would be made the King of an Arab empire that would include the entire area between Egypt and Iran barring the British controlled territories of Kuwait, Aden and the Syrian coast. In the post-war scenario though the Arabs were freed from the Ottoman control, the promised kingdom did not materialize because the Middle East came under the 'Mandate' rule of France and the United Kingdom. Husain's two sons, however, were made Kings of Iraq and Jordan respectively. When the Turkish Grand National Assembly abolished the Caliphate on March 3, 1924, Husain declared himself Caliph of the Islamic world. Nonetheless, soon after Husain was driven out of Arabia by the Saudis who belonged to a rival clan and also had religious differences with Husain because of their Wahabi Islam. The British who had been supporting Husain all these years did not come to his rescue against the Saudis. Husain was forced to flee to Cyprus and finally settled in Amman, Jordan, the kingdom of his son Abdullah. He died in 1931 in Amman and was buried in Jerusalem.
    (Source: Avi Shlaim, *Lion of Jordan*, Penguin Books Ltd., London, 2007)

19. For the details of the meeting with Lloyd George see: Rahman, Rafiqur, *Mohamed Ali: His Life and Speeches*, Mussalman, Calcutta, 1931.
20. Minault, op. cit., p. 89.
21. Ibid., p. 92.
22. See Beg, Mirza Abdul Qadir, *Khilafat and Jazirat al-Arab* (Urdu), Central Khilafat Committee, Bombay, 1920.
23. Minault, op. cit., p. 98.
24. See Helmreich, Paul C., *From Paris to Sèvres: The Partition of the Ottoman Empire at the Peace Conference of 1919–1920*, State University Press, Columbus, Ohio, 1974.
25. The members who resigned fom the membership of the CKC included G.M. Bhurgri, Badruddin Abdullah Koor, Mirza Ali Muhammad Khan, Rahmatullah Chinoy, and Sir Fazalbhau Currimbhai.
26. Quoted by Minault from a speech by Gandhi in Madras, op. cit., pp. 107-8.
27. Ibid., p. 116.
28. See Madhauli, op. cit.; Abdul Ghaffar, *Jamia ki Kahani* (Urdu), Maktaba-e-Jamia, New Delhi, 1965.
29. See Syed Abid Husain's article, 'Jamia Millia ka Maqsad' in *Jamia Jubilee Number* (Urdu), New Delhi, November, 1946.
30. Minault, op. cit., p. 124.
31. Nehru, Jawaharlal, *Autobiography*, Penguin Books India, 2004, pp. 169ff
32. Angora was the ancient name of the present-day capital city, Ankara, of Turkey. It was also known by its Latin name Ancyra. The archaeologists trace the city's history to the Bronze Age Hattic civilization that was followed by the Hittitites in the second century BC. In 1071, the Turkish Sultan Alp Arsalan conquered the city and made it part of the Ottoman Empire. Timur (Tamerlane) defeated the Ottomans in 1402 and took control of the city. However, a year later, Ankara was again the part of the Ottoman Empire.

    In the aftermath of the First World War, the victorious powers, UK, France, Italy, Greece and Armenia had occupied the entire western region of Turkey including Ankara, according to the Treaty of Sevres. The Turkish leader of the nationalist movement and the architect of modern Turkey, Mustafa Kemal Pasha made Ankara the headquarters of his resistance in 1920 and defeated all the forces of occupation. Thereafter, the Treaty of Sevres was replaced by the Treaty of Lausanne and the Republic of Turkey was born on October 29, 1923. Ten days before that Ankara officially became the capital of Turkey in place of Constantinople (Istanbul).
33. Smyrna is the ancient name of the present-day Turkish metropolis Izmir. It is the third largest city of Turkey. The ancient city continued to be referred to as Smyrna in English until the Turkish postal service discontinued the usage of the old name and started the practice of

using only Izmir, which has now been recognized internationally. Izmir is one of the most ancient cities of the world having about 4,000 years of recorded history. However, the excavations discovered in 2004, indicate that the city's past is much older than previously assumed. The findings of the archaeologists from Izmir's Ege University point out that the city was in existence in prehistory.

The city was captured by the Ottoman Sultan, Bayazid I in 1389. However, in 1402, Timur (Tamelane) defeated the Ottoman Sultan and got control of the city. It remained under the control of the Tartars for more than a decade. In 1415, Muhammad (Mehmet) I, recaptured the city and since then it remained under the Ottomans. After the defeat of the Turks in the First World War, the Allied Powers forced Turkey to sign the unjust Treaty of Sevres, according to which the western regions of Turkey, including Izmir, were given to Greece. On May 15, 1919, the Greek forces occupied Izmir. Then Mustafa Kemal started his resistance against the Allied Powers, England, France and Greece to recapture the Turkish territories that were unjustly snatched away from Turkey. When the Khilafatists started collecting money for the Angora and Smyrna Funds, Mustafa Kemal was engaged in a war with Greece to recapture Izmir. Kemal defeated the Greek army on September 8, 1922 and the next day the Turkish army took possession of the city.

34. Minault, op. cit., pp. 156-57.
35. Ibid., p. 141.
36. Ibid., pp. 143-44.
37. Gandhi's article, 'The Brothers' Apology' in *Young India,* quoted by Minault, Ibid., p. 145.
38. Ibid., pp. 138-39.
39. Ibid., p. 139.
40. Ibid., p. 140.
41. Contrary to the popular notion, Islam arrived in India quietly with the Arab traders who were in control of the spice trade many centuries before the emergence of Islam in the Arabian peninsula. They arrived on the western coast in their dhows and conducted their business in absolute peace. The coastal area of present-day Kerala that was usually frequented by the Arab traders came to be known as Malabar, which is the Malayalam corruption of the Arabic word Ma'bar that means passage. Islam, therefore, reached India almost at the same time that it appeared in Mecca in the early seventh century. The first mosque in India was constructed in 629, in the lifetime of the Prophet, at Kodangallur, a town in the district of Thrissur, and at a distance of 35 kilometres from the city of Kochi. It was almost a century later that a young Arab commandant, Muhammad-bin Qasim, conquered Sind.
42. Menon, Sreedhara A., *A Short Survey of Kerala History,* Vishwanathan

Publishers, 2006, p. 361.

43. See *Kerala Development Report*, Government of India Planning Commission, Academic Foundation, 2008, p. 53.
44. V.V. Kunhi Krishnan, *Tenancy Legislation in Malabar-1880-1970*, Northern Book Centre, New Delhi, 1993, pp. 1-24.
45. Qureshi, M. Naeem, *Pan-Islamism in British Indian Politics: A Study of the Khilafat Movement, 1918–1924*, Brill, Leiden, 1999, p. 447.
46. Roland Miller, *The Encyclopaedia of Islam*, Vol. VI , Brill, Leiden, 1988, p. 461.
47. Gandhi in *Young India's* issue dated November 22, 1921, quoted in Minault, op. cit., p. 179.
48. Chaurasia Radhey Shyam, *History of Modern India: 1707 AD to Upto 2000 AD*, Atlantic Publishers & Distributors, New Delhi, 2002, p. 355.
49. Kathryn Tidrick, *Gandhi: A Political and Spiritual Life*, I.B.Tauris Publishers, London, 2006. p. 176.
50. Chaurasia Radhey Shyam, op. cit., p. 355.
51. Kaliquzzaman, op. cit., p. 63.
52. Quoted in Minault, op. cit., p. 185.
53. Ibid., p. 187.
54. Ibid., p. 201.
55. Ibid., pp. 188-91
56. Ali, Zaheer, *Secularism and Its Indian Version*, University of Mumbai, 2011, p. 34.
57. *The Fundamentalism Project*, by Martin E. Marty, R. Scott Appleby, American Academy of Arts and Sciences, University of Chicago Press, 1991 p. 564.
58. "Dayanand and the Shuddhi Movement" in *Indian Political Tradition*, by D.K. Mohanty, Anmol Publications Pvt. Ltd., 1997, p. 116.
59. Minault, op. cit., p. 193.
60. For more details see Jenkins, Philip, *God's Continent* (illustrated, annotated ed.), US: Oxford University Press, 2007, p. 340.
61. Ahmadiya Muslim Jamaat is an Islamic religious movement that started in the late nineteenth century in British India. Its founder, Mirza Ghulam Ahmad (1835–1908), asserted that he had fulfilled the prophecies of the world's reformer during the *end times*, and that he was the Mujaddid (divine reformer), the promised Messiah and Mehdi awaited by the Muslims. He also claimed that he was to herald the eschaton as predicted in the traditions of various religions of the world. He also declared that he was to bring about the final triumph of Islam according to the prediction of the faith. Ahmadi Muslims affirm that Islam as revealed to Muhammad is the final religion for mankind as ordained by the Almighty and through Ahmadiya Jamaat its adherents strive to restore the essence and pristine form of the faith as it existed in the lifetime of the Prophet. The Ahmadis claim that

they are the harbingers of a peaceful revival of Islam to make it the universal faith. Adherents of the Ahmadiya faith believe that Ghulam Ahmad appeared just like Jesus to free the world from violence, wars and bloodshed and restore an age of peace, morality and justice. The Ahmadis claim that they are the harbingers of the peaceful revival of Islam to make it the universal religion of mankind. Mirza Ghulam Ahmad founded the movement on March 23, 1889. After his death, the community was led by a number of community leaders known as Caliphs. Presently the Ahmadiya Jamaat has presence in over 200 countries of the world. They are believed to be the earliest Muslims communities to arrive in Britain and other Western countries. Some of the beliefs of the Ahmadiyas clash with the mainstream Islamic tenets and for that reason most orthodox Muslims denounce Ahmadiyas as Kafirs. For instance, in Pakistan, they are officially declared as non-Muslims.

62. Quoted by Minault, op. cit., pp. 197-98.
63. When Gandhi called off the Non-cooperation movement in the aftermath of the Chaura Chaur tragedy on February 5, 1922, many prominent Congress and Khilafat leaders were disconcerted with the decision. For Gandhi the violent incident was his personal failure because, he thought, he could not properly train his satyagrahis to carry out an anti-government agitation by purely non-violent means. As atonement for the killings he went on fast unto death and to convince all Indians to stop civil resistence. Consequently, most Congressmen heeded Gandhi's call and stopped all sorts of agitations. Nevertheless, many leaders were not convinced. They felt that calling off a hugely successful movement like Non-cooperation merely because of a solitary violent incident was a blunder. In their view the Non-cooperation had seriously rattled the British rulers and it was about to break the back of the Raj. They squarely blamed Gandhi for the fiasco. Therefore, leaders such as Motilal Nehru, Chitranjan Das, Narsimha Chintaman Kelkar, Vallabhbhai Patel, Huseyn Shaheed Suhrawardy and Subhas Chandra Bose formed the Swaraj Party on January 9, 1923. Another controversial issue was entry into the legislative councils. Gandhi and his supporters rejected the entry while the Swarajists were in favour of participating in elections and entering the councils. Despite opposing Gandhi the Swarajists did not split the Congress and as per Gandhi's wish kept the Swaraj Party within the umbrella of INC. Chitranjan Das was appointed the president of the Swaraj Party while Motilal Nehru became the secretary. In the Belgaum session of the INC, attempts were made to win over the Swarajists. The death of Chittaranjan Das in 1925, and with Motilal Nehru rejoining Congress the following year, the Swaraj Party had lost its relevance.

64. *observingliberalpakistan.blogspot.com*
65. Ibid.
66. The Nehru Report was the draft of a Constitution for India prepared by Indians under the British rule. During the implementation of the Montague-Chelmsford Constitutional Reforms in 1919, the foreign rulers had formally assured that henceforth the constitutional reforms for India would be updated every ten years and Indians would also be consulted in future. However, prior to the revision of the next constitutional reforms, the British Parliament constituted an all-white Simon Commission to review the political scene in India and make recommendations for the next constitutional reforms. Indian leaders naturally protested against the breach of trust and a series of demonstrations against the Simon Commission across India started that at some places turned violent. Reacting to this, Lord Birkenhead, the Secretary of State for India, ridiculed the demand of Indians to have a say in the future constitution of their country and disparaged them saying that they were incapable of framing a constitution that would be approved by all the communities of India. Later in a letter to Lord Irwin (Viceroy of India) he wrote: "I am entirely in favour of inducing the malcontents to produce their own proposals, for in the first place I believe them to be quite incapable of surmounting the constitutional and constructive difficulties involved; in the second, if these were overcome, I believe that a unity which can only survive in an atmosphere of generalization would disappear at once."

    In response, the Indian leaders decided to accept the challenge and to concretize their resolve. An All Parties Conference was convened at Delhi in January 1928. The parties that attended it included the Indian National Congress, All India Muslim League, National Liberation Front, Hindu Mahasabha and Central Sikh League. The Conference failed to pass a resolution as no consensus could be reached on the issue of rights of religious minorities. In the second All Parties Conference held the same year, though two sub-committees were constituted, nothing more could be achieved. It was during the third Conference held in May 1928 at Bombay that a seven-member Committee was constituted to draft the future Constitution for India with Motilal Nehru as its chairman and Jawaharlal Nehru as the secretary. The other members of the Committee were Ali Imam, Tej Bahadur Sapru, M.S. Aney, Mangal Singh, Shuaib Qureshi, Subhas Chandra Bose, and G.R. Pradhan. The Committee worked diligently and within three months finalized the draft-constitution that was presented in the fourth All Parties Conference held at Lucknow, in August 1928. The salient features of the draft-constitution, popularly known as the Nehru Report included the following:

    India should be given Dominion Status.

- India should have a parliamentary form of government.
- Indian Legislature (Parliament) should be bi-cameral comprising a Senate and House of Representatives. The Upper Chamber, the Senate, should have two hundred members elected for seven years and the Lower Chamber, House of Representatives, should have five hundred members elected for a five-year term.
- There shall be an executive headed by the Governor-General who will act on the advice of an executive council, which will be responsible to the Parliament.
- India should be a federal state with residuary powers vested in the Centre. The provinces should be linguistically constituted.
- It contained a Bill of Rights.
- India should be a secular country and there shall be no state religion. Men and women should have equal rights.
- There shall be a Supreme Court of India.
- Hindustani written either in Devanagari, Telugu, Kannada, Gujarati, Bengali, Tamil or in Urdu characters shall be the state language. However, the use of the English language shall be permitted.
- There should be no separate electorates for any community or weightage for minorities.

The two Muslim members of the Committee, Ali Imam and Shuaib Quraishi, did not sign the Report; the former because of indisposition and the latter because of disagreement with certain clauses. The Muslim League under the leadership of M.A. Jinnah rejected the Nehru Report mainly because of: a) no separate electorates or weightage was guaranteed to the Muslims as it was provided for in the Lucknow Pact of 1916 and b) the residuary powers were vested in the Centre instead of the provinces. Commenting on the Nehru Report, Jinnah said: "The Committee has adopted a narrow minded policy to ruin the political future of the Muslims. I regret to declare that the report is extremely ambiguous and does not deserve to be implemented." Thus, an opportunity that could have avoided the partition of India was lost and Birkenhead's estimation about Indians was partially proved true.

67. The Simon Commission was a group of 7 Members of the British Parliament led by a chairman that visited India in 1928 to study the Indian political situation, meet the prominent Indian leaders of British India and then recommend constitutional reforms to the British legislature. The group came to be known popularly as the Simon Commission because of its chairman, Sir John Simon. The other members of the group included: Edward Cadogan, Vernon Hartshorn, George Lan-Fox, Donald Howard, Harry Levy Lawson and Clement Attlee. The last one later became the British Prime Minister who had to oversee the partition of the country and transfer of power to Indian

and Pakistani political elites.

The Commission had to face hostile demonstrations, at places violent, wherever it went because contrary to the Indian demand of involvement of Indians in the framing of the constitution of their motherland, the Commission did not include a single Indian. The Indian National Congress and the Muslim League collectively opposed the all-white Simon Commission though it was reported that a few Hindu, Sikh and Muslim leaders favoured cooperation with the members of the Commission. Consequently, the Viceroy, Lord Irwin exploited the opportunity by nominating a few obliging Hindu, Muslim and Sikh leaders on a Committee for Cooperation to assist the Simon Commission. The Committee was composed of: C. Sankaran Nair (Chairman). Arthur Froom, Nawab Ali Khan, Shivdev Singh Uberoi, Zulfiqar Ali Khan, Hari Singh Gour, Abdullah al-Mamun Suhrawardy, Kikabhai Premchand and M. C. Rajah.

In the history of modern India, the Simon Commission is mainly remembered because of the tragic death of a prominent freedom fighter. The members of the Simon Commission reached Lahore on October 30, 1928 and were immediately met by huge groups of black-flag wielding angry protesters. The anti-Commission demonstrations were led by Lala Lajpat Rai. Police using excessive force mercilessly thrashed the demonstrators with batons. Rai was severely injured in the demonstrations and was hospitalized. He, however, succumbed to the injuries and died on November 17, 1928.

68. www.columbia.edu/itc/mealac/pritchett/
69. Ibid.
70. Ibid.
71. Ibid.
72. Ibid.
73. Mushirul Hasan in his Introduction to *My Life: A Fragment*, Manohar, New Delhi, 1999, p. 13.
74. Qoted in Ram Gopal, *Indian Muslims*, Asia Publishing House, Bombay, 1964.

Chapter 5 – Beyond the Movement

1. Prospectus of the All India Khilafat Committee College of Education, Mumbai, p. 5.
2. MSS (Urdu) preserved in the office of the Khilafat College of Education, Mumbai.
3. API news quoted in S.R. Bakshi, *Ali Brothers*, Anmol Publications, New Delhi, 1993, p. 220.
4. Ibid., p. 234.
5. Ibid., p. 221.
6. Ibid.

7. Ibid., p. 219.
8. Ibid.
9. MSS (Urdu), op. cit.
10. Trust Deed preserved in the office of the Khilafat College of Education, Mumbai.
11. Trust Deed preserved in the Office of the Khilafat College of Education, Mumbai.
12. Javed Siddiqui's interview with the author held on August 8, 2015.
13. Mohammed Wajihuddin's feature, "From Inquilab to Kitab", *Times of India*, Mumbai, September 11, 2011.
14. Documents preserved in the office of the Khilafat College of Education, Mumbai.
15. Ibid.
16. Ibid.
17. Ibid.
18. Ibid.
19. Part of the inaugural address quoted in the Prospectus of the All India Khilafat Committee College of Education, 2012-2013, p. 2.
20. Office Document.
21. Ibid.
22. Ibid.
23. *Self-Appraisal Report* of the All India Khilafat Committee College of Education, prepared for submission to the National Assessment and Accreditation Council.
24. MSS (Urdu), op. cit.

Chapter 6 – Conclusion

1. See *Stories of the Prophets, Including Life of Mohammad, the Last of the Prophets*, by Ibn Kathir, Idara Isha'at-e-Diniyat, New Delhi, 2008, pp. 444-445.
2. Ibn al-Dawadari, *Kanz*, 6, Vol. III, nr. 2570, p. 27.
3. Ibid.
4. Quoted by Thomas W. Arnold, *The Caliphate*, Oxford, London, 1924, pp. 49-50.
5. George Saliba, *A History of Arabic Astronomy: Planetary Theories During the Golden Age of Islam*, New York University Press, 1994, pp. 245 and 250.
6. *Chambers Edinburgh Journal*, 1848, library.upenn.edu/webbin/serial?id=chambersedinburgh.
7. See ªükrü Hanioðlu, *A Brief History of the Late Ottoman Empire*, Princeton University Press, 2010.

Index